Using Information Technology

Third Edition

A Practical Introduction to Computers & Communications

BRIEF VERSION

Stacey C. Sawyer

Brian K. Williams

Sarah E. Hutchinson

Irwin
McGraw-Hill

Boston Burr Ridge, IL Dubuque, IA Madison, WI New York San Francisco St. Louis Bangkok Bogotá Caracas
Lisbon London Madrid Mexico City Milan New Delhi Seoul Singapore Sydney Taipei Toronto

Irwin/McGraw-Hill

A Division of The McGraw·Hill Companies

USING INFORMATION TECHNOLOGY: BRIEF VERSION

Photo and other credits are listed in the back of the book.

This book is printed on recycled, acid-free paper containing 10% post consumer waste.

international   1 2 3 4 5 6 7 8 9 0   VNH/VNH   9 3 2 1 0 9 8
domestic   1 2 3 4 5 6 7 8 9 0   VNH/VNH   9 3 2 1 0 9 8

ISBN 0-256-26147-4

Vice president/Editor-in-chief: *Michael W. Junior*
Senior sponsoring editors: *Garrett Glanz & Kyle Lewis*
Developmental editor: *Burrston House, Ltd.*
Marketing manager: *Jodi McPherson*
Senior project manager: *Gladys True*
Senior production supervisor: *Madelyn S. Underwood*
Production management & page layout: *Stacey C. Sawyer, Sawyer & Williams*
Interior designer: *Laurie J. Entringer*
Cover designer: *Matthew Baldwin*
Cover illustrator: *Bob Commander © SIS*
Senior photo research coordinator: *Keri Johnson*
Photo research: *Monica Suder*
Supplement coordinator: *Nancy Martin*
Compositor: *GTS Graphics, Inc.*
Typeface: *10/12 Trump Mediaeval*
Printer: *Von Hoffman Press, Inc.*

Library of Congress Cataloging-in-Publication Data
Sawyer, Stacey C.
    Using information technology: a practical introduction to
  computers & communications: brief version / Stacey C. Sawyer, Brian K. Williams, Sara E.
  Hutchinson. — Brief 3rd ed.
       p.   cm.
    Includes index.
    ISBN 0-256-26147-4
    1. Computers.   2. Telecommunications systems.   3. Information
technology.   I. Williams, Brian K.   II. Hutchinson, Sarah E.
    III. Title
    QA76.5.S2193   1999
    004—dc21   98-21696

http://www.mhhe.com

Brief Contents

Preface to the Instructor

The Audience for & Promises of This Book

USING INFORMATION TECHNOLOGY: A Practical Introduction to Computers & Communications: Brief Version, THIRD EDITION, is intended for use as a concepts textbook to accompany a one-semester or one-quarter introductory course on computers or microcomputers. It is, we hope, a book that will make a difference in the lives of our readers. The **key features** are as follows. We offer:

1. **Emphasis on unification of computer and communications systems.**
2. **Careful revision in response to extensive instructor and student feedback.**
3. **Emphasis on practicality.**
4. **Emphasis throughout on ethics.**
5. **Use of techniques for reinforcing student learning.**
6. **Up-to-the-minute material—in the book and on our Web site.**

We elaborate on these features next.

Key Feature #1: Emphasis on Unification of Computers & Communications

The First Edition of this text broke new ground by emphasizing the technological merger of the computer, communications, consumer electronics, and media industries through the exchange of information in the digital format used by computers. This is the relatively new phenomenon known as **technological convergence.**

Since the First Edition, other texts have also added coverage of the Internet and the World Wide Web. However, we agree with analysts who say the revolution is far broader than this, and we continue to stress the unification of entire industries and technologies and their effects. Thus, the THIRD EDITION continues to embrace the theme of convergence by giving it in-depth treatment in six chapters—the introduction, system software, telecommunications, communications technology, storage and databases, and promises and challenges (Chapters 1, 3, 7, 8, 9, 10). Convergence is also brought out in examples throughout other chapters.

This theme covers much of the technology currently found under such phrases as *the Information Superhighway, the Multimedia Revolution,* and *the Digital Age: mobile computing, the Internet, Web search tools, online services, workgroup computing, the virtual office, video compression, PC/TVs, "intelligent agents,"* and so on.

Key Feature #2: Careful Revision in Response to Extensive Instructor & Student Feedback

Our publisher has told us that the First Edition of *USING INFORMATION TECHNOLOGY* was apparently the most successful new text in the field at that time, with over 300 schools adopting both comprehensive and brief versions. We were delighted to learn that the Second Edition reached an even wider audience. An important reason for this success, we believe, was all the valuable contributions of our reviewers, both instructors and students.

Both the printed version of the Second Edition and the manuscript and proofs of the THIRD EDITION underwent a highly disciplined and wide-ranging reviewing process. This process of expert appraisal drew on instructors who were both users and nonusers, who were from a variety of educational institutions, and who expressed their ideas in both written form and in focus groups.

We also received input from a number of student users and nonusers of the Second Edition. Many indicated their appreciation for the Experience Boxes, as well as such pedagogical devices as section "Previews & Reviews," our unique end-of-chapter Summary, the practical emphasis of the book, and the people-oriented writing.

We have sometimes been overwhelmed with the amount of feedback, but we have tried to respond to all consensus criticisms and countless individual suggestions. Every page of the THIRD EDITION has been influenced by instructor feedback. The result, we think, is **a book addressing the needs of most instructors and students.**

New to this edition! In particular, we have addressed the following matters:

- **Communications material separated into two chapters:** Because of the overwhelming amount of new material, and following the direction of our reviewers, we split the old "Communications" chapter into two chapters. Chapter 7, "Telecommunications," covers online resources, the Internet, and the World Wide Web. Chapter 8, "Communications Technology," covers communications hardware, channels, and networks. (The chapters may be assigned in reverse order without loss of continuity.)

- **Input and output material made one chapter:** The two chapters "Input" and "Output" are combined into a single chapter, which allows us to continue to offer a book of just 10 chapters, which instructors have indicated they prefer.

In addition to these major structural and substantive changes, we have made hundreds of line-by-line and word-by-word adjustments to refine coverage and to conform with instructor's requests.

Key Feature #3: Emphasis on Practicality

As with past editions, we are trying to make this book a "keeper" for students. Thus, we not only cover fundamental concepts but also offer a great deal of **practical advice.** This advice, of the sort found in computer magazines and general-interest computer books, is expressed principally in two kinds of boxes—Experience Boxes and README boxes:

- **The Experience Box:** Appearing at the end of some chapters, the Experience Box is **optional** material that may be assigned at the instructor's discretion. However, students will find the subjects covered are of immediate value: "Getting Started with Computers in College & Going Online"; "Using Software to Access the World Wide Web"; "Good Habits: Protecting Your Computer System, Your Data, & Your Health"; and "Job Searching on the Internet & World Wide Web."

- README boxes: README boxes consist of optional material on practical matters, such as tips for managing your e-mail or staying focused to avoid information overload.

Ethics

Key Feature #4: Emphasis Throughout on Ethics

Many texts discuss ethics in isolation, usually in one of the final chapters. We believe this topic is too important to be treated last or lightly. Thus, **we cover ethical matters in numerous places** throughout the book, as indicated by the special logo shown here in the margin. For example, the all-important question of what kind of software can be legally copied is discussed in Chapter 2 ("Applications Software"), an appropriate place for students just starting software labs. Other ethical matters discussed are the manipulation of truth through digitizing of photographs, intellectual property rights, netiquette, censorship, privacy, and computer crime.

A list of pages with ethics coverage appears on the inside front cover. Instructors wishing to teach all ethical matters as a single unit may refer to this list.

Key Feature #5: Reinforcement for Learning

Having individually or together written nearly two dozen textbooks and scores of labs, the authors are vitally concerned with reinforcing students in acquiring knowledge and developing critical thinking. Accordingly, we offer the following to provide learning reinforcement:

- Interesting writing: Studies have found that textbooks **written in an imaginative style** significantly improve students' ability to retain information. Thus, the authors have employed a number of journalistic devices—such as the short biographical sketch, the colorful fact, the apt direct quote—to make the material as interesting as possible. We also use real anecdotes and examples rather than fictionalized ones.

- Key terms and definitions in boldface: **Each key term AND its definition is printed in boldface** within the text, in order to help readers avoid any confusion about which terms are important and what they actually mean.

- "Preview & Review" presents abstracts of each section for learning reinforcement: Each main section heading throughout the book is followed by **an abstract or précis entitled Preview & Review.** This enables the student to get a preview of the material before reading it and then to review it afterward, for maximum learning reinforcement.

- Innovative chapter Summaries for learning reinforcement: The end-of-chapter Summary is especially innovative—and especially helpful to students. In fact, research through student focus groups has shown that this format was clearly first among five different choices of summary formats. Each concept is discussed under **two columns, headed "What It Is/What It Does" and "Why It's Important."**

Each concept or term is also given a cross-reference page number that refers the reader to the main discussion within the chapter.

In addition, as we discuss next, the term or concept is also given a Key Question number (such as *KQ 2.1, KQ 2.2,* and so on) corresponding to the appropriate Key Question (learning objective) at the beginning of the chapter.

Ethics

- **Key Questions to help students read with purpose:** *New to this edition!* Lists of learning objectives at the start of chapters are common in textbooks—and most students simply skip them. Because we believe learning objectives are excellent instruments for reinforcement, we have crafted ours to make them more helpful to students. We do this in two ways:

  (1) By **phrasing the learning objectives as Key Questions.** These Key Questions appear on the chapter-opening page and again at the start of each chapter section. By phrasing learning objectives as Key Questions we give students a tool to help them read with purpose.

  (2) By **tying terms and concepts in the end-of-chapter Summary to the Key Questions.** That is, in the Summary we have given "KQ" numbers to the terms and concepts that relate to the particular Key Question numbers in the text.

  For example, in Chapter 2, *Key Questions 2.11* ask "When is copying a violation of copyright laws, what is a software license agreement, and what types of agreements are there?" Terms and concepts appearing in the end-of-chapter Summary that relate to these questions—such as "copyright," "freeware," and "intellectual property"—are identified with the notation *KQ 2.11* and the page number in the chapter where they are discussed.

- **Cross-referencing system for key terms and concepts:** Wherever important key terms and concepts appear throughout the text that students might need to remind themselves about, we have added **"check the cross reference"** information, to indicate the first definition or usage of a key term or concept, as in: "use of machine language (✔ p. 120)." In student focus groups, this cross-reference device was found to rank *first* out of 20-plus study/learning aids.

- **Material in "bite-size" portions:** Major ideas are presented in **bite-size form,** with generous use of advance organizers, bulleted lists, and new paragraphing when a new idea is introduced.

- **Short sentences:** Most sentences have been kept short, the majority not exceeding **22–25 words** in length.

- **End-of-chapter exercises:** For practice purposes, students will benefit from several exercises at the end of each chapter: **fill-in-the-blank questions, short-answer questions, multiple-choice questions,** and **true-false questions.** Answers to selected exercises appear upside down at the end of the Exercises section.

  In addition, we present several "Knowledge in Action," end-of-chapter **projects/critical-thinking questions,** generally of a practical nature, to help students absorb the material. In a typical example, students are asked to identify the security threats to which their home computers are vulnerable.

Key Feature #6: Up-to-the-Minute Material—in the Text & on the Irwin/McGraw-Hill Web Site

Writing a text like this is a constant steeplechase of trying to keep up with changing technological developments. Every day seems to bring reports of something new and important. As we write this, our 1998 publication date is only three months away. However, because our publisher has allowed us to do several steps concurrently (writing, reviewing, editing, production), our text includes coverage of the following material:

ActiveX. Cable modems. Cyberspace job hunting. Digital cameras. Digital TV. Divx. DSL. DVD. Extranets. GEO, MEO, and LEO satellite systems. Internet 2. The Merced chip. Net addiction. NGI. Online secondary storage. Portal sites. Radio-frequency identification devices. Set-top boxes. Telephony. VRML. WebTV. Windows 98. XML . . . And more.

Still, we recognize that a Gutenberg-era lag exists between our last-minute scribbling and the book's publication date. And of course we also realize that fast-moving events will unquestionably overtake some of the facts in this book by the time it is in the student's hands. Accordingly, after publication we are periodically offering instructors updated material and other interaction on the Irwin/McGraw-Hill UIT Web Site: **http://www.mhhe.com/cit/concepts/uit**

Complete Course Solutions: Supplements That Work—Four Distinctive Offerings

It's less important how many supplements a textbook has than whether they are truly useful, accurate, and of high quality. Irwin/McGraw-Hill presents **four distinctive kinds of supplement offerings** to complement the text:

1. **Application-software tutorials—four types**
2. **McGraw-Hill Learning Architecture Web-based software**
3. **Classroom presentation software**
4. **Instructor support materials**

We elaborate on these below.

Supplement Offering #1: Application-Software Tutorials—Four Types

Our publisher, Irwin/McGraw-Hill, offers four different series of tutorials, which present four different hands-on approaches to learning various types of application software. An Irwin/McGraw-Hill sales representative can explain the specific software covered by each series.

- Advantage Series tutorials: Written by *Sarah E. Hutchinson* and *Glen J. Coulthard*, manuals in the **Advantage Series for Computer Education** average just over 200 pages each and cover a large number of popular software packages, including the latest versions of Microsoft Office. Each tutorial leads students through step-by-step instructions not only for the most common methods of executing commands but also for alternative methods.

Each session begins with a case scenario and concludes with case problems showing real-world application of the software. "Quick Reference" guides summarizing important functions and shortcuts appear throughout. Boxes introduce unusual functions that will enhance the user's productivity. Hands-on exercises and short-answer questions allow students to practice their skills.

- **Advantage Interactive CD-ROM tutorials:** Offered by Irwin/McGraw-Hill in partnership with *MindQ Publishing*, the **Advantage Interactive** CD-ROM tutorials are based on the printed *Advantage Series* texts described above. The CD-ROMs combine sight, sound, and motion into a truly interactive learning experience. Video clips, simulations, hands-on exercises, and quizzes reinforce every important concept. *Advantage Interactive* tutorials are available for latest versions of Microsoft Office and may be used independently or with corresponding manuals in the *Advantage Series.*

- **O'Leary Series print tutorials:** Written by *Linda* and *Timothy O'Leary*, the **O'Leary Series** manuals are designed for application-specific short courses. Each manual offers a project-based approach that gives students a sense of the real-world capabilities of software applications. Extensive screen captures provide easy-to-follow visual examples for each major textual step, while visual summaries reinforce the concepts, building on students' knowledge. Manuals are available for a wide variety of software applications, including latest versions of Microsoft Office.

- **Interactive Computing Skills CD-ROM tutorials:** Created by *Ken Laudon* and *Azimuth Multimedia*, the **Interactive Computing Skills** CD-ROM tutorials offer complete introductory coverage of software applications, including Microsoft Office 4.3 and 97. Each narrated and highly interactive lesson takes 45–60 minutes to complete. "SmartQuizzes" at the end of the lessons actively test software skills within a simulated software environment. With up to four lessons per disk, *Interactive Computing Skills* is a valuable addition to an instructor's courseware package or an excellent self-study tool for students.

Supplement Offering #2: McGraw-Hill Learning Architecture

New to this edition! The future of interactive, networked education is here today! This exciting Web-based software provides complete course administration, including content customization, authoring, and delivery. With the **McGraw-Hill Learning Architecture (MHLA)** and a standard Web browser, students can take online quizzes and tests, and their scores are automatically graded and recorded. *MHLA* also includes useful features such as e-mail, message boards, and chat rooms, and it easily links to other Internet resources. Your Irwin/McGraw-Hill sales representative can explain *MHLA* in detail.

Supplement Offering #3: Classroom Presentation Software

To help instructors enhance their lecture presentations, Irwin/McGraw-Hill makes available the **CIT Classroom Presentation Tool,** a graphics-intensive set of electronic slides. This CD-ROM-based software helps to clarify topics that may otherwise be difficult to present. Topics are organized to correspond with the text chapters. The *Presentation Tool* also includes electronic files for all of the graphics in the text, allowing instructors to customize their presentations.

Minimum system requirements: IBM PC or compatible with a Pentium processor, 4X CD-ROM drive, and at least 16 MB of RAM, running Windows 95 or later. An LCD panel is needed if the images are to be shown to a large audience.

Supplement Offering #4: Instructor Support Materials

We offer the instructor the following other kinds of supplements and support to complement the text:

- **Instructor's Resource Guide:** This complete guide supports instruction in any course environment. For each chapter, the **Instructor's Resource Guide** provides an overview, chapter outline, lecture notes, notes regarding the boxes (README boxes) from the text, solutions, and suggestions, and additional information to enhance the project and critical thinking sections.

- **Test bank:** The test bank contains over 1200 different questions, which are directly referenced to the text. Specifically, it contains *true/false, multiple-choice,* and *fill-in questions,* categorized by difficulty and by type; *short-essay questions; sample midterm exam; sample final exam;* and *answers to all questions.*

- **Diploma 97—computerized testing software:** Created by *Brownstone Research Group,* **Diploma 97** has been consistently ranked number one in evaluations over similar testing products. *Diploma 97* gives instructors simple ways to write sophisticated tests that can be administered on paper or posted over a campus local area network, an intranet, or the Internet.

  Test results can be merged into *Diploma 97's* gradebook program, which automates grading, curving, and reporting functions. Indeed, thousands of students and hundreds of assignments can be put into the same gradebook file. In addition, teaching programs can be attached to questions to create interactive study guides.

  System requirements: (a) IBM PC or compatible with at least 2 MB of RAM running Windows 3.1 or (b) Macintosh with at least 2 MB of RAM running System 6.01 or later; CD-ROM drive or 3.5-inch floppy-disk drives.

- **Videos:** A selection of 10 video segments of the acclaimed PBS television series, *Computer Chronicles,* is available to qualified adopters. Each video is approximately 30 minutes long. The videos cover topics ranging from computers and politics, to online financial services, to the latest developments in PC technologies.

- **Technical support services:** Irwin/McGraw-Hill's Technical Support is available to instructors on any of our software products, such as the McGraw-Hill Learning Architecture or the CIT Classroom Presentation Tool. Instructors can access the Online Helpdesk at **www.mhhe.com/helpdesk** or by calling toll free 1-800-331-5094.

- **UIT Web site:** It's appropriate that a text with a strong communications focus also find a way to employ the communications technology available. Accordingly, a text-specific Irwin/McGraw-Hill UIT Web is available, located at **http://www.mhhe.com/cit/concepts/uit**

  This Web site was developed as a place to go for periodic updates of text material, relevant links, downloads of supplements, an instructor's forum for sharing information with colleagues, and other value-added features.

Acknowledgment of Focus Group Participants, Survey Respondents, & Reviewers

We are grateful to the following people for their participation in focus groups, response to surveys, or reviews on manuscript drafts or page proofs of all or part of the book. We cannot overstate their importance and contributions in helping us to make this the most market-driven book possible.

INSTRUCTOR FOCUS GROUP PARTICIPANTS

Russell Breslauer
Chabot College

Patrick Callan
Concordia University

Joe Chambers
Triton College

Hiram Crawford
Olive Harvey College

Edouard Desautels
University of Wisconsin—Madison

William Dorin
Indiana University—Northwest

Bonita Ellis
Wright City College

Pat Fenton
West Valley College

Bob Fulkerth
Golden Gate University

Charles Geigner
Illinois State University

Julie Giles
DeVry Institute of Technology

Dwight Graham
Prairie State College

Don Hoggan
Solano Community College

Stan Honacki
Moraine Valley Community College

Tom Hrubec
Waubonsee Community College

Alan Iliff
North Park College

Julie Jordahl
Rock Valley College

John Longstreet
Harold Washington College

Paul Lou
Diablo Valley College

Ed Mannion
California State University—Chico

Jim Potter
California State University— Hayward

Pattie Riden
Western Illinois University

Behrooz Saghafi
Chicago State University

Naj Shaik
Heartland Community College

Charlotte Thunen
Foothill College

James Van Tassel
Mission College

STUDENT FOCUS GROUP PARTICIPANTS

Virginia Amarna
Laney College

Kerry Bassett
California State University—Chico

Jeff Ferreira
Chabot College

Jocelyn Lander
Chabot College

Alfred Lepori
Mission College

Roger Lyle
College of Marin

Susan Malibiran
San Francisco City College

Karey Mathews
Chabot College

Teresa Taganat
San Francisco City College

Robin Torbet
College of Marin

SURVEY RESPONDENTS

Nancy Alderdice
Murray State University

Margaret Allison
University of Texas—Pan American

Angela Amin
Great Lakes Junior College

Connie Aragon
Seattle Central Community College

Gigi Beaton
Tyler Junior College

William C. Brough
University of Texas—Pan American

Jeff Butterfield
University of Idaho

Helen Corrigan-McFadyen
Massachusetts Bay Community College

James Frost
Idaho State University

Candace Gerrod
Red Rocks Community College

Julie Heine
Southern Oregon State College

Jerry Humphrey
Tulsa Junior College

Jan Karasz
Cameron University

Alan Maples
Cedar Valley College

Norman Muller
Greenfield Community College

Paul Murphy
Massachusetts Bay Community College

Sonia Nayle
Los Angeles City College

Janet Olpert
Cameron University

Pat Ormond
Utah Valley State College

Marie Planchard
Massachusetts Bay Community College

Fernando Rivera
University of Puerto Rico—Mayaguez Campus

Naj Shaik
Heartland Community College

Jack Shorter
Texas A&M University

Randy Stolze
Marist College

Ron Wallace
Blue Mountain Community College

Steve Wedwick
Heartland Community College

REVIEWERS

Nancy Alderdice
Murray State University

Margaret Allison
University of Texas—Pan American

Sharon Anderson
Western Iowa Tech Community College

Bonnie Bailey
Morehead State University

David Brent Bandy
University of Wisconsin—Oshkosh

Robert Barrett
Indiana University, Purdue University at Fort Wayne

Anthony Baxter
University of Kentucky

Virginia Bender
William Rainey Harper College

Warren Boe
University of Iowa

Randall Bower
Iowa State University

Phyllis Broughton
Pitt Community College

J. Wesley Cain
City University, Bellevue

Judy Cameron
Spokane Community College

Kris Chandler
Pikes Peak Community College

William Chandler
University of Southern Colorado

John Chenoweth
East Tennessee State University

Ashraful Chowdhury
Dekalb College

Erline Cocke
*Northwest Mississippi Community
College*

Robert Coleman
Pima County Community College

Glen Coulthard
Okanagan University

Robert Crandall
Denver Business School

Thad Crews
Western Kentucky University

Jim Dartt
San Diego Mesa College

Patti Dreven
*Community College of Southern
Nevada*

John Durham
Fort Hays State University

John Enomoto
East Los Angeles College

Ray Fanselau
American River College

Eleanor Flanigan
Montclair State University

Ken Frizane
Oakton Community College

James Frost
Idaho State University

JoAnn Garver
University of Akron

Jill Gebelt
Salt Lake Community College

Charles Geigner
Illinois State University

Frank Gillespie
University of Georgia

Myron Goldberg
Pace University

Sallyann Hanson
Mercer County Community College

Albert Harris
Appalachian State University

Jan Harris
Lewis & Clark Community College

Michael Hasset
Fort Hays State University

Martin Hochhauser
Dutchess Community College

James D. Holland
*Okaloosa-Waltoon Community
College*

Wayne Horn
Pensacola Junior College

Christopher Hundhausen
University of Oregon

Jim Johnson
Valencia Community College

Jorene Kirkland
Amarillo College

Victor Lafrenz
Mohawk Valley Community College

Sheila Lancaster
Gadsden State Community College

Stephen Leach
Florida State University

Paul Leidig
Grand Valley State University

Chang-Yang Lin
Eastern Kentucky University

Paul Lou
Diablo Valley College

Deborah Ludford
Glendale Community College

Peter MacGregor
*Estrella Mountain Community
College*

Donna Madsen
Kirkwood Community College

Kenneth E. Martin
University of North Florida

Curtis Meadow
University of Maine

Timothy Meyer
Edinboro University

Marty Murray
Portland Community College

Charles Nelson
Rock Valley College

Wanda Nolden
Delgado Community College

E. Gladys Norman
Linn-Benton Community College

George Novotny
Ferris State University

Pat Ormond
Utah Valley State College

John Panzica
Community College of Rhode Island

Rajesh Parekh
Iowa State University

Merrill Parker
*Chattanooga State Technical
Community College*

Jim Potter
*California State University—
Hayward*

Leonard Presby
William Patterson State College

Delores Pusins
Hillsborough Community College

Eugene Rathswohl
University of San Diego

Alan Rea
Western Michigan University

Jerry Reed
Valencia Community College

John Rezac
Johnson County Community College

Jane Ritter
University of Oregon

Stan Ross
Newbury College

Judy Scheeren
*Westmoreland County Community
College*

Al Schroeder
Richland College

Earl Schweppe
University of Kansas

Tom Seymour
Minot State University

Elaine Shillito
Clark State Community College

Denis Titchenell
Los Angeles City College

Jack VanDeventer
Washington State University

Jim Vogel
Sanford Brown College

Dale Walikainen
Christopher Newport University

Reneva Walker
Valencia Community College

Patricia Lynn Wermers
North Shore Community College

Ron West
Umpqua Community College

Doug White
Western Michigan University

Edward Winter
Salem State College

Floyd Winters
Manatee Community College

Israel Yost
University of New Hampshire

Eileen Zisk
Community College of Rhode Island

Write to Us

We welcome your response to this book, for we are truly trying to make it as useful as possible. Write to us in care of Kyle Lewis, Sponsoring Editor, Irwin/McGraw-Hill, 1333 Burr Ridge Parkway, Burr Ridge, IL 60521 or via e-mail: **kyle_lewis@mcgraw-hill.com**

Stacey C. Sawyer
Brian K. Williams
Sarah E. Hutchinson

Detailed Contents

Chapter 2

APPLICATIONS SOFTWARE: TOOLS FOR THINKING & WORKING 35

Chapter 3

SYSTEM SOFTWARE: THE POWER BEHIND THE POWER 79

Chapter 4

PROCESSORS: HARDWARE FOR POWER & PORTABILITY   111

Chapter 7

TELECOMMUNICATIONS: THE USES OF ONLINE RESOURCES & THE INTERNET 229

Chapter 8

COMMUNICATIONS TECHNOLOGY: HARDWARE, CHANNELS, & NETWORKS 255

Chapter 9

SYSTEMS: DEVELOPMENT, PROGRAMMING, & LANGUAGES 287

The Digital Age

An Overview of the Revolution in Computers & Communications

Chapter 1

key questions

You should be able to answer the following questions:

1.1 **From the Analog to the Digital Age: The "New Story" of Computers & Communications** What are analog and digital signals, and what is "technological convergence"?

1.2 **Overview of a Computer-&-Communications System: System Elements 1 & 2—People & Procedures** What are the six elements of a computer-and-communications system?

1.3 **System Element 3: Data/Information** What is the difference between data and information, and what are the principal measurements of data?

1.4 **System Element 4: Hardware** What are the five basic operations of computing, and what are the corresponding categories of hardware devices?

1.5 **System Element 5: Software** What is software, and what are the two kinds of software?

1.6 **System Element 6: Communications** How is "communications" defined and how does digital communications present us with the possibility of having an Information Superhighway?

1.7 **Overview of Developments in Computer Technology** What are the three developments in computing, and what are the five types of computers?

1.8 **Overview of Developments in Communications Technology** What are three developments in communications?

1.9 **Computer & Communications Technology Combined: Connectivity & Interactivity** What are connectivity and interactivity?

1.10 **The Ethics of Information Technology** What are some ethical concerns in the field of information technology?

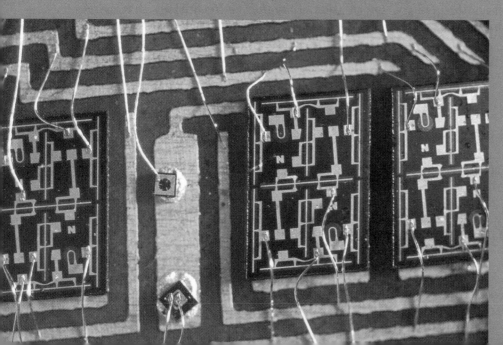

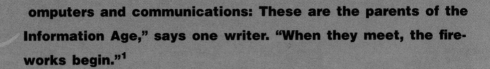

"omputers and communications: These are the parents of the Information Age," says one writer. "When they meet, the fireworks begin."[1]

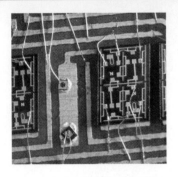

What sort of fireworks are we talking about? Computers and communications are bringing about a revolution that will make—indeed, is making now—profound changes in your life. This wrenching change in human history goes under many names: The Computer Revolution. The Information Revolution. The Communications Revolution. The Binary Age. The Information Age. The Information Society. We prefer to call it the Digital Age, but whatever its name, it is happening in all parts of society and in all parts of the world, and its consequences will reverberate throughout our lifetimes.

The technological systems and industries that the computer and communications revolution is bringing forth may seem overwhelmingly complex. However, the concept on which they are based is as simple as the flick of a light switch: *on* and *off.* Let us begin to see how this works.

1.1 From the Analog to the Digital Age: The "New Story" of Computers & Communications

KEY QUESTIONS

What are analog and digital signals, and what is "technological convergence"?

Preview & Review: Each "Preview & Review" in this book gives you a brief overview of the information discussed in the section that follows it. You can use it again as a review to test your knowledge. This is the first one.

Information technology is technology that merges computers and high-speed communications links. This merger of computer and communications technologies is producing "technological convergence"—the technological coming together of several industries through various devices that exchange information in the electronic format used by computers. The industries include computers, communications, consumer electronics, entertainment, and mass media.

Computers are based on digital, two-state (binary) signals—0 and 1. However, most phenomena in the world are analog, meaning they have the property of continuously varying in strength and/or quantity. Today the word "digital" is used almost interchangeably with "computer."

The essence of all revolution, stated philosopher Hannah Arendt, is the start of a *new story* in human experience. For us, the new story is the arrival of information technology. **Information technology is technology that merges computing with high-speed communications links carrying data, sound, and video.**[2] The most important consequence of information technology is that it is producing a gradual fusion of several important industries in a phenomenon that has been called *technological convergence.*

What Is "Technological Convergence"?

Technological convergence, also known as **digital convergence, is the technological merger of several industries through various devices that exchange information in the electronic, or digital, format used by computers. The industries are computers, communications, consumer electronics, entertainment, and mass media.**

Technological convergence has tremendous significance. It means that from a common electronic base, information can be communicated or delivered in all the ways we are accustomed to receiving it. These include the familiar media of newspapers, photographs, films, recordings, radio, and television. However, it can also be communicated through newer technology—satellite, fiber-optic cable, cellular phone, fax machine, or compact disk, for example. More important, as time goes on, *the same information will be exchanged among many kinds of equipment, using the language of computers.*

The effect of technological convergence on your life could be quite profound. Among other things, it means that you will have to become accustomed to:

- The stepped-up pace of technological change
- The increased need for continuous learning
- Being prepared to interact with people from other cultures and backgrounds
- Continually evaluating the usefulness and reliability of huge quantities of information

Is this consolidation of technologies an overnight phenomenon? Actually, it has been developing over several years, as we explain next.

The Merger of Computer & Communications Technologies

Technological convergence is derived from a combination of two recent technologies—*computers* and *communications.* (■ *See Panel 1.1, next page.*)

- **Computer technology:** It's highly unlikely that anyone reading this book would not have seen a computer by now. Nevertheless, let's define what it is. **A *computer* is a programmable, multiuse machine that accepts data—raw facts and figures—and processes, or manipulates, it into information we can use, such as summaries or totals.** Its purpose is to speed up problem solving and increase productivity.

   If you've actually touched a computer, it's probably been a personal computer, such as the widely advertised desktop or portable models from Apple, IBM, Compaq, Dell, Gateway 2000, NEC, or Packard Bell. However, many other machines, such as automobiles, microwave ovens, and portable phones, use miniature electronic processing devices (microprocessors, or microcontrollers) similar to those that control personal computers.

- **Communications technology:** Unquestionably you've been using communications technology for years. **Communications, or telecommunications, technology consists of electromagnetic devices and systems for communicating over long distances.** The principal examples are telephone, radio, broadcast television, and cable TV.

Before the 1950s, computer technology and communications technology developed independently, like rails in a railroad track that never merge. Since then, however, they have gradually fused together, producing a new information environment.

Why have the worlds of computers and of telecommunications been so long in coming together? The answer is this: *Computers are digital, but most of the world is analog.* Let us explain what this means.

The Digital Basis of Computers

Computers may seem like incredibly complicated devices, but their underlying principle is simple. When you open up a personal computer, what you see is mainly electronic circuitry. And what is the most basic statement that can be made about electricity? Simply this: It can be either *turned on* or *turned off*.

With a two-state on/off arrangement, one state can represent a 1 digit, the other a 0 digit. Because computers are based on on/off or other two-state conditions, they use the *binary system*, which is able to represent any number using only two digits—0 and 1. Today, **digital specifically refers to communications signals or information represented in a two-state (binary) way.** More generally, *digital* is usually synonymous with "computer-based."

In the binary system, each 0 (off) or 1 (on) is called a *bit*—short for *binary digit*. In turn, bits can be grouped in various combinations to represent characters of data—numbers, letters, punctuation marks, and so on. For example, the letter H could correspond to the electronic signal 01001000 (that is, off-on-off-off-on-off-off-off). (A group of eight bits is called a *byte*.)

Digital data, then, consists of data represented by on/off signals, symbolized as 0s and 1s. This is the method of data representation by which computers process and store data and communicate with each other.

The Analog Basis of Life

"The shades of a sunset, the flight of a bird, or the voice of a singer would seem to defy the black or white simplicity of binary representation," points out one writer.[3] Indeed, these and most other phenomena of the world are

■ **PANEL 1.1**

Fusion of computer and communications technology
Today's new information environment came about gradually from two separate streams of technological development.

Computer Technology

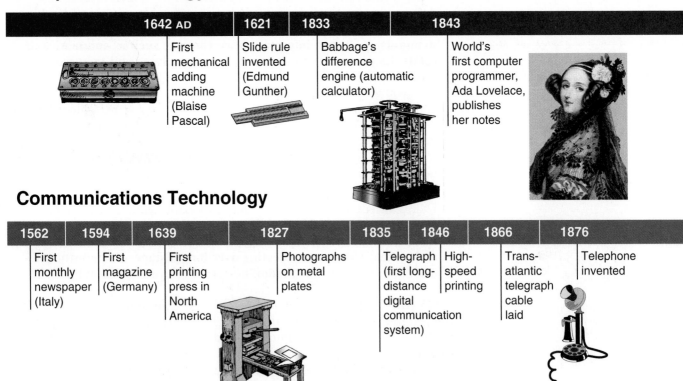

	1642 AD	1621	1833	1843
	First mechanical adding machine (Blaise Pascal)	Slide rule invented (Edmund Gunther)	Babbage's difference engine (automatic calculator)	World's first computer programmer, Ada Lovelace, publishes her notes

Communications Technology

1562	1594	1639	1827	1835	1846	1866	1876
First monthly newspaper (Italy)	First magazine (Germany)	First printing press in North America	Photographs on metal plates	Telegraph (first long-distance digital communication system)	High-speed printing	Trans-atlantic telegraph cable laid	Telephone invented

analog, **continuously varying in strength and/or quantity.** Sound, light, temperature, and pressure values, for instance, can fall anywhere along a continuum or range. The highs, lows, and in-between states have historically been represented with analog devices rather than digital ones. Examples of analog devices are a speedometer, a thermometer, and a pressure sensor, which can measure continuous fluctuations. Thus, *analog data* is transmitted in a continuous form that closely resembles the information it represents. The electrical signals on a telephone line are analog-data representations of the original voices. Telephone, radio, broadcast television, and cable-TV have traditionally transmitted analog data.

The differences between analog and digital transmission are apparent when you look at a drawing of an on/off digital signal and one of a wavy analog signal, such as a voice message appearing on a standard telephone line. In general, for your computer to receive communications signals transmitted over a telephone line, you need a *modem* to translate the telephone line's analog signals into the computer's digital signals. (■ *See Panel 1.2, next page.*)

The modem provides a means for computers to communicate with one another while the old-fashioned copper-wire telephone network—an analog system that was built to transmit the human voice—still exists. Our concern, however, goes far beyond telephone transmission. How can the analog realities of the world be expressed in digital form? How can light, sounds, colors, temperatures, and other dynamic values be represented so that they can be manipulated by a computer? Let us consider this.

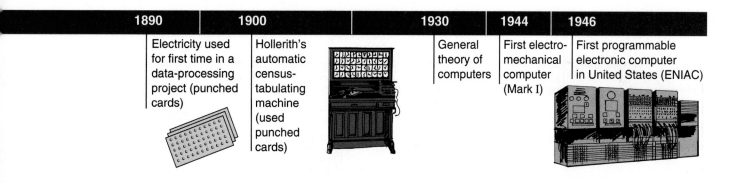

1890	1900		1930	1944	1946
Electricity used for first time in a data-processing project (punched cards)	Hollerith's automatic census-tabulating machine (used punched cards)		General theory of computers	First electro-mechanical computer (Mark I)	First programmable electronic computer in United States (ENIAC)

1888	1894	1895	1912	1915	1928	1939	1946	1947	1948
Radio waves identified	Edison makes a movie	Marconi develops radio; motion-picture camera invented	Motion pictures become a big business	AT&T long-distance service reaches San Francisco	First TV demonstrated; first sound movie	Commercial TV broad-casting	Color TV demon-strated	Transistor invented	Reel-to-reel tape recorder

■ PANEL 1.2

Analog versus digital signals, and the modem
Note the wavy line for an analog signal and the on/off line for a digital signal. (The modem shown here is outside the computer; today most modems are inside the computer's cabinet.)

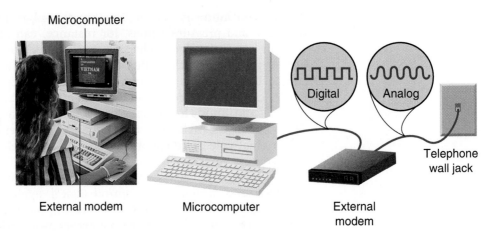

Microcomputer

External modem　　Microcomputer　　External modem

Digital　　Analog

Telephone wall jack

Converting Reality to Digital Form

Suppose you are using an analog tape recorder to record a singer during a performance. The analog process will produce a near duplicate of the sounds. This will include distortions, such as buzzings and clicks, or electronic hums if an amplified guitar is used.

The digital recording process is different. The way in which music is captured for music CDs (compact disks) does not provide a duplicate of a musical performance. Rather, the digital process uses *representative selections (samples)* to record the sounds and produce a copy that is virtually exact and free from distortion and noise. Computer-based equipment takes samples of sounds at regular intervals—nearly 44,100 times a second. The samples are

1952	1963	1964	1967	1969	1970	1971	1975	1977	
UNIVAC computer correctly predicts election of Eisenhower as U.S. President	BASIC developed at Dartmouth	IBM introduces 360 line of computers	Hand-held calculator	ARPA-Net established, led to Internet	Micro-processor chips come into use; floppy disk introduced for storing data	First pocket calculator	First microcomputer (MITs Altair 8800)	Apple II computer (first personal computer sold in assembled form)	

Communications Technology

1950	1952	1957	1961	1968	1975	1976	1977
Cable TV	Direct-distance dialing (no need to go through operator); transistor radio introduced	First satellite launched (Russia's Sputnik)	Push-button telephones	Portable video recorders; video cassettes	Flat-screen TV	First wide-scale marketing of TV computer games (Atari)	First inter-active cable TV

then converted to numbers that the computer uses to express the sounds. The sample rate of 44,100 times per second and the high level of precision fool our ears into hearing a smooth, continuous sound. Similarly, for visual material a computer can take samples of values such as brightness and color. The same is true of other aspects of real-life experience, such as pressure, temperature, and motion.

Are we being cheated out of experiencing "reality" by allowing computers to sample sounds, images, and so on? Actually, people willingly made this compromise years ago, before computers were invented. Movies, for instance, carve up reality into 24 frames a second. Television frames are drawn at 30 lines per second. These processes happen so quickly that our eyes and brains easily jump the visual gaps. Digital processing of analog experience represents just one more degree of compromise.

Let us now look at how a digital computer-and-communications system works. The following sections present a brief overview that is important to an understanding of the rest of the book.

1.2 Overview of a Computer-&-Communications System: System Elements 1 & 2—People & Procedures

KEY QUESTION

What are the six elements of a computer-and-communications system?

Preview & Review: A computer-and-communications system has six elements: (1) people, (2) procedures, (3) data/information, (4) hardware, (5) software, and (6) communications.

People are the most important part—the creators and the beneficiaries—of a computer-and-communications system. Two types of people use information technology— computer professionals and end-users.

Procedures are steps for accomplishing a result. Procedures may be expressed in print-based manuals or online documentation.

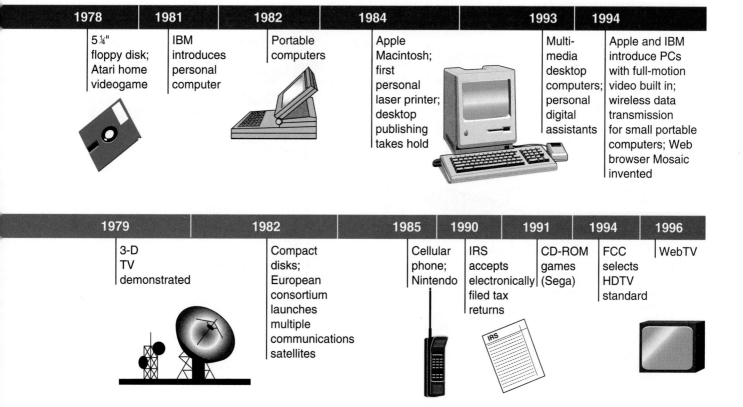

1978	1981	1982	1984	1993	1994
5 ¼" floppy disk; Atari home videogame	IBM introduces personal computer	Portable computers	Apple Macintosh; first personal laser printer; desktop publishing takes hold	Multimedia desktop computers; personal digital assistants	Apple and IBM introduce PCs with full-motion video built in; wireless data transmission for small portable computers; Web browser Mosaic invented

1979	1982	1985	1990	1991	1994	1996
3-D TV demonstrated	Compact disks; European consortium launches multiple communications satellites	Cellular phone; Nintendo	IRS accepts electronically filed tax returns	CD-ROM games (Sega)	FCC selects HDTV standard	WebTV

A *system* is a group of related components and operations that interact to perform a task. A system can be many things: the registration process at your college, the 52 bones in the foot, a weather storm front, the monarchy of Great Britain. Here we are concerned with a technological kind of system. **A *computer-and-communications system* is made up of six elements: (1) people, (2) procedures, (3) data/information, (4) hardware, (5) software, and (6) communications.** (■ *See Panel 1.3.*) We briefly describe these elements in the next six sections and elaborate on them in subsequent chapters.

System Element 1: People

People are the most important part of a computer-and-communications system. People of all levels and skills, from novices to programmers, are the users and operators of the system. The whole point of the system, of course, is to benefit people.

Two types of people use information technology—*computer professionals* and *"end-users."*

- Computer professionals: **A *computer professional,* or an *information technology professional,* is a person who has had extensive education or considerable experience in the technical aspects of using a computer-and-communications system.** For example, a *computer programmer* creates the programs (software) that process the data in a computer system.

- End-users: An end-user is a person probably much like yourself. **An *end-user,* or simply a *user,* is someone with moderate technical**

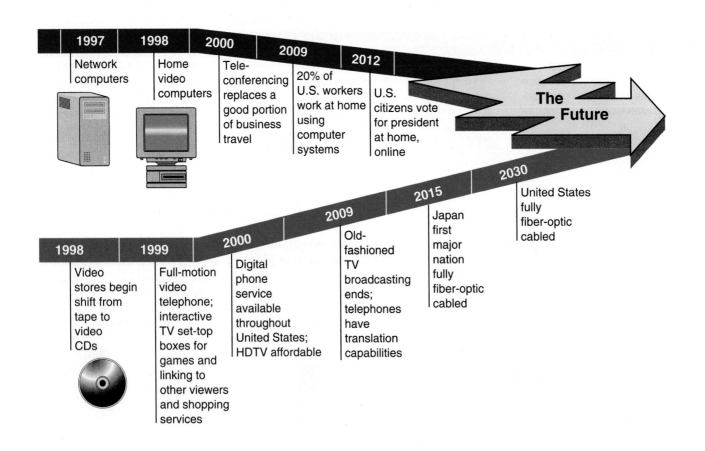

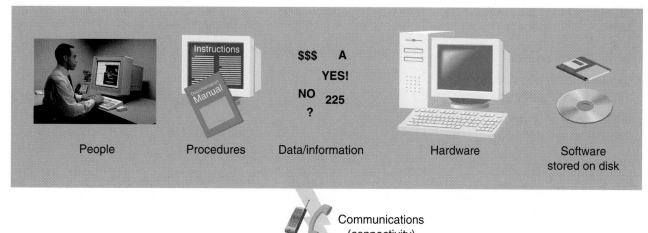

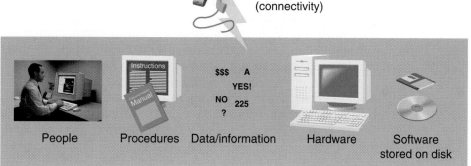

■ PANEL 1.3

A computer-and-communications system

The five basic elements of the system include people, procedures, data/information, hardware, and software. These five system elements are connected to other systems via the sixth element, communications.

knowledge of information technology who uses computers for entertainment, education, or work-related tasks. The user does not understand all the technical nuances of a system but instead usually reacts to the programs and procedures instituted by an information technology professional. For example, you might not know exactly how the Internet works but know how to use it, as did one woman who found the Internet's power as a research and education tool a boon in helping her 12-year-old daughter complete a research project about soap. "In the old days, you'd have had to go to the library, write to the companies for information," she says. "But we sat down together and dialed into Colgate-Palmolive's Web page and Lever Brothers' Web page. . . . It was a blast."[4]

System Element 2: Procedures

Procedures **are descriptions of how things are done—steps for accomplishing a result or rules and guidelines for what is acceptable.** Sometimes procedures are unstated, the result of tradition or common practice. You may find this out when you join a club or are a guest in someone's house for the first time. Sometimes procedures are laid out in great detail in manuals, as is true, say, of tax laws.

When you use a bank automated teller machine (ATM)—a form of computer system—the procedures for making a withdrawal or a deposit are given in on-screen messages. In other computer systems, procedures are spelled out in manuals. Manuals, called *documentation,* contain instructions, rules, or guidelines to follow when using hardware or software. When you buy a microcomputer or a software package, it comes with documentation, or procedures. Nowadays, in fact, many such procedures come not only in a book or pamphlet but also on a computer disk, which presents directions on your display screen. Many companies also offer documentation on the Internet.

1.3 System Element 3: Data/Information

Preview & Review: The distinction is made between raw data, which is unprocessed, and information, which is processed data. Units of measurement of data/information capacity include kilobytes, megabytes, gigabytes, and terabytes.

KEY QUESTIONS

What is the difference between data and information, and what are the principal measurements of data?

Though used loosely all the time, the word *data* has some precise and distinct meanings.

"Raw Data" Versus Information

Data can be considered the raw material—whether in paper, electronic, or other form—that is processed by the computer. In other words, **data consists of the raw facts and figures that are processed into information.**

Information **is summarized data or otherwise manipulated data that is useful for decision making.** Thus, the raw data of employees' hours worked and wage rates is processed by a computer into the information of paychecks and payrolls. Some characteristics of useful information are that it is *relevant, timely, accurate, concise,* and *complete.*

Actually, in ordinary usage the words *data* and *information* are often used synonymously. After all, one person's information may be another person's data. The "information" of paychecks and payrolls may become the "data" that goes into someone's yearly financial projections or tax returns.

Units of Measurement for Capacity: From Bytes to Terabytes

A common concern of computer users is "How much data can this gadget hold?" The gadget might be a diskette, a hard disk, or a computer's main memory (all terms we'll explain shortly). The question is a crucial one. If you have too much data, the computer may not be able to handle it. Or if a software package takes up too much storage space, it cannot be run on a particular computer.

We mentioned that computers deal with "on" and "off" electrical states, which are represented as 0s and 1s, called *bits*. Bits are combined in groups of eight, called *bytes*, to hold the equivalent of a character. A *character* is a single letter, number, or special symbol (such as a punctuation mark or dollar sign). Examples of characters are A, 1, and ?.

A computer system's data/information storage capacity is represented by bytes, kilobytes, megabytes, gigabytes, and terabytes:

- **Kilobyte:** A *kilobyte*, abbreviated K or KB, is equivalent to approximately 1000 bytes (or characters). More precisely, 1 kilobyte is 1024 (2^{10}) bytes, but the figure is commonly rounded off. Kilobytes are a common unit of measure for the data-holding (memory) capacity of personal computers.

- **Megabyte:** A *megabyte*, abbreviated M or MB and sometimes called a "meg," is about 1 million bytes. Some software programs require 16 or more megabytes, or about 16 million bytes, of memory.

- **Gigabyte:** A *gigabyte*, G or GB, is about 1 billion bytes. Pronounced "*gig*-a-bite," this unit of measure—sometimes called a "gig"—is used not only with large computers but also with newer personal computers to represent hard-disk storage capacities.

- **Terabyte:** A *terabyte*, T or TB, is about 1 trillion bytes, or 1000 gigabytes.

1.4 System Element 4: Hardware

KEY QUESTIONS

What are the five basic operations of computing, and what are the corresponding categories of hardware devices?

Preview & Review: The basic operations of computing consist of (1) input, (2) processing, (3) output, and (4) storage. Communications (5) adds an extension capability to each operation.

Hardware devices are often categorized according to which of these five operations they perform. (1) Input hardware includes the keyboard, mouse, and scanner. (2) Processing and memory hardware consists of the CPU (the processor) and main memory. (3) Output hardware includes the display screen, printer, and sound devices. (4) Secondary-storage hardware stores data on diskette, hard disk, magnetic-tape devices, and CD-ROM. (5) Communications hardware includes modems.

As we said earlier, a *system* is a group of related components and operations that interact to perform a task. Once you know how the pieces of the system fit together, you can then make better judgments about any one of them. And you can make knowledgeable decisions about buying and operating a computer system.

The Basic Operations of Computing

How does a computer system process data into information? It usually goes through four operations: *(1) input, (2) processing, (3) output,* and *(4) storage.* (■ *See Panel 1.4, next page.*)

1 **Input operation:** In the *input* operation, data is entered or otherwise captured electronically and is converted to a form that can be processed by the computer. The means for "capturing" data (the raw, unsorted facts) is input hardware, such as a keyboard.

2 **Processing operation:** In the *processing* operation, the data is manipulated to process or transform it into information (such as summaries or totals). For example, numbers may be added or subtracted.

3 **Output operation:** In the *output* operation, the information obtained from the data is produced in a form usable by people. Examples of output are printed text, sound, and charts and graphs displayed on a computer screen.

4 **Secondary-storage operation:** In the *storage* operation, data, information, and programs are permanently stored in computer-processable form. Diskettes are examples of materials used for storage.

Often these four operations occur so quickly that they seem to be happening simultaneously.

Where does *communications* fit in here? In the four operations of computing, communications offers an *extension* capability. Data may be input from afar, processed in a remote area, output in several different locations, and stored in yet other places. And information can be transmitted to other computers, whether 3 feet away or halfway around the world. All this is done through a wired or wireless communications connection to the computer.

Hardware Categories

Hardware is what most people think of when they picture computers. ***Hardware consists of all the machinery and equipment*** in a computer system. The hardware includes, among other devices, the keyboard, the screen, the printer, and the computer or processing device itself.

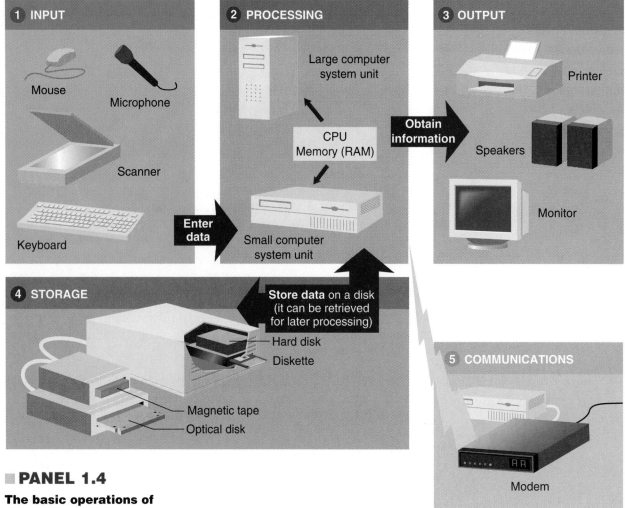

1 INPUT

Mouse

Microphone

Scanner

Keyboard

Enter data

2 PROCESSING

Large computer system unit

CPU
Memory (RAM)

Small computer system unit

Obtain information

3 OUTPUT

Printer

Speakers

Monitor

4 STORAGE

Store data on a disk (it can be retrieved for later processing)

Hard disk

Diskette

Magnetic tape

Optical disk

5 COMMUNICATIONS

Modem

■ **PANEL 1.4**

The basic operations of computing

A computer goes through four operations: (1) input of data, (2) processing of data into information, (3) output of information, and (4) storage of information. Communications (5) extends the computer system's capabilities.

In general, computer hardware is categorized according to which of the five computer operations it performs:

- Input
- Processing and memory
- Output
- Secondary storage
- Communications

Regardless of the operations they perform, external devices that are connected to the main computer cabinet are referred to as "peripheral devices," or simply "peripherals." **A *peripheral device* is any piece of hardware that is connected to a computer.** Examples are the keyboard, mouse, monitor, and printer.

We describe hardware in detail elsewhere (Chapters 4–8), but the following offers a quick overview to help you gain familiarity with terms.

Input Hardware

***Input hardware* consists of devices that allow people to put data into the computer in a form that the computer can use.** For example, input may be by means of a *keyboard, mouse, microphone,* or *scanner.* The keyboard is self-explanatory.

Keyboard

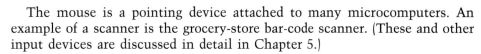

Mouse—two types

The mouse is a pointing device attached to many microcomputers. An example of a scanner is the grocery-store bar-code scanner. (These and other input devices are discussed in detail in Chapter 5.)

Processing & Memory Hardware

The brains of the computer are the *processing* and *main memory* devices, housed in the computer's system unit. The *system unit*, or system cabinet, houses the electronic circuitry called the *CPU (central processing unit)*, which does the actual processing, and *main memory*, which supports processing. (These are discussed in detail in Chapter 4.)

Microprocessor

The CPU is the computing part of the computer. It controls and manipulates data to produce information. In a personal computer the CPU is usually a single, fingernail-size "chip" called a *microprocessor*, with electrical circuits printed on it. This microprocessor and other components necessary to make it work are mounted on a main circuit board called a *motherboard.*

Memory—also known as *main memory, RAM (random access memory),* or *primary storage*—is working storage. Memory is the computer's "work space," where data and programs for immediate processing are held. Computer memory is contained on memory chips mounted on the motherboard. Memory capacity is important because it determines how much data can be processed at once and how big and complex a program may be used to process the data.

Despite its name, memory does not remember. That is, once the power is turned off, all the data and programs within memory simply vanish. This is why data/information must also be stored in relatively permanent form on disks and tapes, which are called *secondary storage* to distinguish them from main memory's *primary storage.*

Output Hardware

Screen

Output hardware consists of devices that translate information processed by the computer into a form that humans can understand. We are now so exposed to products that are output by some sort of computer that we don't consider them unusual. Examples are grocery receipts, bank statements, and grade reports. More recent forms are digital recordings and even digital radio.

As a personal computer user, you will be dealing with three principal types of output hardware—*screens, printers,* and *sound output devices.* (These and other output devices are discussed in detail in Chapter 5.) The *screen* is the display area of a computer. A *printer* is a device that converts computer output into printed images. Printers are of many types, some noisy, some quiet, some able to print carbon copies, some not.

Many computers emit chirps and beeps. Some go beyond those noises and contain sound processors and speakers that can play digital music or human-like speech. High-fidelity stereo sound is becoming more important as computer and communications technologies continue to merge.

Printer

Secondary-Storage Hardware

Main memory, or primary storage, is *temporary* storage. It works with the CPU chip on the motherboard inside the computer cabinet to hold data and programs for immediate processing. Secondary storage, by contrast, is *permanent* storage. It is not on the motherboard (although it may still be inside the system cabinet). ***Secondary storage* consists of devices that store data and programs permanently on disk or tape.**

You may hear people use the term "storage media." *Media* refers to the material that stores data, such as disk or magnetic tape. For microcomputers, the principal storage media are *diskette (floppy disk), hard disk, magnetic tape,* and *CD-ROM.* (■ *See Panel 1.5.*) (These and other secondary-storage devices are discussed in detail in Chapter 6.)

A *diskette,* or *floppy disk,* is a removable round, flexible disk that stores data as magnetized spots. The disk is contained in a plastic case to prevent the disk surface from being touched. The most common size is *3½ inches* in diameter.

To use a diskette, you need a disk drive in your computer. A *disk drive* is a device that holds and spins the diskette inside its case; it "reads" data from and "writes" data to the disk. The words *read* and *write* are used a great deal in computing. *Read* means that the data represented in magnetized spots on the disk (or tape) are converted to electronic signals and transmitted to the memory in the computer. *Write* means that the electronic information processed by the computer is recorded onto disk (or tape).

Diskettes are made out of a magnetic, plastic-type material, which is what makes them "floppy." They are also removable. By contrast, a *hard disk* is a disk platter made out of metal and covered with a magnetic recording surface. It also holds data represented by the presence (1) and absence (0) of magnetized spots. Hard-disk drives read and write data in much the same way that diskette drives do. However, there are three significant differences. First, hard-disk drives can handle thousands of times more data than diskettes do. Second, hard-disk drives are often located in the system cabinet, in which case they are not removable. (External hard-disk drives such as the Zip, Jaz, and Syquest models are also available; they use removable hard-disk cartridges that can store large amounts of data.) Third, hard disks read and write data much faster than diskettes do.

Moviemakers used to love to represent computers with banks of spinning reels of magnetic tape. Indeed, with early computers, "mag tape" was the principal method of secondary storage. The magnetic tape used for computers is made from the same material as that used for audiotape and videotape. That is, *magnetic tape* is made of flexible plastic coated on one side with a magnetic material; again, data is represented by the presence and absence of magnetized spots. Because of its drawbacks (described in Chapter 6), nowadays tape—along with hard-disk cartridges—is used mainly to provide low-cost duplicate storage. A tape that is a duplicate or copy of another form of

Diskette

■ PANEL 1.5

Secondary storage for microcomputers

(Left) Examples of diskette and CD-ROM drives (the hard-disk drive has no exterior opening). *(Middle)* Inside of hard-disk drive. *(Right)* External Zip hard-disk drive with hard-disk cartridge.

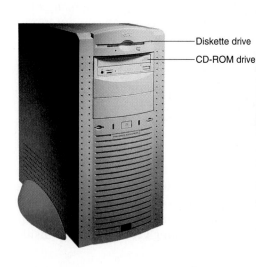

Diskette drive
CD-ROM drive

CD-ROM

storage is referred to as a *backup*. Because hard disks sometimes fail ("crash"), personal computer users who don't wish to do backup using a lot of diskettes may use magnetic tape or hard-disk cartridges instead.

If you have been using music CDs (compact disks), you are already familiar with optical disks. An *optical disk* is a disk that is written and read by lasers. *CD-ROM*, which stands *for compact disk—read-only memory*, is only one kind of optical-disk format that is used to hold text, graphics, and sound. CD-ROMs can hold hundreds of times more data than diskettes, and can hold more data than many hard disks. A newer type of optical disk called *DVD-ROM* has more than ten times the capacity of a CD-ROM.

Communications Hardware

Computers can be "stand-alone" machines, meaning that they are not connected to anything else. Indeed, many students tote around portable personal computers on which they use word processing or other programs to help them with their work. However, the *communications* component of the computer system *vastly* extends the range of a computer—for example, via connection to the Internet, which is actually a worldwide electronic network of smaller connected networks.

The dominant communications lines developed during this century use analog transmission. Thus, for many years the principal form of direct connection was via standard copper-wire telephone lines. Hundreds of these twisted-pair copper wires are bundled together in cables and strung on telephone poles or buried underground. As mentioned, a modem is communications hardware required to translate a computer's digital signals into analog form for transmission over telephone wires. Although copper wiring still exists in most places, it is gradually being supplanted by two other kinds of direct connections: coaxial cable and fiber-optic cable. Eventually, all transmission lines will accommodate digital signals. (Communications hardware and related issues are covered in detail in Chapters 7 and 8.)

1.5 System Element 5: Software

KEY QUESTIONS

What is software, and what are the two kinds of software?

Preview & Review: Software comprises the instructions that tell the computer what to do. In general, software is divided into applications software and system software.

Applications software is software that has been developed to solve a particular problem, to perform useful work on specific tasks, or to provide entertainment. Applications software may be custom or packaged.

System software, which includes operating systems, enables the applications software to run on the computer.

Software, or programs, consists of the instructions that tell the computer how to perform a task. Software is written in special code by programmers, and the software is then copied by the manufacturer onto a storage medium, such as CD-ROM. The code on the CD-ROM is translated in the user's computer into the 0/1, off/on signals discussed earlier (✔ p. 4). In most instances, the words *software* and *program* are interchangeable. (We discuss software in detail in the next two chapters.)

There are two major types of software:

- **Applications software:** This may be thought of as the kind of software that people use to perform a specific task, such as word processing software used to prepare documents and game software used to entertain.

● System software: This may be thought of as the underlying software that the computer uses to manage its own internal activities and run applications software. System software acts as the interpreter that allows you and your applications software to access the physical hardware devices and other resources.

Although you may not need a particular applications program, you must have system software or you will not even be able to "boot up" (start) your computer.

Applications Software

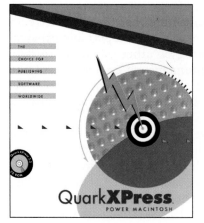

Applications software is software that has been developed to solve a particular problem, to perform useful work on specific tasks, or to provide entertainment. Applications software may be either *custom* or *packaged.*

Custom software is software designed and developed for a particular customer. This is the kind of software that you would hire a computer programmer—a software creator—to develop for you. Such software would perform a task that could not be readily done with standard off-the-shelf packaged software available from a computer store or mail-order house.

Packaged software, or a *software package,* is the kind of off-the-shelf program developed for sale to the general public. This is the principal kind that will be of interest to you. Examples of packaged software that you will most likely encounter are word processing programs, spreadsheet programs, and office suites. (We discuss these in Chapter 2.)

System Software

As the user, you interact mostly with the applications software and let the applications software interact with the system software. **System software controls the allocation and usage of hardware resources and enables the applications software to run.**

System software consists of several programs, the most important of which is the operating system. The *operating system* acts as the master control program that runs the computer. It handles such activities as running and storing programs and storing and processing data. The purpose of the operating system is to allow applications to operate by standardizing access to shared resources such as disks and memory. Examples of operating systems are MS-DOS, Windows 95 and 98, Windows NT, Unix, and the Macintosh operating system (MacOS). (We discuss these operating systems in detail in Chapter 3.)

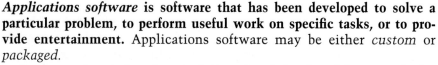

1.6 System Element 6: Communications

KEY QUESTIONS

How is "communications" defined, and how does digital communications present us with the possibility of having an Information Superhighway?

Preview & Review: "Communications" refers to the electronic transfer of data. The kind of data being communicated is rapidly changing from analog to digital. The Information Superhighway is a metaphor for the fusion of telephones and networked computers with television and radio programming.

Communications is defined as the electronic transfer of data from one place to another. Of all six elements in a computer-and-communications system, communications is probably experiencing the most changes at this point.

As we mentioned, until now, most data being communicated has been analog data. Recently, however, the notion of a *digital* electronic highway has roared into everyone's consciousness. Some say this so-called *Information Superhighway* promises to provide an almost endless supply of electronic interactive services. Others say it is surrounded "by more hype and inflated expectations than any technological proposal of recent memory."[5] What, in fact, is this electronic highway? Does it or will it really exist?

Parts of this idea have been raised before. Indeed, in many ways the Information Superhighway is a 1990s dusting off of earlier concepts of "the wired nation." In 1978, for example, James Martin wrote *The Wired Society,* which considered the social impacts of various telecommunications technologies. In its current form, however, **the Information Superhighway may be said to be a vision or a metaphor for a fusion of the two-way wired and wireless capabilities of telephones and networked computers with television and radio's capacity to transmit hundreds of programs. The resulting interactive digitized traffic would include movies, TV shows, phone calls, databases, shopping services, and online services.** This superhighway, it is hoped, would link all homes, schools, businesses, and governments.

1.7 Overview of Developments in Computer Technology

KEY QUESTIONS

What are the three developments in computing, and what are the five types of computers?

Preview & Review: Computers have developed in three directions: smaller, more powerful, and less expensive.

Today the five types of computers are microcontrollers, microcomputers, minicomputers, mainframes, and supercomputers.

Microcontrollers are embedded in machines such as cars and kitchen appliances.

Microcomputers may be personal computers (PCs) or workstations. PCs include desktop and floorstanding units, laptops, notebooks, subnotebooks, pocket PCs, and pen computers. Workstations are sophisticated desktop microcomputers used for technical purposes.

Minicomputers/midrange computers are intermediate-size machines.

Mainframes are the traditional size of computer and are used in large companies to handle millions of transactions.

The high-capacity machines called supercomputers are the fastest calculating devices and are used for large-scale projects.

Any of these last four types of computers may be used as a server, a central computer in a network.

A human generation is not a very long time, about 30 years. During the short period of one and a half generations, computers have come from nowhere to transform society in unimaginable ways. One of the first computers, the outcome of military-related research, was delivered to the U.S. Army in 1946. ENIAC—short for Electronic Numerical Integrator And Calculator—weighed 30 tons, was 80 feet long and two stories high, and required 18,000 vacuum tubes. However, it could multiply a pair of numbers in the then-remarkable time of three-thousandths of a second. This was the first general-purpose, programmable electronic computer, the grandfather of today's lightweight handheld machines.

The Three Directions of Computer Development

Since the days of ENIAC, computers have developed in three directions:

- **Smaller size:** Everything has become smaller. ENIAC's old-fashioned radio-style vacuum tubes gave way to the smaller, faster, more reliable transistor. A *transistor* is a small device used as a gateway to transfer electrical signals along predetermined paths (circuits).

The next step was the development of tiny integrated circuits. *Integrated circuits* are entire collections of electrical circuits or pathways etched on tiny squares of silicon half the size of your thumbnail. *Silicon* is a natural element found in sand that is purified to form the base material for making computer processing devices.

- **More power:** In turn, miniaturization of hardware components allowed computer makers to cram more power into their machines, providing faster processing speeds and more data storage capacity.

- **Less expense:** The miniaturized processor in a personal desktop computer performs the same sort of calculations once performed by a computer that filled an entire room. However, processor costs are only a fraction of what they were 15 years ago; the fastest processors can be had today for less than $1000, whereas 15 years ago this same processing power might have cost more than $1 million.

Five Kinds of Computers

Generally speaking, the larger the computer, the greater its processing power. Computers are often classified into five sizes: tiny, small, medium, large, and superlarge. (■ *See Panel 1.6.*)

- **Microcontrollers:** ***Microcontrollers*, also called *embedded computers*, are the tiny, specialized microprocessors installed in "smart" appliances and automobiles.** These microcontrollers enable microwave ovens, for example, to store data about how long to cook your potatoes and at what temperature.

- **Microcomputers—personal computers:** ***Microcomputers* are small computers that can fit on or beside a desk or are portable.** Microcomputers are considered to be of two types: personal computers and workstations.

  Personal computers (PCs) **are desktop, tower, or portable computers that can run easy-to-use programs such as word processing or spreadsheets.** PCs come in three sizes, as follows.

  (1) **Desktop and tower units:** Even though many personal computers today are portable, buyers of new PCs often opt for nonportable systems, for reasons of price, power, or flexibility. For example, the television-tube-like (CRT, or cathode-ray tube) monitors that come with desktops have display screens that are easier to read than those of many portables. Moreover, you can stuff a desktop's roomy system cabinet with add-on circuit boards and other extras, which is not possible with portables.

  Desktop PCs are those in which the system cabinet sits on a desk, with keyboard in front and monitor often on top. A difficulty with this arrangement is that the system cabinet's "footprint" can deprive you of a fair amount of desk space. *Tower PCs* are those in which the system cabinet sits as a "tower" on the desk or on the floor next to the desk, giving you more usable desk space.

  (2) **Laptops: A** *laptop computer* **is a portable computer equipped with a flat display screen and weighing about 2–11 pounds.** The top of the computer opens up like a clamshell to reveal the screen. The two principal types of laptop computers are *notebooks* and *subnotebooks,* a category sometimes called *ultralights.*

  A *notebook computer* **is a portable computer that weighs 4–9 pounds and is roughly the size of a thick notebook,** perhaps 8½ by 11 inches. Notebook PCs can easily be tucked into a briefcase or backpack or simply under your arm. Notebook computers can be just as powerful as some desktop machines. Indeed, we are now at the point where a notebook may fill just about all the needs of a desktop.

A *subnotebook computer* weighs 1.8–4 pounds. To save weight, subnotebooks in the past have often had external hard-disk drives, which were available as separate units.

(3) **Pocket PCs:** *Pocket personal computers,* or *handhelds,* weigh about 1 pound or so and can fit in a jacket pocket. These PCs are useful in specific situations, as when a driver of a package-delivery truck must feed hourly status reports to company headquarters. Other pocket PCs have more general applications as electronic diaries and pocket organizers.

In general, pocket PCs may be classified into three types: (a) *Electronic organizers* are specialized pocket computers that mainly store appointments, addresses, and "to do" lists. Recent versions feature wireless links to other computers for data transfer. (b) *Palmtop computers* are PCs that are small enough to hold in one hand and operate with the other. (c) *Pen computers* lack a keyboard or a mouse

■ PANEL 1.6

The principal types of computers—and the microprocessor that powers them

(Clockwise from left top) Six types of computers, ranging from large to small. *(Center)* A microprocessor, the miniaturized circuitry that does the processing in computers. A PC may have only one of these, a supercomputer thousands.

Supercomputer

Mainframe computer

Microcontroller

Microprocessor

Workstation

Personal computer

Minicomputer

but allow you to input data by writing directly on the screen with a stylus, or pen. Pen computers are useful for package-delivery drivers who must get electronic signatures as proof of delivery and for more general purposes, like those of electronic organizers and PDAs.

Personal digital assistants (PDAs), or *personal communicators,* are small, pen-controlled, handheld computers that, in their most developed form, can do two-way wireless messaging.

- Microcomputers—workstations: Workstations look like desktop PCs but are far more powerful. Traditionally, **workstations were sophisticated machines that fit on a desk, cost many thousands of dollars, and were used mainly by engineers and scientists for technical purposes.** However, workstations have long been used for computer-aided design and manufacturing, software development, and scientific modeling. Workstations have caught the eye of the public mainly for their graphics capabilities, such as those used to breathe three-dimensional life into movies such as *Jurassic Park* and *Titanic.*

- Minicomputers/midrange computers: *Minicomputers* **are machines midway in cost and capability between microcomputers and mainframes. They can be used as single-user workstations. When used in a system tied by network to several hundred terminals for many users they are known as** *midrange computers.* Traditionally, minicomputers have been used to serve the needs of medium-size companies or of departments within larger companies, often for accounting or design and manufacturing (CAD/CAM). Now many minicomputers are being replaced by groups of PCs and workstations in networks.

- Mainframes: The large computers called *mainframes* are the oldest category of computer system. **Occupying specially wired, air-conditioned rooms and capable of great processing speeds and data storage,** *mainframes* **traditionally have been water- or air-cooled computers that are about the size of a Jeep and that range in price from $50,000 to $5 million.** Such machines are typically operated by professional programmers and technicians in a centrally managed department within a large company. Examples of such companies are banks, insurance companies, and airlines, which handle millions of transactions.

- Supercomputers: **Typically priced from $225,000 to over $30 million,** *supercomputers* **are high-capacity machines that require special air-conditioned rooms and are the fastest calculating devices ever invented.** Supercomputer users are those who need to model complex phenomena. Examples are automotive engineers who simulate cars crashing into walls and airplane designers who simulate air flowing over an airplane wing. "Supers," as they are called, are also used for oil exploration and weather forecasting. The most powerful computer, Janus, located at the Sandia National Laboratories in Albuquerque, New Mexico, and built by Intel, enables scientists to simulate the explosion of a nuclear bomb.

New communications lines have made possible supercomputing power that is truly awesome. In 1995 the National Science Foundation and MCI Communications, the nation's No. 2 long-distance provider, established a giant, 14,000-mile network called the Very-High-Performance Backbone Network Service (VBNS), which links the five most important concentrations of supercomputers into what they called a new Internet. With this arrangement a scientist sitting at a terminal or workstation anywhere in the country could have access to all the power of these fast machines simultaneously.

Servers

The word "server" does not describe a size of computer but rather a particular way in which a computer is used. Nevertheless, because of the principal concerns of this book—the union of computers and communications—servers deserve separate discussion here. (This topic is also included in Chapters 7 and 8.)

A *server*, or *network server*, is a central computer that holds databases and programs for many PCs, workstations, or terminals, which are called clients. These clients are linked by a wired or wireless network. The entire network is called a *client/server network*. In small organizations, servers can store files and transmit electronic mail between departments. In large organizations, servers can house enormous libraries of financial, sales, and product information. The surge in popularity of the World Wide Web has also led to an increased demand for servers at tens of thousands of Web sites.

1.8 Overview of Developments in Communications Technology

KEY QUESTION

What are three developments in communications?

Preview & Review: Communications, or telecommunications, has had three important developments: better communications channels, the use of networks, and new sending and receiving devices.

Throughout the 1980s and early 1990s, telecommunications made great leaps forward. Three of the most important developments were:

- Better communications channels
- Networks
- New sending and receiving devices

Better Communications Channels

Data may be sent by wired or wireless connections. The old kinds of telephone connections—that is, copper wire—have begun to yield to the more efficient wired forms, such as coaxial cable and, more important, fiber-optic cable (Chapter 8), which can transmit vast quantities of information in both analog and digital form.

Even more interesting has been the expansion of wireless communication. Federal regulators have permitted existing types of wireless channels to be given over to new uses, as a result of which we now have many more kinds of two-way radio, cellular telephone, and paging devices than we had previously.

Networks

When you hear the word "network," you may think of a *broadcast network*, a group of radio or television broadcasting stations that cut costs by airing the same programs. Here, however, we are concerned with ***communications networks*, which connect one or more telephones and computers and associated devices.** The principal difference is that *broadcast networks transmit messages in only one direction*, whereas *communications networks transmit in both directions*. Communications networks are crucial to technological convergence, for they allow information to be exchanged electronically.

A communications network may be large or small, public or private, wired or wireless or both. In addition, smaller networks may be connected to larger ones. For instance, a *local area network (LAN)* may be used to connect users located near one another, as in the same building. On some college campuses, for example, microcomputers in the rooms in residence halls are linked throughout the campus by a LAN.

New Sending & Receiving Devices

Part of the excitement about telecommunications in the last decade or so has been the development of new devices for sending and receiving information. Two examples are the *cellular phone* and the *fax machine.*

Cellular phone

Fax machine

- **Cellular phones:** *Cellular telephones* use a system that divides a geographical service area into a grid of "cells." In each cell, low-powered, portable, wireless phones can be accessed and connected to the main (wire) telephone network.

  The significance of the wireless, portable phone is not just that it allows people to make calls from their cars. Most important is its effect on worldwide communications. Countries with underdeveloped wired telephone systems, for instance, can use cellular phones as a fast way to install better communications. Such technology gives these nations a chance of joining the world economy.

- **Fax machines:** *Fax* stands for "facsimile," which means "a copy"; more specifically, *fax* stands for "facsimile transmission." A *fax machine* scans an image and sends a copy of it in the form of electronic signals over transmission lines to a receiving fax machine. The receiving machine re-creates the image on paper. Fax messages may also be sent to and from microcomputers.

  Fax machines have been commonplace in offices and even many homes for some time, and new uses have been found for them. For example, some newspapers offer facsimile editions, which are transmitted daily to subscribers' fax machines. These editions look like the papers' regular editions, using the same type and headline styles, although they have no photographs. Toronto's *Globe & Mail* offers people who will be away from Canada a four-page fax that summarizes Canadian news. The *New York Times* sends a faxed edition, transmitted by satellite, to island resorts and to cruise ships in mid-ocean. (Networks, fax machines, modems and related topics are covered in detail in Chapters 7 and 8.)

1.9 Computer & Communications Technology Combined: Connectivity & Interactivity

KEY QUESTION

What are connectivity and interactivity?

Preview & Review: Trends in information technology involve connectivity and interactivity.

Connectivity, or online information access, refers to connecting computers to one another by modem or network and communications lines. Connectivity provides, among other things, the benefits of voice mail, e-mail, telecommuting, teleshopping, databases, online services and networks, and electronic bulletin board systems.

Interactivity refers to the back-and-forth "dialog" between a user and a computer or communications device. Interactive devices include multimedia computers, personal digital assistants, and "smart boxes"—TV/PCs and WebTVs.

Under development are different versions of a device that combines telephone, television, and personal computer. This device would deliver digitized entertainment, communications, and information.

Alaska commercial salmon fisherman Blanton Fortson says he is such a frequent user of portable technology—on his boat, in his home, even on his airplane—that he has to wear baggy pants to carry it all around. For example, he says, "I'm often in the woods running, hiking, or biking and almost always reachable by digital pager. My home is wired, and I maintain a dedicated phone-line link between home and office-network zones. . . . With the combination of [a laptop computer] and cellular technology, I find that I very rarely need to be tied to any specific location in order to take care of business."[6]

Fortson is a beneficiary of two trends that will no doubt intensify as information technology continues to proliferate. These trends are:

- Connectivity
- Interactivity

Connectivity: Online Information Access

As we discussed, small telecommunications networks may be connected to larger ones. This is called **connectivity, the ability to connect computers to one another by modem or network and communications lines to provide online information access.** It is this connectivity that is the foundation of the latest advances in the Digital Age.

The connectivity of telecommunications has made possible many kinds of activities. Although we cover these activities in more detail in Chapters 7 and 8, briefly they are as follows:

- Voice mail: *Voice mail* acts like a telephone answering machine. Incoming voice messages are digitized and stored for your retrieval later. Retrieval is accomplished by dialing into your "mailbox" number from any telephone. You can get your own personal voice-mail setup by paying a monthly fee to a telephone company.

- E-mail: An alternative system is e-mail. *E-mail,* or *electronic mail,* is a software-controlled system that links computers by wired or wireless connections. It allows users, through their keyboards, to post messages and to read responses on their computer screens. Whether the network is a company's small local area network or a worldwide network, e-mail allows users to send messages anywhere on the system.

- Telecommuting: In standard commuting, one takes transportation (car, bus, train) from home to work and back. In *telecommuting,* one works at home and communicates with ("commutes to") the office by computer and communications technology. Already about 7.6 million Americans—not including business owners or independent contractors—telecommute three or more days a month, according to Link Resources.[7] If the definition is expanded to include self-employed contractors, part-timers, and even people who simply bring work home from the office at night, there may be 32.7 million work-at-home households.[8]

- Teleshopping: Teleshopping is the computer version of cable-TV shop-at-home services. With *teleshopping,* microcomputer users dial into a telephone-linked computer-based shopping service listing prices and descriptions of products, which may be ordered through the computer. You charge the purchase to your credit card, and the teleshopping service sends the merchandise to you by mail or other delivery service. Although most people seem to prefer buying merchandise in a store or via mail catalog, online car shopping seems to have some appeal, according to one survey. As one observer put it, on the Web "you don't have some guy in your face giving you a hard sell."[9]

- **Databases:** A database may be a large collection of data located within your own unconnected personal computer. Here, however, we are concerned with databases located elsewhere. These are libraries of information at the other end of a communications connection that are available to you through your microcomputer. A *database* is a collection of electronically stored data. The data is integrated, or cross-referenced, so that different people can access it for different purposes.

  For example, suppose an unfamiliar company offered you a job. To find out about your prospective employer, you could go online to gain access to some helpful databases. Examples are Business Database Plus, Magazine Database Plus, and TRW Business Profiles. You could then study the company's products, review financial data, identify major competitors, or learn about recent sales increases or layoffs. You might even get an idea of whether you would be happy with the "corporate culture."

- **Computer online services:** Established major commercial online services include America Online, CompuServe, Microsoft Network, and Prodigy. A *computer online service* is a commercial information service that, for a fee, makes various services available to subscribers through their telephone-linked microcomputers.

  Among other things, consumers can research information in databases, go teleshopping, make airline reservations, or send messages via e-mail to others using the service. They can also dial into *electronic bulletin board systems (BBSs)*, centralized information sources and message-switching systems for particular computer-linked interest groups, many accessible through the Internet. For example, there are BBSs on such varying subjects as fly-fishing, clean air, ecology, genealogy, San Diego entertainment, Cleveland city information, and adult chat.

- **The Internet and World Wide Web:** Through a computer online service or other means (such as with an Internet service provider, or ISP) you may also gain access to the greatest network of all, the Internet. **The *Internet* is an international network connecting approximately 140,000 smaller networks that link computers at academic, scientific, government, and commercial institutions.** The heart of the Internet is a backbone of high-speed communications lines that route data among thousands of other computer systems. The best-known part of the Internet is the ***World Wide Web*, which stores information in multimedia form—sounds, photos, video, as well as text.** An estimated 40 million to 55 million adults in the United States now have access to the Internet at home or work.[10] The number of microcomputers connected to the Internet worldwide is predicted to reach 268 million by 2001.[11]

Interactivity: The Examples of Multimedia Computers, Wireless Pocket PCs, & Various PC/TVs

Screens from the interactive game *Riven*. The user moves through the game's environment, and various things happen, to which the user may or may not respond.

The movie rolls on your PC/TV screen. The actors appear. Instead of passively watching the plot unfold, however, you are able to determine different plot developments by pressing keys on your keyboard. This is an example of interactivity. As we mentioned earlier, **interactivity means that the user is able to make an immediate response to what is going on and modify the processes. That is, there is a dialog between the user and the computer or communications device.** Video games, for example, are interactive. Interactivity allows users to be active rather than passive participants in the technological process.

Among the types of interactive devices are multimedia computers, wireless pocket PCs, and various kinds of "smart boxes" that work as a "converged" computer/TV.

- **Multimedia computers:** The word "multimedia," one of the buzzwords of the '90s, has been variously defined. Essentially, however, **multimedia refers to technology that presents information in more than one medium, including text, graphics, animation, video, music, and voice.**

  Multimedia personal computers are powerful microcomputers that include sound and video capability, run CD-ROM disks, and allow users to play games or perform interactive tasks.

- **Wireless pocket PCs:** In 1988, handheld electronic organizers were introduced, consisting of tiny keypads and barely readable screens. They were unable to do much more than store phone numbers and daily "to do" lists.

  Five years later, electronic organizers began to be supplanted by personal digital assistants, such as Apple's Newton. Personal digital assistants (PDAs) are simply wireless pocket-sized personal computers—small pen-controlled, handheld computers that, in their most developed form, can do two-way wireless messaging. Instead of pecking at a tiny keyboard, you can use a special pen to write out commands on the computer screen. The newer generation of wireless pocket PCs can be used not only to keep an appointment calendar and write memos but also to access the Internet and send and receive faxes and e-mail. With a wireless pocket PC, then, you can immediately get information from some remote location—such as the microcomputer on your desk at home—and, if necessary, update it.

- **"Smart boxes" & PC/TVs:** Envisioning a world of cross-breeding among televisions, telephones, and computers, enterprising manufacturers have been developing different kinds of "smart boxes," set-top control boxes or so-called PC/TVs (or TV/PCs) that merge the personal computer with the television set. With fully developed PC/TVs, consumers are able to watch movies, view multiple cable channels, make phone calls, fax documents, exchange e-mail, do teleshopping, and browse the Internet and the Web. Set-top boxes or PC/TVs provide two-way interactivity not only with video games but also with online entertainment, news, and educational programs.

  WebTV, which delivers the World Wide Web to ordinary television sets with an inexpensive set-top box, is one of several possible *TV computers* (telecomputers) that might be called an *Internet access*

PC-TV

device. Other types of TV computers are *online game players* that not only let you play games but also cruise the Web, exchange e-mail, write letters, and do drawings on your TV. Another is the *full-blown PC-TV combination,* the joining of full-function, multimedia PCs with big-screen TVs, such as Gateway 2000's Destination, a home-entertainment setup built around a PC and a 31-inch TV, and Thomson and Compaq's PC Theatre, a high-powered microcomputer paired with a 36-inch multimedia monitor.

Another variation is the *network computer*—a cheap, stripped-down computer that connects people to networks and that is available for under $500. Instead of having all the complex memory and storage capabilities built in, the network computer (available from Sun Microsystems, IBM, Oracle, and others) is "hollowed out," designed to serve as an entry point to the online world, which is supposed to contain all the software, data, and other resources anyone would need. Many network computers use the TV as a display, but they can also be coupled with a computer monitor or have a built-in screen.

README

Practical Matters: Too Much, Too Fast—Staying Focused to Avoid Information Overload

One of the basic features of the World Wide Web is that it offers *hypertext*—highlighted words and phrases—that Web travelers can use to link up with related words and phrases. But with the Web offering *70 million* or more "home pages," the technology presents all the possibilities for being simply a stupefying waste of time. Says well-known computer journalist John Dvorak, "the Web and the Net revolution have removed the natural barriers between us and the carloads of information we would normally never see."[12]

How, then, to keep yourself from being overwhelmed by information overload on the Web? Dvorak offers the following suggestions for creating "filters" to cut down on all the noise:

● *Stay focused on what you're trying to find:* If you're doing research on the Web, the biggest problem is *staying focused.* Dvorak gives this example of how following random links can be a time killer: "You begin your session looking for a coffee distribu-

tor, . . . and at that site, you see a link to a site on rare chocolates. You jump to that site, and before you know it, you've learned more than you ever wanted to know about the history of the chocolates. Enough already." Thus, remember why you're online in the first place.

● *Limit your time online:* Plan to go on the Web just for 45 minutes or an hour, and *stick with* the plan. If you don't, you'll find yourself up in front of the computer until 4 A.M.

● *Use your printer frequently:* When you see interesting material online, don't try to read it all then and there. Rather, use your computer's printer to print it out immediately for reading later. "That way," says Dvorak, "you can gather as much information as possible without spending all night online or chasing useless links." (When paper costs and waste are at issue, it's best to save material you want to read later to your hard disk.)

1.10　The Ethics of Information Technology

Ethics

Preview & Review: Ethical issues pervade all aspects of the use of information technology, as will be noted with a special logo—shown below, left—throughout the book.

Every computer user will have to wrestle with ethical issues related to the use of information technology. *Ethics* is defined as a set of moral values or principles that govern the conduct of an individual or a group. Indeed, ethical questions arise so often in connection with information technology that we have decided to note them wherever they appear in this book with the symbol shown in the margin.

Here, for example, are some important ethical concerns pointed out by Tom Forester and Perry Morrison in their book *Computer Ethics*.[13]

- **Speed and scale:** Great amounts of information can be stored, retrieved, and transmitted at a speed and on a scale not possible before. Despite the benefits, this has serious implications "for data security and personal privacy [as well as employment]," they say, because information technology can never be considered totally secure against unauthorized access.

- **Unpredictability:** Computers and communications are pervasive, touching nearly every aspect of our lives. However, compared to other pervasive technologies—such as electricity, television, and automobiles—information technology is a lot less predictable and reliable.

- **Complexity:** The on/off principle underlying computer systems may be simple, but the systems themselves are often incredibly complex. Indeed, some are so complex that they are not always understood even by their creators. "This," say Forester and Morrison, "often makes them completely unmanageable," producing massive foul-ups or spectacularly out-of-control costs.

These concerns are only a few of many. You'll read about others as you work through the book.

Summary

Note to the reader: "KQ" refers to Key Questions; see the first page of each chapter. The number ties the summary term to the appropriate section in the book.

What It Is/What It Does

Why It's Important

analog (p. 5, KQ 1.1) Refers to nondigital (noncomputer-based) forms of data transmission that can vary continuously, including voice and video. Telephone lines and radio, television, and cable-TV hookups have historically been analog transmissions media. Analog is the opposite of digital.

You need to know about analog and digital forms of communication to understand what is required for you to connect your computer to other computer systems and information services. Computers cannot communicate directly over analog lines. A modem and communications software are usually required to connect a microcomputer user to other computer systems and information services.

applications software (p. 16, KQ 1.5) Software that has been developed to solve a particular problem, perform useful work on general-purpose tasks, or provide entertainment.

Applications software such as word processing, spreadsheet, database manager, graphics, and communications packages have become commonly used tools for increasing people's productivity.

communications (p. 3, KQ 1.1, 1.6) The sixth element of a computer-and-communications system; the electronic transfer of data from one place to another.

Communications systems using electronic connections have helped to expand human communication beyond face-to-face meetings.

communications network (p. 21, KQ 1.8) System of interconnected computers, telephones, or other communications devices that can communicate with one another.

Communications networks allow users to share applications and data; without networks, information could not be electronically exchanged.

computer (p. 3, KQ 1.1) Programmable, multiuse machine that accepts data—raw facts and figures—and processes (manipulates) it into useful information, such as summaries and totals.

Computers greatly speed up problem solving and other tasks, increasing users' productivity.

computer-and-communications system (p. 8, KQ 1.2) System made up of six elements: people, procedures, data/information, hardware, software, and communications.

Users need to understand how the six elements of a computer-and-communications system relate to one another in order to make knowledgeable decisions about buying and using a computer system.

computer professional (p. 8, KQ 1.2) Person who has had formal education in the technical aspects of using computer-and-communications systems; also called an *information technology professional.*

Computer professionals create and manage the software and systems that enable users (end-users) to accomplish many types of business, professional, and educational tasks and increase their productivity.

What It Is/What It Does	**Why It's Important**

connectivity (p. 23, KQ 1.9) Ability to connect devices by telecommunications lines to other devices and sources of information.

Connectivity is the foundation of the latest advances in the Digital Age. It provides online access to countless types of information and services.

data (p. 10, KQ 1.2, 1.3) Consists of the raw facts and figures that are processed into information; third element in a computer-and-communications system. For computing, data is measured in kilobytes, megabytes, gigabytes, and terabytes.

Users need data to create useful information.

digital (p. 4, KQ 1.1) Term used synonymously with *computer;* refers to communications signals or information represented in a binary, or two-state, way—1s and 0s, on and off.

Putting data into digital form allows computers to transmit voice, text, sound, graphics, color, and animation. The whole concept of an Information Superhighway is based on the existence of digital communications.

electronic organizer (p. 19, KQ 1.7) Specialized pocket computer that mainly stores appointment, addresses, and "to do" lists; recent versions feature wireless links to other computers for data transfer.

Puts in electronic form the kind of day-to-day personal information formerly kept in paper form.

end-user (p. 8, KQ 1.2) Also called a *user;* a person with moderate technical knowledge of information technology who uses computers for entertainment, education, or work-related tasks.

End-users are the people for whom most computer-and-communications systems are created (by computer professionals).

hardware (p. 11, KQ 1.2, 1.4) Fourth element in a computer-and-communications system; refers to all machinery and equipment in a computer system. Hardware is classified into five categories: input, processing and memory, output, secondary storage, and communications.

Hardware design determines the type of commands the computer system can follow. However, hardware runs under the control of software and is useless without it.

information (p. 10, KQ 1.2, 1.3) In general, refers to summarized data or otherwise manipulated data. Technically, data comprises raw facts and figures that are processed into information. However, information can also be raw data for the next person or job, so sometimes the terms are used interchangeably. Information/data is the third element in a computer-and-communications system.

The whole purpose of a computer (and communications) system is to produce (and transmit) usable information.

Information Superhighway (p. 17, KQ 1.6) Vision or metaphor for a fusion of the two-way wired and wireless capabilities of telephones and networked computers with television and radio's capacity to transmit hundreds of programs. The resulting interactive digitized traffic would include movies, TV shows, phone calls, databases, shopping services, and online services.

The Information Superhighway is envisioned as fundamentally changing the nature of communications and hence society, business, government, and personal life.

What It Is/What It Does	**Why It's Important**
information technology (p. 2, KQ 1.1) Technology that merges computing with high-speed communications links carrying data, sound, and video.	Information technology is bringing about the gradual fusion of several important industries in a phenomenon called *digital convergence* or *technological convergence.*
input hardware (p. 12, KQ 1.4) Devices that allow people to put data into the computer in a form that the computer can use; that is, they perform *input operations.* Input devices include a keyboard, mouse, pointer, scanner, or microphone.	Useful information cannot be produced without input data.
interactivity (p. 25, KQ 1.9) Situation in which the user is able to make an immediate response to what is going on and modify processes; that is, there is a dialog between the user and the computer or communications device.	Interactive devices allow the user to actively participate in a technological process instead of just reacting to it.
Internet (p. 24, KQ 1.9) International network connecting approximately 36,000 smaller networks that link computers at academic, scientific, and commercial institutions.	The Internet makes possible the sharing of all types of information and services for millions of people all around the world.
laptop computer (p. 18, KQ 1.7) Portable computer equipped with a flat display screen and weighing 2–11 pounds. The top of the computer opens up like a clamshell to reveal the screen.	Laptop and other small computers have provided users with computing capabilities in the field and on the road.
mainframe (p. 20, KQ 1.7) Second-largest computer available, after the supercomputer; occupies a specially wired, air-conditioned room, is capable of great processing speeds and data storage, and costs $50,000– $5 million.	Mainframes are used by large organizations (banks, airlines) that need to process millions of transactions.
microcomputer (p. 18, KQ 1.7) Small computer that can fit on or beside a desktop or is portable; uses a single microprocessor for its CPU. A microcomputer may be a workstation, which is more powerful and is used for specialized purposes, or a personal computer (PC), which is used for general purposes.	The microcomputer has lessened the reliance on mainframes and has enabled more ordinary users to use computers.
microcontroller (p. 18, KQ 1.7) Also called an *embedded computer;* the smallest category of computer.	Microcontrollers are built into "smart" electronic devices, as controlling devices.
minicomputer (p. 20, KQ 1.7) Also known as a *midrange computer;* computer midway in cost and capability between a microcomputer and a mainframe and costing $20,000–$250,000.	Minicomputers can be used as single units or in a system tied by network to as many as several hundred terminals for many users. Many minicomputers are being replaced by networked microcomputers.

What It Is/What It Does	Why It's Important

multimedia (p. 25, KQ 1.9) Refers to technology that presents information in more than one medium, including text, graphics, animation, video, music, and voice.

Use of multimedia is becoming more common in business, the professions, and education as a means of improving the way information is communicated.

notebook computer (p. 18, KQ 1.7) Type of portable computer weighing 4–9 pounds and measuring about 8½ x 11 inches.

Notebooks have more features than many subnotebooks yet are lighter and more portable than laptops.

output hardware (p. 13, KQ 1.4) Consists of devices that translate information processed by the computer into a form that humans can understand; that is, the devices perform *output operations.* Common output devices are monitors and printers. Sound is also a form of computer output.

Without output devices, computer users would not be able to view or use their work.

palmtop computer (p. 19, KQ 1.7) Type of pocket personal computer, weighing less than 1 pound, that is small enough to hold in one hand and operate with the other.

Unlike other pocket PCs, palmtops use the same software as IBM microcomputers and so are compatible with larger computers.

pen computer (p. 19, KQ 1.7) Type of portable computer; it lacks a keyboard or mouse but allows users to input data by writing directly on the display screen with a pen (stylus).

Pen computers are useful for specific tasks, such as for signatures to show proof of package delivery, and some general purposes, such as those fulfilled by electronic organizers and personal digital assistants.

peripheral device (p. 12, KQ 1.4) Any hardware device that is connected to a computer. Examples are keyboard, mouse, monitor, printer, and disk drives.

Most of a computer system's input and output functions are performed by peripheral devices.

personal computer (PC) (p. 18, KQ 1.7) Type of microcomputer; desktop, floor-standing (tower), or portable computer that can run easy-to-use programs, such as word processing or spreadsheets.

The PC is designed for one user at a time and so has boosted the popularity of computers.

personal digital assistant (PDA) (p. 20, KQ 1.7) Also known as *pocket communicator;* type of handheld pocket personal computer, weighing 1 pound or less, that is pen-controlled and that in its most developed form can do two-way, wireless messaging.

PDAs may supplant book-style personal organizers and calendars, as well as allow transmission of personal messages.

pocket personal computer (p. 19, KQ 1.7) Also known as a *handheld computer;* a portable computer weighing 1 pound or less. Three types of pocket PCs are electronic organizers, palmtop computers, and personal digital assistants.

Pocket PCs are useful to help workers with specific jobs, such as delivery people and parking control officers.

What It Is/What It Does	Why It's Important

procedures (p. 9, KQ 1.2) Descriptions of how things are done; steps for accomplishing a result or rules and guidelines for what is acceptable. Procedures are the second element in a computer-and-communications system.

In the form of documentation, procedures help users learn to use hardware and software.

secondary storage (p. 14, KQ 1.4) Refers to devices and media that store data and programs permanently— such as disks and disk drives, tape and tape drives. These devices perform *storage operations.*

Without secondary storage media, users would not be able to save their work.

server (p. 21, KQ 1.7) Computer in a network that holds databases and programs for multiple users.

The server enables many users to share equipment, programs, and data.

software (p. 15, KQ 1.2, 1.5) Also called *programs;* step-by-step instructions that tell the computer hardware how to perform a task. Software represents the fifth element of a computer-and-communications system.

Without software, hardware would be useless.

subnotebook computer (p. 19, KQ 1.7) Type of portable computer, weighing 1.8–4 pounds.

Subnotebooks are lightweight and thus extremely portable; however, they may lack features found on notebooks and other larger portable computers.

supercomputer (p. 20, KQ 1.7) High-capacity computer that is the fastest calculating device ever invented; costs $225,000–$30 million.

Used principally for research purposes, airplane design, oil exploration, weather forecasting, and other activities that cannot be handled by mainframes and other less powerful machines.

system software (p. 16, KQ 1.5) Software that controls the computer and enables it to run applications software. System software, which includes the operating system, allows the computer to manage its internal resources.

Applications software cannot run without system software.

technological convergence (p. 2, KQ 1.1) Also called *digital convergence;* refers to the technological merger of several industries through various devices that exchange information in the electronic, or digital, format used by computers. The industries are computers, communications, consumer electronics, entertainment, and mass media.

From a common electronic base, the same information may be exchanged among many organizations and people using any of a multitude of information technology devices.

World Wide Web (p. 24, KQ 1.9) The part of the Internet that stores information in multimedia form—sounds, photos, and video as well as text.

The most widely known part of the Internet, the Web stores information in multimedia form—sounds, photos, video, as well as text.

workstation (p. 20, KQ 1.7) Type of microcomputer; desktop or floor-standing (tower) machine that costs $3700 or more and is used mainly for technical purposes.

Workstations are used for scientific and engineering purposes and also for their graphics capabilities.

Exercises

Self-Test Exercises

1. The _____ refers to the part of the Internet that stores information in multimedia form.

2. Whereas most of the world is _____, computers deal with data in _____ form.

3. In _____, one works at home and communicates with the office by computer and communications technology.

4. A _____ computer is less powerful than a supercomputer, but more powerful than a minicomputer.

5. The term _____ is used to describe a programmable, multiuse machine that accepts data and manipulates it into information.

Short-Answer Questions

1. List the six main elements of a computer and communications system.

2. What is the function of the system unit in a computer system?

3. What is the difference between system software and applications software?

4. Why is it important to have a computer with more main memory rather than less?

5. Which hardware category has the most in common with a filing cabinet?

Multiple-Choice Questions

1. A kilobyte is equal to approximately:
   a. 1000 bytes
   b. 10,000 bytes
   c. 1 million bytes
   d. 1 billion bytes
   e. None of the above

2. Which of the following converts computer output into printed images?
   a. keyboard
   b. mouse
   c. scanner
   d. printer
   e. All of the above

3. Which of the following enables digital data to be transmitted over the phone lines?
   a. keyboard
   b. mouse
   c. scanner
   d. modem
   e. All of the above

4. Which of the following computer types typically costs the least and has the smallest main memory capacity?
   a. supercomputer
   b. mainframe computer
   c. workstation
   d. microcomputer
   e. microcontroller

5. What hardware category does magnetic tape fall into?
   a. input
   b. processing and memory
   c. output
   d. storage
   e. communications

True/False Questions

T F 1. Computers are continually getting larger and more expensive.

T F 2. Mainframe computers process faster than microcomputers.

T F 3. Main memory is a software component.

T F 4. System software consists of several programs, the most important of which is the operating system.

T F 5. An end-user is someone with considerable experience in the technical aspects of using a computer.

Knowledge in Action

1. Determine what types of computers are being used where you work or go to school. Microcomputers? Minicomputers? Any mainframe or supercomputers? In which departments are the different types of computers used? What are they being used for? How are they connected to other computers?

2. Identify some of the problems of information overload in one or two departments in your school or place of employment—or in a local business, such as a real estate firm, health clinic, pharmacy, or accounting firm. What types of problems are people having? How are they trying to solve them? Are they rethinking their use of computer-related technologies?

3. Imagine a business you could start or run at home. What type of business is it? What type of computer do you think you'll need? Describe the computer system in as much detail as possible, including hardware components in all five areas we discussed. Keep your notes and then refine your answers after you have completed the course.

4. Can you envision yourself using a supercomputer in your planned profession or job? If yes, how? What other type(s) of computer do you envision yourself using?

5. How do you think technological, or digital, convergence will affect you in the next five years? For example, will it affect how you currently perform your job or obtain access to education? Do you think that technological convergence is a good thing? Why? Why not?

6. Other than the topics already addressed in this chapter, do you have any ethical concerns about how computers and communications systems are being used today? What are they?

Applications Software

Tools for Thinking & Working

key questions

You should be able to answer the following questions:

2.1   **How to Think About Software** What is applications software, and what are the five general categories of applications software?

2.2   **Common Features of Software** What are some common features of the graphical software environment?

2.3   **Word Processing** What can you do with word processing software that you can't do with pencil and paper?

2.4   **Spreadsheets** What can you do with an electronic spreadsheet that you can't do with pencil and paper and a standard calculator?

2.5   **Database Software** What is database software, and what is personal information management (PIM) software?

2.6   **Financial Software** What is the purpose of financial software?

2.7   **Software for Cyberspace: Communications, E-Mail, Web Browsers** What do communications, e-mail, and Web-browser programs do?

2.8   **Integrated Software & Suites** What are integrated software packages and software suites, and how do they differ?

2.9   **Specialty Software** What are the principal uses of programs for desktop publishing, presentation graphics, project management, computer-aided design, drawing and painting, groupware, and multimedia authoring software?

2.10   **When Software Causes Problems** What are two principal drawbacks of new applications software, and what can you do about them?

2.11   **Ethics & Intellectual Property Rights: When Can You Copy?** When is copying a violation of copyright laws, what is a software license agreement, and what types of agreements are there?

That's how one writer in 1993 described a new kind of software called a *Web browser*, designed to help computer users find their way around the Internet, particularly the sound-and-graphics part of it known as the World Wide Web.[1] The global "network of networks," the Internet is rich in information but can be baffling to navigate without assistance. The developers of the first Web browser had tried to remove that difficulty. Indeed, they had hoped their program might become the first "killer app"—killer application—of network computing. That is, it would be a breakthrough development that would help millions of people become comfortable using electronic computer networks, a technology formerly used by only a relative few.

The name of the first Web browser was Mosaic, but it was not to become the software that would make the Internet available to everyone, being overtaken in a matter of months by Netscape Navigator. Now Netscape itself is on the defensive, fighting the aggressive marketing of Microsoft and its Internet Explorer. As this is written, developers are engaged in a titanic struggle to come up with the defining tool that will simplify users' abilities to summon text, as well as sound and images, from among the Internet's many information sources.

Nevertheless, the search for highly useful applications shows how truly important software is. Without software, your computer is only about as useful as a doorstop.

2.1 How to Think About Software

KEY QUESTIONS

What is applications software, and what are the five general categories of applications software?

Preview & Review: Applications software enables users to perform work on specific tasks or to participate in different forms of entertainment.

The five types of applications software may be considered to be (1) entertainment software, (2) home/personal software, (3) education/reference software, (4) productivity software, and (5) specialty software.

Over the long course of time, luckily for us, software for personal computers has generally become easier to use. At one time, for instance, users had to learn cryptic commands such as "format a: /n:9 /t:40." Now they can use a mouse to point to words and images on a screen.

In this chapter, we'll discuss the various types of applications software. We'll also consider how software is changing and how you can deal with it.

The Most Popular Uses of Software

Let's get right to the point: What do most people use software for? The answer hasn't changed in years. If you don't count games and communication, by far the most popular applications are (1) word processing and (2) spreadsheets, according to the Software Publishers Association.[2] Small-business owners, according to one study, say the software they use most often is word processing (by 94% of those surveyed), spreadsheet (75%), database management (67%), and desktop publishing (51%).[3]

Interestingly, most people use only a few basic features of word processing and spreadsheet programs, and they use them for rather simple tasks. For example, 70% of all documents produced with word processing software are one-page letters, memos, or simple reports. And 70% of the time people use spreadsheets simply to add up numbers.[4]

This is important information. If you are this type of user, you may have no more need for fancy software and hardware than an ordinary commuter has for an expensive Italian race car. However, you may be in a profession in which you need to become a "power user," having to learn a great number of features in order to keep ahead in your career.

The Two Kinds of Software: Applications & System

As stated in Chapter 1, *software,* or *programs,* consists of the instructions that tell the computer how to perform a task. **Applications software is software that has been developed to solve a particular problem, to perform useful work on specific tasks, or to provide entertainment.** As the user, you interact with the applications software. In turn, *system software* (covered in the next chapter) enables the applications software to interact with the computer. It also helps the computer manage its internal resources. (■ *See Panel 2.1.*)

If you buy a new microcomputer in a store, you will find that some packaged software has already been installed on it. This typically includes system software and various types of applications software compatible with it.

Versions, Releases, & Compatibility

Every year or so, software developers find ways to enhance their products and put forth new versions or new releases. Although not all software developers use the terms consistently, their accepted definitions are as follows.

- **Version:** A *version* is a major upgrade in a software product. Traditionally versions have been indicated by numbers such as 1.0, 2.0, 3.0, and so forth. The higher the number preceding the decimal point, the more recent the version. In recent years, a number of software developers have departed from this system. Microsoft, for instance, decided to call the new operating system that it launched in 1995 "Windows 95" instead of "Windows 4.0." Windows 98 would have been Windows 5.0.

- **Release:** A *release* is a minor upgrade. Releases are usually indicated by a change in number after the decimal point—3.0, then 3.1, then

■ PANEL 2.1

Applications software and system software
You interact principally with the applications software. The applications software interacts with components of the system software, which in turn interacts directly with the computer. (Sometimes, however, you do interact directly with the system software.)

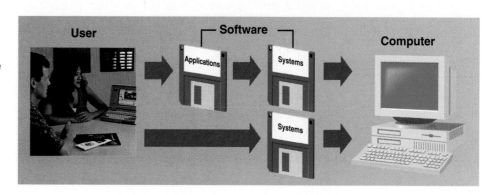

perhaps 3.11, then 3.2, and so on. Some releases are now also indicated by the year they are marketed.

When you buy a new software version or release, you must make sure it is compatible with your existing system. *Compatible* means that documents created with earlier versions of the software can be processed successfully on later versions. *Compatible* also means that a new version of an applications program will run with the system software you are currently using. To avoid problems of incompatibility, be sure to read the compatibility requirements printed on the software package you are considering buying.

The Five Categories of Applications Software

Software can change the way we act, even the way we think. Some readers may intuitively understand this because they grew up playing video games. Indeed, some observers hold that video games are not quite the time wasters we have been led to believe, that these forms of entertainment can be a step to something else. That is, they say, video games are "training wheels" for using more sophisticated software that can help us be more productive.

Applications software may be classified in many ways. We use five categories. (■ *See Panel 2.2.*)

1. Entertainment software
2. Home/personal software
3. Education/reference software
4. Productivity software
5. Specialty software

■ **PANEL 2.2**

The five categories of applications software

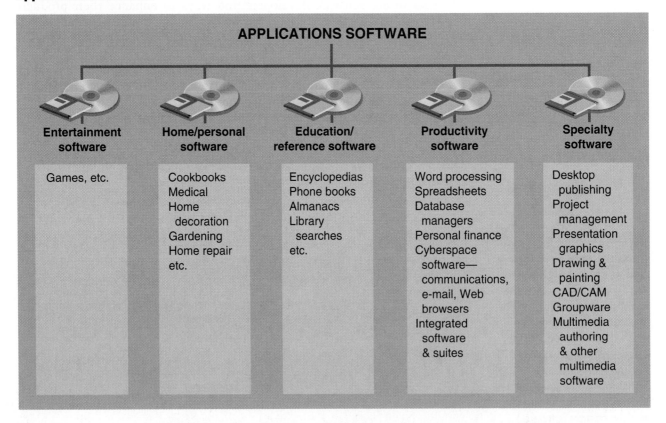

APPLICATIONS SOFTWARE

Entertainment software	Home/personal software	Education/ reference software	Productivity software	Specialty software
Games, etc.	Cookbooks Medical Home decoration Gardening Home repair etc.	Encyclopedias Phone books Almanacs Library searches etc.	Word processing Spreadsheets Database managers Personal finance Cyberspace software— communications, e-mail, Web browsers Integrated software & suites	Desktop publishing Project management Presentation graphics Drawing & painting CAD/CAM Groupware Multimedia authoring & other multimedia software

Let us consider them briefly.

● **Entertainment software—the serious matter of video games:** Video games might seem frivolous, but they are more important than you might think. Important enough that they generated $3.5 billion in sales in the United States in 1996.[5]

It was Pong—an electronic version of table tennis introduced by Atari in 1972—that popularized computers in the home. "Pong was the first time people saw computers as friendly and approachable," states one technology writer. "It launched a video game boom that . . . prepared an entire generation for interaction with a blinking and buzzing computer screen."[6]

Pong was followed by Space Invaders and Pac-Man, and then by Super Mario, which begot Sonic the Hedgehog, which led to Mortal Kombat I and II, and so on. In 1986 Nintendo began to reshape the market when it introduced 8-bit entertainment systems. *Bit numbers* measure how much data a computer chip can process at one time. Bit (✔ p. 4) numbers are important because the higher the bit number, the greater the screen resolution (clarity), the more varied the colors, and the more complex the games.[7] Since then, video game hardware—which, after all, is just a form of computer hardware—has increased in power just as microcomputers have. In the 1990s, video game hardware manufacturers—Sega, 3DO, Atari, Sony, Nintendo—upped the ante to 16 bits, then 32 bits, until finally 64-bit machines appeared on the market.

Of course, there are other categories of entertainment software, ranging from interactive movies to gambling. We will describe these from time to time throughout the book.

● **Home/personal software:** Swiftly Seasoned, the Jenny Craig Cookbook, and the Completely Interactive Cookbook are examples of software cookbooks, one of several kinds of home/personal software. Other software in this category includes home repair, home decoration, gardening, genealogy, travel planning, and the like. PlanetWare North European Travel Planner, for example, is a CD-ROM offering attractions, maps, hotels, and restaurants (and currency, tours, and pictures) from France to Finland.

● **Educational/reference software:** Because of the popularity of video games, many educational software companies have been blending educational content with action and adventure—as in MathBlaster or the problem-solving game Commander Keen. They hope this marriage will help students be more receptive to learning. After all, as one writer points out, players of Nintendo's Super Mario Brothers must "become intimately acquainted with an alien landscape, with characters, artifacts, and rules completely foreign to ordinary existence. . . . Children assimilate this essentially useless information with astonishing speed."[8] Why not, then, design software that would educate as well as entertain?

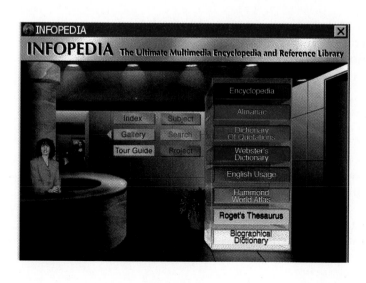

Computers alone won't boost academic performance, but they can have a positive effect on student achievement in all major subject areas, preschool through college, according to an independent consulting firm, New York's Interactive Educational Systems Design. Skills improve when students use programs that are self-paced or contain interactive video, the consultants found after analyzing 176 studies done over 5 years. This is particularly true for low-achieving students. The reason, says a representative of the firm, is that this kind of educational approach is "a different arena from the one in which they failed, and they have a sense of control."[9]

In addition to educational software, library search and reference software have become popular. For instance, there are CD-ROMs with encyclopedias, phone books, mailing lists, maps, and reproductions of famous art. With the CD-ROM encyclopedia Microsoft Encarta, for example, you can search for, say, music in 19th-century Russia, then listen to an orchestral fragment from Tchaikovsky's *1812 Overture*.

- **Productivity software:** Productivity software consists of programs found in most offices, in many homes, and probably on all campuses, on personal computers and on larger computer systems. Their purpose is simply to make users more productive at performing particular tasks. Productivity software is probably the most important type of software you will learn to use.

  The most popular kinds of productivity tools are *word processing software; spreadsheet software; database software, including personal information managers; financial software, including personal finance programs; software for cyberspace (communications, e-mail, Web browsers); and integrated software and suites.*

  We describe productivity software in more detail shortly.

- **Specialty software:** Whatever your occupation, you will probably find it has specialized software available to it. This is so whether your career is as an architect, building contractor, chef, dairy farmer, dance choreographer, horse breeder, lawyer, nurse, physician, police officer, tax consultant, or teacher.

  Some programs help lawyers or advertising people, for instance, keep track of hours spent on particular projects for billing purposes. Other programs help construction estimators pull together the costs of materials and labor needed to estimate a job.

  Later in this chapter we describe the following kinds of specialty software: *desktop publishing; presentation graphics; project management; computer-aided design; drawing and painting programs; groupware; and multimedia authoring software.*

Before we discuss specific productivity and specialty software programs, however, let's first cover some of the common features of much of the software—both applications and systems—used today.

2.2 Common Features of Software

KEY QUESTION

What are some common features of the graphical software environment?

Preview & Review: In a graphical environment, software packages share some basic features. They use special-purpose keys, function keys, and a mouse to issue commands and choose options. Their interfaces include menus, windows, icons, buttons, and dialog boxes to make it easy for people to use the program.

Software packages are also accompanied by tutorials and documentation.

You may already be familiar with basic computer concepts such as the cursor, the mouse pointer, dialog boxes, and so on, as well as keyboard components such as function keys. If not, the following discussion provides a brief review of some features common to both applications software and system software.

Features of the Keyboard

We describe the keyboard as an input device in Chapter 5. Here, however, we explain some aspects of the keyboard because it and the mouse are the means for manipulating software.

Besides letter, number, and punctuation keys and often a calculator-style numeric keypad, computer keyboards have special-purpose and function keys. Sometimes keystrokes are used in combinations called *macros,* or *keyboard shortcuts.*

- **Special-purpose keys:** *Special-purpose keys* **are used to enter, delete, and edit data and to execute commands.** An example is the Esc (for "Escape") key. The Enter key, which you will use often, tells the computer to execute certain commands and to start new paragraphs in a document. Commands are instructions that cause the software to perform specific actions. For example, pressing the Esc key commands the computer, via software instructions, to cancel an operation or leave ("escape from") the current mode of operation.

  Special-purpose keys are generally used the same way regardless of the applications software package being used. Most keyboards include the following special-purpose keys: Esc, Ctrl, Alt, Del, Ins, Home, End, PgUp, PgDn, Num Lock, and a few others. (*Ctrl* means Control, *Del* means Delete, *Ins* means Insert, for example.)

- **Function keys:** *Function keys,* **labeled F1, F2, and so on, are positioned along the top or left side of the keyboard. They are used to execute commands specific to the software being used.** For example, one applications software package may use F6 to exit a file, whereas another may use F6 to underline a word.

  Many software packages come with printed templates that you can attach to the keyboard. Like the explanation of symbols on a road map, the template describes the purpose of each function key and certain combinations of keys.

- **Macros:** Sometimes you may wish to reduce the number of keystrokes required to execute a command. To do this, you use a macro. **A** *macro,* **also called a** *keyboard shortcut,* **is a single keystroke or command—or a series of keystrokes or commands—used to automatically issue a longer, predetermined series of keystrokes or commands.** Thus, you can consolidate several activities into only one or two keystrokes. The user names the macro and stores the corresponding command sequence; once this is done, the macro can be used repeatedly.

  Although many people have no need for macros, others who find themselves continually repeating complicated patterns of keystrokes say they are quite useful.

The User Interface: GUIs, Menus, Windows, Icons, Buttons, & Dialog Boxes

The first thing you look at when you call up any applications software on the screen is the user interface. **The** *user interface* **is the user-controllable part of the software that allows you to communicate, or interact, with it.** The type of user interface is usually determined by the system software (discussed in the next chapter). However, because this is what you see on the screen before you can begin using the applications software, we will briefly describe it here.

The kind of interface now used by most people is the graphical user interface. **With a *graphical user interface*, or *GUI* (pronounced "gooey"), you may use graphics (images) and menus as well as keystrokes to choose commands, start programs, and see lists of files and other options.**

Common features of GUIs are *menus, windows, icons, buttons,* and *dialog boxes.*

- **Menus: A *menu* is a list of available commands presented on the screen.** Menus may appear as menu bars, pull-down menus, or pop-up menus.

Menu bar

  A *menu bar* is a line of command options across the top or bottom of the screen. Examples of commands, which you activate with a mouse or with key combinations, are File, Edit, and Help.

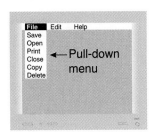
Pull-down menu

  A *pull-down menu,* also called a *drop-down menu,* is a list of command options that "drops down" from a selected menu bar item at the top of the screen. For example, you might use the mouse to "click on" (activate) a command (for example, File) on the menu bar, which in turn would yield a pull-down menu offering further commands. Choosing one of these options may produce further menus called *cascading,* or *fly-out, menus.*

  A *pop-up menu,* usually activated by a shortcut (macro) or a mouse click, is a list of command options that can "pop up" anywhere on the screen. Pop-up menus are not connected to a menu bar as are drop-down menus.

  A particularly useful option on the menu bar is the **Help option, which offers assistance on how to perform various tasks,** such as printing out a document. Help offers a built-in electronic instruction and reference manual.

- **Windows:** A particularly interesting feature of GUIs is the use of windows. **A *window* is a rectangular area that appears on the screen and displays information from a particular part of a program.** A display screen may show more than one window—for instance, one might show information from a word processing program, another information from a spreadsheet.

  A window (small w) should not be confused with Windows (capital W)—the program known as Microsoft Windows—which is the most popular form of system software for the personal computer. However, as you might expect, Windows features extensive use of windows.

- **Icons: An *icon* is a picture used in a GUI to represent a command, a program, a file, or a task.** For example, a picture of a diskette might represent the command "Save (store) this document." Icons are activated by a mouse or other pointing device.

Button on Toolbar

Save changes?
yes no cancel

- **Buttons:** A *button* is a simulated on-screen button (kind of icon) that is activated ("pushed") by a mouse or other pointing device to issue a command, such as "OK" and "Cancel."
- **Dialog box:** A *dialog box* is a box that appears on the screen and displays a message requiring a response from you, such as clicking on "yes" or "no" or typing in the name of a file. A dialog box is used to collect additional information from the user before performing a command or completing a task.

Tutorials & Documentation

How are you going to learn a given software program? Most commercial packages come with tutorials and documentation.

- **Tutorials:** A *tutorial* is an instruction book or program that takes you through a prescribed series of steps to help you learn how to use the product. For instance, our publisher offers several how-to books, known as the *Advantage Series,* that enable you to learn different kinds of software. Tutorials can also be provided as part of the software package.
- **Documentation:** *Documentation* is a user guide or reference manual that is a narrative and graphical description of a program. Documentation may be print-based, but today it is usually available on CD-ROM, as well as via the Internet. Documentation may be instructional, but features and functions are usually grouped by category for reference purposes. For example, in word processing documentation, all features having to do with printing are grouped together so you can easily look them up if you have forgotten how to perform them.

Let us now consider the various forms of applications software used as productivity tools. Then we will cover specialty programs.

2.3 Word Processing

KEY QUESTION

What can you do with word processing software that you can't do with pencil and paper?

Preview & Review: Word processing software allows you to use computers to create, edit, format, print, and store text material, among other things.

The typewriter, that long-lived machine, has gone to its reward. Indeed, if you have a manual typewriter, it is becoming as difficult to get it repaired as it is to find a blacksmith. Today, word processing software offers a much-improved way to deal with documents.

Word processing software allows you to use computers to format, create, edit, print, and store text material, among other things. (■ *See Panel 2.3, next page.*) Popular word processing programs are Microsoft Word and Corel Word-Perfect for PCs, and Word and WordPerfect for the Macintosh.

Word processing software allows users to maneuver through a document and *delete, insert,* and *replace* text, the principal correction activities. It also offers such additional features as *creating, editing, formatting, printing,* and *saving.*

■ **PANEL 2.3**

Word processing screen
This Microsoft Word 97 screen shot shows a pull-down Format menu that offers, among other things, several options for styling text.

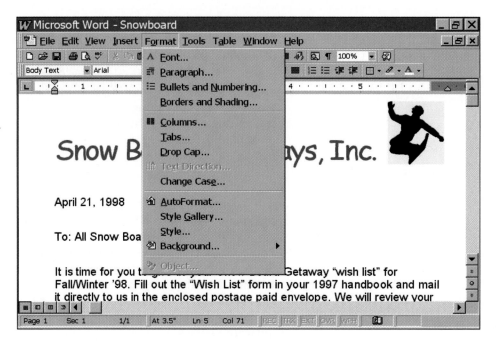

Creating Documents

Creating a document means entering text using the keyboard. Word processing software has three features that affect this process—the *cursor, scrolling,* and *word wrap.*

- ● Cursor: **The *cursor* is the movable symbol on the display screen that shows you where you may enter data or commands next.** The symbol is often a blinking rectangle or I-beam. You can move the cursor on the screen using the keyboard's directional arrow keys or a mouse. Wherever the cursor is located, that point is called the *insertion point.*

- ● Scrolling: ***Scrolling* is the activity of moving quickly upward or downward through the text or other screen display.** A standard computer screen displays only 20–22 lines of standard-size text. Of course, most documents are longer than that. Using the directional arrow keys, or the mouse and a scroll bar located at the side of the screen, you can move ("scroll") through the display screen and into the text above and below it.

- ● Word wrap: *Word wrap* automatically continues text on the next line when you reach the right margin. That is, the text "wraps around" to the next line.

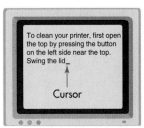

Scrolling

Editing Documents

Editing is the act of making alterations in the content of your document. Some features of editing are *insert and delete, undelete, find and replace, cut/copy and paste, spelling checker, grammar checker,* and *thesaurus.*

- ● Insert and delete: *Inserting* is the act of adding to the document. You simply place the cursor wherever you want to add text and start typing; the existing characters will be pushed along.

  Deleting is the act of removing text, usually using the Delete or Backspace keys.

The *Undelete command* allows you to change your mind and restore text that you have deleted. Some word processing programs offer as many as 100 layers of "undo," allowing users who delete several paragraphs of text, but then change their minds, to reinstate one or more of the paragraphs.

- **Find and replace:** The *Find*, or *Search*, *command* allows you to find any word, phrase, or number that exists in your document. The *Replace command* allows you to automatically replace it with something else.

- **Cut/Copy and paste:** Typewriter users were accustomed to using scissors and glue to "cut and paste" to move a paragraph or block of text from one place to another in a manuscript. With word processing, you select (highlight) the portion of text you want to copy or move. Then you can use the *Copy* or *Cut command* to move it to a special area in the computer's memory called the *clipboard*. Once the material is on the clipboard, you can "paste," or transfer, it anywhere in the existing document or in a new document.

- **Spelling checker, grammar checker, thesaurus:** Many writers automatically run their completed documents through a *spelling checker*, which tests for incorrectly spelled words. (Some programs, such as Microsoft Word 97, have an "Auto Correct" function that automatically fixes such common mistakes as transposed letters— "teh" instead of "the.") Another feature is a *grammar checker*, which flags poor grammar, wordiness, incomplete sentences, and awkward phrases.

  If you find yourself stuck for the right word while you're writing, you can call up an on-screen *thesaurus*, which will present you with the appropriate word or alternative words.

Formatting Documents

Formatting means determining the appearance of a document. There are many choices here.

- **Font:** You can decide what font—that is, what typeface and type size—you wish to use. You can specify what parts of it should be <u>underlined</u>, *italic*, or **boldface.**

- **Spacing and columns:** You can choose whether you want the lines to be *single-spaced* or *double-spaced* (or something else). You can specify whether you want text to be *one column* (like this page), *two columns* (like many magazines and books), or *several columns* (like newspapers).

- **Margins and justification:** You can indicate the dimensions of the *margins*—left, right, top, and bottom—around the text.

  You can specify whether the text should be *justified* or not. *Justify* means to align text evenly between left and right margins, as, for example, is done with most newspaper columns and this text. *Left-justify* means to not align the text evenly on the right side, as in many business letters ("ragged right").

- **Pages, headers, footers:** You can indicate *page numbers* and *headers* or *footers*. A *header* is common text (such as a date or document name) that is printed at the top of every page. A *footer* is the same thing printed at the bottom of every page.

● Other formatting: You can specify *borders* or other decorative lines, *shading*, *tables*, and *footnotes*. You can even pull in ("import") *graphics* or drawings from files in other software programs.

It's worth noting that word processing programs (and indeed most forms of applications software) come from the manufacturer with *default settings*. **Default settings are the settings automatically used by a program unless the user specifies otherwise, thereby overriding them.** Thus, for example, a word processing program may automatically prepare a document single-spaced, left-justified, with 1-inch right and left margins unless you alter these default settings.

Printing Documents

Most word processing software gives you several options for printing. For example, you can print *several copies* of a document. You can print *individual pages* or a *range of pages*. You can even preview a document before printing it out. *Previewing (print previewing)* means viewing a document on screen to see what it will look like in printed form before it's printed. Whole pages are displayed in reduced size.

Saving Documents

Saving means to store, or preserve, the electronic files of a document permanently on diskette, hard disk, or CD-ROM, for example. Saving is a feature of nearly all applications software, but anyone accustomed to writing with a typewriter will find this activity especially valuable. Whether you want to make small changes or drastically revise your word processing document, having it stored in electronic form spares you the tiresome chore of having to retype it from scratch. You need only call it up from the storage medium and make just those changes you want, then print it out again.

2.4   Spreadsheets

KEY QUESTION

What can you do with an electronic spreadsheet that you can't do with pencil and paper and a standard calculator?

Preview & Review: Spreadsheet software allows users to create tables and financial schedules by entering data into rows and columns arranged as a grid on a display screen. If one (or more) numerical value or formula is changed, the software calculates the effect of the change on the rest of the spreadsheet.

Spreadsheet software also allows users to create analytical graphics charts to present data.

What is a spreadsheet? Traditionally, it was simply a grid of rows and columns, printed on special light-green paper, that was used by accountants and others to produce financial projections and reports. A person making up a spreadsheet often spent long days and weekends at the office penciling tiny numbers into countless tiny rectangles. When one figure changed, all the rest of the numbers on the spreadsheet had to be recomputed—and ultimately there might be wastebaskets full of jettisoned worksheets.

In the late 1970s, Daniel Bricklin was a student at the Harvard Business School. One day he was staring at columns of numbers on a blackboard when he got the idea for computerizing the spreadsheet. The result, VisiCalc, was the first of the electronic spreadsheets. **An *electronic spreadsheet*, also called simply a *spreadsheet*, allows users to create tables and financial schedules by entering data and formulas into rows and columns arranged as a grid on a display screen.**

The electronic spreadsheet quickly became the most popular small-business program. Unfortunately for Bricklin, VisiCalc was shortly surpassed by Lotus 1-2-3, a sophisticated program that combines the spreadsheet with database and graphics programs. Today the principal spreadsheets are Microsoft Excel, Lotus 1-2-3, and Quattro Pro.

Principal Features

The arrangement of a spreadsheet is as follows. (■ *See Panel 2.4.*)

- **Columns, rows, and labels:** In the spreadsheet's frame area (work area), lettered *column headings* appear across the top ("A" is the name of the first column, "B" the second, and so on), and numbered *row headings* appear down the left side ("1" is the name of the first row, "2" the second, and so forth). Labels are any descriptive text, such as APRIL, RENT, or GROSS SALES.

- **Cells, cell addresses, values, and spreadsheet cursor:** The place where a row and a column intersect is called a *cell,* and its position is called a *cell address.* For example, "A1" is the cell address for the top left cell, where column A and row 1 intersect. A selection (group) of cells is called a *range.* A number or date entered in a cell is called a *value.* The values are the actual numbers used in the spreadsheet—dollars, percentages, grade points, temperatures, or whatever. A *cell pointer,* or *spreadsheet cursor,* indicates where data is to be entered. The cell pointer can be moved around like a cursor in a word processing program.

- **Formulas, functions, and recalculation:** Now we come to the reason the electronic spreadsheet has taken offices by storm. Formulas are instructions for calculations. For example, a formula might be =SUM(A5:A15), meaning "Sum (add) all the numbers in the cells with cell addresses A5 through A15."

■ PANEL 2.4

Electronic spreadsheet
An important feature of Lotus 1-2-3 for Windows and other electronic spreadsheets is their *recalculation* feature: When a number is changed, all related numbers on the spreadsheet are recomputed.

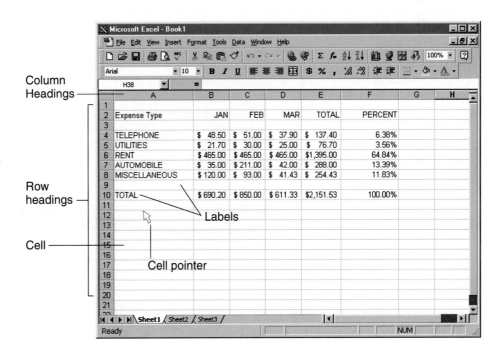

Functions are built-in formulas that perform common calculations. For instance, a function might average a range of numbers or round off a number to two decimal places.

After the values have been plugged into the spreadsheet, the formulas and functions can be used to calculate outcomes. What is revolutionary, however, is the way the spreadsheet can easily do recalculation. **Recalculation is the process of recomputing values,** either as an ongoing process as data is being entered or afterward, with the press of a key. With this simple feature, the hours of mind-numbing work required to manually rework paper spreadsheets became a thing of the past.

- **The "what if" world:** The recalculation feature has opened up whole new possibilities for decision making. As a user, you can create a plan, put in formulas and numbers, and then ask yourself, "What would happen if we change that detail?"—and immediately see the effect on the bottom line. You could use this if you're considering buying a car. Any number of things can be varied: total price ($15,000? $20,000?), down payment ($2,000? $3,000?), interest rate on the car loan (7%? 8%?), or number of months to pay (36? 48?). You can keep changing the "what if" possibilities until you arrive at a monthly payment figure that you're comfortable with.

Analytical Graphics: Creating Charts

A nice feature of spreadsheet packages is the ability to create analytical graphics. **Analytical graphics, or business graphics, are graphical forms that make numeric data easier to analyze** than when it is in the form of rows and columns of numbers, as in electronic spreadsheets. Whether viewed on a monitor or printed out, analytical graphics help make sales figures, economic trends, and the like easier to comprehend and analyze.

The principal examples of analytical graphics are *bar charts, line graphs,* and *pie charts.* (■ *See Panel 2.5.*) Quite often these charts can be displayed or printed out so that they look three-dimensional. Spreadsheets can even be linked to more exciting graphics, such as digitized maps.

■ PANEL 2.5

Analytical graphics
Bar charts, line graphs, and pie charts are used to display numerical data in graphical form.

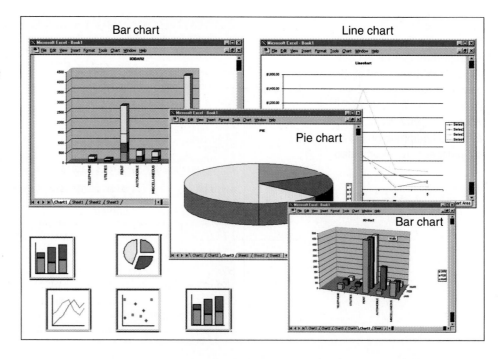

2.5 Database Software

KEY QUESTIONS

What is database software, and what is personal information management (PIM) software?

Preview & Review: A database is a computer-based collection of interrelated files. Database software is a program that controls the structure of a database and access to the data.

Personal information management (PIM) software is specialized database software that helps track and manage information used on a daily basis, such as addresses, appointments, lists, and miscellaneous notes.

In its most general sense, a database is any electronically stored collection of data in a computer system. In its more specific sense, **a *database* is a collection of interrelated files** in a computer system. These computer-based files are organized according to their common elements, so that they can be retrieved easily. (Databases are covered in detail in Chapter 6.) Sometimes called a *database manager* or *database management system (DBMS)*, ***database software* is a program that controls the structure of a database and access to the data.**

The Benefits of Database Software

Because it can access several files at one time, database software is much better than the old file managers (also known as flat-file management systems) that used to dominate computing. A *file manager* is a software package that can access only one file at a time. With a file manager, you could call up a list of, say, all students at your college majoring in psychology. You could also call up a separate list of all students from Indiana. But you could not call up a list of psychology majors from Indiana, because the relevant data is kept in separate files. Most database software allows you to do that.

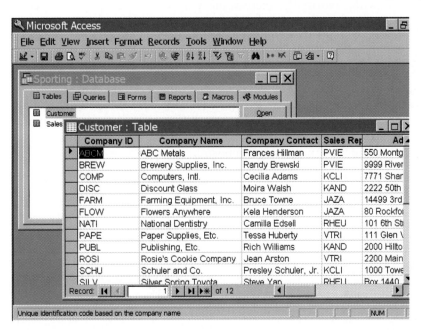

Databases are a lot more interesting than they used to be. Once they included only text. The Digital Age has added new kinds of information—not only documents but also pictures, sound, and animation. It's likely, for instance, that your personnel record in a future company database will include a picture of you and perhaps even a clip of your voice. If you go looking for a house to buy, you will be able to view a real estate agent's database of video clips of homes and properties without leaving the realtor's office.

Today the principal database programs are Microsoft Access, Microsoft Visual FoxPro, dBASE, Paradox, and Claris Filemaker Pro. These programs also allow users to attach multimedia—sound, motion, and graphics—to forms.

Databases have gotten easier to use, but they still can be difficult to set up. Even so, the trend is toward making such programs easier for both database creators and database users.

Principal Features of Database Software

Some features of databases are as follows:

- **Organization of a database:** A database is organized—from smallest to largest items—into *fields, records,* and *files.*

  A *field* is a unit of data consisting of one or more characters. An example of a field is your name, your address, or your driver's license number.

  A *record* is a collection of related fields. An example of a record would be your name and address and driver's license number.

  A *file* is a collection of related records. An example of a file could be one in your state's Department of Motor Vehicles. The file would include everyone who received a driver's license on the same day, including their names, addresses, and driver's license numbers.

- **Retrieve and display:** The beauty of database software is that you can locate records in the file quickly. For example, your college may maintain several records about you—one at the registrar's, one in financial aid, one in the housing department, and so on. Any of these records can be called up on a computer screen for viewing and up-dating. Thus, if you move, your address field will need to be changed in all records. The database is quickly corrected by finding your name field. Once the record is displayed, the address field can be changed.

- **Sort:** With database software you can easily change the order of records in a file. Normally, records are entered into a database in the order they occur, such as by the date a person registered to attend college. However, all these records can be sorted in different ways. For example, they can be rearranged by state, by age, or by Social Security number.

- **Calculate and format:** Many database programs contain built-in mathematical formulas. This feature can be used, for example, to find the grade-point averages for students in different majors or in different classes. Such information can then be organized into different formats and printed out in sophisticated reports.

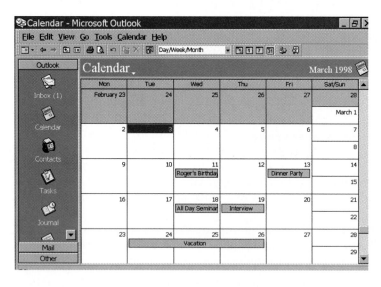

Personal Information Managers

Pretend you are sitting at a desk in an old-fashioned office. You have a calendar, Rolodex-type address file, and notepad. Most of these items could also be found on a student's desk. How would a computer and software improve on this arrangement?

Many people find ready uses for specialized types of database software known as personal information managers. **A *personal information manager (PIM)* is software to help you keep track of and manage information you use on a daily basis, such as addresses, telephone numbers, appointments, "to do" lists, and miscellaneous notes.** Some programs feature phone dialers, outliners (for roughing out ideas in outline form), and ticklers (or reminders). With a PIM, you can key in notes in any way you like and then retrieve them later based on any of the words you typed.

Popular PIMs are Lotus Organizer, Microsoft Outlook, and Act. Lotus Organizer, for example, looks much like a paper datebook on the screen—down to simulated metal rings holding simulated paper pages. The program has screen images of section tabs labeled Calendar, To Do, Address, Notepad, Planner, and Anniversary. The Notepad section lets users enter long documents, including text and graphics, that can be called up at any time.

2.6 Financial Software

KEY QUESTION

What is the purpose of financial software?

Preview & Review: Financial software includes personal-finance managers, entry-level accounting packages, and business financial-management software. Personal-finance managers let you keep track of income and expenses, write checks, do online banking, and plan financial goals.

Besides word processing, spreadsheet, and database software, the next most important program for business is financial software. **Financial software is a growing category that ranges from personal-finance managers to entry-level accounting programs to business financial-management packages.**

Personal-Finance Managers

Personal-finance managers **let you keep track of income and expenses, write checks, do online banking, and plan financial goals.** Such programs don't promise to make you rich, but they can help you manage your money, maybe even get you out of trouble.

Many personal-finance programs, such as Quicken and Microsoft Money, include a calendar and a calculator, but the principal features are the following:

- Tracking of income and expenses: The programs allow you to set up various account categories for recording income and expenses, including credit card expenses.
- Checkbook management: All programs feature checkbook management, with an on-screen check writing form and check register that look like the ones in your checkbook. Checks can be purchased to use with your computer printer.
- Reporting: All programs compare your actual expenses with your budgeted expenses. Some will compare this year's expenses to last year's.
- Income tax: All programs offer tax categories, for indicating types of income and expenses that are important when you're filing your tax return.
- Other: Some of the more versatile personal-finance programs also offer financial-planning and portfolio-management features.

Other Financial Software

Besides personal-finance managers, financial software includes small business accounting and tax software programs, which provide virtually all the forms you need for filing income taxes. Tax programs such as TaxCut and Turbo Tax make complex calculations, check for mistakes, and even unearth deductions you didn't know existed. Tax programs can be linked to personal finance software to form an integrated tool.

A lot of financial software is of a general sort used in all kinds of enterprises, such as accounting software, which automates bookkeeping tasks, or payroll software, which keeps records of employee hours and produces reports for tax purposes.

Some programs go beyond financial management and tax and accounting management. For example, Business Plan Pro, Management Pro, and Performance Now can help you set up your own business from scratch.

Finally, there are investment software packages, such as StreetSmart from Charles Schwab and Online Xpress from Fidelity, as well as various retirement planning programs.

2.7 Software for Cyberspace: Communications, E-Mail, Web Browsers

KEY QUESTION

What do communications, e-mail, and Web-browser programs do?

Preview & Review: Communications software manages the transmission of data between computers. Electronic mail (e-mail) software enables users to exchange letters and documents between computers.

Web browsers are software programs that allow people to view information at Web sites in the form of colorful, on-screen magazine-style "pages" with text, graphics, and sound. Using a browser, users can access search tools known as directories and search engines.

The term *cyberspace* was coined by William Gibson in his novel *Neuromancer* to refer to a futuristic computer network that people use by plugging their brains into it. Today **cyberspace has come to mean the online or digital world in general and the Internet and its World Wide Web in particular.**

Three software tools for accessing cyberspace are *communications software, e-mail software,* and *Web browsers.*

Communications Software

***Communications software,* or *data communications software,* manages the transmission of data between computers.** For most microcomputer users, this sending and receiving of data is by way of a modem and a telephone line. A *modem* (✔ p. 5) is an electronic device that allows computers to communicate with each other over telephone lines. The modem translates the digital signals of the computer into analog signals that can travel over telephone lines to another modem, which translates the analog signals back to digital. When you buy a modem, you often get communications software with it. Popular microcomputer communications programs are Crosstalk, QuickLink, and Procomm Plus.

Communications software gives you these capabilities:

- **Online connections:** You can connect to online services such as America Online (AOL) and Microsoft Network (MSN) and to networks, such as those used within an office (a local area network, or LAN) or the Internet.

- **Use of financial services:** You can order discount merchandise, look up airline schedules and make reservations, follow and engage in stock trading, and even do some home banking and bill paying.

- **Automatic dialing services:** You can set your software to answer for you if someone tries to call your computer, to dial certain telephone numbers automatically, and to automatically redial after a certain time if a line is busy.

- **Remote access connections:** While traveling you can use your portable computer to exchange files via modem with your computer at home.

- **File transfer:** You can obtain a file from a computer at the other end of a communications line and *download* it to your personal computer—that is, transfer it onto your computer's hard disk. You can also do the reverse—*upload* a file of data from your computer and transfer it elsewhere.

- **Fax support:** You can fax messages from your computer to others' computers or fax machines and receive their fax messages in your computer.

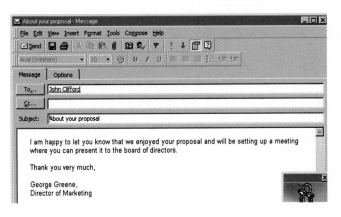

Electronic Mail Software

Electronic mail software, **or** ***e-mail software,*** **enables users to send letters and files from one computer to another.** Many organizations have "electronic mailboxes." If you were a sales representative, for example, such a mailbox would allow you to transmit a report you created on your word processor to a sales manager in another area. Or you could route the same message to a number of users on a distribution list. Popular e-mail software packages include Eudora, Microsoft Outlook, Lotus CC:Mail, and Pegasus Mail.

Web Browsers

The Internet, that network of thousands of interconnected networks, "is just a morass of data, dribbling out of servers [computers] around the world," says one writer. "It is unfathomably chaotic, mixing items of great value with cyber-trash." This is why so-called browsers have caught people's imaginations, he states. "A browser cuts a path through the tangled growth and even creates a form of memory, so each path can be retraced."[10]

The most exciting part of the Internet is probably that fast-growing region or subset of it known as the World Wide Web. The *World Wide Web,* or simply *the Web,* consists of hundreds of thousands of intricately interlinked sites called "home pages" set up for on-screen viewing in the form of colorful magazine-style "pages" with text, images, and sound.

To be connected to the World Wide Web, you need a setup with an online service (✔ p. 24) or a commercial Internet service provider (described in the Experience Box at the end of Chapter 3 and also in Chapter 7), who will usually give you a "browser" for actually exploring the Web. (The reverse is also true: Some Web browsers you buy will help you find an Internet service provider.) **A *Web browser,* or simply *browser,* is software that enables you to "browse through" and view Web sites.** You can move from page to page by "clicking on" or using a mouse to select an icon or by typing in the address of the page. The accompanying drawing explains what the parts of a Web electronic address mean. (■ *See Panel 2.6, next page.*)

There are several browsers available, including some relatively unsophisticated ones offered by Internet service providers and some by commercial online services such as America Online or Compuserve. However, the recent battle royal to find the "killer app" browser has been between Netscape, which produces Navigator, and Microsoft, which produces Internet Explorer. As of mid-1998, Netscape was still leading with 54% (down from 70%) of the browser market to Microsoft's 39%.[11] However, Microsoft had increased its market share by making Internet Explorer available free as part of new releases of its Windows operating system. Because most new microcomputers come

Back
Takes you back to pages previously viewed.

Bookmarks
A list of sites can be created so the user can quickly jump to the ones used frequently (also called *favorite places*).

Home
Takes you back to the introductory screen (the one you see when you first load your browser).

Browser vendor screen
Technical support, browser copies, and browser updates.

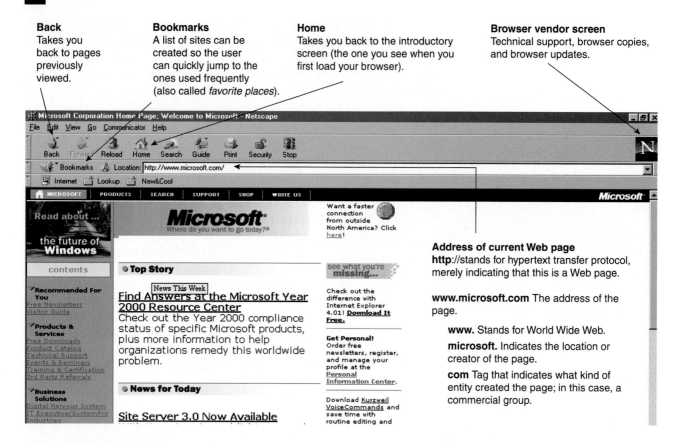

Address of current Web page
http://stands for hypertext transfer protocol, merely indicating that this is a Web page.

www.microsoft.com The address of the page.

> **www.** Stands for World Wide Web.
>
> **microsoft.** Indicates the location or creator of the page.
>
> **com** Tag that indicates what kind of entity created the page; in this case, a commercial group.

■ PANEL 2.6

What's a Web browser?
This screen from Netscape Navigator illustrates some components of a home page (Web site). From here you can move to other pages.

equipped with this operating system, and therefore Microsoft's Internet Explorer, buyers of new computers had less incentive to choose Netscape's browser. Netscape thereupon changed its strategy and also began giving away its browser. It also made public the "source code" that is the key to the program's inner workings, hoping that thousands of developers would tinker with the program and devise improvements that could be incorporated into the next version of the product.

Remember that online services and ISPs are *not the same* as browsers. The online services and ISPs are commercial enterprises that provide *communications* software that enables you to connect your computer with them via modem and phone lines. Because you pay the service/ISP a monthly subscription fee, you may continue to use whatever services the company offers, including e-mail, teleshopping, investing, and the like. Browsers are software used to access the Web *after* you are online with an online service or ISP. With a browser you may access Web sites that offer services or activities that are also available from an online service—there is some overlap.

Web Search Tools: Directories & Search Engines

Once you're in your browser, you need to know how to find what you're looking for. Search tools are of two basic types—*directories* and *search engines.*

- Directories: **Web directories are indexes classified by topic.** One of the foremost examples is Yahoo! *(http://www.yahoo.com),* which provides you with an opening screen offering several general categories. Directory information is collected and ranked by people.

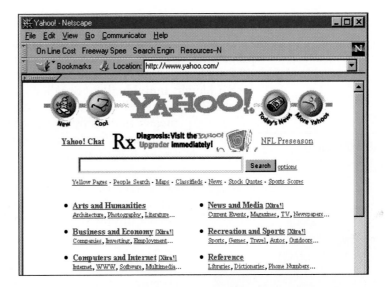

- Search engines: **Web *search engines* allow you to find specific documents through keyword searches.** An example of one useful search engine is AltaVista *(http://www.altavista.com)*. Search engine information is collected and ranked by software programs (sometimes called *spiders*).

According to a 1997 Baruch College–Harris Poll, which surveyed 1000 U.S. households, 21% of adults—the equivalent of 40 million people—use the Internet and/or the Web. The most common activity, by 82% of Net users, is research, followed by education (75%), news (68%), and entertainment (61%).[12]

2.8 Integrated Software & Suites

KEY QUESTIONS

What are integrated software packages and software suites, and how do they differ?

Preview & Review: Integrated software packages combine the basic features of several applications programs—for example, word processing, spreadsheet, database manager, graphics, and communications—into one software package. Software suites are full-fledged versions of several applications programs bundled together.

What if you want to take data from one program and use it in another—say, call up data from a database and use it in a spreadsheet? You can try using separate software packages, but one may not be designed to accept data from the other. Two alternatives are the collections of software known as *integrated software* and *software suites*.

Integrated Software: "Works" Programs

***Integrated software packages* combine the most commonly used features of several applications programs—such as word processing, spreadsheet, database, graphics, and communications—into one software package.** These so-called "works" collections—the principal representatives are AppleWorks, Claris-Works, Lotus Works, Microsoft Works, and PerfectWorks—give good value because the entire bundle often sells for $100 or less.

Integrated software packages are less powerful than separate programs used alone, such as a word processing or spreadsheet program used by itself. But that may be fine, because single-purpose programs may be more complicated and demand more computer resources than necessary.

Software Suites: "Office" Programs

Software suites, or simply *suites,* are applications—like spreadsheets, word processing, graphics, and communications—with a standard user interface that are bundled together and sold for a fraction of what the programs would cost if bought individually. "Bundled" and "unbundled" are jargon words frequently encountered in software and hardware merchandising. *Bundled*

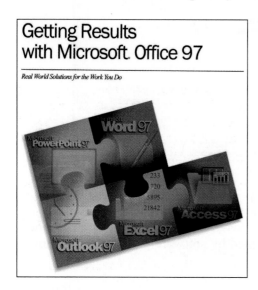

**Getting Results
with Microsoft Office 97**

Real World Solutions for the Work You Do

means that components of a system are sold together for a single price. *Unbundled* means that a system has separate prices for each component.

Three principal suites, sometimes called "office" programs, are available. Microsoft's Office 97 is available in both "standard" and "professional" versions. IBM's Lotus SmartSuite 97 comes in one version. Corel's WordPerfect Suite 8 is the "standard" version and Office Professional is the "professional" version.

Although lower price is what makes suites attractive to many corporate customers, the software has other benefits as well. Software makers have tried to integrate the "look and feel" of the separate programs within the suites to make them easier to use. "All applications in a suite look and function similarly," says one writer. "You learn one, you learn them all. And they're integrated, passing information back and forth easily without compatibility problems—in theory, at least."[13]

A trade-off, however, is that such packages require a lot of hard-disk storage capacity. The standard edition of Office 97 hogs 120 megabytes and Corel gobbles up 157 megabytes of hard-disk space. (Compare with the "works" program ClarisWorks at 13 megabytes.)

2.9 Specialty Software

KEY QUESTION

What are the principal uses of programs for desktop publishing, presentation graphics, project management, computer-aided design, drawing and painting, groupware, and multimedia authoring software?

Preview & Review: Specialty software includes the following programs. (1) Desktop publishing (DTP) combines text and graphics in a highly sophisticated manner to produce high-quality output for commercial printing. (2) Presentation graphics uses graphics and data/information from other software tools to communicate or make a presentation of data to others. (3) Project management software is used to plan, schedule, and control the people, costs, and resources required to complete a project on time. (4) Computer-aided design (CAD) programs are for designing products and structures. (5) Drawing programs allow users to design and illustrate objects and products, and painting programs allow them to simulate painting on screen. (6) Groupware is used on a network and allows users within the same building or on different continents to share ideas and update documents. (7) Multimedia authoring software enable users to integrate multimedia elements—text, images, sound, motion, animation—into a logical sequence of events.

After learning some of the productivity software just described, you may wish to extend your range by becoming familiar with more specialized programs. For example, you might first learn word processing and then move on to desktop publishing, the technology used to prepare much of today's printed information. Or you may find yourself in an occupation that requires you to learn some very specific kinds of software. We will consider the following specialized tools, although these are but a handful of the thousands of programs available:

- Desktop publishing
- Presentation graphics
- Project management
- Computer-aided design
- Drawing and painting
- Groupware
- Multimedia authoring

Desktop Publishing

Once you've become comfortable with a word processor, could you then go on and learn to do what Margaret Trejo did? When Trejo, then 36, was laid off from her job because her boss couldn't meet the payroll, she was stunned. "Nothing like that had ever happened to me before," she said later. "But I knew it wasn't a reflection on my work. And I saw it as an opportunity."[14]

Today Trejo Production is a successful desktop-publishing company in Princeton, New Jersey, using Macintosh equipment to produce scores of books, brochures, and newsletters. "I'm making twice what I ever made in management positions," says Trejo, "and my business has increased by 25% every year."

Not everyone can set up a successful desktop-publishing business, because many complex layouts require experience, skill, and knowledge of graphic design. Indeed, use of these programs by nonprofessional users can lead to rather unprofessional-looking results. Nevertheless, the availability of microcomputers and reasonably inexpensive software has opened up a career area formerly reserved for professional typographers and printers.

Desktop publishing, abbreviated DTP, involves using a microcomputer and mouse, scanner, laser or ink-jet printer, and DTP software for mixing text and graphics to produce high-quality output for commercial printing. Often the printer is used primarily to get an advance look before the completed job is sent to a typesetter for even higher-quality output. Professional DTP programs are QuarkXPress and PageMaker. Microsoft Publisher is a "low-end," consumer-oriented DTP package. Some word processing programs, such as Word and WordPerfect, also have many DTP features, though at nowhere near the level of the packages just mentioned.

Desktop publishing has the following characteristics:

- **Mix of text with graphics:** Desktop-publishing software allows you to precisely manage and merge text with graphics. As you lay out a page on-screen, you can make the text "flow," liquid-like, around graphics such as photographs. You can resize art, silhouette it, change the colors, change the texture, flip it upside down, and make it look like a photo negative.

- **Varied type and layout styles:** As do word processing programs, DTP programs provide a variety of fonts, or typestyles, from readable Times Roman to staid Tribune to wild Jester and Scribble. Additional fonts can be purchased on disk or downloaded online. You can also create all kinds of rules, borders, columns, and page numbering styles.

- **Use of files from other programs:** It's usually not efficient to do word processing, drawing, and painting with the DTP software. Thus, text is usually composed on a word processor, artwork is created with drawing and painting software, and photographs are scanned in using a scanner and then manipulated and stored using photo-manipulation software. Prefabricated art may also be obtained from disks containing *clip art,* or "canned" images that can be used to illustrate DTP documents. The DTP program is used to integrate all these files. You can look at your work on the display screen as one page or as two facing pages (in reduced size). Then you can see it again after it is printed out on a printer. (■ *See Panel 2.7.*)

Presentation Graphics Software

Computer graphics can be highly complicated, such as those used in special effects for movies (such as *Titanic* or *Twister*). Here we are concerned with just one kind of graphics called presentation graphics.

Presentation graphics **are part of presentation software, which uses graphics and data/information from other software tools to communicate or make a presentation of data to others,** such as clients or supervisors. Presentations may make use of some analytical graphics—bar, line, and pie charts—but they usually look much more sophisticated, using, for instance, different texturing patterns (speckled, solid, cross-hatched), color, and three-dimensionality. (■ *See Panel 2.8.*) Examples of well-known presentation graphics packages are Microsoft PowerPoint, WordPerfect Presentations, ASAP from Software Publishing Group, and Gold Disk's Astound.

In general, presentation graphics are displayed electronically or output as 35-millimeter slides. Presentation graphics packages often come with slide sorters, which group together a dozen or so slides in miniature. The person making the presentation can use a mouse or keyboard to bring the slides up for viewing or even start a self-running slide show.

■ PANEL 2.7

How desktop publishing uses other files

Text is composed on a word processor, graphics are drawn with drawing and painting programs, and photographs and other artwork are scanned in with a scanner. Data from these files is integrated using desktop-publishing software, and the pages are printed out on a laser or ink-jet printer.

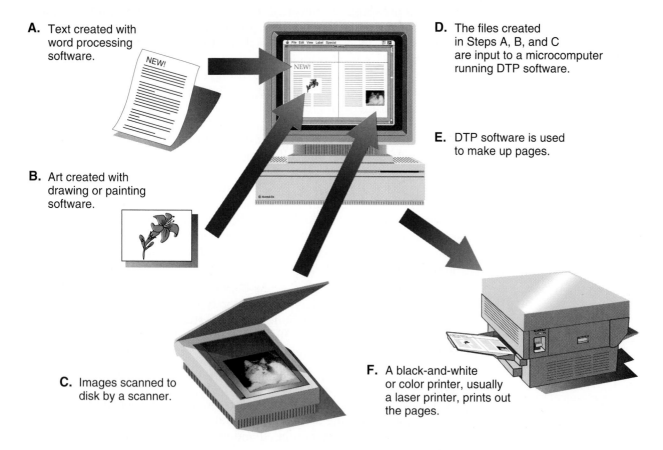

A. Text created with word processing software.

B. Art created with drawing or painting software.

C. Images scanned to disk by a scanner.

D. The files created in Steps A, B, and C are input to a microcomputer running DTP software.

E. DTP software is used to make up pages.

F. A black-and-white or color printer, usually a laser printer, prints out the pages.

■ PANEL 2.8
Presentation graphics

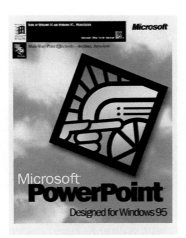

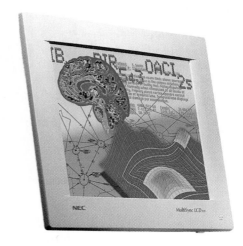

Project Management Software

The kind of database program we called a personal information manager (PIM) can help you schedule your appointments and do some planning. That is, it can help you manage your own life. But what if you need to manage the lives of others to accomplish a full-blown project, such as steering a political campaign or handling a nationwide road tour for a band? Strictly defined, a *project* is a one-time operation consisting of several tasks and multiple resources that must be organized toward completing a specific goal within a given period of time. The project can be small, such as an advertising campaign for an in-house advertising department, or large, such as construction of an office tower or a jetliner.

Project management software is a program used to plan, schedule, and control the people, costs, and resources required to complete a project on time. For instance, the associate producer on a feature film might use such software to keep track of the locations, cast and crew, materials, dollars, and schedules needed to complete the picture on time and within budget. The software would show the scheduled beginning and ending dates for a particular task—such as shooting all scenes on a certain set—and then the date that task was actually completed. Examples of project management software are Harvard Project Manager, Microsoft Project, Suretrack Project Manager, and ManagerPro.

Computer-Aided Design

Computers have long been used in engineering design. **Computer-aided design (CAD) programs are software programs for the design of products, structures, civil engineering drawings, and maps.** CAD programs, which are available for microcomputers, help architects design buildings and workspaces and engineers design cars, planes, electronic devices, roadways, bridges, and subdivisions. One advantage of CAD software is that the product can be drawn in three dimensions and then rotated on the screen so the designer can see all sides. (■ *See Panel 2.9, next page.*) Examples of CAD programs for beginners are Autosketch and CorelCAD.

A variant on CAD is *CADD,* for *computer-aided design and drafting,* software that helps people do drafting. CADD programs include symbols (points, circles, straight lines, and arcs) that help the user put together graphic elements, such as the floor plan of a house. An example is Autodesk's Auto-CAD.

■ **PANEL 2.9**

CAD: example of computer-aided design
(Left) CAD model of wire connections. *(Right)* CAD modeling of a stadium for the 1996 Olympics in Atlanta, Georgia.

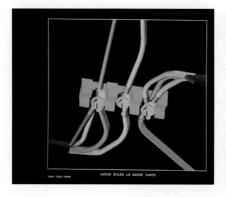 

CAD/CAM—for computer-aided design/computer-aided manufacturing—software **allows products designed with CAD to be input into an automated manufacturing system that makes the products.** For example, CAD and its companion CAM brought a whirlwind of enhanced creativity and efficiency to the fashion industry. Some CAD systems, says one writer, "allow designers to electronically drape digital-generated mannequins in flowing gowns or tailored suits that don't exist, or twist imaginary threads into yarns, yarns into weaves, weaves into sweaters without once touching needle to garment."[15] The designs and specifications are then input into CAM systems that enable robot pattern-cutters to automatically cut thousands of patterns from fabric with only minimal waste. Whereas previously the fashion industry worked about a year in advance of delivery, CAD/CAM has cut that time to 8 months—a competitive edge for a field that feeds on fads.

Drawing & Painting Programs

John Ennis was trained in realistic oil painting, and for years he used his skill creating illustrations for covers and dust jackets for book publishers. Now he "paints" using a computer, software, and mouse. The greatest advantage, he says, is that if "I do a brush stroke in oil and it's not right, I have to take a rag and wipe it off. With the computer, I just hit the 'undo' command."[16]

It may be no surprise to learn that commercial artists and fine artists have begun to abandon the paintbox and pen and ink for software versions of palettes, brushes, and pens. The surprise, however, is that an artist can use mouse and pen-like stylus to create computer-generated art as good as that achievable with conventional artist's tools. More surprising, even *nonartists* can be made to look good with these programs.

There are two types of computer art programs: drawing and painting.

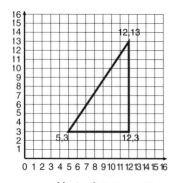

Vector image

● Drawing programs: **A *drawing program* is graphics software that allows users to design and illustrate objects and products.** CAD and drawing programs are similar. However, CAD programs provide precise dimensioning and positioning of the elements being drawn, so that they can be transferred later to CAM programs. Also, CAD programs lack the special effects for illustrations that come with drawing programs. Some drawing programs are CorelDRAW, Adobe Illustrator, Macromedia Freehand, and Sketcher.

Drawing programs create *vector images (see left)*—images created from mathematical calculations.

● Painting programs: ***Painting programs* are graphics programs that allow users to simulate painting on screen.** A mouse or a tablet stylus is used to simulate a paintbrush. The program allows you to select "brush" sizes, as well as colors from a color palette. Examples of

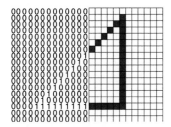

Raster image

painting programs are MetaCreations' Painter, Adobe Photoshop, Corel PhotoPaint, and JASC's PaintShop Pro.

Painting programs produce *raster images* made up of little dots *(see left).*

Groupware

Most microcomputer software is written for people working alone. **Group-ware, also known as *collaboration software*, is software that is used on a network and allows users in the same building or even continents away working on the same project to share ideas and update documents.** Groupware improves productivity by keeping you continually notified about what your colleagues are thinking and doing, and they about you. "Like e-mail," one writer points out, "groupware became possible when companies started linking PCs into networks. But while e-mail works fine for sending a message to a specific person or group—communicating one-to-one or one-to-many—groupware allows a new kind of communication: many-to-many."[17]

The standard for groupware was set in 1989 with the introduction of Lotus Notes, which dominates the market today with 9 million users. Other principal programs are Microsoft's Exchange, Novell's GroupWise, and Netscape's Communicator. Original versions of groupware allowed e-mail, discussion groups, customizable databases, scheduling, and network security. Newer versions enable users to get access to Web pages and even send Web pages to each other.

Multimedia Authoring Software

As mentioned in Chapter 1 (✔ p. 25), *multimedia* refers to technology that presents information in more than one form: text, graphics, animation, video, music, and voice. **Multimedia authoring software, or simply *authoring software*, enables users to create multimedia applications that integrate text, images, sound, motion, and animation.** Basically, authoring tools allow you to sequence and time the occurrence of events, determining which graphics, sound, text, and video files shall come into the action at what point. Among the various kinds of authoring software are Macromedia Authorware, Macromedia Director, Asymetrix IconAuthor, Asymetrix Toolbook, and Action! for Macintosh and Windows.

2.10 When Software Causes Problems

KEY QUESTIONS

What are two principal drawbacks of new applications software, and what can you do about them?

Preview & Review: Software can come with many more features than you'll ever need—this is sometimes called *bloatware*. Software can also come with many flaws—this is called *shovelware*. Instruction manuals, help software, telephone help lines, commercial how-to books, and knowledgeable friends can help users deal with bloatware and shovelware.

In Issaquah, Washington, reported an Associated Press news story, a man was coaxed out of his home by police officers "after he pulled a gun and shot several times at his personal computer, apparently in frustration."[18]

Experienced computer users will recognize the phrase "apparently in frustration" as an understatement. Fortunately, newcomers will likely be spared these agonies with software because they will be operating at rather basic levels (and can seek help in computer classrooms from their instructors or staff members).

Some Drawbacks of New Software: Bloatware & Shovelware

Not everything is wrong with new programs or, of course, people wouldn't be using them. Nevertheless, let us consider a couple of significant drawbacks that often characterize new software and what you can do about them.

- **"Bloatware"—too many features:** Some software has become so crowded, or bloated, with features that it has led to the term "bloatware." The reason for all these features, of course, is the software industry's strategy of planned obsolescence—to make buyers want to abandon their old programs and rush out to buy new ones.

  Many computer users don't understand how to use all the software features they already have. Yet when Microsoft's Office 97 came on the market, supplanting Office 95, it contained *4500 commands*—far more than the few dozen or even few hundred that most people would use.[19]

- **"Shovelware"—full of flaws:** "In the computer world, as in horseshoes, close is good enough," says Stephen Manes, computer columnist for the *New York Times*. "In the computer world, products are considered perfectly acceptable when they almost work the way they are supposed to."[20]

  This second drawback is even more distressing than the first. Software makers are in such a hurry to ship, or shovel, their products out the door to market that it has inspired a new word: "shovelware." And a lot of shovelware was developed so hastily that it doesn't work right.

Help for Software Users

Fortunately, there are a number of sources of user assistance—although even here, forewarned is forearmed.

- **Instruction manuals:** User guides or instruction manuals printed on paper have traditionally accompanied a box of applications software diskettes or CD-ROMs. Sometimes these are just what you need. Sometimes, however, you need to know what you need help with, and it may be difficult to define the problem. In addition, these guides may be a puzzle to anyone not trained as a programmer because they are often written by the very people who developed the software. And experts are not always able to anticipate the problems of the inexpert.

- **Help software:** In place of paper manuals, software publishers are now relying more on "Help" programs on a diskette or CD-ROM accompanying the software, which contain a series of Help menus. However, these, too, may feature technospeak that is baffling to newcomers. Also, like paper manuals, help programs may suffer the drawbacks of having been rushed out at the last minute.

  Help programs may also be available through the Internet. The problem with trying to use the Net or the Web, of course, is: How do you go online to solve the problem of your computer not working if your computer isn't working? Or how do you access the Internet to get advice on how to fix your software and simultaneously fix your software? (It helps to have two computers.)

- **Telephone help lines:** If you encounter a software glitch, it's possible you could use a help line to call a customer-support technician at the program's manufacturer. The tech would then try to talk you through the problem or might refer you to a Web site from which you could obtain a file that would remedy your problem.

  Both software and hardware makers have long offered telephone help lines for customers. If your computer breaks down, you may find that your hardware company still offers emergency advice for free (although you may have to pay the phone company's long-distance tolls). However, software manufacturers now invariably charge for help calls if you've had the software longer than 30–90 days.

- **Commercial how-to books:** Because of the inadequacies in user support by the software developers themselves, an entire industry has sprung up devoted to publishing how-to books. These are the kind of books found both in computer stores and in general bookstores such as Barnes & Noble or Borders. Examples are the "For Dummies" or "Complete Idiot's" books (such as *Adobe PhotoShop for Dummies* and *The Complete Idiot's Guide to Microsoft Office 97 Professional*).

- **Knowledgeable friends:** Believe it or not, nothing beats having a knowledgeable friend: your instructor, a student more advanced than you, or someone with a technical interest in computers. We can't stress enough how important it is to get to know people—from your classes, from computer user groups (including online Internet groups), from family friends, or whatever—who can lend aid and expertise when your computer software gives you trouble.

2.11 Ethics & Intellectual Property Rights: When Can You Copy?

KEY QUESTIONS

When is copying a violation of copyright laws, what is a software license agreement, and what types of agreements are there?

Preview & Review: Intellectual property consists of the products of the human mind. Such property can be protected by copyright, the exclusive legal right that prohibits copying it without the permission of the copyright holder.

Software piracy, network piracy, and plagiarism violate copyright laws.

Public domain software, freeware, and shareware can be legally copied, which is not the case with proprietary (commercial) software.

Ethics

Information technology has presented legislators and lawyers—and you—with some new ethical questions regarding rights to intellectual property. *Intellectual property* consists of the products, tangible or intangible, of the human mind. There are three methods of protecting intellectual property. They are *patents* (as for an invention), *trade secrets* (as for a formula or method of doing business), and *copyrights* (as for a song or a book).

What Is a Copyright?

Of principal interest to us is copyright protection. **A *copyright* is the exclusive legal right that prohibits copying of intellectual property without the permission of the copyright holder.** Copyright law protects books, articles, pamphlets, music, art, drawings, movies—and, yes, computer software. Copyright protects the *expression* of an idea but not the idea itself. Thus, others may copy your idea for, say, a new video game but not your particular variant of it. Copyright protection is automatic and lasts a minimum of 50 years; you do not have to register your idea with the government (as you do with a patent) in order to receive protection.

These matters are important because the Digital Age has made the act of copying far easier and more convenient than in the past. Copying a book on a photocopier might take hours, so people usually feel they might as well buy the book. Copying a software program onto another diskette, however, might take just seconds.

Piracy, Plagiarism, & Ownership of Images & Sounds

Three copyright-related matters deserve our attention: software and network piracy, plagiarism, and ownership of images and sounds.

- **Software and network piracy:** It may be hard to think of yourself as a pirate (no sword or eyepatch) when all you've done is make a copy of some commercial software for a friend. However, from an ethical standpoint, an act of piracy is like shoplifting the product off a store shelf.

  Piracy is theft or unauthorized distribution or use. **Software piracy is the unauthorized copying of copyrighted software.** One way is to copy a program from one diskette to another. Another is to download (transfer) a program from a network and make a copy of it. **Network piracy is using electronic networks for the unauthorized distribution of copyrighted materials in digitized form.** Record companies, for example, have protested the practice of computer users' sending unauthorized copies of digital recordings over the Internet. Both types of piracy are illegal.

  The easy rationalization is to say that "I'm just a poor student, and making this one copy or downloading only one digital recording isn't going to hurt anyone." But it is the single act of software piracy multiplied millions of times that is causing the software publishers a billion-dollar problem. They point out that the loss of revenue cuts into their budget for offering customer support, upgrading products, and compensating their creative people. Piracy also means that software prices are less likely to come down; if anything, they are more likely to go up.

- **Plagiarism:** *Plagiarism* **is the expropriation of another writer's text, findings, or interpretations and presenting it as one's own.** Information technology puts a new face on plagiarism in two ways. On the one hand, it offers plagiarists new opportunities to go far afield for unauthorized copying. On the other hand, the technology offers new ways to catch people who steal other people's material.

  Electronic online journals are not limited by the number of pages, and so they can publish papers that attract a small number of readers. In recent years, there has been an explosion in the number of such journals and of their academic and scientific papers. This proliferation may make it harder to detect when a work has been plagiarized, because few readers will know if a similar paper has been published elsewhere. In addition, the Internet has spawned many companies that market prewritten term papers to students—a practice that some states are making illegal.

  Yet information technology may also be used to identify plagiarism. Scientists have used computers to search different documents for identical passages of text. In 1990, two "fraud busters" at the

National Institutes of Health alleged after a computer-based analysis that a prominent historian and biographer had committed plagiarism in his books. The historian, who said the technique turned up only the repetition of stock phrases, was later exonerated in a scholarly investigation.[21]

- **Ownership of images and sounds:** Computers, scanners, digital cameras, and the like make it possible to alter images and sounds to be almost anything you want. What does this mean for the original copyright holders? Images can be appropriated by scanning them into a computer system, then altered or placed in a new context.

These are the general issues you need to consider when you're thinking about how to use someone else's intellectual property in the Digital Age. Now let's see how software fits in.

Public Domain Software, Freeware, & Shareware

No doubt most of the applications programs you will study in conjunction with this book will be commercial software packages, with brand names such as Microsoft Word or Excel. However, there are a number of software products—many available over communications lines from the Internet—that are available to you as *public domain software, freeware,* or *shareware.*

- **Public domain software:** ***Public domain software* is software that is not protected by copyright and thus may be duplicated by anyone at will.** Public domain programs—usually developed at taxpayer expense by government agencies—have been donated to the public by their creators. They are often available through sites on the Internet (or electronic bulletin boards) or through computer users groups. A users group is a club, or group, of computer users who share interests and trade information about computer systems.

  You can duplicate public domain software without fear of legal prosecution. (Beware: Downloading software through the Internet may introduce some problems in the form of bad code called *viruses* into your system. We discuss viruses, and how to prevent them, in the Chapter 6 Experience Box.)

- **Freeware:** ***Freeware* is software that is available free of charge.** Freeware is distributed without charge, also usually through the Internet or computer users groups.

  Why would any software creator let the product go for free? Sometimes developers want to see how users respond, so they can make improvements in a later version. Sometimes it is to further some scholarly purpose, such as to create a standard for software on which people are apt to agree because there is no need to pay for it.

  Freeware developers often retain all rights to their programs, so that technically you are not supposed to duplicate and distribute them further. Still, there is no problem with your making several copies for your own use.

- **Shareware:** ***Shareware* is copyrighted software that is distributed free of charge but requires users to make a contribution in order to continue using it.** Shareware, too, is distributed primarily through communications connections such as the Internet.

  Sometimes "trialware" versions of shareware are available via the Internet. This type of software is limited in functionality (it's a watered-down version of the real thing), or the period of time that the software will work is self-limited. After the trial period is over, the user pays a fee to obtain the fully functional version, or the software simply becomes useless.

Though copying shareware is permissible, because it is copyrighted you cannot use it as the basis for developing your own program in order to compete with the developer.

Proprietary Software & Types of Licenses

***Proprietary software* is software whose rights are owned by an individual or business,** usually a software developer. The ownership is protected by the copyright, and the owner expects you to buy a copy in order to use it. The software cannot legally be used or copied without permission.

Software manufacturers don't sell you the software so much as sell you a license to become an authorized user of it. What's the difference? In paying for a ***software license,* you sign a contract in which you agree not to make copies of the software to give away or for resale.** That is, you have bought only the company's permission to use the software and not the software itself. This legal nicety allows the company to retain its rights to the program and limits the way its customers can use it.[22] The small print in the licensing agreement allows you to make one copy (backup copy or archival copy) for your own use.

Experience Box

Getting Started with Computers in College & Going Online

Students who come to college with a personal computer as part of their luggage are certainly ahead of the game. If you don't have one, however, there are other options.

If You Don't Own a Personal Computer

If you don't have a PC, you can probably borrow someone else's sometimes. However, if you have a paper due the next day, you may have to defer to the owner, who may also have a deadline. When borrowing, then, you need to plan ahead and allow yourself plenty of time.

Virtually every campus now makes computers available to students, either at minimal cost or essentially for free as part of the regular student fees. This availability may take two forms:

- **Library or computer labs:** Even students who have their own computers may sometimes want to use the computers available at the library or campus computer lab. These may have special software or better printers than most students have.

- **Dormitory computer centers or dorm-room terminals:** Some campuses provide dormitory-based computer centers (for example, in the basement). Even if you have your own computer, it's nice to know about these for backup purposes.

  More and more campuses are also providing computers or terminals within students' dormitory rooms. These are usually connected by a campuswide local area network (LAN) to lab computers and administrative systems. Often, however, they also allow students to communicate over phone lines to people in other states.

  Of course, if the system cannot accommodate a large number of students, all the computers may be in high demand come term-paper time. Clearly, owning a computer offers you convenience and a competitive advantage.

If You Do Own a Personal Computer

Perhaps someone gave you a personal computer, or you acquired one, before you came to college. It will probably be one of two types: (1) a PC, such as from IBM, Gateway, Compaq, Dell, Hewlett-Packard, Packard Bell NEC; or (2) an Apple Macintosh.

If all you need to do is write term papers, nearly any microcomputer will do. Indeed, you may not even need to have a printer, if you can find other ways to print out things. The University of Michigan, for instance, offers "express stations" or "drive-up windows." These allow students to use a diskette or connect a computer to a student-use printer to print out their papers. Or, if a friend has a compatible computer, you can ask to borrow it and the printer for a short time to print your work.

You should, however, take a look around you to see *if your present system is appropriate for your campus and your major.*

- **The fit with your campus:** Most campuses are known as PC schools; however, "Macs" (Apple Macintoshes) are used at some schools. Why should choice of machine matter? The answer is that diskettes can't always be read interchangeably among the two main types of microcomputers. Thus, if you own the system that is out of step for your campus, you may find it difficult to swap files or programs with others. Nor will you be able to borrow their equipment to finish a paper if yours breaks down. Call the dean of students' office or otherwise ask around to find which system is most popular.

- **The fit with your major:** Speech communications, foreign language, physical education, political science, biology, and English majors probably don't need a fancy computer system (or even any system at all). Business, engineering, architecture, and journalism majors may have special requirements. For instance, an architecture major doing computer-aided design (CAD) projects or a journalism major doing desktop publishing will need reasonably powerful systems. A history or nursing major, who will mainly be writing papers, will not. Of course, you may be presently undeclared or undecided about your major. Even so, it's a good idea to find out what kinds of equipment and programs are being used in the majors you are contemplating.

How to Get Your Own Personal Computer

Buying a personal computer, like buying a car, often requires making a trade-off between power and expense.

Power Many computer experts try to look for a personal computer system with as much power as possible. The word *power* has different meanings when describing software and hardware:

- **Powerful software:** Applied to software, "powerful" means that the program is flexible. That is, it can do many different things. For example, a word processing program that can include graphics in documents is more powerful than one that cannot.

- **Powerful hardware:** Applied to hardware, "powerful" means that the equipment (1) is fast and (2) has *great capacity.*

  A fast computer will process data more quickly than a slow one. With an older computer, for example, it may take several seconds to save, or store on a disk, a 50-page term paper. On a newer machine, it might take less than a second.

  A computer with great capacity can run complex software and process voluminous files. *This is an especially important matter if you want to be able to run the latest releases of software.*

Will computer use make up an essential part of your major, as it might if you are going into engineering, business, or graphic arts? If so, you may want to try to acquire powerful hardware and software. People who really want (and can afford) their own desktop publishing system might buy a new Macintosh PowerPC with color ink-jet printer, scanner, and Quark page makeup software and PhotoShop photo manipulation software, among other programs. This might well cost $8000. Most students, of course, cannot afford anything close to this.

Expense If your major does not require a special computer system, a microcomputer can be acquired for relatively little.

What's the *minimum* you should get? Probably a microcomputer with 32 megabytes of memory (✔ p. 13) and one diskette drive, one hard-disk drive, a CD-ROM drive, and an external hard-disk unit such as a Zip drive with removable Zip cartridges to use for backup. (However, 64 or more megabytes of memory may be needed if you're going to run graphic-intensive programs. Because software memory requirements are increasing, check with some knowledgeable friends about recommended minimum memory before buying a computer.)

Buying a New Computer Fierce price wars among microcomputer manufacturers and retailers have made hardware more affordable. One reason PCs have become so widespread is that non-PC microcomputer manufacturers early on were legally able to copy, or "clone," IBM machines (the original PCs) and offer them at cut-rate prices. For a long time, Apple Macintoshes were considerably more expensive, although this has changed somewhat. (In part this was because other manufacturers were unable to offer inexpensive Mac clones.)

When buying hardware, make sure the system software that comes with it is at least Windows 95 for a PC and at least System 8 for the Macintosh. Also, look to see if any applications software, such as word processing or spreadsheet programs, comes "bundled" with it. In this case, *bundled* means that software is included in the selling price of the hardware. This arrangement can be a real advantage, saving you several hundred dollars.

There are several sources for inexpensive new computers, as follows:

- **Student-discount sources:** With a college ID card, you're probably entitled to a student discount (usually 10 to 20%) through the campus bookstore or college computer resellers. In addition, during the first few weeks of the term, many campuses offer special sales on computer equipment. Campus resellers also provide on-campus service and support and can help students meet the prevailing campus standards while satisfying their personal needs.

  Note that some private educational discount companies can sell software to students that is discounted up to and above 70%. A few examples are Solomon Computer Student Discount Offers *(www.surfshop.net/users/solomon/student.htm),* Student Discount Network *(www.discount-net.com),* Software Services *(www.swservices.com/student.htm),* and Indelible Blue *(www.indelible-blue.com/press/academic.html).*

- **Computer superstores:** These are big chains such as Computer City, CompUSA, and Microage. Computers are also sold at department stores, warehouse stores such as Costco and Sam's Club, office-supply chains such as Staples and Office Depot, and electronics stores such as the Good Guys and Circuit City.

- **Mail-order houses:** Companies like Dell Computer and Gateway 2000 found they could sell computers inexpensively while offering customer support over the phone. Their success inspired IBM, Compaq, and others to plunge into the mail-order business.

  The price advantage of mail-order companies has eroded with the rise of computer superstores. Moreover, the lack of local repair and service support can be a major disadvantage. Still, if you're interested in this route, look for a copy of the phone-book-size magazine *Computer Shopper,* which carries ads from most mail-order vendors. (Make sure the mail-order house offers warranties and brand-name equipment.)

Checklist Here are some decisions you should make before acquiring a computer:

- **What software will I need?** Although it may sound backward, you should select the software before the hardware. This is because you want to choose software that will perform the kind of work you want to do. First find the kind of programs you want—word processing, spreadsheet, Web browser, PIM, graphics, or whatever. Check out the memory and other hardware requirements for those programs. Then make sure you get a system to fit them.

  The advice to start with software before hardware has always been standard for computer buyers. However, it is becoming increasingly important as programs with extensive graphics come on the market. Graphics tend to require a lot of memory, hard-disk storage, and screen display area.

- **Do I want a desktop or a portable?** Look for a computer that fits your work style. For instance, you may want a portable if you spend a lot of time at the library. Some students even use portables to take notes in class. If you do most of your work in your room or at home, you may find it more comfortable to have a desktop PC. Though not portable, the monitors of desktop computers are usually easier to read.

Actually, however, portables have come so far along that you'll probably have no trouble reading the screens on the latest models. Keep in mind, however, that the keyboards on portables are smaller.

Whatever type of computer you buy, make sure it is an established brand-name computer.

● **Is upgradability important?** The newest software being released is so powerful (meaning flexible) that it requires increasingly more powerful hardware. That is, the software requires hardware that is fast and has great main memory and storage capacity. Be sure to ask the salesperson how the hardware can be upgraded to accommodate increased memory and storage needs later.

● **Do I want a PC or a Macintosh?** Although the situation is changing, until recently the division between PCs on the one hand and Apple Macintoshes on the other was fundamental. Neither could run the other's software or exchange files of data without special equipment and software. We mentioned that some campuses and some academic majors tend to favor one type of microcomputer over the other. Outside of college, however, the business world tends to be dominated by PCs. In a handful of areas—education, graphic arts, and desktop publishing, for example—Macintoshes are preferred.

Getting Started Online

Computer networks have transformed life on campuses around the country, becoming a cultural and social force affecting everybody. How do you join this vast world of online information and interaction?

Hardware & Software Needed Besides a microcomputer with a hard disk, you need a modem to send messages from one computer to another via a phone line. Nowadays modems come installed on most computers. If not, you can have a store install an internal modem as an electronic circuit board on the inside of the computer, or you can buy an external modem, a box-shaped unit that is hooked up to the outside of the computer.

To go online, you'll need communications software, which may come bundled with any computer you buy or is sold on diskettes or CD-ROMs in computer stores. However, many modems come with communications software when you buy them. Or, if you sign up for an online service, it will supply the communications program you need to use its network.

Your modem will connect to a standard telephone wall jack. (When your computer is in use, it prevents you from using the phone, and callers trying to reach you will hear a busy signal. If you have call waiting, it will cut off your online session and ring the call through. Check with your telephone company about how to turn off call waiting when you are online.)

Getting Connected: Starting with an Online Service Unless you already have access to a campus network, probably the easiest first step for using this equipment is to sign up with a commercial online service, such as America Online, CompuServe, Microsoft Network, or Prodigy.

You'll need a credit card in order to join because online services charge a monthly fee, typically about $20. All online services have introductory offers that allow you a free trial period. You can get instructions and a free start-up communications disk by phoning their toll-free 800 numbers. You'll also find promotional offers at computer stores or promotional diskettes shrink-wrapped inside computer magazines on newsstands.

The chart below lists the leading online services, costs, phone numbers, and other details. Rates are subject to change. All have special introductory offers.

America Online   800-827-6364
www.aol.com
50 free hours with download of trial software; then $21.95 per month.
Call the 800 number for CD-ROM version.

CompuServe   800-848-8199
www.compuserve.com
Order online or via phone. 1 month free with trial software; then $24.95 per month for unlimited use, or $9.95 per month for 5 hours and $2.95 per hour thereafter.

Prodigy   800-776-3449
www.prodigy.com
Order online or via phone. 1 month free, then $19.95 per month.

Microsoft Network   800-free-msn
www.microsoft.com
Order online or via phone. $69.50 per year for unlimited use, or $19.95 per month for unlimited use, or $6.95 per month for 5 hours and $2.50 per hour thereafter.

Notes: Check the service's system requirements for running their software before you order it. If you download the software online, ask the service how long it will take. (If you have a slow modem, it could take hours!) All software comes in PC versions and Mac versions.

Summary

What It Is/What It Does	Why It's Important
analytical graphics (p. 48, KQ 2.4) Also called *business graphics;* graphical forms representing numeric data. The principal examples are bar charts, line graphs, and pie charts. Analytical graphics programs are a type of applications software.	Numeric data is easier to analyze in graphical form than in the form of rows and columns of numbers, as in electronic spreadsheets.
applications software (p. 37, KQ 2.1) Software that solves a particular problem, performs useful work on tasks, or provides entertainment.	Applications software such as word processing, spreadsheet, database manager, graphics, and communications packages are used to increase people's productivity, and video games have become a big business by providing new forms of entertainment with the side effect of teaching new users how to use a computer.
button (p. 43, KQ 2.2) Simulated on-screen button (kind of icon) that is activated ("pushed") by a mouse or other pointing device to issue a command.	Buttons make it easier for users to enter commands.
communications software (p. 52, KQ 2.7) Applications software that manages the transmission of data between computers. Also called *data communications software.*	Communications software is required to transmit data via modems in a communications system.
computer-aided design (CAD) (p. 59, KQ 2.9) Applications software programs for designing products and structures and making civil engineering drawings and maps.	CAD programs help architects design buildings and work spaces and engineers design cars, planes, and electronic devices. With CAD software, a product can be drawn in three dimensions and then rotated on the screen so the designer can see all sides.
computer-aided design/computer-aided manufacturing (CAD/CAM) (p. 60, KQ 2.9) Applications software that allows products designed with CAD to be input into a computer-based manufacturing system (CAM) that makes the products.	CAD/CAM systems have greatly enhanced creativity and efficiency in many industries.
copyright (p. 63, KQ 2.11) Body of law that prohibits copying of intellectual property without the permission of the copyright holder.	Copyright law aims to prevent people from taking credit for and profiting unfairly from other people's work.

What It Is/What It Does	Why It's Important

cursor (p. 44, KQ 2.3) The movable symbol on the display screen that shows the user where data or commands may be entered next, that is, where the *insertion point* is. The cursor is moved around with the keyboard's directional arrow keys or an electronic mouse.

All applications software packages use cursors to show users where their current work location is on the screen.

cyberspace (p. 52, KQ 2.7) The online or digital world in general and the Internet and its World Wide Web in particular.

By adding communications capabilities to a computer to access cyberspace, the user can reach libraries, databases, and individuals all over the world.

database (p. 49, KQ 2.5) Collection of interrelated files in a computer system that is created and managed by database software. These files are organized so that those parts with a common element can be retrieved easily.

Online database services provide users with enormous research resources. Businesses and organizations use databases to keep track of transactions and increase people's efficiency.

database software (p. 49, KQ 2.5) Applications software for maintaining a database. It controls the structure of a database and access to the data.

Database manager software allows users to organize and manage huge amounts of data.

default settings (p. 46, KQ 2.3) Settings automatically used by a program unless the user specifies otherwise, thereby overriding them.

Users need to know how to change default settings in order to customize their documents.

desktop publishing (DTP) (p. 57, KQ 2.9) Producing high-quality printed output for commercial printing using DTP software and a microcomputer, mouse, and scanner to mix text and graphics, including photos. Text is usually composed first on a word processor, artwork is created with drawing and painting software, and photographs are scanned in using a scanner, or clip-art drawings or photos may be used. A laser or ink-jet printer is used to get an advance look.

Desktop publishing has reduced the number of steps, the time, and the money required to produce professional-looking printed projects.

dialog box (p. 43, KQ 2.2) With graphical user interface (GUI) software, a box that appears on the screen and displays a message requiring a response from the user—for example, Y for "Yes" or N for "No."

Dialog boxes are only one aspect of GUIs that make software easier for people to use.

documentation (p. 43, KQ 2.2) User's guide or reference manual that is a narrative and graphical description of a program. Documentation may be instructional, but usually features and functions are grouped by category.

Documentation helps users learn software commands and use of function keys, solve problems, and find information about system specifications.

drawing program (p. 60, KQ 2.9) Applications software that allows users to design and illustrate objects and products.

Drawing programs and CAD are similar. However, drawing programs provide special effects that CAD programs do not.

electronic mail (e-mail) software (p. 53, KQ 2.7) Software that enables computer users to send letters and files from one computer to another.

E-mail allows businesses and organizations to quickly and easily send messages to employees and outside people without resorting to paper messages.

electronic spreadsheet (p. 46, KQ 2.4) Also called *spreadsheet;* applications software that allows users to create tables and financial schedules by entering data and formulas into rows and columns arranged as a grid on a display screen. If data is changed in one cell, values in other cells specified in the spreadsheet will automatically recalculate.

The electronic spreadsheet became such a popular small-business applications program that it has been held directly responsible for making the microcomputer a widely used business tool.

financial software (p. 51, KQ 2.6) A growing category of software that ranges from *personal-finance managers* to entry-level accounting programs to business financial-management packages.

Financial software uses the power of computers to handle basic mathematical tasks, giving the user the time and information to decide on a financial course of action.

freeware (p. 65, KQ 2.11) Software that is available free of charge.

Freeware is usually distributed through the Internet. Users can make copies for their own use but are not free to make unlimited copies.

function keys (p. 41, KQ 2.2) Computer keyboard keys that are labeled F1, F2, and so on; usually positioned along the top or left side of the keyboard.

Function keys are used to issue commands. These keys are used differently depending on the software.

graphical user interface (GUI) (p. 42, KQ 2.2) User interface that uses images, menus, buttons, dialog boxes, and windows as well as keystrokes to let the user choose commands, start programs, and see file lists.

GUIs are easier to use than command-driven interfaces and menu-driven interfaces; they permit liberal use of the electronic mouse as a pointing device to move the cursor to a particular icon or place on the display screen. The function represented by the icon can be activated by pressing ("clicking") buttons on the mouse.

groupware (p. 61, KQ 2.9) Applications software that is used on a network and allows a group of users working together on the same project to share ideas and update documents. Also called *collaboration software,* it can serve users in the same building or continents apart.

Groupware improves productivity by keeping users continually notified about what colleagues are thinking and doing, and vice versa.

Help option (p. 42, KQ 2.2) Also called *Help screen;* offers on-screen instructions for using software. Help screens are accessed via a function key or by using the mouse to select Help from a menu.

Help screens provide a built-in electronic instruction manual.

icon (p. 42, KQ 2.2) In a GUI, a picture that represents a command, program, file, or task.

The icon's function can be activated by pointing at it with the mouse pointer and clicking on it. The use of icons has simplified the use of computers.

integrated software package (p. 55, KQ 2.8) Applications software that combines in one package the commonly used features of several applications programs—usually electronic spreadsheets, word processing, database management, graphics, and communications. Often called "works" programs.

Integrated software packages offer greater flexibility than separate single-purpose programs.

What It Is/What It Does	**Why It's Important**

macro (p. 41, KQ 2.2) Software feature that allows a single keystroke or command to be used to automatically issue a predetermined series of keystrokes or commands. Also called a *keyboard shortcut.*

Macros increase productivity by consolidating several command keystrokes into one or two.

menu (p. 42, KQ 2.2) List of available commands displayed on the screen.

Menus are used in graphical user interface programs to make software easier for people to use.

multimedia authoring software (p. 61, KQ 2.9) Applications software that enables users to create multimedia applications that integrate text, images, sound, motion, and animation. Also called *authoring software.*

Offers tools that make it possible to sequence and time the files used in a multimedia presentation, and to add user interaction screens.

network piracy (p. 64, KQ 2.11) The use of electronic networks for unauthorized distribution of copyrighted materials in digitized form.

If piracy is not controlled, people may not want to let their intellectual property and copyrighted material be dealt with in digital form.

painting program (p. 60, KQ 2.9) Applications programs that simulate painting on the screen using a mouse or tablet stylus like a paintbrush.

Painting programs can render sophisticated illustrations.

personal-finance manager (p. 51, KQ 2.6) Applications software that helps users track income and expenses, write checks, do online banking, and plan financial goals.

Personal-finance software can help people manage their money more effectively.

personal information manager (PIM) (p. 50, KQ 2.5) Applications software to help the user keep track of and manage information used daily, such as addresses, telephone numbers, appointments, "to do" lists, and miscellaneous notes.

PIMs offer an electronic version of essential daily tools all in one place.

plagiarism (p. 64, KQ 2.11) Expropriation of another writer's text, findings, or interpretations and presenting them as one's own.

Information technology offers plagiarists new opportunities to go far afield for unauthorized copying, yet it also offers new ways to catch these people.

presentation graphics (p. 58, KQ 2.9) Professional-looking graphics used to communicate information to others, such as in training, sales, formal reports, and kiosks. Presentation graphics are part of presentation software, which uses data/information and graphics from other software tools to create a presentation.

Presentation graphics programs may make use of analytical graphics—bar, line, and pie charts—but they look much more sophisticated, using texturing patterns, complex color, and dimensionality.

project management software (p. 59, KQ 2.9) Applications software used to plan, schedule, and control the people, costs, and resources required to complete a project on time.

Project management software increases the ease and speed of planning and managing complex projects.

What It Is/What It Does	**Why It's Important**

proprietary software (p. 66, KQ 2.11) Software whose rights are owned by an individual or business.

Ownership of proprietary software is protected by copyright. This type of software must be purchased to be used. Copying is restricted.

public domain software (p. 65, KQ 2.11) Software that is not protected by copyright and thus may be duplicated by anyone at will.

Public domain software offers lots of software options to users who may not be able to afford a lot of commercial software. Users may make as many copies as they wish.

recalculation (p. 48, KQ 2.4) In electronic spreadsheets, the process of recomputing values automatically when data changes.

Recalculation is what makes electronic spreadsheets valuable: as information changes, the user just enters the data and the computer does the recalculating.

scrolling (p. 44, KQ 2.3) The activity of moving quickly upward or downward through text or other screen display, using directional arrow keys or mouse.

Normally a computer screen displays only 20–22 lines of text. Scrolling enables users to view an entire document, no matter how long.

search engines (p. 55, KQ 2.7) Software search tools that allow Web users to search for specific documents through keyword searches. Search engine information is collected by software programs.

Search engines make it easy for users to find Web sites they may be interested in.

shareware (p. 65, KQ 2.11) Copyrighted software that is distributed free of charge, usually over the Internet, but that requires users to make a contribution in order to continue using it.

Along with public domain software and freeware, shareware offers yet another inexpensive way to obtain new software.

software license (p. 66, KQ 2.11) Contract by which users agree not to make copies of proprietary software to give away or to sell.

Software manufacturers don't sell people software so much as sell them licenses to become authorized users of the software.

software piracy (p. 64, KQ 2.11) Unauthorized copying of copyrighted software—for example, copying a program from one floppy disk to another or downloading a program from a network and making a copy of it.

Software piracy represents a serious loss of income to software manufacturers and is a contributor to high prices in new programs.

software suite (p. 56, KQ 2.8) Several applications software packages—like spreadsheets, word processing, graphics, communications, and groupware—bundled together and sold for a fraction of what the programs would cost if bought individually. Often called "office" programs.

Software suites can save users a lot of money.

special-purpose keys (p. 41, KQ 2.2) Computer keyboard keys used to enter, delete, and edit data and execute commands—for example, Esc, Alt, and Ctrl.

All computer keyboards have special-purpose keys. The user's software program determines how these keys are used.

tutorial (p. 43, KQ 2.2) Instruction book or program that takes users through a prescribed series of steps to help them learn the product.

Tutorials, which accompany applications software packages, enable users to practice new software in a graduated fashion, thereby saving them the time they would have used trying to teach themselves.

What It Is/What It Does	Why It's Important
user interface (p. 41, KQ 2.2) Part of a software program that presents on the screen the alternative commands by which the user communicates with the system and that displays information.	Some user interfaces are easier to use than others. Most users prefer a graphical user interface.
Web browser (p. 53, KQ 2.7) Software that enables people to view Web sites on their computers.	Without browser software, users cannot use the part of the Internet called the World Wide Web.
Web directories (p. 54, KQ 2.7) Web indexes classified by topic. Directory information is collected by people rather than by software as in search engines.	Web directories make it easy for users to find Web sites they may be interested in.
window (p. 42, KQ 2.2) Feature of graphical user interfaces; rectangle that appears on the screen and displays information from a particular part of a program.	Using the windows feature, an operating system (or operating environment) can display several windows on a computer screen, each showing a different application program such as word processing, spreadsheets, and graphics.
word processing software (p. 43, KQ 2.3) Applications software that enables users to create, edit, revise, store, and print text material.	Word processing software allows a person to use a computer to easily create, edit, copy, save, and print documents such as letters, memos, reports, and manuscripts.

Self-Test

1. A(n) _____ is a window that appears on the screen and requires a response from you.

2. _____ is the activity of moving quickly upward or downward through text or other screen elements.

3. A(n) _____ is a major upgrade in a software product. A(n) _____ is a minor upgrade.

4. The type of software most suited to creating tables and financial schedules is _____ software.

5. _____ software controls how a collection of interrelated files are organized and access to their data.

Short-Answer Questions

1. What is the difference between integrated software and a software suite?

2. What do the abbreviations CAD and CAM mean?

3. List at least three resources for software users who are in need of helpful assistance.

4. What is the difference between software piracy and network piracy?

5. List the five categories of application software.

Multiple-Choice Questions

1. Which of the following would you most likely use to design products, structures, civil engineering drawings, and maps?
   a. communications software
   b. electronic-mail software
   c. computer-aided design software
   d. desktop publishing software
   e. All of the above

2. Which of the following terms is used to describe software that is full of flaws?
   a. bloatware
   b. badware
   c. shovelware
   d. bugware
   e. All of the above

3. Which of the following is distributed free of charge but requires users to make a contribution later on?
   a. public domain software
   b. shareware
   c. freeware
   d. proprietary software
   e. All of the above

4. Which of the following is a type of specialty software?
   a. desktop publishing
   b. presentation graphics
   c. project management
   d. drawing and painting programs
   e. All of the above

True/False Questions

T F 1. Word processing and database management are the two most popular software applications.

T F 2. Although software documentation may be accessed online, today it is usually only available in printed form.

T F 3. A spreadsheet is composed of fields, records, and files.

T F 4. Groupware software allows users located in the same building or in different countries to collaborate on projects and update documents.

T F 5. You can access the World Wide Web using multimedia authoring software.

Knowledge in Action

1. Attend a meeting of a computer users' group in your area. What is the overall purpose of the group? Software support? Hardware support? In what ways? Does it cost money to be a member? How many members are there? How does the group get new members? If you were looking to join a user group, would you be interested in joining this group? Why/why not?

2. What is your opinion about the issue of free speech on an electronic network? Research some recent legal decisions in various countries, as well as some articles on the topic, and then give a short report about what you think. Should the contents of messages be censored? If so, under what conditions?

3. Prepare a short report about how you would use an electronic spreadsheet to organize and manage your personal finances and to project outcomes of changes. What column headings (labels) would you use? Row headings? What formula relationships would you want to establish among which cells? (For example, if your tuition increased by $2000, how would that affect the monthly amount set aside to buy a car or take a trip?)

4. Picture yourself in your future job. What types of current applications software do you see yourself using? What are you producing with this software? What kinds of new applications software would you invent to help you do your job better?

5. Research what is meant by the phrase *digital office*. What would a digital office look like? How is this different from today's offices? What companies are involved in digital-office technologies? Perform your research using the Web and current computer periodicals.

Extra Information: More About Fonts

Examples of fonts:

ABCDEFGHIJK   10-point Times Roman regular

ABCDEFGHIJK 14-point Ariel Bold

*ABCDEFGHIJK*24-point Trump Medieval Italic

Type glossary:

Font   A character set in a particular size and type design (typeface)
Point   Unit of measurement of type size; 12 points equal 1 pica.
Pica   Unit of measurement of page elements, such as margin width; 6 picas equal 1 inch.
Leading Unit of measurement between lines of type; for example, space (10 + 2 = 12) between lines.
           10/12 lines would be closer together than 10/14 lines.

Type basics:

Many characteristics give fonts different looks—from the ornate to the plain, text-book style. Some fonts are more readable and better for reports and documents. Some are unique or formal and may be better for a logo or invitation.

But how do font designers give their fonts different looks? One of the most common ways to change a font is to add a *serif* or leave the font *sans serif* (without a serif). This serif is a little "foot" or "hat" added to the letters. Designers also can adjust some of the type characteristics, maybe making a loop a little wider, raising an ascender, or giving a jaunty lift to the ear on a *g*. They can change the *pitch* of letters, which is how much horizontal room they get. The pitch may be *fixed* or *monospaced,* meaning each letter gets the same amount of room, or it may be *proportional*, so that the spacing depends on the width of the particular character. Finally, they can give letters or numerals a different weight, which is the thickness, or a different style, such as straight up or italics.

f i tness
Monospaced type

fitness
Proportional type

To give you an idea of what designers have to play around with, here we've assembled a chart illustrating the names of all the parts of a typeface design.

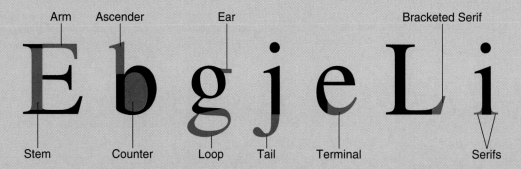

Arm   Ascender   Ear   Bracketed Serif

EbgjeLi

Stem   Counter   Loop   Tail   Terminal   Serifs

System Software

The Power Behind the Power

key questions

You should be able to answer the following questions:

3.1 **Three Components of System Software** What are the three basic components of system software?

3.2 **The Operating System** What are the principal functions of the operating system?

3.3 **Common Microcomputer Operating Systems: The Changing Platforms** What are the principal operating systems and operating environments for personal computers, and what are their principal characteristics?

3.4 **Utility Programs: Software to Make Your Computer Run Smoother** How do utility programs interact with and extend an operating system's features and capabilities?

3.5 **The Network Computer: Is the Web Changing Everything?** How could the network computer make the choice of PC operating system irrelevant?

What we need is a science called practology, a way of thinking about machines that focuses on how things will actually be used.

So says Alan Robbins, a professor of visual communications, on the subject of machine *interfaces*—the parts of a machine that people actually manipulate.[1] An interface is a machine's "control panel," ranging from the volume and tuner knobs on an old radio to all the switches and dials on the flight deck of a jetliner. You may have found, as Robbins thinks, that on too many of today's machines—digital watches, VCRs, even stoves—the interface is often designed to accommodate the machine or some engineering ideas rather than the people actually using them. Good interfaces are intuitive—that is, based on prior knowledge and experience—like the twin knobs on a 1940s radio, immediately usable by both novices and sophisticates. Bad interfaces, such as a software program with a bewildering array of menus and icons, force us to relearn the required behaviors every time. Of course, you can prevail over a bad interface if you repeat the procedures often enough.

How well are computer hardware and software makers doing at giving us useful, helpful interfaces? The answer is: getting better all the time, but they still have some leftovers from the past to get rid of. For instance, PC keyboards still come with a SysReq (for "System Request") key, which was once used to get the attention of the central computer but now is rarely used.

In time, as interfaces are refined, it's possible computers will become no more difficult to use than a car. Until then, however, for smoother computing you need to know something about how system software works. Today people communicate one way, computers another. People speak words and phrases; computers process bits and bytes. For us to communicate with these machines, we need an intermediary, an interpreter. This is the function of system software. We interact mainly with the applications software, which interacts with the system software, which controls the hardware.

3.1 Three Components of System Software

KEY QUESTION

What are the three basic components of system software?

Preview & Review: System software comprises three basic components: the operating system, utility programs, and language translators.

As we've said, *software*, or *programs*, consists of the instructions that tell the computer how to perform a task. Software is of two types—*applications software* and *system software*. As Chapter 2 described, *applications software* is software that can perform useful work on general-purpose tasks, such as word processing or spreadsheets, or that is used for entertainment. **System software enables the applications software to interact with the computer and helps the computer manage its internal and external resources.** System software is required to run applications software; however, the reverse is not true. Buyers of new computers will find the system software has already been installed by the manufacturer.

There are three basic types of system software that you need to know about—*operating systems, utility programs,* and *language translators.*

- Operating systems: An operating system is the principal component of system software in any computing system. We describe it at length in the next section.

- **Utility programs:** *Utility programs* are generally used to support, enhance, or expand existing programs in a computer system. Most system software bundles utility programs for performing common tasks such as merging two files into one file or performing backup. Other external, or commercial, utility programs (such as Norton Utilities) are available separately—for example, a utility to recover damaged files. We describe external utility programs later in this chapter.

- **Language translators: A *language translator* is software that translates a program written by a programmer in a language such as C—for example, a word processing program—into machine language (0s and 1s), which the computer can understand.**

The components of system software are diagrammed below. (■ *See Panel 3.1.*)

3.2 The Operating System

KEY QUESTION

What are the principal functions of the operating system?

Preview & Review: The operating system manages the basic operations of the computer. These operations include booting the computer and management of storage media. Another feature is the user interface, which may be command-driven, menu-driven, graphical, or network. Other operations are managing computer resources and managing files. The operating system also manages tasks, through multitasking, multiprogramming, time-sharing, or multiprocessing.

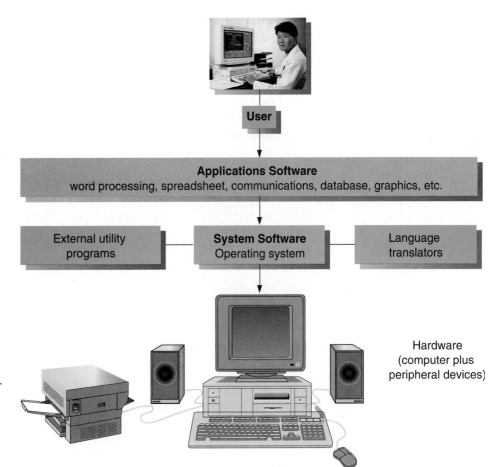

■ PANEL 3.1

The three components of system software

An operating system is required for applications software to run on your computer. The user usually works with the applications software but can bypass it to work directly with the system software for certain tasks.

The *operating system (OS)* consists of the master system of programs that manage the basic operations of the computer. These programs provide resource management services of many kinds, handling such matters as the control and use of hardware resources, including disk space, memory, CPU time allocation, and peripheral devices. The operating system allows you to concentrate on your own tasks or applications rather than on the complexities of managing the computer.

Different sizes and makes of computers have their own operating systems. In general, an operating system written for one kind of hardware will not be able to run on another kind of machine. Microcomputer users may readily experience the aggravation of such incompatibility when they acquire a microcomputer. Should they get an Apple Macintosh with Macintosh system software, which won't run PC programs? Or should they get a PC (such as IBM, Compaq, or Dell), which won't run Macintosh programs?

Before we try to sort out these perplexities, we should see what operating systems do that deserve our attention. We consider:

- Booting
- Managing storage media
- User interface
- Managing computer resources
- Managing files
- Managing tasks

Booting

The operating system begins to operate as soon as you turn on, or "boot," the computer. The term ***booting* refers to the process of loading an operating system into a computer's main memory from disk.** This loading is accomplished by a program (called the *bootstrap loader* or *boot routine*) that is stored permanently in the computer's electronic circuitry.

When you turn on the machine, programs called *diagnostic routines* first start up and test the main memory, the central processing unit (✔ p. 16), and other parts of the system to make sure they are running properly. As these programs are running, the display screen may show the message "Testing RAM" (main memory).

Next, other programs (indicated on your screen as "BIOS," for basic input/output system) will be copied to main memory to help the computer interpret keyboard characters or transmit characters to the display screen or to a diskette.

Then the boot program obtains the operating system, usually from hard disk, and loads it into the computer's main memory (✔ p. 16). The operating system remains in main memory until you turn the computer off. With newer operating systems, the booting process puts you into a graphically designed starting screen, from which you choose the applications programs you want to run or the files you want to open.

Managing Storage Media

If you have not entered a command to start an applications program, what else can you do with the operating system? One important function is to perform common repetitive tasks involved with managing storage media.

An example of such a task is formatting of blank diskettes. Before you can use a blank diskette you've just bought, you may have to format it. ***For-***

matting, or *initializing,* **electronically prepares a diskette so it can store data or programs.** Nowadays, however, it's easier to buy preformatted diskettes, which bear the label "Formatted IBM" or "Formatted Macintosh."

Providing a User Interface

Many operating-system functions are never apparent on the computer's display screen. What you do see is the user interface (✔ p. 42). **The *user interface* is the user-controllable part of the operating system that allows you to communicate, or interact, with it.**

There are four types of user interfaces, for both operating systems and applications software: *command-driven; menu-driven; graphical;* and, most recently, *network.* (■ *See Panel 3.2.)*

- Command-driven interface: **A *command-driven interface* requires you to enter a command by typing in codes or words.** An example of such a command might be DIR (for "directory"). This command instructs the computer to display a directory list of all folder and file names on a disk.

■PANEL 3.2

Types of user interfaces

(Top left) A command-driven interface, as in MS-DOS, requires typing of codes or words. *(Middle)* A menu-driven interface contains menus offering displayed lists of options. *(Bottom right)* A graphical user interface, such as Windows 98, allows users to select programs, commands, files, and other items represented by pictorial figures (icons), as well as use various types of menus.

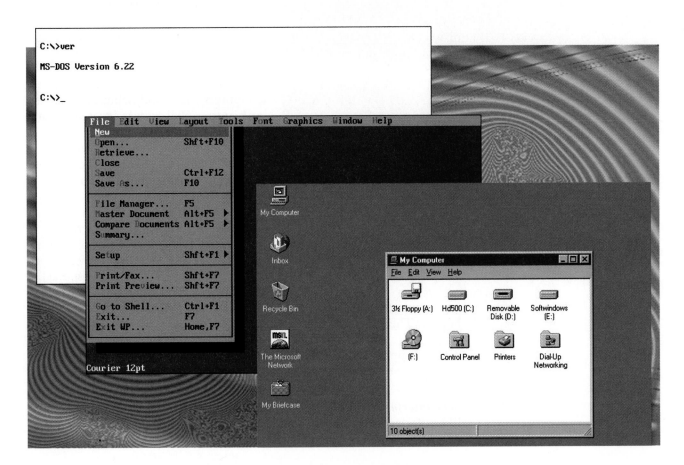

You type a command at the point on the display screen where the cursor follows the prompt, such as following "C:\>". In general, C:\ refers to the hard disk and > is a *system prompt*, asking you for a command. After you type in the command, you press the Enter key to execute the command.

The command-driven interface is the type found on PCs with the DOS operating system (discussed shortly).

- **Menu-driven interface:** **A *menu-driven interface* allows you to use cursor-movement (arrow) keys to choose a command from a menu.** Like a restaurant menu, **a *menu* offers you options to choose from—in this case, commands available for manipulating data,** such as Print or Edit.

  Menus are easier to use than command-driven interfaces, especially for beginners, because users can choose from lists of options rather than having to remember the code for specific commands. The disadvantage of menus, however, is that they are slower to use. Thus, some software programs offer both features—menus for novice users and keyboard commands for experienced users.

- **Graphical user interface (GUI):** The easiest interface to use, **the *graphical user interface* allows you to use graphics (images) and menus as well as keystrokes to choose commands, start programs, and see lists of files and other options** (✔ p. 42). Some of these images take the form of icons. ***Icons* are small pictorial figures that represent tasks, procedures, and programs.** For example, you might select the picture of a trash can to delete a file you no longer want.

Items on a desktop

Another feature of the GUI is the use of windows (✔ p. 42). ***Windows* "divide" the display screen into rectangular sections.** Each window may show a different display, such as a word processing document in one and a spreadsheet in another.

On both Windows and Macintosh computers, the windowing capabilities built into a GUI appear layered on or above a common base, or "canvas," known as a desktop. **A *desktop* presents icons on the computer screen according to principles used for organizing the top of a businessperson's desk.** Thus, a user can move on-screen items on the desktop among directories and folders.

Finally, the GUI permits liberal use of the mouse. The mouse is used as a pointing device to move the cursor to a particular place on the display screen or to point to an icon or button. The function represented by the icon can be activated by pressing ("clicking") buttons on the mouse. Or, using the mouse, you can pick up and slide ("drag") an image from one side of the screen to the other or change its size.

- **Network user interface (NUI):** The latest interface is the ***network user interface*, or *NUI* (pronounced "new-ee"), which offers a browser-like interface that helps users interact with online programs and files.**

NUIs started out being designed for network computers (NCs) (✔ p. 26), but they are finding their way onto regular PCs as well. Basically, network interfaces look like GUIs.

Managing Computer Resources

Suppose you are writing a report using a word processing program and want to print out a portion of it while continuing to write. How does the computer manage both tasks?

Behind the user interface, the operating system acts like a police officer directing traffic. This activity is performed by the **supervisor, or kernel, the central component of the operating system. The supervisor, which manages the CPU, resides in (is "resident in") main memory while the computer is on and directs other "nonresident" programs to perform tasks to support applications programs.**

The operating system also manages memory—it keeps track of the locations within main memory where the programs and data are stored. It can swap portions of data and programs between main memory and secondary storage, such as your computer's hard disk. This capability allows a computer to hold only the most immediately needed data and programs within main memory. Yet it has ready access to programs and data on the hard disk, thereby greatly expanding memory capacity.

Managing Files

Files of data and programs are located in many places on your hard disk and other secondary-storage devices. The operating system allows you to find them. If you move, rename, or delete a file, the operating system manages such changes and helps you locate and gain access to it. For example, you can *copy*, or duplicate, files and programs from one disk to another. You can *back up*, or make a duplicate copy of, the contents of a disk. You can *erase*, or remove, from a disk any files or programs that are no longer useful. You can *rename*, or give new file names to, the files on a disk.

Managing Tasks

A computer is required to perform many different tasks at once. In word processing, for example, it accepts input data, stores the data on a disk, and prints out a document—seemingly simultaneously. Some computers' operating systems can also handle more than one program at the same time—word processing, spreadsheet, database searcher—displaying them in separate windows on the screen. Others can accommodate the needs of several different users at the same time. All these examples illustrate process, or task, management—a "task" being an operation such as storing, printing, or calculating.

Among the ways operating systems manage tasks in order to run more efficiently are *multitasking, multiprogramming, time-sharing,* and *multiprocessing.* (Not all operating systems can do all these things.)

- **Multitasking: for one user—executing more than one program concurrently.** You may be writing a report on your computer with one program while another program searches an online database for research material. How does the computer handle both programs at once?

The answer is that the operating system directs the processor (CPU) to spend a predetermined amount of time executing the instructions for each program, one at a time. In essence, a small amount of each program is processed, and then the processor moves to the remaining programs, one at a time, processing small parts of each. This cycle is repeated until processing is complete. The processor speed is usually so fast that it may seem as if all the programs are being executed at the same time. However, the processor is still executing only one instruction at a time, no matter how it may appear to the user.

- **Multiprogramming: for multiple users—executing different users' programs concurrently.** As with multitasking, the CPU spends a certain amount of time executing each user's program, but it works so quickly that it seems as though all the programs are being run at the same time.

- **Time-sharing: for multiple users—executing different users' programs in round-robin fashion.** Time-sharing is used when several users are linked by a communications network to a single computer. The computer will first work on one user's task for a fraction of a second, then go on to the next user's task, and so on.

- **Multiprocessing: for single or multiple users—simultaneous processing of two or more programs by multiple computers.** With multiprocessing, two or more computers or processors linked together perform work simultaneously, meaning at precisely the same time. This can entail processing instructions from different programs or different instructions from the same program.

  One type of multiprocessing is *parallel processing*, whereby several full-fledged CPUs work together on the same tasks, sharing memory. Parallel processing is often used in large computer systems designed to keep running if one of the CPUs fails. These systems are called *fault-tolerant* systems; they have several CPUs and redundant components, such as memory and input, output, and storage devices. Fault-tolerant systems are used, for example, in airline reservation systems.

How do multitasking and time-sharing differ? With *multitasking,* the processor directs the programs to take turns accomplishing small tasks or events within the programs. These events may be making a calculation, searching for a record, printing out part of a document, and so on. Each event may take a different amount of time to accomplish. With *time-sharing,* the computer spends a fixed amount of time with each program before going on to the next one.

How do multiprocessing and multitasking differ? *Multiprocessing* goes beyond *multitasking,* which works with only one microprocessor. In both cases, the processing is so fast that, by spending a little bit of time working on each of several programs in turn, a number of programs can be run at the same time. With both multitasking and multiprocessing, the operating system keeps track of the status of each program so that it knows where it left off and where to continue processing. But the multiprocessing operating system is much more sophisticated than multitasking.

Operating system functions are shown in the chart on the following page. *(See ■ Panel 3.3.)*

■ PANEL 3.3

Basic operating system functions

Booting	Managing Storage Media	User Interface	Managing Computer Resources	Managing Files	Managing Tasks
Uses diagnostic routines to test system for equipment failure Stores BIOS programs in main memory Loads operating system into computer's main memory	Formats diskettes Displays information about operating system version Displays disk space available	Provides a way for user to interact with the operating system —can be command-driven, menu-driven, graphical, or network	Via the supervisor, manages the CPU and directs other programs to perform tasks to support applications programs Keeps track of locations in main memory where programs and data are stored (memory management) Moves data and programs back and forth between main memory and secondary storage (swapping).	Copies files/ programs from one disk to another Backs up files/programs Erases (deletes) files/programs Renames files	May be able to perform multitasking, multiprogramming, time-sharing, or multiprocessing

3.3 Common Microcomputer Operating Systems: The Changing Platforms

KEY QUESTIONS

What are the principal operating systems and operating environments for personal computers, and what are their principal characteristics?

Preview & Review: A computer platform is defined by its processor model and its operating system. The principal microcomputer operating system on new personal computers is Windows 95 and 98. Other microcomputer operating systems and operating environments are DOS, Macintosh operating system, Windows 3.x, OS/2, Novell's NetWare, Unix, Windows NT, and Windows CE.

Platform **refers to the particular processor model and operating system on which a computer system is based.** (We discuss processor models in Chapter 4.) Today the principal platform is that dominated by Windows 95, and its successor, Windows 98. (■ *See Panel 3.4, next page.*) How did this come about—especially when people were able to get the essential elements using other operating systems, such as that offered by Apple's Macintosh? The personal computer technology finally culminating in Windows 95 was actually invented more than 20 years ago by researchers at Xerox's Palo Alto Research Center (PARC) in northern California. Xerox executives asked about the profitability of marketing the PARC personal computer, which in those days, says one former researcher, "had the same ring to it as 'personal nuclear reactor' would have today."[2] When PARC scientists couldn't answer that, the PC was

▪ PANEL 3.4

Market share of operating systems

In 1998, operating systems by Microsoft—DOS, Windows 3.x, Windows NT, and Windows 95 and 98—dominated 90% of the market for new microcomputers, according to Dataquest.

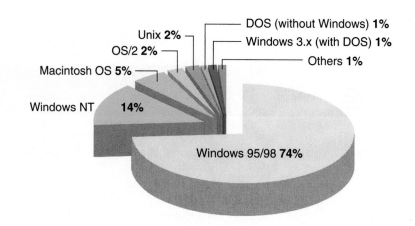

DOS (without Windows) **1%**
Windows 3.x (with DOS) **1%**
Others **1%**
Unix **2%**
OS/2 **2%**
Macintosh OS **5%**
Windows NT **14%**
Windows 95/98 **74%**

relegated to in-house use. At about that time, PARC gave a tour to Steve Jobs, who saw the PC. Later, as a founder of Apple Computer, Jobs used the PARC technology to create the Lisa PC, which was succeeded by the Macintosh, launched in 1984. Microsoft's Windows for DOS then followed in 1990. Now we have Windows 95, Windows 98, and Windows NT.

Principal Microcomputer Operating Systems in Use Today

Windows 95/98 may be the most popular operating system, but other operating systems are still being used on microcomputers throughout the world. Probably most of these, such as DOS, are so-called legacy systems. *Legacy systems* are the millions of older computer systems used in offices and homes today that employ outdated yet still functional technology, which you may find yourself having to use at some point.

In the rest of this section, we'll discuss the following:

- DOS
- Macintosh operating system
- Windows 3.x
- OS/2
- Windows 95
- Novell's NetWare
- Unix
- Windows NT
- Windows CE
- Windows 98

Before we proceed, however, we need to define what an *operating environment* is, because some people have trouble distinguishing it from an *operating system*. An *operating environment*—also known as a *windowing environment*, or *shell*—provides a graphical user interface or a menu-driven interface as an outer layer to an operating system. The best-known operating environment is Microsoft Windows 3.x, which adds a graphical user interface to DOS, which is the operating system.

DOS: The Old-Timer

DOS (rhymes with "boss")—for *Disk Operating System*—runs primarily on **PCs,** such as those made by AST, Compaq, Dell, Gateway 2000, Hewlett-Packard, IBM, NEC, and Packard Bell. There are two main operating systems calling themselves DOS:

- **Microsoft's MS-DOS:** DOS is sold under the name *MS-DOS* by Microsoft; the "MS," of course, stands for Microsoft. Microsoft launched its original version, MS-DOS 1.0, in 1981, and there have been many upgrades since then.
- **IBM's PC-DOS:** Microsoft licenses a version to IBM called *PC-DOS.* The "PC" stands for "Personal Computer." The most recent version is PC-DOS 7, released March 1995.

DOS is a command-driven operating system. For example, to format a diskette in drive A (the diskette drive designation), you would insert your diskette into the drive and then type, after the C:\>, CD\DOS, and then FORMAT A:. The command DISKCOPY copies the contents of one disk to another disk; DIR, for "directory," displays the names of files on a disk.

Two years before Windows 95 came on the scene, there were reportedly more than 100 million users of DOS, which made it the most popular software ever adopted—of any sort.[3] Today more Windows (3.x, 95, 98, NT) operating systems are being used, but DOS is still an important legacy system.

Macintosh Operating System: For the Love of Mac

The *Macintosh operating system (Mac OS)* **runs only on Apple Macintosh computers or on Mac clones,** such as those formerly made by Power Computing, Motorola, and Umax Computer Systems. The Mac set the standard for icon-oriented, easy-to-use graphical user interfaces, which generated a strong legion of fans. (■ *See Panel 3.5.)*

■ PANEL 3.5

Macintosh operating system

The icons, pull-down menus, and windows of the Apple Macintosh operating system give the Mac an ease of use that has generated many loyal fans. The screen shown here is from System 8.

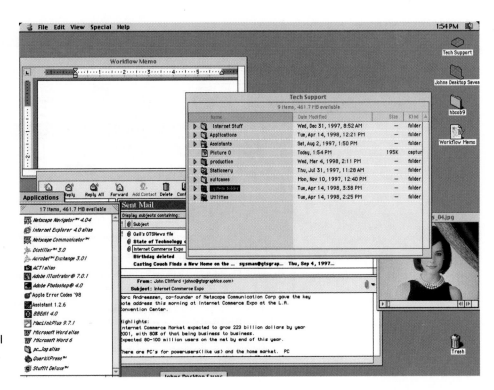

Unfortunately, PC and Macintosh microcomputers are different platforms—they are designed around different microprocessors—so it was impossible to combine the best of both. PC computers use microprocessors built by Intel (the 80286, 80386, 80486, Pentium, Pentium Pro, Pentium MMX, and Pentium II chips). Macintoshes are built around microprocessors made by Motorola (the 68000, 68020, 68030, 68040, and PowerPC chips). Intel chips could not run Macintosh programs, and Motorola chips could not run DOS or Windows programs.

Thus, because of price, and because in pre-PC times businesses were already accustomed to using IBM equipment, DOS-equipped (and later Windows-equipped) PCs have tended to rule the day in most offices. Apple also lost ground because during the 1990s it failed to upgrade and improve the Mac OS. And while Apple dallied, Microsoft came out with Windows 95 and managed to nearly match all of the Mac system's best features.

The latest version of the operating system for desktops is Mac OS 8; a version called Rhapsody is available to run on servers. Scheduled for release in the fall of 1999, Mac OS X (Roman numeral 10; the system is called "OS 10") combines elements of Mac OS 8 and Rhapsody.

Windows 3.x: Windows for DOS

Microsoft's *Windows 3.x* is an operating *environment* (not operating system) that lays a graphical user interface shell around the DOS operating system and extends DOS capabilities. (■ *See Panel 3.6.*) Actually, there is no Windows "3.x": this is simply shorthand for the three releases of Windows 3.0, 3.1, and 3.11.

As we mentioned, a *window* is a rectangular portion of the display area with a title on top. With Windows 3.x, which supports multitasking, you can display several windows on the screen, each showing a different application.

■PANEL 3.6

Windows 3.x screen

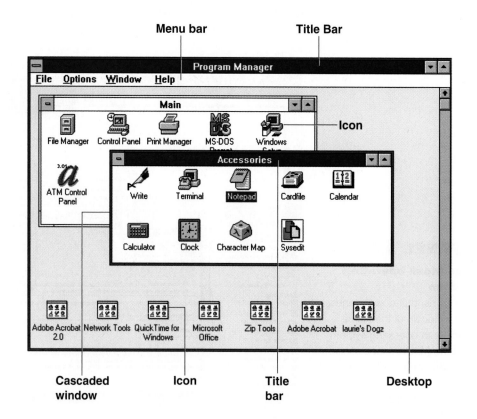

Although far easier to use than DOS, Windows 3.x is not as easy to use as the Mac. This is because Windows 3.x sits atop the old command-driven DOS operating system, which requires certain compromises on ease of use. Windows 95 solved this problem.

OS/2: IBM's Entry in the OS Sweepstakes

OS/2 (there is no OS/1) was released by International Business Machines in 1987 as IBM's contender for the next mainstream operating system. **OS/2—for *Operating System/2*—is designed to run on many recent IBM and compatible microcomputers.** Like Windows, it has a graphical user interface, called the Workplace Shell (WPS), which uses icons resembling documents, folders, printers, and the like. OS/2 can also run most DOS, Windows, and OS/2 applications simultaneously. This means that users don't have to throw out their old applications software to take advantage of new features. Lastly, this operating system was designed to connect everything from small hand-held personal computers to large mainframes.

In late 1994 IBM unveiled a souped-up version with the *Star Trek*–like name of OS/2 Warp. However, despite spending $2 billion on OS/2 in its long struggle against Windows 3.x, the company failed to increase its market share. Nevertheless, IBM continues to support its approximately 10 million Warp users—the latest version is OS/2 Warp Server, which can handle system management for networks. Upgrades are available online and can be downloaded from IBM's Web site.

Windows 95: The Successor to Windows 3.x

Released in August 1995, **Windows 95, the successor to Windows 3.x, is not just an operating environment but rather a true PC operating system.** Unlike Windows 3.x, it does not require the separate DOS program, although DOS commands can still be used. The graphical user interface is not just a shell; it is integrated into the operating system.

Following are just some of the features of Windows 95:

- **Clean "Start":** Upon booting, you'll first see a clean "desktop" with program icons and, in the "tray area" at the bottom of the screen, you'll see a button labeled Start at the left and some date and volume controls at the right. (■ *See Panel 3.7, next page.*)

- **Better menus:** Unlike Windows 3.x, the menus in Windows 95 let you quickly see what's stored on your disk drives and make tracking and moving files easier.

- **Long file names:** Whereas file names in DOS and Windows 3.x have to be limited to eight characters plus a three-character extension (for example, PSYCHRPT.NOV), file names under Windows 95 can be up to 256 characters in length (PSYCHOLOGY REPORT FOR NOVEMBER). (Macintosh OS and OS/2 have always permitted long file names.)

- **The "Recycle Bin":** This feature allows you to delete complete files and then get them back if you change your mind.

- **32-bit instead of 16-bit:** The new software is a 32-bit program, whereas most Windows 3.x software is 16-bit. *Bit numbers* refer to how many bits of data a computer chip, and software written for it, can process at one time. Such numbers are important because they refer to the amount of information the hardware and software can use at any one

Start button: Click for an easy way to start using the computer.

Microsoft Network: Click here to connect to the Microsoft Network, the company's online service.

My Briefcase: Allows you to synchronize files in two computers—say, an office PC and a laptop.

Recycle Bin: Allows you to dispose of files—or retrieve them later.

Network Neighborhood: If your PC is linked to a network of PCs, click here to get a glimpse of everything available on the network.

My Computer: Gives you a quick overview of all the files and programs installed in your PC.

Document: Multitasking capabilities allow people to smoothly run more than one program at once.

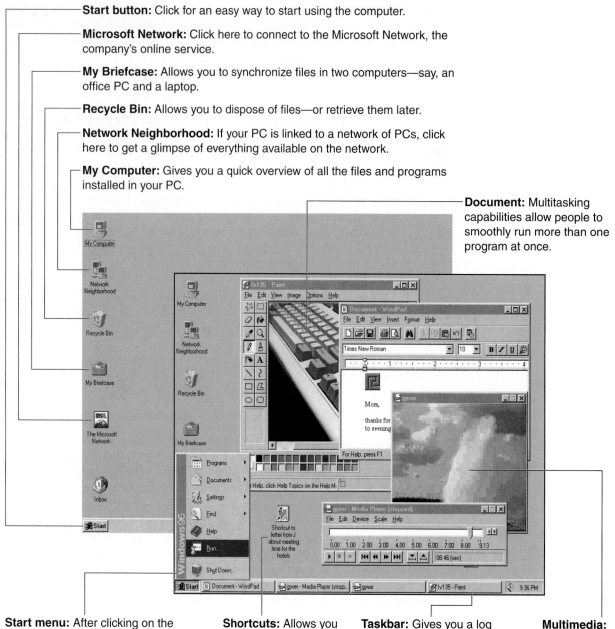

Start menu: After clicking on the start button, a menu appears, giving you a quick way to handle common tasks. You can launch programs, call up documents, change system settings, get help, and shut down your PC.

Shortcuts: Allows you to immediately launch often-used files and programs.

Taskbar: Gives you a log of all programs you have opened. To switch programs, click on the buttons that appear in the taskbar.

Multimedia: Windows 95 features sharper graphics and improved video capabilities compared to Windows 3.x.

■ PANEL 3.7

Windows 95 screens

time. This doesn't mean that 32-bit software will necessarily be twice as fast as 16-bit software, but it does promise that new 32-bit applications software will offer better performance efficiency and features once software developers take advantage of the design.

- **Plug and play:** It has always been easy to add new hardware components to Macintoshes. It used to be extremely difficult with PCs. *Plug and play* refers to the ability to add a new hardware component to a computer system and have it work without needing to perform complicated technical procedures.

More particularly, *Plug and Play* is a standard developed for PCs by Microsoft and chip maker Intel and incorporated into Windows 95 to eliminate user frustration when one is adding new components. Now when you add a new printer or modem that is built to plug-and-play standards, your PC will recognize that a new peripheral has been added and then automatically set it up.

In its first 12 months, Windows 95 sold an unprecedented 40 million copies, most of them preloaded on (bundled with) new PCs.[4] Now there are reportedly 100 million copies in use.[5]

If Windows 95 is the name Microsoft gave to what would have been called "Windows 4.0," then Windows 98 is the name for "Windows 5.0." We discuss Windows 98 in another few pages.

Novell's NetWare: PC Networking Software

So far we have described operating systems (and operating environments) pretty much in the chronological order in which they appeared. Except for OS/2, these operating systems were principally designed to be used with stand-alone desktop machines, not large systems of networked computers. Now let us consider the three important operating systems designed to work with networks: NetWare, Unix, and Windows NT.

Novell, of Orem, Utah, is the maker of NetWare. **NetWare is a popular network operating system (NOS) for coordinating microcomputer-based local area networks (LANs) throughout a company or a campus.** LANs allow PCs to share programs, data files, and printers and other devices.

Novell thrived as corporate data managers realized that networks of PCs could exchange information more cheaply than the previous generation of mainframes and midrange computers. Today the company still holds half the corporate network software market, with about 50 million people using its software. However, this market share is down from earlier times, owing to the rise of the Internet and competition from Microsoft. In 1998, the company was scheduled to rush out an update of NetWare—code-named Moab—that may help Novell reposition itself as a leader in network software technology.

Unix: The Operating System for Multiple Users

Unix was invented more than two decades ago by American Telephone & Telegraph, making it one of the oldest operating systems. **Unix is a multitasking operating system for multiple users that has built-in networking capability and versions that can run on all kinds of computers.** Because it can run with relatively simple modifications on different types of computers—from micros to mainframes—Unix is called a "portable" operating system. (■ *See Panel 3.8, next page.*)

The primary users of Unix are government agencies, universities, research institutions, large corporations, and banks, which use the software for everything from airplane-parts design to currency trading. Unix is also used for Web-site management. Indeed, the developers of the Internet built the system around Unix because of the operating system's ability to keep large systems with hundreds of processors churning out transactions day in and day out for years without fail.

■**PANEL 3.8**
Unix screen

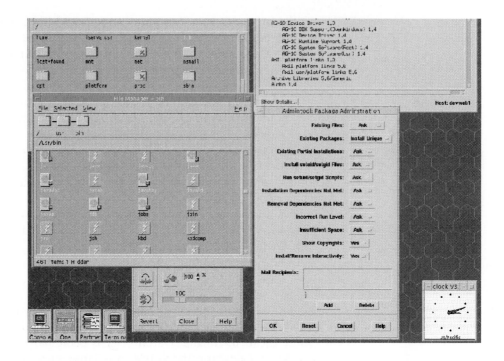

Today there are a number of Unix variations. (Examples: SCO UnixWare, Solaris, AIX, HP-UX.) The "flavor" that seems to be becoming most popular, however, is a Unix-like operating system called *Linux,* shareware (✔ p. 65) that is freely distributed over the Internet. One expert contends that "There is more Linux running Internet servers than all other OSs [operating systems] combined."[6]

Windows NT: Microsoft's Software for Business Networks

Unveiled by Microsoft in 1993, **Windows NT, for *New Technology*, is a multitasking, multiuser, multiprocessing network operating system with a graphical user interface.** Multiuser systems are used to support computer *workgroups.* A *workgroup* is a group of computers connected with networking hardware and software so that users can share resources, such as files and databases.

Unlike the early Windows 3.x *operating environment,* Windows NT is a true *operating system,* which (like Windows 95) interacts directly with the hardware. It runs not only NT-specific applications but also programs written for DOS, Windows 3.x, and Windows 95.

The operating system comes in two basic versions:

● **Windows NT Workstation:** This version supports one or two processors, looks exactly like Windows 95 and runs most of the programs written for Windows 95. Its power benefits graphics artists, engineers, and others who use workstations and who do intensive computing at their desks.

● **Windows NT Server:** Users of this version consist of those tied together in "client/server" networks with "file server" computers. A *client/server network* is a type of local area network (LAN). The "client" is the requesting PC or workstation (usually running a version of Windows) and the "server" is the supplying file-server or mainframe computer, which maintains databases and processes requests from the client. A *file server* is a high-speed computer in a LAN that stores the programs and files shared by the users.

Windows CE: Scaled-Down Windows for Handheld Computing Devices

In late 1996, Microsoft released **Windows CE, a greatly slimmed-down version of Windows 95 for handheld computing devices.** It has some of the familiar Windows look and feel and includes rudimentary word processing, spreadsheet, e-mail, Web browsing, and other software. The devices on which Windows CE is supposed to run include pocket-sized computers, electronic Rolodex-type organizers, and digital TV set-top boxes.

Windows 98: End of the Line for DOS, Windows 3.x, & Windows 95 Software Code?

Released in 1998, **the *Windows 98* operating system features what Microsoft calls True Web Integration—a graphical user interface, or "desktop," that not only acts like Web browser software but also allows users access to data on the Internet as easily as if it were stored on the user's hard disk.** From a visual standpoint, with True Web Integration it would make no difference to users whether information was out on the Web or stored somewhere in a user's own PC. By incorporating the Web browser within the operating system, the new design seemed to take dead aim at Microsoft's principal browser competitor, the popular Netscape Navigator, which must be installed separately.

Besides the browser integration, other significant features are:

- **Free Internet content via TV:** Computers equipped with television reception will be able to receive free, over an unused portion of the television broadcast spectrum, Internet information such as news, sports, weather, and entertainment. The content is supported by advertising.

- **Changes in the "desktop":** The Desktop, the screen that first appears when Windows is loaded, not only lists all your programs but also your favorite Web sites. A feature called Active Desktop changes the background of the desktop into a Web page that enables you to view live content from the Web, such as scrolling stock prices or sports scores.

- **System software to support new hardware:** Special system software ("drivers") will support not only television tuners but also new types of disk players and other leading-edge hardware devices.

Despite the hoopla over Windows 98, Microsoft is actually trying to urge consumers to move toward Windows NT. Says one report, "Windows 98 is likely to be the last major release of an operating system based on the line of software code that extends from its original DOS system through Windows 3.1 to Windows 95."[7]

3.4 Utility Programs: Software to Make Your Computer Run Smoother

Preview & Review: Utility programs either enhance existing functions or provide services not performed by other system software. They include backup, data recovery, file defragmentation, disk repair, virus protection, data compression, and memory management. Multiple-utility packages are available.

KEY QUESTION

How do utility programs interact with and extend an operating system's features and capabilities?

"You wouldn't take a cruise on a ship without life preservers, would you?" asks one writer. "Even though you probably wouldn't need them, the terrible *what if* is always there. Working on a computer without the help and assurance of utility software is almost as risky."[8]

The "what if" being referred to is an unlucky event, such as your hard-disk drive "crashing" (failing), risking loss of all your programs and data; or your computer system being invaded by someone or something (a virus) that disables it.

Utility programs are special programs that either enhance existing functions or provide services not provided by other system software programs. Most computers come with utilities built in for free as part of the system software (Windows 95/98 offers several of them), but they may also be bought separately as external utility programs.

Some Specific Utility Tasks

The principal services offered by utilities are the following.

- **Backup:** If you have only one utility it should be this one. With a *backup utility*, which makes a duplicate of every file on your hard disk on diskettes or other removable storage medium (such as a Zip cartridge), if your hard disk fails, you can be back in business with your data and programs intact. A backup utility is integral with Windows 95 and 98.

- **Data recovery:** A *data-recovery utility* is used to resurrect, or "undelete," a file or information that has been accidentally deleted. The data or program you are trying to recover may be on a hard disk or a diskette. *Undelete* means to undo the last delete operation that has taken place.

- **File defragmentation:** Over time, as you delete old files from your hard disk and add new ones, something happens: the files become fragmented. **Fragmentation is the scattering of portions of files about the disk in nonadjacent areas, thus greatly slowing access to the files.**

  When a hard disk is new, the operating system puts files on the disk contiguously (next to one another). However, as you update a file over time, new data for that file is distributed to unused spaces. These spaces may not be contiguous to the older data in that file. It takes the operating system longer to read these fragmented files. A *defragmenter utility program*, commonly called a "defragger," will find all the scattered files on your hard disk and reorganize them as contiguous files, which will speed up the drive's operation. An example of this utility is Norton Speed Disk.

- **Disk repair:** There are all kinds of small glitches that can corrupt the data and programs on your hard-disk drive. For instance, a power surge in the house electricity may cause your files to become cross-linked. A *disk-repair utility* will check your hard-disk drive for defects and make repairs on the spot or mark the bad areas. An example of this utility is Norton's Disk Doctor.

- **Virus protection:** Few things can make your heart sink faster than the sudden failure of your hard disk. One exception is the realization that your computer system has been invaded by a virus. **A *virus* consists of hidden programming instructions that are buried within an applications or systems program. They copy themselves to other programs, causing havoc.** Sometimes the virus is merely a simple prank that pops up a message. ("Have a nice day.") Sometimes, however, it can destroy programs and data. Viruses are spread when people exchange diskettes or download (make copies of) information from computer networks.

  Fortunately, antivirus software is available. ***Antivirus software* is a utility program that scans hard disks, diskettes, and memory to detect viruses.** Some utilities destroy the virus on the spot. Others notify you of possible viral behavior. Because new viruses are constantly being created, you need the type of antivirus software that can detect unknown viruses. Examples of antivirus software are Norton AntiVirus, Dr. Solomon's Anti-Virus Toolkit, McAfee VirusScan, and Webscan.

- **Data compression:** As you continue to store files on your hard disk, it will eventually fill up. You then have four choices: You can delete old files to make room for the new. You can buy a new hard disk with more capacity and transfer the old files and programs to it. You can add an external hard drive with removable disk cartridges. Or you can buy a data compression utility.

  ***Data compression utilities* remove redundant elements, gaps, and unnecessary data from a computer's storage space so less space (fewer bits) is required to store or transmit data.** With a data compression utility, files can be made more compact for storage on your hard-disk drive. The files are then "stretched out" again when you need them. Examples of data compression programs are DriveSpace 2 Stacker from Stac Electronics, Double Disk from Verisoft Systems, and SuperStor Pro from AddStor.

- **Memory management:** Different microcomputers have different types of memory, and different applications programs have different memory requirements. *Memory-management utilities* are programs that determine how to efficiently control and allocate memory resources.

  Memory-management programs may be activated by software *drivers*. **Drivers are small software programs that allow the operating system to communicate with hardware devices,** such as a mouse or printer. Many basic drivers come with the operating system. If, however, you buy a new peripheral device, such as a CD-ROM drive, a driver will come packaged with it, and you'll have to install it on your computer's hard-disk drive before the device will operate.

Multiple-Utility Packages

Some utilities are available singly, but others are available as "multipacks." These multiple-utility packages provide several utility disks bundled in one box, affording considerable savings. Examples are Symantec's Norton Desktop, 911 Utilities from Microcom, and PC Tools from Central Point Software.

3.5   The Network Computer: Is the Web Changing Everything?

KEY QUESTION

How could the network computer make the choice of PC operating system irrelevant?

Preview & Review: New computers might follow the model of network PCs, without their own operating systems, and be dominated by Web browsers to access the Web and applications software located anywhere on the network. Instead of networks having "fat client" computers loaded with software and doing most of their own processing, "fat servers" would perform most of the processing for "thin clients," network PCs that are relatively cheap and leave the upgrading to the network.

Nothing stands still. In a matter of just a couple of years, the Internet and the World Wide Web have dramatically changed the picture for system software.

Software for Online Computing: Today Versus Tomorrow

As we've seen, there are different platforms—the Macintosh platform versus the PC platform, for example, or Unix versus Windows NT. Developers of applications software, such as word processors or database managers, need to make different versions if they are to run on all the platforms.

Networking complicates things even further. "Text, photos, sound files, video, and other kinds of data come in so many different formats that it's nearly impossible to maintain the software needed to use them," points out one writer. So far, users have had to "steer their own way through the complex, upgrade-crazy world of computing."[9]

Is this now changing? Let's consider today's model versus tomorrow's proposed model.

- **Today's model—more user responsibility:** Today microcomputer users who wish to access online data sources must provide not only their own computer, modem, and communications software but also their own operating system software and applications software. (■ *See Panel 3.9, top.*)

  In addition, you must also take responsibility for making sure your computer system will be compatible with others you have to deal with. For instance, if a Macintosh user sends you a file to run on your PC, it's up to you to take the trouble to use special software that will translate the file so it will work on your system.

- **Tomorrow's model—more service provider responsibility:** What if the responsibility for ensuring compatibility between different systems were left to online service providers? In tomorrow's model, you would use your browser to access the World Wide Web and take advantage of applications software anywhere on the network. (■ *See Panel 3.9, bottom.*)

  In this arrangement, it will not matter what operating system you use. Applications software will become nearly disposable. You will download applications software and pay a few cents or a few dollars for each use. You could store frequently used software on your own computer. You will not need to worry about buying the right software, since it can be provided online whenever you need to accomplish a task.

■PANEL 3.9

Online personal computing—today and tomorrow

(Top) Today users provide their own operating system software and their own applications software and are usually responsible for installing them on their personal computers. They are also responsible for any upgrades of hardware and software. Data can be input or downloaded from online sources. *(Bottom)* Tomorrow, according to this model, users would not have to worry about operating systems or even about having to acquire and install (and upgrade) their own applications software. Using a universal Web browser, they could download not only data but also different kinds of applications software from an online source.

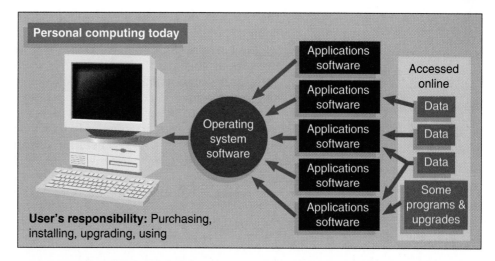

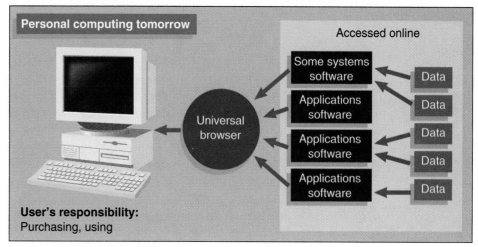

Fat Clients Versus Thin Clients: Bloatware or Network Computers?

We see today's and tomorrow's models expressed in the concepts of *fat clients* versus *thin clients.*

- **Fat clients—computers with bloatware:** As we mentioned in Chapter 2 (✔ p. 62), *bloatware* is a colloquial name for software that is so crowded ("bloated") with features—it is afflicted with "featuritis"—that it requires a powerful microprocessor and enormous amounts of main memory and hard-disk storage capacity to run efficiently.

  When on a network, computers with bloatware are known as fat clients. That is, in a client/server network arrangement, a *fat client* is a client computer that performs most or all of the application processing; little or no processing is done by the network server.

- **Thin clients—slimmed-down network computers:** To staunch the continual expansion in bloatware, engineers proposed the notion of a stripped-down computer known as the network computer. Here muscular microprocessors and operating systems are replaced by a "hollowed-out" computer costing $500 or less that serves as a mere terminal or entry point to the online universe. Thus, the network computer—which might not even have a hard disk—is a peripheral of the Internet, with most software, processing, and information needs being supplied by remote servers.

The network computer is known as a thin client. In a client/server network arrangement, a *thin client* is a client computer that performs little or no application processing. All or most processing is done by the server, which is thus known as a *fat server*.

The thin-client/fat-server strategy is to replace existing bloatware-stuffed desktop computers with a new generation of ultracheap network computers. At present there are two standards of network computers. One standard (called the NC Reference Profile) is backed by Apple, IBM, Netscape, Oracle, Sun, and others. The other standard is backed by Microsoft and chipmaker Intel.

The concept of the network computer has raised some interesting questions:[10-12]

- **Would the browser really become the OS?** Would a Web browser or some variant become the operating system? Or will existing operating systems expand, as in the past, taking over browser functions?

- **Would communications functions really take over?** Would communications functions become the entire computer, as proponents of the network computer contend? Or would they simply become part of the personal computer's existing repertoire of skills?

- **Would an NC really be easy to use?** Would a network computer really be user friendly? At present, features such as graphical user interfaces require lots of hardware and software.

- **Aren't high-speed connections required?** Even users equipped with the fastest modems would find downloading even small programs ("applets") time-consuming. Doesn't the network computer ultimately depend on faster connections than are possible with the standard telephone lines and modems now in place?

- **Doesn't the NC run counter to computing trends?** Most trends in computing have moved toward personal control and access, as from the mainframe to the microcomputer. Wouldn't a network computer that leaves most functions with online sources run counter to that trend?

- **Would users go for it?** Would computer users really prefer scaled-down generic software that must be retrieved from the Internet each time it is used? Would a pay-per-use system tied to the Internet really be cheaper in the long run? Why would anyone buy a $500 stripped-down box when he or she can get a full-fledged computer for prices that are rapidly dropping below $1000?[13]

Using Software to Access the World Wide Web

We cover the Internet, the Web, and other communications topics in detail in Chapters 7 and 8. However, you may want to get online and use the Web now. If so, the following discussion is designed to help.

What's the easiest way to use the Internet, that international conglomeration of thousands of smaller networks? Getting on the sound-and-graphics part of it known as the World Wide Web is no doubt the best choice. Increasingly, system software is coming out with features for accessing and exploring the Net and the Web. This Experience Box, however, describes ways to tour both the Net and the Web independent of whatever system software you have.

The Web resembles a huge encyclopedia filled with thousands of general topics or so-called Web sites that have been created by computer users and businesses around the world. The entry point to each Web site is a home page, which may offer cross-reference links to other pages. Pages may be in multimedia form—meaning they can include text, graphics, sound, animation, and video.

To get on the Net and the Web, you need a microcomputer, a modem, a telephone line, and communications software. (For details about the initial setup, review pages 67–69 in the Experience Box at the end of Chapter 2.) You then need to gain access to the Web and, finally, to get a browser. Some browsers come in kits that handle the setup for you, as we will explain.

Gaining Access to the Web

There are three principal ways of getting connected to the Internet: (1) through school or work, (2) through commercial online services, or (3) through an Internet service provider.

Connecting Through School or Work The easiest access to the Internet is available to students and employees of universities and government agencies, most colleges, and certain large businesses. If you're involved with one of these, you can simply ask another student or coworker with an Internet account how you can get one also. In the past, college students have often been able to get a free account through their institutions. However, students living off campus may not be able to use the connections of campus computers.

Connections through universities and business sites are called *dedicated*, or *direct*, connections and consist of local area networks and high-speed phone lines (called T1 or T3 carrier lines) that typically cost thousands of dollars to install and maintain every month. Their main advantage is their high speed, so that the graphic images and other content of the Web unfold more quickly. (Note that if you are connected to the Internet via some of the special high-speed *digital* lines, you won't need a modem.)

Connecting Through Online Services The large commercial online services—such as America Online, CompuServe, Microsoft Network, or Prodigy—also offer access to the Internet. (See the Experience Box at the end of Chapter 2 for information.) Some offer their own Web browsers, but some (such as America Online, or AOL) offer Netscape Navigator and Internet Explorer. Commercial online services may also charge more than independent Internet service providers, although they are probably better organized and easier for beginners.

Web access through online services is usually called a *dial-up connection.* As long as you don't live in a rural area, there's no need to worry about long-distance telephone charges; you can generally sign on ("log on") by making a local call. When you receive membership information from the online service, it will tell you what to do.

Connecting Through Internet Service Providers Internet service providers (ISPs) are local or national companies that provide public access to the Internet for a fee. Examples of national companies include PSI, UUNet, Netcom, and Internet MCI. Telephone companies such as AT&T and Pacific Bell have also jumped into the fray by offering Internet connections. Most ISPs offer a flat-rate monthly fee for an unlimited number of hours of use. The connections offered by ISPs may offer faster access to the Internet than those of commercial online services.

The whole industry of Internet connections is still new enough that many ISP users and online service users have had problems with uneven service (such as busy signals or severing of online "conversations"). Often ISPs signing up new subscribers aren't prepared to handle traffic jams caused by a great influx of newcomers.

You can also ask someone who is already on the Web to access for you the worldwide list of ISPs at *http://www.thelist. com.* Besides giving information about each provider in your area, "thelist" provides a rating (on a scale of 1 to 10) by users of different ISPs.

Accessing the Web: Browser Software

Once you're connected to the Internet, you need a Web browser. This software program will help you to get whatever information you want on the Web by clicking your mouse pointer on words or pictures the browser displays on your screen.

The two-best known browsers are Netscape Navigator and Microsoft's Internet Explorer.

Features of Browsers What kinds of things should you consider when selecting a browser? Here are some features:

- **Price:** Some browsers are free (freeware, ✔ p. 65). Some are free to students only or come free with membership in an online service or ISP—America Online, for instance, offers browsers for both PCs and Macintoshes. Some may be acquired for a price separately from any online connection.

  You can get a kit that offers other features besides a browser. For instance, Macintosh users can buy the Apple Internet Connection Kit, which contains the browser Netscape Navigator/Communicator and several other programs. (They include Claris E-mailer Lite, News Watcher, Fetch, Alladin Stuffit Expander, NCSA Telnet, Adobe Acrobat Reader, Sparkle, Real Audio, MacTCP, MacPPP, and Apple Quicktime VR Player). The kit comes with an Apple Internet Dialer application that helps you find an Internet service provider.

- **Ease of setup:** Especially for a beginner, the browser should be easy to set up. Ease of setup favors the university/business dedicated lines or commercial online services, of course, which already have browsers. If not provided by your online service or ISP, the browser should be compatible with it. Most online services allow you to use browsers besides their own.

- **Ease of use:** If you have a multimedia PC, the browser should allow you to view and hear all of the Web's multimedia—not only text and images but also sounds and video. It should be easy to use for saving "hot lists" of frequently visited Web sites and for saving text and images to your hard disk. Finally, the browser should allow you to do "incremental" viewing of images, so that you can go on reading or browsing while a picture is slowly coming together on your screen, rather than having to wait with browser frozen until the image snaps into view.

Surfing the Web

Once you are connected to the Internet and have used your browser to access the Web, your screen will usually display the browser's home page. (■ *See Panel 3.10.*) (You can determine whose home page you want to see after you load your browser.)

Web Untanglers Where do you go from here? You'll find that unlike a book, there is no page 1 where everyone is supposed to start reading, and unlike an encyclopedia, the entries are not in alphabetical order. Moreover, there is no definitive listing of everything available.

There are, however, a few search tools for helping you find your way around, which can be classified as directories and search engines (✔ p. 55).

■ PANEL 3.10

Home page for a Web browser

(*Top*) Netscape Navigator's home page. (*Bottom*) Microsoft's Internet Explorer home page.

Web Addresses: URLs Getting to a Web location is easy if you know the address. Just choose, in most cases, Open location (Find location) from the browser's file menu, and then type in the address. Web addresses usually start with *http* (for Hypertext Transfer Protocol) and are followed by a colon and double slash (://). For example, to reach the home page of Yahoo!, you would type the address: *http://www.yahoo.com*. Your browser uses the address to connect you to the computer of the Web site; then it downloads (transfers) the Web page information to display it on your screen. (In most cases now, you can skip the *http://* and just start with *www.*)

If you get lost on the Web, you can return to your opening home page by clicking on the Home button.

Nowadays you see Web site addresses appearing everywhere, in all the mass media, and some of it's terrific and some of it's awful. For a sample of the best, try Yahoo!'s What's Cool list (*http://www.yahoo.com/Entertainment/ COOL_Links*). For less-than-useful information, try Worst of the Web (*http://turnpike.net/metro/mirsky/Worst.html*).

How to Use Directories & Search Engines

How can you best explore the Net and the Web? The key, says personal computing writer Michael Martin, is to apply two simple concepts, both of which derive from methods we are accustomed to using for finding information in other areas of life: *browsing* and *hunting*.[14]

- **Directories—for browsing:** Browsing, says Martin, "involves looking in a general area of interest, then zooming in on whatever happens to catch your attention." For example, he says, a basketball fan would head for the sports section of the newspaper, check the basketball news and scores on the front page, then skim other pages for related sports information.

  Directories—Yahoo! is the best known—arrange resources by subject and thus are best for people who browse.

- **Search engines—for hunting:** Hunting "is what we do when we want specific information," Martin says. In his example, if you were hopelessly nearsighted and wanted to hunt up specifics on the latest advances in laser treatment, you might check with an ophthalmologist, a university library, the National Eye Institute, and so on.

  Search engines, such as AltaVista, Excite, HotBot, Infoseek, and Lycos are for those who want specifics.

If you use Netscape Navigator/Communicator, you can quickly access directories by clicking the Net Directory button and access search engines by clicking the Net Search button. We explain some of the principal directories and search engines below.

Directories: For Browsing *Directories* provide lists of Web sites covering several categories. As we mentioned earlier, directories are managed and organized by people. These are terrific tools if you want to find Web sites pertinent to a general topic you're interested in, such as bowling, heart disease, or the Vietnam War. For instance, in Yahoo! you might click your mouse on one of the general headings listed on the menu, such as Recreation or Health, then proceed to click on menus of subtopics until you find what you need.

Some general directories are the following:

- **Yahoo!** *(http://www.yahoo.com)* is the most popular of the Web directories and lists half a million Web sites. The home page lists several topics, with some subtopics listed beneath. Among other things, Yahoo! features a weekly list of "cool sites" and Cool Links connections (look for the sunglasses "cool" icon). Unlike other directories, it does not review sites, and its descriptions are rather brief.

- **Magellan** *(http://www.mckinley.com)* allows users to search 50 million Web sites. It also offers detailed overviews of more than 60,000 Web sites chosen and reviewed by Magellan's experts. Overviews include a short review and a percentage sign that rates a resource for relevance.

- **Netguide Live** *(http://www.netguide.com)* has fewer Web site listings than Yahoo! but, unlike Yahoo!, offers reviews and evaluations of the sites listed.

- **The Mining Company** *(http://www.miningco.com)* includes comprehensive Web sites for over 500 topics, run by outside experts who compile lists of sites that deal with their areas of expertise. Each site is devoted to a single topic, complete with site reviews, feature articles, and discussion areas.

- **Galaxy** *(http://www.einet.net)* calls itself "the professional's guide to a world of information" and employs professional information specialists to organize and classify Web pages. It includes resources for professionals in nine categories, including business, law, medicine, government, and science.

- **The Argus Clearinghouse** *(http://www.clearinghouse. net/index.html)* is a directory of directories, or "virtual library"; that is, it is maintained by "digital librarians" who identify, select, evaluate, and organize resources. Argus provides a list of subject-specific directories on topics ranging from arts and entertainment to social science and social issues.

- **The Internet Public Library** *(http://www.ipl.org)* is another "virtual library." It began in 1995 in the School of Information and Library Studies at the University of Michigan and has the goal of providing library services to the Internet community. Besides offering Web searches and lists of books and periodicals, it maintains its own collection of over 12,000 hand-picked and organized Internet resources.

Search Engines: For Specifics *Search engines*, such as AltaVista, are best when you're trying to find very specific information—the needle in the haystack. Search engines are Web pages containing forms into which you type keywords to suggest the subject you're searching for. The search engine then scans its database and presents you with a list of Web sites matching your search criteria. (Search engines are managed and organized by machines and software.)

The search engine's database is created by spiders (also known as crawlers or robots), software programs that scout the Web looking for new sites. When the spider finds a new page, it adds its Internet address (URL), title, and usually the headers starting each section to an index in the search engine's database. The principal search engines add index information about new pages every day.

Writer Richard Scoville points out that the bigger the database, the greater your chances for success in your search. For example, he says, he queried several engines with the keywords *recipe wheat beer*. "The massive Lycos database gave us 437 *hits* (matched pages) in return. InfoSeek and Open Text Index gave us around 200 each; others, less than 100."[15]

Important search engines include the following:

- **AltaVista** *(http://www.altavista.digital.com)*, probably the largest and probably best known of the search engines, has over 100 million indexed Web pages, roughly twice as many as its competitors. It also takes care of all the searches that spill over from Yahoo! Thus, if you start your search on Yahoo! and can't find what you're looking for there, you'll automatically be switched to AltaVista. If you're worried you might miss a Web site, AltaVista is the search engine to use first. Along with HotBot, it should be one of the first Web searching tools you use.

- Excite *(http://www.excite.com)* is considered both a directory and a search engine and has 50 million indexed pages and 140,000 Yahoo!-style listings. Besides searching by exact words, it also searches by concept. For example, a query for "martial arts" finds sites about *kick-boxing* and *karate* even if the original search term isn't in the page.[16] After you do a search, Excite will also suggest words to use to narrow the query. In addition, it ranks the documents as to relevancy—that is, as to how well they fit your original search criteria.

- HotBot *(http://www.hotbot.com)* reindexes its 54 million Web pages every two weeks, which can often yield more recent material than is found using other search engines. In fact, you can find only up-to-date pages by limiting your search to those pages that have changed only in the last 3–6 months. Like Excite, HotBot offers relevancy rankings. Along with AltaVista, HotBot should be one of the first search tools you use when you're looking for something.

- InfoSeek *(http://www.infoseek.com)* is a blend of search engine, directory, and news service. It has 60 million Web pages and an extensive directory and ranks results according to relevance to your search criteria. InfoSeek also searches more than the Web, indexing Usenet newsgroups and several non-Internet databases. Once you complete a search, you can search with those results, by constructing a new query and clicking on the "Search These Results" button.

- Lycos *(http://www.lycos.com)*, which combines directory and search services, offers 30 million indexed pages. It also offers a list of interesting Web sites called A2Z, which indicates the most popular pages on the Web, as measured by the number of hypertext links, or "hits," from other Web sites pointing to them. The Lycos relevancy rankings are among the strongest of the search engines.

The best way to make a search engine useful is to be extremely specific when formulating your keywords. More on this below.

Metasearch Engines

Metasearch engines are search tools that let you use several search engines to track down information, although you are somewhat restricted compared to using single search en-

gines. Most metasearch engines also include directories, such as Yahoo! Examples of these "one-stop-shopping" sites are Savvy Search *(http://www.cs.colostate.edu/~dreiling/smartform.html)* and MetaCrawler *(http://www.cs.washington.edu/research/projects/ai/metacrawler/www/home.html)*.

Tips for Searching

Here are some rules that will help improve your chances for success in operating a search engine:[17,18]

- **Read the instructions!** Every search site has an online search manual. Read it.

- **Make your keywords specific:** The more narrow or distinctive you can make your keywords, the more targeted will be your search. Say *drag racing* or *stock-car racing* rather than *auto racing*, for example. Also try to do more than one pass and try spelling variations: *drag racing, dragracing, drag-racing.* In addition, think of synonyms, and write down related key terms as they come to mind. Finally, be sure to enclose phrases within quotation marks—"drag racing" or "jet plane"— so the search tool will know that the words belong together.

- **Use AND, OR, and NOT:** Use connectors as a way of making your keyword requests even more specific. In Martin's example, if you were looking for a 1965 Mustang convertible, you could search on the three terms "1965," "Mustang," and "convertible." However, since you want all three together, try linking them with a connector: "Mustang AND convertible AND 1965." You can also sharpen the keyword request by using the word NOT for exclusion—for example, "Mustang NOT horse."

- **Don't bother with "natural language" queries:** Some search engines will let you do *natural language queries,* which means you can ask questions as you might in conversation. For example, you could ask, "Who was the Indianapolis 500 winner in 1998?" You'll probably get better results by entering "Indianapolis 500 AND race AND winner AND 1998."

- **Use more than one search engine:** "We found surprisingly little overlap in the results from a single query performed on several different search engines," writes Scoville. "So to make sure that you've got the best results, be sure to try your search with numerous sites."

All these search tools are constantly adding new features, such as easier interfaces. But whichever you end up using, you'll find that they can turn the Web from a playground or novelty into a source of real value. For additional search tips, check out Search Engine Watch: *(http://www.searchenginewatch.com)* and Internet Searching Strategies *(http://www.rice.edu/Fondren/Netguides/strategies.html)*.

Summary

Summary

What It Is/What It Does	**Why It's Important**
antivirus software (p. 97, KQ 3.4) Software utility that scans hard disks, floppy disks, and microcomputer memory to detect viruses; some antivirus utilities also destroy viruses.	Computer users must find out what kind of antivirus software to install on their systems in order to protect them against damage or shutdown.
booting (p. 82, KQ 3.2) Refers to the process of loading an operating system into a computer's main memory from disk.	When a computer is turned on, a program (called the *bootstrap loader* or *boot routine*) stored permanently in the computer's electronic circuitry obtains the operating system from the floppy disk or hard disk and loads it into main memory. Only after this process is completed can the user begin work.
command-driven interface (p. 83, KQ 3.2) Type of user interface that requires users to enter a command by typing in codes or words.	The command-driven interface is used on IBM and IBM-compatible computers with the DOS operating system.
data compression utility (p. 97, KQ 3.4) Software utility that removes redundant elements, gaps, and unnecessary data from computer files so less space is required to store or transmit data.	Many of today's files, with graphics, sound, and video, require too much storage space; data compression utilities allow users to reduce the space they take up.
desktop (p. 84, KQ 3.2) Graphical user interface screen of an operating system; it serves as a basic screen that presents icons on the computer screen representing items ready for use on the top of a businessperson's desk.	Items can be manipulated as on a desktop—open a folder to check information, to work on a project, or to move a file to another folder.
DOS (disk operating system) (p. 89, KQ 3.3) Microcomputer operating system that runs primarily on PCs. DOS is sold under the names MS-DOS by Microsoft Corporation and PC-DOS by IBM.	DOS is the second most common microcomputer operating system after the various Windows systems, making it an important *legacy system.*
driver (p. 97, KQ 3.4) Small software programs that allow the operating system to communicate with peripheral hardware, such as a mouse or printer.	Drivers are needed so that the computer's operating system will know how to handle the data and run the peripheral device. A user who buys a new piece of peripheral hardware and hooks it up to a system will also probably have to install that hardware's driver software on the hard disk.
formatting (p. 83, KQ 3.2) Also called *initializing;* a computer process that electronically prepares a diskette so it can store data or programs.	Before using a new diskette, the user has to format it unless it is labeled as formatted.

What It Is/What It Does	Why It's Important

fragmentation (p. 96, KQ 3.4) The scattering of parts of files on nonadjacent areas of a hard disk, which slows down access to the files.

Fragmentation causes operating systems to run slower; to solve this problem, users can buy a file defragmentation software utility.

graphical user interface (GUI) (p. 84, KQ 3.2) User interface that uses icons and menus as well as keystrokes to allow the user to choose commands, start programs, and see lists of files and other options.

GUIs are easier to use than command-driven interfaces and menu-driven interfaces; they permit liberal use of the electronic mouse as a pointing device to move the cursor to a particular icon, button, or menu option on the display screen. The function represented by the screen item can be activated by pressing ("clicking") buttons on the mouse.

icon (p. 84, KQ 3.2) Small pictorial figure that represents a task, procedure, or program.

The function represented by the icon can be activated by pointing at it with the mouse pointer and pressing ("clicking") on the mouse. The use of icons has simplified the use of computers.

language translator (p. 81, KQ 3.1) System software that translates a program written in a computer language (such as BASIC) into the language that the computer can understand (machine language—0s and 1s).

Without language translators, software programmers would have to write all programs in machine language, which is difficult to work with.

Macintosh operating system (Mac OS) (p. 89, KQ 3.3) Operating system used on Apple Macintosh computers or on Mac clones.

Although not used in as many offices as DOS and Windows, the Macintosh operating system is easier to use.

menu (p. 84, KQ 3.2) List on the computer screen of commands available for manipulating data.

Menus are used in graphical user interface programs to make software easier to use: the user can choose from a list instead of having to remember commands.

menu-driven interface (p. 84, KQ 3.2) User interface that allows users to choose a command from a menu.

Like a restaurant menu, a software menu offers options to choose from—in this case commands available for manipulating data. Two types of menus are available, menu bars and pull-down menus. Menu-driven interfaces are easier to use than command-driven interfaces.

NetWare (p. 93, KQ 3.3) A popular network operating system, from Novell, for orchestrating microcomputer-based local area networks (LANs) throughout a company or campus.

NetWare allows PCs to share data files, printers, and file servers.

network user interface (NUI) (p. 84, KQ 3.2) A browser-like interface that helps users interact with on-line programs and files.

NUIs were originally designed for network computers where most software is located on another computer, but they are coming into use on PCs.

operating system (OS) (p. 82, KQ 3.1, 3.2) Principal piece of system software in any computer system; consists of the master set of programs that manage the basic operations of the computer. The operating system remains in main memory until the computer is turned off.

These programs act as an interface between the user and the computer, handling such matters as running and storing programs and storing and processing data. The operating system allows users to concentrate on their own tasks or applications rather than on the complexities of managing the computer.

What It Is/What It Does

Why It's Important

OS/2 (Operating System/2) (p. 91, KQ 3.3) Microcomputer operating system designed to run on many recent IBM and IBM-compatible microcomputers.

OS/2 and its most recent version, Warp, offered a true operating system with a graphical user interface for PCs before Windows 95 was available. OS/2 and Warp can run most DOS, Windows, and OS/2 applications programs simultaneously, which means users who switch to OS/2 can keep their applications. Also, OS/2 is designed to connect everything from handheld computers to mainframes.

platform (p. 87, KQ 3.3) Refers to the particular processor model and operating system on which a computer system is based—for example, IBM platform or Macintosh platform.

Users need to be aware that, without special arrangements or software, different platforms are not compatible.

supervisor (p. 85, KQ 3.2) Also called *kernel;* central component of the operating system as the manager of the CPU. It resides in main memory while the computer is on and directs other programs to perform tasks to support applications programs.

Were it not for the supervisor program, users would have to stop one task—for example, writing—and wait for another task to be completed—for example, printing out of a document.

system software (p. 80, KQ 3.1) Software that enables applications software to interact with the computer and helps the computer manage its internal resources. A computer's system software contains an operating system, utility programs, and language translators.

Applications software cannot run without system software.

Unix (p. 93, KQ 3.3) Operating system for multiple users, with built-in networking capability, the ability to run multiple tasks at one time, and versions that can run on all kinds of computers.

Because it can run with relatively simple modifications on many different kinds of computers, from micros to minis to mainframes, Unix is said to be a "portable" operating system. The main users of Unix are government agencies, universities, research institutions, large corporations, and banks that use the software for everything from designing airplane parts to currency trading.

user interface (p. 83, KQ 3.2) The part of the operating system that allows users to communicate, or interact, with it. There are four types of user interfaces: command-driven, menu-driven, graphical user, and network user.

User interfaces are necessary for users to be able to use a computer system.

utility programs (p. 96, KQ 3.1, 3.4) System software that either enhances existing functions or provides services not offered by other system software programs.

Many operating systems have utility programs built in for common purposes such as copying the contents of one disk to another. Other, external utility programs are available on separate diskettes to, for example, recover damaged or erased files.

virus (p. 97, KQ 3.4) Hidden programming instructions that are buried within an application or system program and that copy themselves to other programs, often causing damage.

Viruses can cause users to lose data or files or even shut down entire computer systems.

What It Is/What It Does	Why It's Important

windows (p. 84, KQ 3.2) Feature of graphical user interfaces; causes the display screen to divide into sections. Each window is dedicated to a specific purpose.

Using the windows feature, an operating system (or operating environment) can display several windows on a computer screen, each showing a different application program, such as word processing, spreadsheets, and graphics.

Windows 3.x (p. 90, KQ 3.3) Operating environment made by Microsoft that places a graphical user interface shell around the DOS operating system and extends DOS's capabilities.

The Windows 3.x operating environment made DOS easier to use, but only with Windows 95 did Windows become a true operating system.

Windows 95 (p. 91, KQ 3.3) Successor to Windows 3.x for DOS; this is a true operating system for PCs, rather than just an operating environment.

Windows 95 has become by far the most common system software on new microcomputers.

Windows 98 (p. 95, KQ 3.3) Latest release of the Windows operating system; uses a graphical user interface that acts like Web browser software and allows users to access data on the Internet as if it were stored on their hard disk.

Besides offering access to the Internet directly from the desktop, Windows 98 has new drivers to support television tuners and new types of disk players and other new hardware.

Windows CE (p. 95, KQ 3.3) A greatly slimmed-down version of Windows 95 for handheld computing devices. It includes basic word processing, spreadsheet, e-mail, Web browsing, and other software, and has a Windows look and feel.

A handheld computer, organizer, or TV set-top box with an operating system compatible with that of a desktop computer can readily exchange information with that computer.

Windows NT (New Technology) (p. 94, KQ 3.3) Network operating system that has multitasking, multiuser, and multiprocessing capabilities and a graphical user interface.

Multiuser systems like Windows NT are used to support computer workgroups. Windows NT comes in two versions, the Workstation version to support users who need a powerful system and no more than 10 computers in a network, and the more expensive Server version to support up to 32 processors in a LAN.

Exercises

Self-Test

1. A(n) _____ is software that translates a program written by a programmer into machine language.

2. _____ programs are special programs that either enhance existing functions or provide services not provided by other system software programs.

3. Software _____ are programs that allow the operating system to communicate with hardware devices.

4. _____ software is a program that scans hard disks, diskettes, and memory to detect viruses.

5. _____ utilities remove redundancies from a computer's storage space so less space is required to store or transmit data.

Short-Answer Questions

1. Why does a computer need system software?
2. What does the term *booting* mean?
3. What is a GUI?
4. What does the term *platform* refer to?
5. What is the difference between multitasking and time-sharing?

Multiple-Choice Questions

1. Which of the following is a multitasking, multiuser, multiprocessing network operating system?
   a. Windows 3.1
   b. Windows 95
   c. Windows NT
   d. DOS
   e. None of the above

2. Which of the following allows Microsoft Windows users to easily join and share data among applications?
   a. GUI
   b. OLE
   c. OS/2
   d. NUI
   e. NOS

3. Which of the following refers to the execution of two or more programs by multiple computers?
   a. multiprocessing
   b. multitasking
   c. time-sharing
   d. multiprogramming
   e. All of the above

4. Which of the following isn't an example of a file-management command?
   a. format
   b. copy
   c. rename
   d. erase
   e. All of the above

True/False Questions

T F 1. The operating system remains in main memory at all times when your computer is on.

T F 2. Applications software starts up the computer and functions as the principal coordinator of all hardware components.

T F 3. Command-driven interfaces allow you to use graphics and menus to start programs.

T F 4. A program that can defragment a disk is commonly referred to as a *defragger*.

T F 5. An example of a thin client is a network computer.

Knowledge in Action

1. If you have been using a particular microcomputer for two years and are planning to upgrade the version of systems software you are using, what issues must you consider before you go ahead and buy the new version?

2. If your computer runs Windows 95 or Windows 98, choose Settings, Control Panel from the Start menu to obtain information about your computer system. What are the current settings of your computer display (monitor)? Keyboard? Modem? Mouse? What other settings can you view in the Control Panel window?

3. Do you think the network computer will become a standard fixture in homes and businesses in the near future? If so, when? Research your answer on the Web and/or using current computer magazines.

4. What system software is used on the computer at your school, work, or home? Why was this software selected? Do you find this software easy to use? Would you prefer another type of system software or version upgrade? If so, why?

5. Locate someone who is using DOS and Windows 3.1. Why hasn't this person switched to Windows 95? Is the reason related to the existing hardware? Existing software? Other?

Answers

Self-Test Questions
1. language translator 2. utility 3. drivers
4. antivirus 5. data compression

Short-Answer Questions
1. Without system software, your computer wouldn't even be able to start. It is the principal coordinator of all hardware components and applications software programs. 2. The process of loading an operating system into a computer's main memory from disk is known as booting. 3. GUI stands for graphical user interface. A GUI allows you to use graphics and menus (as well as keystrokes) to choose commands, start programs, and see lists of files and other options. 4. The term platform refers to the type of processor model and operating system on which a computer system is based. 5. Whereas multitasking refers to the execution of more than one program concurrently for a single user, timesharing refers to the processing of several programs for several users.

Multiple-Choice Questions
1. c 2. b 3. a 4. a

True/False Questions
1. t 2. f 3. f 4. t 5. t

Processors
Hardware for Power & Portability

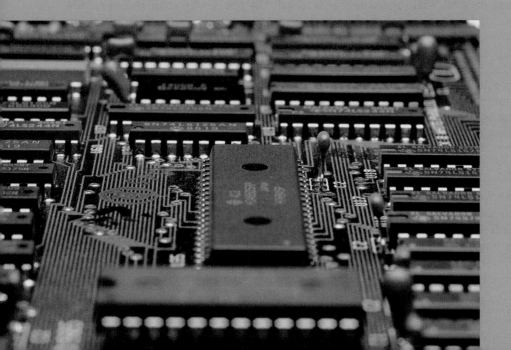

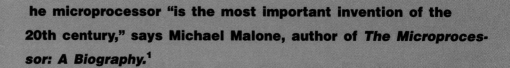

he microprocessor "is the most important invention of the 20th century," says Michael Malone, author of *The Microprocessor: A Biography.*[1]

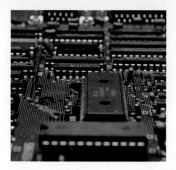

Quite a bold claim, considering the incredible products that have issued forth during the past nearly 100 years. More important than the airplane? More than television? More than atomic weapons?

However, Malone argues, the case for the exalted status of this thumbnail-size information-processing device is demonstrated, first, by its pervasiveness in the important machines in our lives, from computers to transportation. Second, "The microprocessor is, intrinsically, something special," he says. "Just as [the human being] is an animal, yet transcends that state, so too the microprocessor is a silicon chip, but more." Why? Because it can be programmed to recognize and respond to patterns in the environment, as humans do.

Indeed, this *is* something different. Until now, nothing that was inorganic—that was nonliving—was quite so adaptable.

4.1 Microchips, Miniaturization, & Mobility

KEY QUESTION

What are the differences between transistors, integrated circuits, chips, and microprocessors?

Preview & Review: Computers used to be made from vacuum tubes. Then came the tiny switches called transistors, followed by integrated circuits made from silicon, a common mineral. Integrated circuits called microchips, or chips, are printed and cut out of "wafers" of silicon. The microcomputer microprocessors, which process data, are made from microchips. They are also used as microcontrollers in other instruments, such as phones and TVs.

The microprocessor has presented us with a gift that we may barely appreciate—that of *portability* and *mobility* in electronic devices.

In 1955, for instance, portability was exemplified by the ads showing a young woman holding a Zenith television set accompanied by the caption: IT DOESN'T TAKE A MUSCLE MAN TO MOVE THIS LIGHTWEIGHT TV. That "lightweight" TV weighed a hefty 45 pounds. Today, by contrast, there is a handheld Casio color TV weighing a mere 6.2 ounces.

Similarly, tape recorders have gone from RCA's 35-pound machine in 1953 to today's Sony microcassette recorder of 3.5 ounces. Portable computers began in 1982 with Osborne's advertised "24 pounds of sophisticated computing power." Since then they have come down in weight and size so that now we have notebooks (4–9 pounds), subnotebooks (about 1.8–4 pounds), and pocket PCs (1 pound or less).

Had the transistor not arrived, as it did in 1947, the Age of Portability and consequent mobility would never have happened. To us a "portable" telephone might have meant the 40-pound backpack radiophones carried by some American GIs through World War II, rather than the 6-ounce shirtpocket cellular models available today.

From Vacuum Tubes to Transistors to Microchips

Old-time radios used vacuum tubes—small lightbulb-size electronic tubes with glowing filaments. The last computer to use these tubes, the ENIAC, which was turned on in 1946, employed 18,000 of them. Unfortunately, a tube failure occurred on average once every 7 minutes. Since it took more than 15 minutes to find and replace the faulty tube, it was difficult to get any useful computing work done. Moreover, the ENIAC was enormous, occupying 1500 square feet and weighing 30 tons.

The transistor changed all that. **A *transistor* is essentially a tiny electrically operated switch that can alternate between "on" and "off" many millions of times per second.** The transistor transfers electricity across a *resistor*, made of a material somewhat resistant to the current (thus the name: *trans*fer re*sistor*). Transistors make up *logic gates*, of which there are several types designed to respond differently to particular patterns of electrical pulses. Gates make up a *circuit*, which is an electronic pathway as well as a set of electronic components that perform a particular function in an electronic system. Circuits make up a logical device, such as a CPU (✔ p. 13).

The first transistors were one-hundredth the size of a vacuum tube, needed no warm-up time, consumed less energy, and were faster and more reliable. (■ *See Panel 4.1.*) Moreover, they marked the beginning of a process of miniaturization that has not ended yet. In 1960 one transistor fit into an area about a half-centimeter square.

Initially, transistors were made individually and then formed into an electronic circuit using wires and solder. Today transistors are part of an **integrated circuit; that is, an entire electronic circuit, including wires, is all formed together on a single "chip," or piece, of special material, usually silicon,** as part of a single manufacturing process. An integrated circuit embodies what is called *solid-state technology. Solid state* means that the electrons are traveling through solid material—in this case silicon. They do not travel through a vacuum, as was the case with the old radio vacuum tubes.

What is silicon, and why use it? *Silicon* is an element that is widely found in clay and sand. It is used not only because its abundance makes it cheap but also because it is a semiconductor. A *semiconductor* is material whose electrical properties are intermediate between a good conductor of electricity and a nonconductor of electricity. (An example of a good conductor of

■ PANEL 4.1

Shrinking components

The lightbulb-size 1940s vacuum tube was replaced in the 1950s by a transistor one-hundredth its size. Today's transistors are much smaller, being microscopic in size.

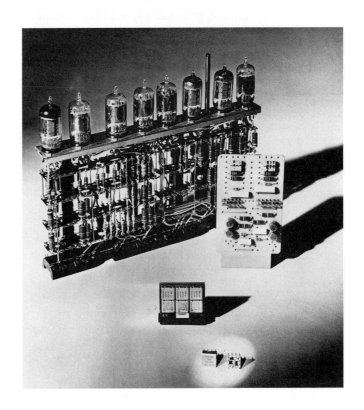

electricity is copper in household wiring; an example of a nonconductor is the plastic sheath around that wiring.) Because it is only a semiconductor, silicon has partial resistance to electricity. As a result, when good-conducting metals are overlaid on the silicon, the electronic circuitry of the integrated circuit can be created.

A computer's electronic circuitry is printed on a chip less than 1 centimeter square and about half a millimeter thick. **A *chip*, or *microchip*, is a tiny piece of silicon that contains millions of microminiature electronic circuit components,** mainly transistors.

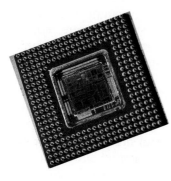

Miniaturization Miracles: Microchips, Microprocessors, & Micromachines

There are different kinds of microchips—for example, microprocessor, memory, logic, communications, graphics, and math coprocessor chips. We discuss some of these later in this chapter. Perhaps the most important is the microprocessor chip. **A *microprocessor* ("microscopic processor" or "processor on a chip") is the miniaturized circuitry of a computer processor—the part that processes, or manipulates, data into information.** When modified for use in machines other than computers, microprocessors are called *microcontrollers,* or *embedded computers* (✔ p. 18).

Mobility

Smallness—in TVs, phones, radios, camcorders, CD players, and computers—is now largely taken for granted. In the 1980s portability, or mobility, meant trading off computing power and convenience in return for smaller size and weight. Today, however, we are getting close to the point where we don't have to give up anything. As a result, experts have predicted that small, powerful, wireless personal electronic devices will transform our lives far more than the personal computer has done so far. "[T]he new generation of machines will be truly personal computers, designed for our mobile lives," wrote one reporter in 1992. "We will read office memos between strokes on the golf course and answer messages from our children in the middle of business meetings."[2] Today such activities are becoming commonplace.

4.2 The CPU & Main Memory

KEY QUESTIONS

How do the CPU and main memory work, and what are the four different kinds of processing speeds?

Preview & Review: The central processing unit (CPU)—the "brain" of the computer—consists of the control unit and the arithmetic/logic unit (ALU). Main memory holds data in storage temporarily; its capacity varies in different computers. Registers are staging areas in the CPU that store data during processing.

The operations for executing a single program instruction are called the *machine cycle,* which has an instruction cycle and an execution cycle.

Processing speeds are expressed in four ways: megahertz, MIPS, flops, and fractions of a second.

How is the information in "information processing" in fact processed? As we indicated, this is the job of the circuitry known as the microprocessor. This device, the "processor on a chip" found in a microcomputer, is also called the *CPU.* The CPU works hand in hand with other circuits known as *main memory* to carry out processing.

CPU

The *CPU,* for *central processing unit,* the "brain" of the computer, follows the instructions of the software to manipulate data into information. The CPU consists of two parts: (1) the control unit and (2) the arithmetic/logic unit. The two components are connected by a kind of electronic "roadway" called a *bus.* (■ *See Panel 4.2.*)

- **The control unit:** The *control unit* **tells the rest of the computer system how to carry out a program's instructions.** It directs the movement of electronic signals between main memory and the arithmetic/logic unit. It also directs these electronic signals between main memory and the input and output devices.

- **The arithmetic/logic unit:** The *arithmetic/logic unit,* or *ALU,* **performs arithmetic operations and logical operations and controls the speed of those operations.**

    As you might guess, *arithmetic operations* are the fundamental math operations: addition, subtraction, multiplication, and division.

    Logical operations are comparisons. That is, the ALU compares two pieces of data to see whether one is equal to (=), greater than (>), or less than (<) the other. (The comparisons can also be combined, as in "greater than or equal to" and "less than or equal to.")

The capacities of CPUs are expressed in terms of *word size.* **A *word* is the number of bits that may be manipulated or stored at one time by the CPU.** Often the more bits in a word, the faster the computer. An 8-bit computer— that is, one with an 8-bit-word processor—will transfer data within each CPU chip itself in 8-bit chunks. A 32-bit-word computer is faster, transferring data in 32-bit chunks. Other things being equal, a 32-bit computer processes 4 bytes in the time a 16-bit computer processes 2 bytes.

Main Memory

Main memory—variously known as *memory, primary storage, internal memory,* or *RAM* (for random access memory)—is working storage. It has three tasks. (1) It holds data for processing. (2) It holds instructions (the programs) for processing the data. (3) It holds processed data (that is,

■ PANEL 4.2

The CPU and main memory
The two main CPU components (control unit and ALU), the registers, and main memory are connected by a kind of electronic "roadway" called a *bus.* (Registers are temporary data storage holding areas.)

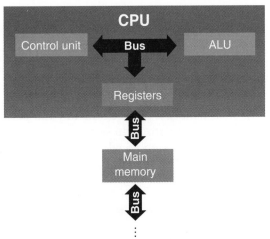

To expansion slots and input/output devices

information) waiting to be sent to an output or secondary-storage device. Main memory is contained on special microchips called *RAM chips,* as we describe in a few pages. This memory is in effect the computer's short-term capacity. It determines the total size of the programs and data files the computer can work on at any given moment.

There are two important facts to know about main memory:

- Its contents are temporary: Once the power to the computer is turned off, all the data and programs within main memory simply vanish. This is why data must also be stored on disks and tapes—called "secondary storage" to distinguish them from main memory's "primary storage."

  Thus, main memory is said to be *volatile.* **Volatile storage is temporary storage; the contents are lost when the power is turned off.** Consequently, if you kick out the connecting power cord to your computer, whatever you are currently working on will immediately disappear. This impermanence is the reason you should *frequently save* your work in progress to a secondary-storage medium such as a diskette. By "frequently," we mean every 3–5 minutes.

- Its capacity varies in different computers: The size of main memory is important. It determines how much data can be processed at once and how big and complex the programs are that can be used to process it. This capacity varies with different computers, and older machines generally have less RAM.

  For example, the original IBM PC, introduced in 1979, held only about 64,000 bytes (characters), or 64 kilobytes, of data or instructions. By contrast, new microcomputers can have 128 million bytes (megabytes) or more of memory—a 2000-fold increase.

Registers: Staging Areas for Processing

The control unit and the ALU also use registers, or special areas that enhance the computer's performance. (■ *Refer back to Panel 4.2.*) **Registers are high-speed storage areas that temporarily store data during processing.** It could be said that main memory (RAM) holds material that will be used "a little bit later." Registers hold material that is to be processed "immediately." The computer loads the program instructions and data from main memory into the registers just prior to processing, which helps the computer process faster.

Machine Cycle: How an Instruction Is Processed

How does the computer keep track of the data and instructions in main memory? Like a system of post-office mailboxes, it uses addresses. An *address* is the location, designated by a unique number, in main memory in which a character of data or of an instruction is stored during processing. To process each character, the control unit of the CPU retrieves that character from its address in main memory and places it into a register. This is the first step in what is called the *machine cycle.*

The *machine cycle* **is a series of operations performed to execute a single program instruction. The machine cycle consists of two parts: an instruction cycle, which fetches and decodes, and an execution cycle, which executes and stores.** (■ *See Panel 4.3.*)

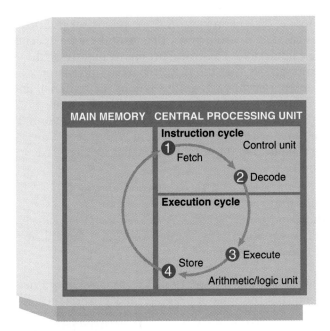

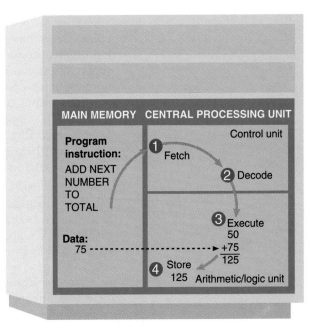

■ PANEL 4.3

The machine cycle

(Left) The machine cycle executes instructions one at a time during the instruction cycle and execution cycle. *(Right)* Example of how the addition of two numbers, 50 and 75, is processed and stored in a single cycle.

System Clock

When people talk about a computer's "speed," they mean how fast it can do processing—turn data into information. Every microprocessor contains a system clock. **The *system clock* controls how fast all the operations within a computer take place.** The system clock uses fixed vibrations from a quartz crystal to deliver a steady stream of digital pulses to the CPU. The faster the clock, the faster the processing, assuming the computer's internal circuits can handle the increased speed.

Processing speeds may be expressed in megahertz (MHz), with 1 MHz equal to 1 million cycles per second. The original IBM PC had a clock speed of 4.77 MHz. At the time of this book's publication, Intel chips were running at speeds up to 450 MHz. The Alpha chip was running at 500 MHz.

Categories of Processing Speeds

With transistors switching off and on perhaps millions of times per second, the tedious repetition of the machine cycle occurs at blinding speeds.

There are four main ways in which processing speeds are measured:

- For microcomputers—megahertz: Microcomputer microprocessor speeds are usually expressed in *megahertz (MHz),* **millions of machine cycles per second,** which is also the measure of a microcomputer's clock speed. For example, a 333-MHz Pentium II–based microcomputer processes 333 million machine cycles per second.

- For workstations, minicomputers, and mainframes—MIPS: Processing speed can also be measured according to the number of instructions processed per second that a computer can process, which today is in the millions. *MIPS* is a measure of a computer's processing speed; MIPS stands for *millions of instructions per second* that the processor can perform. A high-end microcomputer or workstation might perform at 100 MIPS or more, a mainframe at 200–1200 MIPS.

- **For supercomputers—flops:** The abbreviation *flops* stands for *floating-point operations per second*, a floating-point operation being a special kind of mathematical calculation. This measure, used mainly with supercomputers, is expressed as *megaflops* (mflops, or millions of floating-point operations per second), *gigaflops* (gflops, or billions), and *teraflops* (tflops, or trillions). The U.S. supercomputer known as Option Red cranks out 1.34 teraflops. (To put this in perspective, if a person were able to do one arithmetic calculation every second, it would take him or her about 31,000 years to do what Option Red does in a single second.)

- **Another measurement—fractions of a second:** Another way to measure machine cycle times is in fractions of a second. A *millisecond* is one-thousandth of a second. A *microsecond* is one-millionth of a second. A *nanosecond* is one-billionth of a second. A *picosecond* is one-trillionth of a second.

Now that you know where data and instructions are processed, we need to review how those data and instructions are represented in the CPU, registers, buses, and RAM.

4.3 How Data & Programs Are Represented in the Computer

KEY QUESTIONS

How is data capacity represented in a computer, and how do coding schemes, parity bits, and machine language work?

Preview & Review: Computers use the two-state 0/1 binary system to represent data. A computer's capacity for data is expressed in bits, bytes, kilobytes, megabytes, gigabytes, or terabytes. Two binary coding schemes are ASCII-8 and Unicode. Accuracy checks use parity bits.

Human-language-like programming languages are processed as 0s and 1s by the computer in machine language.

As we've explained, electricity is the basis for computers and communications because electricity can be either *on* or *off*. This two-state situation allows computers to use the *binary system* to represent data and programs.

Binary System: Using Two States

The decimal system that we are used to has 10 digits (0, 1, 2, 3, 4, 5, 6, 7, 8, 9). By contrast, **the *binary system* has only two digits: 0 and 1.** Thus, in the computer the 0 can be represented by the electrical current being off and the 1 by the current being on. All data and programs that go into the computer are represented in terms of these binary numbers. (■ *See Panel 4.4.*)

For example, the letter H is a translation of the electronic signal 01001000, or off-on-off-off-on-off-off-off. When you press the key for H on the computer keyboard, the character is automatically converted into the series of electronic impulses that the computer can recognize.

How Capacity Is Expressed

How many 0s and 1s will a computer or a storage device such as a hard disk hold? To review what we covered in Chapter 1, the following terms are used to denote capacity.

- **Bit:** In the binary system, **each 0 or 1 is called a *bit*, which is short for "binary dig*it*."**

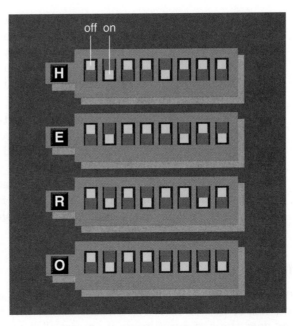

■ PANEL 4.4

Binary data representation
How the letters H-E-R-O are represented in one type of off/on, 0/1 binary code (ASCII-8).

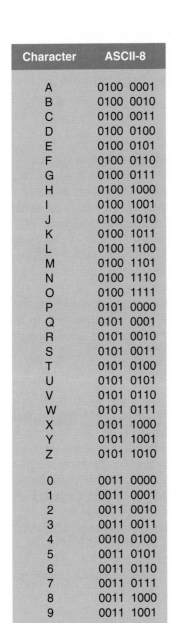

Character	ASCII-8
A	0100 0001
B	0100 0010
C	0100 0011
D	0100 0100
E	0100 0101
F	0100 0110
G	0100 0111
H	0100 1000
I	0100 1001
J	0100 1010
K	0100 1011
L	0100 1100
M	0100 1101
N	0100 1110
O	0100 1111
P	0101 0000
Q	0101 0001
R	0101 0010
S	0101 0011
T	0101 0100
U	0101 0101
V	0101 0110
W	0101 0111
X	0101 1000
Y	0101 1001
Z	0101 1010
0	0011 0000
1	0011 0001
2	0011 0010
3	0011 0011
4	0010 0100
5	0011 0101
6	0011 0110
7	0011 0111
8	0011 1000
9	0011 1001

■ PANEL 4.5

ASCII-8 binary code
There are many more characters than those shown here, such as punctuation marks, Greek letters, and math symbols.

- **Byte:** To represent letters, numbers, or special characters (such as ! or *), bits are combined into groups. **A group of 8 bits is called a *byte*, and a byte represents one character, digit, or other value.** (As we mentioned, in one scheme, 01001000 represents the letter *H*.) The capacity of a computer's memory or a diskette is expressed in numbers of bytes or multiples such as kilobytes and megabytes.

- **Kilobyte:** A *kilobyte (K, KB)* is about 1000 bytes. (Actually, it's precisely 1024 bytes, but the figure is commonly rounded.) The kilobyte was a common unit of measure for memory or secondary-storage capacity on older computers.

- **Megabyte:** A *megabyte (M, MB)* is about 1 million bytes (1,048,576 bytes). Measures of microcomputer primary-storage capacity today are expressed in megabytes.

- **Gigabyte:** A *gigabyte (G, GB)* is about 1 billion bytes (1,073,741,824 bytes). This measure was formerly used mainly with "big iron" types of computers, but now is typical of secondary storage (hard disk) capacity of today's microcomputers.

- **Terabyte:** A *terabyte (T, TB)* represents about 1 trillion bytes (1,009,511,627,776 bytes).

Binary Coding Schemes

Letters, numbers, and special characters are represented within a computer system by means of *binary coding schemes*. That is, the off/on 0s and 1s are arranged in such a way that they can be made to represent characters, digits, or other values. When you type a word on the keyboard (for example, HERO), the letters are converted into bytes—eight 0s and 1s for each letter. The bytes are represented in the computer by a combination of eight transistors, some of which are closed (representing the 0s) and some of which are open (representing the 1s).

One popular coding scheme, *ASCII-8*, uses eight bits to form each byte. (**■** *See Panel 4.5.*) One newer coding scheme, Unicode, uses 16 bits.

- **ASCII-8:** Pronounced "askey," **ASCII stands for American Standard Code for Information Interchange and is the binary code most widely used with microcomputers.** ASCII originally used seven bits, but a zero was added in the left position to provide an eight-bit code, which offers more possible combinations with which to form characters, such as math symbols and Greek letters.

- Unicode: A subset of ASCII, **Unicode uses two bytes (16 bits) for each character,** rather than one byte (8 bits). Instead of the 256 character combinations of ASCII-8, Unicode can handle 65,536 character combinations, thus allowing almost all the written languages of the world to be represented using a single character set. Although each Unicode character takes up twice as much memory space and hard-disk space as each ASCII character, conversion to the Unicode standard seems likely.

The Parity Bit

Dust, electrical disturbance, weather conditions, and other factors can cause interference in a circuit or communications line that is transmitting a byte. How does the computer know if an error has occurred? Detection is accomplished by use of a parity bit. **A parity bit, also called a check bit, is an extra bit attached to the end of a byte for purposes of checking for accuracy.**

Parity schemes may be *even parity* or *odd parity*. In an even-parity scheme, for example, the ASCII letter H (01001000) contains two 1s. Thus, the ninth bit, the parity bit, would be 0 in order to make the sum of the bits come out even. With the letter O (01001111), which has five 1s, the ninth bit would be 1 to make the byte come out even. The system software in the computer automatically and continually checks the parity scheme for accuracy. (If the message "Parity Error" appears on your screen, you need a technician to look at the computer to see what is causing the problem.)

Machine Language

Why won't word processing software that runs on an Apple Macintosh run (without special arrangements) on an IBM microcomputer? It's because each computer has its own machine language. **Machine language is a binary-type programming language that the computer can run directly.** To most people an instruction written in machine language is incomprehensible, consisting only of 0s and 1s. However, it is what the computer itself can understand, and the 0s and 1s represent precise storage locations and operations.

How do people-comprehensible program instructions become computer-comprehensible machine language? Special system programs called *language translators* rapidly convert the instructions into machine language—language that computers can understand. This translating occurs virtually instantaneously, so that you are not aware it is happening.

4.4 The Microcomputer System Unit

KEY QUESTION

What are the names and functions of the main parts of the system unit?

Preview & Review: The system unit, or cabinet, contains the following electrical components: the power supply, the motherboard, the CPU chip, specialized processor chips, RAM chips, ROM chips, other forms of memory (cache, VRAM, flash), expansion slots and boards, bus lines, ports, and PC (PCMCIA) slots and cards.

Because the type of computer you will most likely be working with is the microcomputer, we'll now take a look at what's inside the microcomputer's system unit.

What is inside the gray or beige box that we call "the computer"? **The box or cabinet is the *system unit;* it contains the electrical and hardware components that make the computer work.** These components actually do the processing in information processing.

The system unit of a desktop microcomputer does not include the keyboard or printer. Usually it also does not include the monitor or display screen (although it did in early Apple Macintoshes and some Compaq Presarios). It usually does include a hard-disk drive, a diskette drive, a CD-ROM drive, and sometimes a tape drive. We describe these and other *peripheral devices*—**hardware that is outside the central processing unit**—in the chapters on input/output and secondary storage. Here we are concerned with eleven parts of the system unit, as follows:

- Power supply
- Motherboard
- CPU chip
- Specialized processor chips
- RAM chips
- ROM chips
- Other forms of memory—cache, VRAM, flash
- Expansion slots and boards
- Bus lines
- Ports
- PC (PCMCIA) slots and cards

These are terms that appear frequently in advertisements for microcomputers. After reading this section, you should be able to understand what these ads are talking about.

Power Supply

The electricity available from a standard wall outlet is alternating current (AC), but a microcomputer runs on direct current (DC). **The *power supply* is a device that converts AC to DC to run the computer.** (■ *See Panel 4.6, next page.*) The on/off switch in your computer turns on or shuts off the electricity to the power supply. Because electricity can generate a lot of heat, a fan inside the computer keeps the power supply and other components from becoming too hot.

Motherboard

The *motherboard*, or *system board*, is the main circuit board in the system unit. (■ *See Panel 4.6, next page.*)

The motherboard consists of a flat board that fills the bottom of the system unit. (It is accompanied by the power-supply unit and fan and probably one or more disk drives.) This board contains the "brain" of the computer, the CPU or microprocessor; electronic memory (RAM) that assists the CPU; and some sockets, called *expansion slots,* where additional circuit boards, called *expansion boards,* may be plugged in.

■ PANEL 4.6

System unit and motherboard components

(Top) Motherboard. *(Bottom)* System unit.

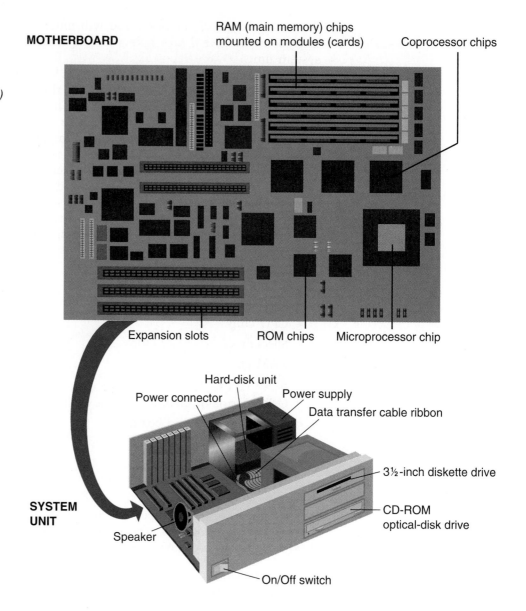

MOTHERBOARD

RAM (main memory) chips mounted on modules (cards)

Coprocessor chips

Expansion slots   ROM chips   Microprocessor chip

SYSTEM UNIT

Hard-disk unit

Power connector   Power supply

Data transfer cable ribbon

3½-inch diskette drive

CD-ROM optical-disk drive

Speaker

On/Off switch

CPU Chip

Most personal computers today use CPU chips (microprocessors) of two kinds—those based on the model made by Intel and those based on the model made by Motorola.

- **Intel-type chips:** About 90% of microcomputers use Intel-type microprocessors. Indeed, the Microsoft Windows operating system is designed to run on Intel chips. As a result, people in the computer industry tend to refer to the Windows/Intel joint powerhouse as *Wintel.*

   Intel-type chips are made principally by Intel Corporation—but also by Advanced Micro Devices, Cyrix, DEC, and others—for PCs such as IBM, Compaq, Dell, Gateway 2000, NEC, and Packard Bell.

   Intel used to identify its chips by numbers—8086, 8088, 80286, 80386, 80486, the latter abbreviated in common parlance to simply '286, '386, and '486. The higher the number, the faster the processing

The Pentium II processor comes in a cartridge that is inserted in a slot on the motherboard.

speed. Since 1993, Intel has marketed its chips under the names *Pentium, Pentium Pro, Pentium MMX,* and *Pentium II.* The Pentium II, which came out in late 1997, allows users to install more demanding multimedia programs, such as three-dimensional visualization tools.

- **Motorola-type chips:** ***Motorola-type chips* are made by Motorola for Apple Macintosh computers and its clones,** such as those formerly made by Power Computing and by Motorola itself. These chip numbers include the 68000, 68020, 68030, and 68040. Since 1993, Motorola has joined forces with IBM and Apple to produce the PowerPC family of chips. With certain hardware or software add-ons, a PowerPC can run PC as well as Mac applications software.

Two principal designs—what computer people call "architectures"—for microprocessors are CISC and RISC:

- **CISC:** ***CISC chips—CISC* stands for *complex instruction set computing*—are used mostly in PCs and in conventional mainframes.** CISC chips can support a large number of instructions, although this number gets in the way of processing speeds.

- **RISC:** ***RISC chips—RISC* stands for *reduced instruction set computing*—are used mainly in workstations,** such as those made by Sun Microsystems, Hewlett-Packard, and Digital Equipment Corporation. With RISC chips, a great many seldom-used instructions are eliminated. Thus, RISC-equipped workstations have been found to work up to 10 times faster than conventional computers.

The development of new chips is popularly known to follow what is called *Moore's law.* Named for the legendary cofounder of Intel, Gordon Moore, Moore's law reflects his observation that, as one journalist paraphrased it,

> The number of components [transistors] that can be packed on a computer chip doubles every 18 months while the price stays the same. Essentially, that means that computer power per dollar doubles every 18 months.[3]

Amazingly, this "law" has held true for more than 30 years, with power increasing and prices falling at a spectacular rate. For instance, in 1961 a chip had only 4 transistors, in 1971 it had 2300, and in 1979 it had 30,000. The 1997 Pentium II has 7.5 million transistors. The 2000 chip code-named Merced will have 40 million transistors according to one report, between 20 million and 50 million according to another.[4,5] (■ *See Panel 4.7, next page.)* The chief operating officer of Intel has predicted that PCs in the year 2011 will use a microprocessor chip that has as many as a billion transistors.[6]

Specialized Processor Chips

A motherboard usually has slots for plugging in specialized processor chips. Two in particular that you may encounter are math and graphics coprocessor chips. A *math coprocessor chip* helps programs using lots of mathematical equations to run faster. A *graphics coprocessor chip* enhances the performance of programs with lots of graphics and helps create complex screen displays. Specialized chips significantly increase the speed of a computer system.

RAM Chips

RAM, for random access memory, is memory that temporarily holds data and instructions that will be needed shortly by the CPU. RAM is what we have been calling *main memory, internal memory,* or *primary storage.* It operates like a chalkboard that is constantly being written on, then erased, then written on again. (The term *random access* comes from the fact that data can be stored and retrieved at random—from anywhere in the electronic RAM chips—in approximately equal amounts of time, no matter what the specific data locations are.)

Like the microprocessor, RAM consists of circuit-inscribed silicon chips attached to the motherboard. **RAM chips are often mounted on a small circuit board, such as a SIMM or DIMM, which is plugged into the motherboard. A *SIMM* (for *single inline memory module*) has multiple RAM chips on one side. A *DIMM* (for *dual inline memory module*) has multiple RAM chips on both sides.**

The two principal types of RAM chips are *DRAM* (for *dynamic random access memory*), used for most main memory, and *SRAM* (for *static random access memory*), used for some specialized purposes within main memory. A newer type of DRAM chip is the *EDO* (for *extended data out*) *RAM* chip.

Microcomputers come with different amounts of RAM. In many cases, additional

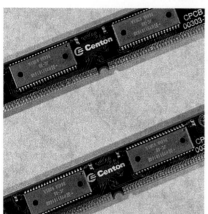

Memory chip modules
(SIMMs)

■ PANEL 4.7

Moore's law: Intel CPU chips' transistor explosion

How the number of transistors in Intel CPU chips has grown. Moore's law states that the number of transistors on a chip doubles every 18 months while price stays the same.

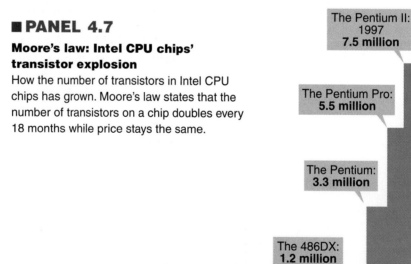

The Merced:
2000
40 million (est.)

The Pentium II:
1997
7.5 million

The Pentium Pro:
5.5 million

The Pentium:
3.3 million

The 486DX:
1.2 million

The 386DX:
275,000

The 4004:
2300

Transistors (in millions)

Year

RAM chips can be added by plugging a memory-expansion card into the motherboard, as we will explain. The more RAM you have, the faster the computer operates, and the better your software performs.

Having enough RAM has become a critical matter! Before you buy a software package, look at the outside of the box or check the manufacturer's Web site to see how much RAM is required. Windows 95 supposedly will run with 4 megabytes of RAM, but a realistic minimum is 16 megabytes. One powerful IBM-compatible microcomputer, the Micron XKU 300, has *128 megabytes* of RAM.

ROM Chips

Unlike RAM, which is constantly being written on and erased, **ROM, which stands for *read only memory* and is also known as *firmware*, cannot be written on or erased by the computer user without special equipment.** (■ *Refer back to Panel 4.6.)* ROM chips contain programs that are built in at the factory; these are special instructions for basic computer operations, such as those that start the computer or put characters on the screen.

There are variations of the ROM chip that allow programmers to vary information stored on the chip and also to erase it.

Other Forms of Memory

The performance of microcomputers can be enhanced further by adding other forms of memory, as follows.

- Cache memory: Pronounced "cash," **cache memory is a special high-speed memory area that the CPU can access quickly.** Cache memory can be located on the microprocessor chip or elsewhere on the motherboard. Cache memory is used in computers with very fast CPUs. The most frequently used instructions are kept in cache memory so the CPU can look there first. This allows the CPU to run faster because it doesn't have to take time to swap instructions in and out of main memory. Large, complex programs benefit the most from having a cache memory available.

- Video memory: ***Video memory* or *video RAM (VRAM)* chips are used to store display images for the monitor.** The amount of video memory determines how fast images appear and how many colors are available. Video memory chips are particularly desirable if you are running programs that display a lot of graphics.

- Flash memory: Used primarily in notebook and subnotebook computers, ***flash memory*, or *flash RAM*, cards consist of circuitry on credit-card-size cards that can be inserted into slots connected to the motherboard.** Unlike standard RAM chips, flash memory is *nonvolatile.* That is, it retains data even when the power is turned off. Flash memory can be used not only to simulate main memory but also to supplement or replace hard-disk drives for permanent storage.

READ ME

Practical Matters: Preventing Problems from Too Much or Too Little Power to Your Computer

"When the power disappears, so can your data," writes *San Jose Mercury News* computer columnist Phillip Robinson. "I say this with authority, sitting here in the dark in the wake of severe storms that have hit my part of California."[7] (Deprived of use of his computer, Robinson dictated his column by phone.)

Too little electricity can be devastating to your data. Too much electricity can be devastating to your computer hardware.

Here are a few things you can do to keep both safe:[8–11]

● **Back up data regularly:** If you faithfully make backup (duplicate) copies of your data every few minutes as you're working, then if your computer has power problems you'll be able to get back in business fairly quickly once the machine is running again.

● **Use a surge protector to protect against too much electricity:** Plug all your hardware into a surge protector (suppressor), which will prevent damage to your equipment if there is a power surge. (You'll know you've experienced a power surge when the lights in the room suddenly get very bright.)

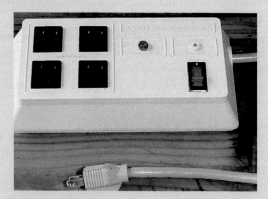

Surge protector

● **Use a voltage regulator to protect against too little electricity:** Plug your computer into a voltage regulator to adjust for power sags or brownouts. If power is too low for too long, it's as though the computer were turned off.

● **Consider using a UPS to protect against complete absence of electricity:** Consider plugging your computer into a UPS, or uninterruptible power supply. (A low-cost one, available at electronics stores, sells for about $150.) The UPS is kind of a short-term battery that will keep your computer running long enough for you to save your data before you turn off the machine after a power failure.

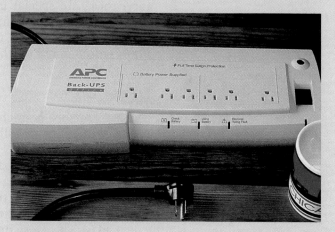

UPS unit

● **Turn ON highest-power-consuming hardware first:** When you turn on your computer system, you should turn on the devices that use the most power first. This will avoid causing a power drain on smaller devices. The most common advice is to turn on (1) external drives and/or scanners, (2) system unit, (3) monitor, (4) printer—in that order.

● **Turn OFF lowest-power-consuming hardware first:** When you turn off your system, follow the reverse order—first printer, then monitor, and so on. This avoids causing a power surge to the smaller devices.

● **Unplug your computer system during lightning storms:** Unplug all your system's components—including phone lines—during thunder and lightning storms. If lightning strikes your house or the power lines, it can ruin your equipment.

Expansion Slots & Boards

Today all new microcomputer systems can be expanded. *Expandability* refers to a computer's capacity for adding more memory or peripheral devices. Having expandability means that when you buy a PC you can later add devices to enhance its computing power. This spares you from having to buy a completely new computer.

Expandability is made possible with expansion slots and expansion boards. **Expansion slots are sockets on the motherboard into which you can plug expansion cards. Expansion cards, or** *add-on boards,* **are circuit boards that provide more memory or control peripheral devices. (■** *Refer back to Panel 4.6.)* The words *card* and *board* are used interchangeably. Some slots may be needed right away for ordinary functions, but if your system unit leaves enough slots open, you can use them for expansion later.

Among the types of expansion cards are the following.

- **Expanded memory:** Memory expansion cards (SIMMs or DIMMs) allow you to add RAM chips, giving you more main memory.
- **Display adapter or graphics adapter cards:** These allow you to adapt different kinds of color video display monitors for your computer.
- **Controller cards:** *Controller cards* are circuit boards that allow your CPU to work with the computer's various peripheral devices. For example, a disk controller card allows the computer to work with different kinds of hard-disk and diskette drives.
- **Other add-ons:** You can also add special circuit boards for modems, fax, sound, and networking, as well as math or graphics coprocessor chips.

Bus Lines

A *bus line,* **or simply** *bus,* **is an electrical pathway through which bits are transmitted within the CPU and between the CPU and other devices in the system unit.** There are different types of buses (address bus, control bus, data bus), but for our purposes the most important is the **expansion bus, which carries data between RAM and the expansion slots.** To obtain faster performance, some users will use a bus that avoids RAM altogether. **A bus that connects expansion slots directly to the CPU is called a** *local bus.* **(■** *See Panel 4.8.)*

■ PANEL 4.8

Buses

Buses are the electrical pathways that carry bits within the CPU and from the CPU to peripheral devices. Expansion buses connect RAM with expansion slots. Local buses avoid RAM and connect expansion slots directly with the CPU.

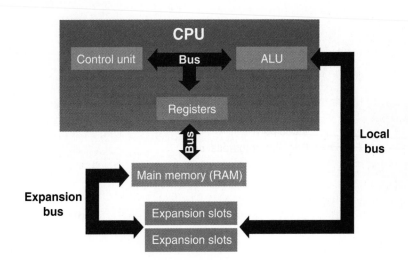

A bus resembles a multilane highway: The more lanes it has, the faster the bits can be transferred. The old-fashioned 8-bit-word bus of early microprocessors had only eight pathways. It was therefore four times slower than the 32-bit bus of later microprocessors, which had 32 pathways. Intel's Pentium chip is a 64-bit processor. Some supercomputers contain buses that are 128 bits. Today there are several principal expansion bus standards, or "architectures," for microcomputers.

Ports

A *port* is a socket on the outside of the system unit that is connected to a board on the inside of the system unit. A port allows you to plug in a cable to connect a peripheral device, such as a monitor, printer, or modem, so that it can communicate with the computer system.

Ports are of several types. (■ *See Panel 4.9.*)

- Game ports: *Game ports* **allow you to attach a joystick or similar gameplaying device to the system unit.** Not all microcomputers will have these.

- Parallel ports: **A *parallel port* allows lines to be connected that will enable 8 bits to be transmitted simultaneously,** like cars on an eight-lane highway. Parallel lines move information faster than serial lines do, but they can transmit information efficiently only up to 15 feet. Thus, parallel ports are used principally for connecting printers.

- Serial ports: **A *serial port,* or *RS-232 port,* enables a line to be connected that will send bits one after the other on a single line,** like cars on a one-lane highway. Serial ports—frequently labeled "COM" for communications—are used principally for communications lines, modems, and mice. In the Macintosh, serial ports are also used for the printer.

- Video adapter ports: *Video adapter ports* **are used to connect the video display monitor outside the computer to the video adapter card inside the system unit.** Monitors may have either a 9-pin plug or a

■ PANEL 4.9

Ports

Shown are the backs of a PC and a Macintosh.

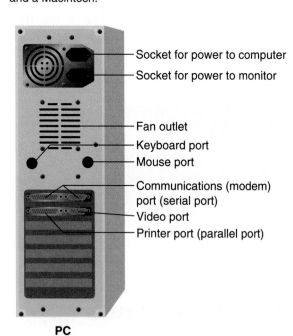

PC

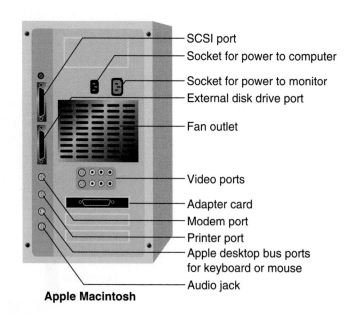

Apple Macintosh

15-pin plug. The plug must be compatible with the number of holes in the video adapter card.

- **SCSI ports:** Pronounced "scuzzy" (and **short for *small computer system interface*), a *SCSI port* provides an interface for transferring data at high speeds for up to 15 SCSI-compatible devices.** These devices include external hard-disk drives, CD-ROM drives, scanners, and magnetic-tape backup units. SCSI devices are linked together in what is called a *daisy chain*—a set of devices connected in a series along an extended cable. Sometimes the equipment on the chain is inside the computer, an internal daisy chain; sometimes it is outside the computer, an external daisy chain.

- Infrared ports: When you use a handheld remote unit to change channels on a TV set, you're using invisible radio waves of the type known as infrared waves. **An *infrared port* allows a computer to make a cableless connection with infrared-capable devices,** such as some printers. This type of connection requires an unobstructed line of sight between transmitting and receiving ports, and they can only be a few feet apart.

Why are so many ports needed? Why can't plugging peripherals into a computer be as easy as plugging in a lamp in your living room? Fortunately, new technology promises simplification. Several companies (Intel, Microsoft, IBM, Compaq, and others) have agreed on something called the ***Universal Serial Bus (USB),* which allows up to 127 peripherals to be connected through just one general-purpose port.**

Plug-In Cards: PC (PCMCIA) Slots & Cards

Although its name doesn't exactly roll off the tongue, PCMCIA has probably changed mobile computing more dramatically than any other technology today. **Short for *Personal Computer Memory Card International Association, PCMCIA* is a completely open, relatively new bus standard for portable computers.** *PC cards*—renamed because it's easier to say—**are cards approximately 2.1 by 3.4 inches in size that contain peripherals and can be plugged into slots in microcomputers.** The PC cards may be used to hold credit-card-size modems, sound boards, hard disks, extra memory, and even pagers and cellular communicators.

At present there are four sizes for PC cards—I (thin), II (thick), III (thicker), and IV (thickest). Type I is used primarily for flash memory cards. Type II, the kind you'll find most often, is used for fax modems and adapters for local area networks (LANs). Type III is for rotating disk devices, such as hard-disk drives. Type IV is for large-capacity hard-disk drives.

PC card

Not much bigger than a credit card, a PC card fits in a small slot on the side of a computer. PC cards are typically used to provide extra memory or a modem.

4.5 Computers, Obsolescence, & the Environment

KEY QUESTION

What are two adverse effects of computers?

Preview & Review: Information technology has had some adverse effects on the environment, including environmental pollution and energy consumption.

Where has miniaturization taken us today? How about making computers small enough to wear?

Indeed, PC evolution has already gone from palmtops to "smart clothes." Steve Mann, 35, a scientist and inventor who received his Ph.D. from the Massachusetts Institute of Technology, spends his waking hours wearing a wireless wearable system. For instance, his eyeglasses contain a tiny display

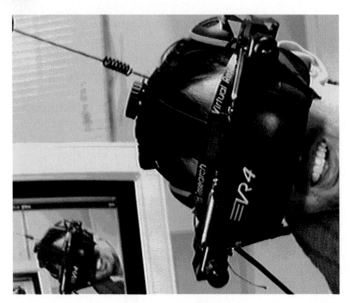

Steve Mann and his wireless wearable system

screen and a microcamera (which he calls *aremac*—"camera" spelled backwards) that are connected to the World Wide Web. When he got lost in downtown Boston one day, he retraced his steps by calling up images he had just sent to his Web page. "My visual memory prosthetic told me how to get back," he said.[12] Mann's cyberclothes also provide a cellular phone, pager, Walkman, dictating machine, camcorder, laptop computer, microphone, and earphones.

Obsolescence

The advances in wearable computers suggest just how fast the pace of technological change is—and consequently how fast the rate of obsolescence. Because obsolescence in PC systems occurs about every three years, numerous computers, printers, monitors, fax machines, and so on have wound up as junk in landfills, although some are stripped by recyclers for valuable metals. However, a better idea, if you have an old-fashioned PC, is to consider donating it to an organization that can make use of it. Don't abandon it in a closet. Don't dump it in the trash. "Even if you have no further use for a machine that seems horribly antiquated," writes *San Jose Mercury News* technology editor Dan Gillmor, "someone else will be grateful for all it will do."[13]

Ethics

Energy Consumption & "Green PCs"

Besides recycling old computers, there are some environment-friendly things you can do with new computers. All the computers and communications devices discussed in this book run on electricity. Much of this is simply wasted. To reduce the amount of electricity such equipment uses, the U.S. Environmental Protection Agency launched Energy Star, a voluntary program to encourage the use of computers that consume a minimum amount of power. As a result, manufacturers now make Energy Star–compliant "green PCs," as well as energy-saving monitors and printers. In most cases, they go into a "sleep" mode after several minutes of not being used. When you press a key, they go back to full power.

If your equipment does not have the Energy Star logo, there are other things you can do to save energy. For one thing, you can turn off the PC, monitor, and printer if you're not planning to use them for an hour or more. And certainly don't leave them on 24 hours a day. People used to think a computer system would be worn out by repeatedly being turned on and off, but that's no longer true. Hard disks, for example, are built to last an average of 10,000 starts and stops. That means, says computer columnist Lawrence Magid, "that you could expect to turn the computer on and off once a day for 27 years before you would wear it out."[14]

Summary

What It Is/What It Does	Why It's Important
American Standard Code for Information Interchange (ASCII) (p. 120, KQ 4.3) Binary code used in microcomputers. ASCII originally used seven bits to form a character, but a zero was added in the left position to provide an eight-bit code, providing 256 possible combinations with which to form other characters and marks.	ASCII is the binary code most widely used with microcomputers.
arithmetic/logic unit (ALU) (p. 115, KQ 4.2) The part of the CPU that performs arithmetic operations and logical operations and that controls the speed of those operations.	Arithmetic operations are the fundamental math operations: addition, subtraction, multiplication, and division. Logical operations are comparisons, such as is equal to (=), greater than (>), or less than (<).
binary system (p. 118, KQ 4.3) A two-state system.	Computer systems use a binary system for data representation; two digits, 0 and 1, refer to the presence or absence of electrical current or a pulse of light.
bit (p. 118, KQ 4.3) Short for *binary digit,* which is either a 1 or a 0 in the binary system of data representation in computer systems.	The bit is the fundamental element of all data and information stored in a computer system.
bus (p. 127, KQ 4.4) Electrical pathway through which bits are transmitted within the CPU and between the CPU and other devices in the system unit. There are different types of buses (address bus, control bus, data bus, input/output bus).	The larger a computer's buses, the faster it operates.
byte (p. 119, KQ 4.3) A group of 8 bits.	A byte holds the equivalent of a character—such as a letter or a number—in ASCII and other leading computer data-representation coding schemes. It is also the basic unit used to measure the storage capacity of main memory and secondary-storage devices.
cache memory (p. 125, KQ 4.4) Special high-speed memory area on the CPU or another chip that the CPU can access quickly. A copy of the most frequently used instructions is kept in the cache memory so the CPU can look there first.	Cache memory allows the CPU to run faster because it doesn't have to take time to swap instructions in and out of main memory. Large, complex programs benefit the most from having a cache memory available.

What It Is/What It Does	Why It's Important

central processing unit (CPU) (p. 115, KQ 4.2) The processor; it follows the software's instructions to manipulate data to produce information. In a microcomputer the CPU is usually contained on a single integrated circuit called a *microprocessor*. The CPU consists of two parts, the control unit and the arithmetic/logic unit, connected by a bus.

The CPU is the "brain" of the computer.

chip (microchip) (p. 114, KQ 4.1) Microscopic piece of silicon that contains thousands of microminiature electronic circuit components, mainly transistors.

Chips have made possible the development of small computers.

complex instruction set computing (CISC) (p. 123, KQ 4.4) Design that allows a microprocessor to support a large number of instructions, although the processing speed is slowed by that number compared to the reduced number supported by RISC chips.

CISC chips are used mostly in PCs and conventional mainframes.

control unit (p. 115, KQ 4.2) The part of the CPU that tells the rest of the computer system how to carry out a program's instructions.

The control unit directs the movement of electronic signals between main memory and the arithmetic/logic unit. It also directs these electronic signals between the main memory and input and output devices.

dual inline memory module (DIMM) (p. 124, KQ 4.4) Small circuit board plugged into the motherboard and carrying multiple *RAM* chips on both sides.

A DIMM's RAM chips can be used to increase a computer's working memory.

expansion bus (p. 127, KQ 4.4) Bus that carries data between RAM and the expansion slots.

Without buses, computing would not be possible.

expansion card (p. 127, KQ 4.4) Add-on circuit board that provides more memory or a new peripheral-device capability. (The words *card* and *board* are used interchangeably.) Expansion cards are inserted into expansion slots inside the system unit.

Users can use expansion cards to upgrade their computers instead of having to buy entire new systems.

expansion slot (p. 127, KQ 4.4) Socket on the motherboard into which users may plug an expansion card.

See expansion board.

flash memory (p. 125, KQ 4.4) Used primarily in notebook and subnotebook computers; flash memory, or a flash RAM card, consists of circuitry on credit-card-size cards that can be inserted into slots connecting to the motherboard.

Unlike standard RAM chips, flash memory is nonvolatile—it retains data even when the power is turned off. Flash memory can be used not only to simulate main memory but also to supplement or replace hard-disk drives for permanent storage.

game port (p. 128, KQ 4.4) External electrical socket on the system unit that allows users to connect a joystick or similar game-playing device to an internal circuit board.

A game port allows a microcomputer to be made into a game machine.

What It Is/What It Does	**Why It's Important**

gigabyte (G, GB) (p. 119, KQ 4.3) Approximately 1 billion bytes (1,073,741,824 bytes); a measure of storage capacity.

Gigabyte is used to express the storage capacity of large computers, such as mainframes, although it is also applied to some microcomputer secondary-storage devices.

infrared port (p. 129, KQ 4.4) Allows a computer to make a cableless connection with infrared-capable devices, such as some printers. The connection is the same as the one between a remote control and a TV, requiring an unobstructed line of sight for the infrared radio waves to travel up to several feet between devices.

Infrared connections allow hookups without a cable trailing between two devices.

integrated circuit (p. 113, KQ 4.1) An entire electrical circuit, or pathway, etched a on tiny square, or chip, of silicon half the size of a person's thumbnail. In a computer, different types of integrated circuits perform different types of operations.

The integrated circuit has enabled the manufacture of the small, powerful, and relatively inexpensive computers used today.

Intel-type chips (p. 122, KQ 4.4) CPU chips designed for PCs; they are based on the model made by Intel Corporation, but other makers include Cyrix, Advanced Micro Devices, and DEC.

The majority of microcomputers run on Intel-type chips, including Intel's line of 8086 through '486 chips and the Pentium and Pentium MMX chips.

kilobyte (K, KB) (p. 119, KQ 4.3) Unit for measuring storage capacity; equals 1024 bytes (usually rounded off to 1000 bytes).

The sizes of stored electronic files are often measured in kilobytes.

local bus (p. 127, KQ 4.4) Bus that connects expansion slots to the CPU, bypassing RAM.

A local bus is faster than an expansion bus.

machine cycle (p. 116, KQ 4.2) Series of operations performed by the CPU to execute a single program instruction; it consists of two parts: an *instruction cycle* and an *execution cycle.*

The machine cycle is the essence of computer-based processing.

machine language (p. 120, KQ 4.3) Binary code (language) that the computer uses directly. The 0s and 1s represent precise storage locations and operations.

For a program to run, it must be in the machine language of the computer that is executing it.

main memory (p. 115, KQ 4.2) Also known as *memory, primary storage, internal memory,* or *RAM* (for *random access memory*). Main memory is working storage that holds (1) data for processing, (2) the programs for processing the data, and (3) data after it is processed and is waiting to be sent to an output or secondary-storage device.

Main memory determines the total size of the programs and data files a computer can work on at any given moment.

megabyte (M, MB) (p. 119, KQ 4.3) About 1 million bytes (1,048,576 bytes).

Most microcomputer main memory capacity is expressed in megabytes.

What It Is/What It Does	**Why It's Important**

megahertz (MHz) (p. 117, KQ 4.2) Measurement of transmission frequency; 1 MHz equals 1 million beats (cycles) per second.

Generally, the higher the megahertz rate, the faster a computer can process data.

microprocessor (p. 114, KQ 4.1) A CPU (processor) consisting of miniaturized circuitry on a single chip; it controls all the processing in a computer.

Microprocessors enabled the development of microcomputers and electronic controls for other devices.

motherboard (p. 121, KQ 4.4) Also called *system board;* the main circuit board in the system unit of a microcomputer.

It is the interconnecting assembly of essential components, including CPU, main memory, other chips, and expansion slots.

Motorola-type chips (p. 123, KQ 4.4) CPU chips made by Motorola for Apple Macintosh and its clones.

Motorola chips have provided Macintoshes and Power-PCs with a powerful CPU.

parallel port (p. 128, KQ 4.4) External electrical socket on the system unit that allows a parallel device, which transmits 8 bits simultaneously, to be connected to an internal board.

Enables microcomputer users to connect to a printer using a cable.

parity bit (p. 120, KQ 4.3) Also called a *check bit;* an extra bit attached to the end of a byte.

Enables a computer system to check for errors during transmission (the check bits are organized according to a particular coding scheme designed into the computer).

PC cards (p. 129, KQ 4.4) Small cards that contain peripherals and can be plugged into slots in portable computers. Based on the PCMCIA standard.

See Personal Computer Memory Card International Association.

peripheral device (p. 121, KQ 4.4) Hardware that is outside the central processing unit, such as input/output and secondary-storage devices.

These devices are used to get data into and out of the CPU and to store large amounts of data that cannot be held in the CPU at one time.

Personal Computer Memory Card International Association (PCMCIA) (p. 129, KQ 4.4) Completely open, nonproprietary bus standard for portable computers.

This standard enables users to insert credit-card-size peripheral devices, called *PC cards,* such as modems, memory cards, hard disks, sound boards, and even pagers and cellular communicators into their computers.

port (p. 128, KQ 4.4) Connecting socket on the outside of the computer system unit that is connected to an expansion board on the inside of the system unit. Types of ports include parallel, serial, video adapter, game, SCSI, and USB.

A port enables users to connect by cable or infrared signals a peripheral device such as a monitor, printer, or modem so that it can communicate with the computer system.

power supply (p. 121, KQ 4.4) Device in the computer that converts AC current from the wall outlet to the DC current the computer uses.

The power supply enables the computer (and peripheral devices) to operate.

RAM chip (p. 124, KQ 4.4) An integrated circuit that provides *random access memory;* it is mounted on a small SIMM or DIMM circuit board that is plugged into the motherboard.

Adding RAM chips speeds up a computer by keeping more software capabilities and data immediately available for the CPU to use.

random access memory (RAM) (p. 124, KQ 4.4) Also known as *main memory* or *primary storage;* type of memory that temporarily holds data and instructions needed shortly by the CPU. RAM is a volatile type of storage.

RAM is the working memory of the computer; it is the workspace into which applications programs and data are loaded and then retrieved for processing.

read-only memory (ROM) (p. 125, KQ 4.4) Also known as *firmware;* a memory chip that permanently stores instructions and data that are programmed during the chip's manufacture. ROM is a nonvolatile form of storage.

ROM chips are used to store special basic instructions for computer operations such as those that start the computer or put characters on the screen.

reduced instruction set computing (RISC) (p. 123, KQ 4.4) Type of design in which the complexity of a microprocessor is reduced by reducing the amount of superfluous or redundant instructions.

With RISC chips, a computer system gets along with fewer instructions than those required in conventional computer systems. RISC-equipped workstations work up to 10 times faster than conventional workstations.

register (p. 116, KQ 4.2) High-speed circuit that is a staging area for temporarily storing data during processing.

The computer loads the program instructions and data from the main memory into the staging areas of the registers just prior to processing.

serial port (p. 128, KQ 4.4) Also known as *RS-232 port;* external electrical socket on the system unit that allows a serial device, which transmits 1 bit at a time, to be connected to an internal board.

Serial ports are used principally for connecting communications lines, modems, and mice to microcomputers.

single inline memory module (SIMM) (p. 124, KQ 4.4) Small circuit board plugged into the motherboard that carries RAM chips on one side.

A SIMM's RAM chips can be used to increase a computer's main memory capacity.

small computer system interface (SCSI) port (p. 129, KQ 4.4) Pronounced "scuzzy"; an interface for transferring data at high speeds for up to 15 SCSI-compatible devices.

SCSI ports are used to connect external hard-disk drives, magnetic-tape backup units, scanners, and CD-ROM drives to the computer system.

system clock (p. 117, KQ 4.2) Internal timing device that uses a quartz crystal to generate a uniform electrical frequency from which digital pulses are created.

The system clock controls the speed of all operations within a computer. The faster the clock, the faster the processing.

system unit (p. 121, KQ 4.4) The box or cabinet that contains the electrical components that do the computer's processing; usually includes processing components, RAM chips (main memory), ROM chips (read-only memory), power supply, expansion slots, and disk drives but not keyboard, printer, or often even the display screen.

The system unit protects many important processing and storage components.

What It Is/What It Does

terabyte (p. 119, KQ 4.3) Approximately 1 trillion bytes (1,009,511,627,776 bytes); a measure of capacity.

transistor (p. 113, KQ 4.1) Semiconducting device that acts as a tiny electrically operated switch, switching between "on" and "off" many millions of times per second.

Unicode (p. 120, KQ 4.3) A binary coding scheme that uses 2 bytes (16 bits) for each character, rather than 1 byte (8 bits), providing 65,536 possible characters that could represent almost all the written languages of the world.

Universal Serial Bus (USB) (p. 129, KQ 4.4) Allows up to 127 peripherals to be connected through just one general-purpose port. The USB connecting the port inside the computer will interpret the signals from each peripheral device and tell the computer to recognize it.

video adapter port (p. 128, KQ 4.4) Electrical socket that connects the video display monitor outside the computer to the video adapter card inside the system unit.

video memory (p. 125, KQ 4.4) Video RAM (VRAM) chips are used to store display images for the monitor.

volatile storage (p. 116, KQ 4.2) Temporary storage, as in main memory (RAM).

word (p. 115, KQ 4.2) Also called *bit number;* group of bits that may be manipulated or stored at one time by the CPU.

Why It's Important

Some forms of mass storage, or secondary storage for mainframes and supercomputers, are expressed in terabytes.

Transistors act as electronic switches in computers. They are more reliable and consume less energy than their predecessors, electronic vacuum tubes.

Because Unicode can provide character sets for Chinese, Japanese, and other languages that don't use the Roman alphabet, it is likely to become the standard code, though the need to convert existing software applications and databases will make the change a slow one.

The user can easily connect printers, modems, mice, keyboards, and CD-ROM drives in a daisy-chain style without worrying about adding ports.

The video adapter port enables users to have different kinds of monitors, some having higher resolution and more colors than others.

The amount of video memory determines how fast images appear and how many colors are available on the display screen. Video memory chips are useful for programs displaying lots of graphics.

The contents of volatile storage are lost when power to the computer is turned off.

Often the more bits in a word, the faster the computer. An 8-bit-word computer will transfer data within each CPU chip in 8-bit chunks. A 32-bit-word computer is faster, transferring data in 32-bit chunks.

Exercises

Self-Test

1. A(n) _____ bit is an extra bit attached to a byte for purposes of checking for accuracy.

2. _____ is a binary programming language that the computer can run directly.

3. The _____ is often referred to as the *brain* of the computer.

4. The _____ controls how fast the operations within a computer take place. (system clock)

5. A(n) _____ is about 1,000 bytes (1,024) bytes.

   A(n) _____ is about 1 million bytes (1,048,576 bytes).

   A(n) _____ is about 1 billion bytes (1,073,741,824 bytes).

Short-Answer Questions

1. What is the function of the ALU in a microcomputer system?

2. What is the purpose of a parity scheme? How does it work?

3. What is the function of registers in a computer system?

4. List at least five electrical components commonly found in a microcomputer's system unit.

5. Why is it important that your computer be expandable?

Multiple-Choice Questions

1. Which of the following are used to hold data and instructions that will be used shortly by the CPU?
   a. RAM chips
   b. ROM chips
   c. peripheral devices
   d. cache memory
   e. All of the above

2. Which of the following coding schemes is widely used on microcomputers?
   a. ASCII-8
   b. Unicode
   c. Microcode
   d. All of the above

3. Which of the following is accessed when you switch on your computer?
   a. RAM chip
   b. ROM chip
   c. coprocessor chip
   d. microprocessor chip
   e. All of the above

4. Which of the following can be used in portable computers to replace the hard disk?
   a. cache memory
   b. video RAM
   c. flash memory
   d. ROM
   e. None of the above

5. Which of the following is used to measure processing speeds in supercomputers?
   a. megahertz
   b. MIPS
   c. flops
   d. picoseconds
   e. None of the above

True/False Questions

T F 1. Microcomputer processing speeds are usually measured in MIPS.

T F 2. The machine cycle is composed of the instruction cycle and execution cycle.

T F 3. Computer programmers write in programming languages that resemble machine language.

T F 4. Today's microprocessors have more transistors than those in the 1970s.

T F 5. Main memory is nonvolatile.

Knowledge in Action

1. Describe the latest microprocessor chip released by Intel. Who are the intended users of this chip? How is this chip better than its predecessor? Perform your research using current computer magazines and periodicals and/or the Internet.

2. Develop a binary system of your own (use any two states, objects, or conditions) and encode the following: I am a rocket scientist.

3. Look through some computer magazines and identify advertised microcomputer systems. Decide what microcomputer might be the best one for you to use based on your processing requirements (if necessary, pick a hypothetical job and identify some probable processing requirements). Describe the microcomputer you would choose and why. Compare this microcomputer to others you saw advertised using the following categories: (a) name and brand of computer, (b) microprocessor model, (c) RAM capacity, (d) availability of cache memory, and (f) cost.

4. Look through several computer magazines and list all the coprocessor chips and add-on boards mentioned. Next to each listed item, write down what it does and what type of computer system it's compatible with. Then, note an application (task) for which each item could be useful.

Input & Output

Taking Charge of Computing & Communications

've talked to people who've been separated for years but didn't get divorced because they couldn't afford an attorney," says Heather Fisher, a spokeswoman for Utah's QuickCourt. "They're really excited about this."[1]

Coca-Cola kiosk at a trade fair

What they're excited about, according to Fisher, are particular kinds of electronic kiosks that are designed to help people in filling out paperwork for no-fault divorces. With these machines, which QuickCourt makes and sells to state governments, people can get officially unmarried quickly and inexpensively.

Whatever you may think of the idea of the high-tech divorce, it's clear that the ATM, long a standby for people needing fast cash during evenings and weekends, is growing up. Across the United States, the new generation of kiosks is being used by governments to enable people not only to learn about tourist attractions and bus routes but also to get vehicle license plates, garage-sale permits, and information on property taxes. These super-ATMs also have commercial uses, not only doling out $20 bills, but selling stamps, printing out checks, and making movie and plane tickets available.[2,3] Says one report, "They work 24 hours a day and never demand overtime. They're never in a surly mood. Though occasionally they run out of paper."[4]

The kiosk is an example of a device that presents the two faces of the computer that are important to humans: that is, it allows you to *input* data and to *output* information. In this chapter, we discuss what the principal input and output devices are and how you can make use of them.

5.1   Input Hardware

KEY QUESTION

What are the three general types of input hardware?

Preview & Review: Input hardware devices are classified as three types: keyboards, pointing devices, and source data-entry devices.

***Input hardware* consists of devices that translate data into a form the computer can process.** The people-readable form may be words like the ones in these sentences, but the computer-readable form consists of 0s and 1s, or off and on electrical signals.

Input hardware devices are categorized as three types: *keyboards, pointing devices,* and *source data-entry devices.* (■ *See Panel 5.1.*)

Keyboards

In a computer, a ***keyboard* is a device that converts letters, numbers, and other characters into electrical signals that are machine-readable by the computer's processor.** The keyboard may look like a typewriter keyboard with which some special keys have been added. Or it may look like the keys on a bank ATM or the keypad of a pocket computer. Or it may even be a Touch-Tone phone, network computer, or cable-TV set-top box.

Pointing Devices

***Pointing devices* control the position of the cursor or pointer on the screen.** Pointing devices include *mice, trackballs, pointing sticks,* and *touchpads; light pens; digitizing tablets;* and *pen-based systems.*

■ PANEL 5.1

Summary of input devices

CATEGORIES OF INPUT HARDWARE		
KEYBOARD HARDWARE	**POINTING DEVICES**	**SOURCE DATA–ENTRY**

Keyboards
Touch-Tone devices
Set-top boxes
	Mice, trackballs,
	  pointing sticks,
	  touchpads
	Light pens
	Digitizing tablets
	Pen computers
		Scanning devices
		Bar-code readers
		Mark- and character-
		  recognition devices
		Fax machines
		Imaging systems

		Other input devices Audio-input devices Video-input devices Digital cameras Sensors Radio-frequency identification Voice recognition systems Human-biology devices

Source Data-Entry Devices

Source data-entry devices refer to the many forms of data-entry devices that are not keyboards or pointing devices. **Source data-entry devices create machine-readable data on magnetic media or paper or feed it directly into the computer's processor.** Source data-entry devices include *scanning devices, sensors, audio-input devices, voice-recognition systems, video-input devices, electronic cameras,* and *human-biology input devices.*

Quite often a computer system will combine keyboard, pointing devices, and source data-entry devices. In the next sections we discuss the three types of input hardware in more detail.

5.2 Keyboard Input

KEY QUESTION

What are the different types of keyboard hardware?

Preview & Review: Keyboard-type devices include computer keyboards, Touch-Tone devices, and cable-TV set-top boxes.

Even if you aren't a ten-finger touch typist, you can use a keyboard. Yale University computer scientist David Gelernter, for instance, lost the use of his right hand and right eye in a mail bombing by the Unabomber. However, he expressed not only gratitude at being alive but also recognition that he could continue to use a keyboard even with his limitations. "In the final analysis," he wrote in an online message to colleagues, "one decent typing hand and an intact head is all you really need. . . ."[5]

Here we describe the following keyboard-type devices: *computer keyboards, Touch-Tone devices,* and *set-top boxes.*

Computer Keyboards

Conventional computer keyboards have all the keys that typewriter keyboards have plus others unique to computers. The keyboard is built into laptop computers or attached to desktop computers with a cable. Wireless keyboards (which use an infrared signal) are available for those who find portable computer keyboards too small for efficient typing.

The illustration opposite shows keyboard functions. (■ *See Panel 5.2.*)

Touch-Tone Devices

The *Touch-Tone,* or *push-button, telephone* can be used like a dumb terminal to send data to a computer. For example, one way FedEx customers can request pickup service for their packages is by pushing buttons on their phones. Another common device is the *card dialer,* or *card reader,* used by merchants to verify credit cards over phone lines with a central computer.

Interactive TV Set-Top Boxes

If you receive television programs from a cable-TV service instead of free through the air, you may have a decoder device called a set-top box. A *set-top box* works with a keypad, such as a handheld wireless remote control, to allow cable-TV viewers to change channels or, in the case of interactive systems, to exercise other commands. What is new, however, is that set-top boxes are heading in the direction of PC/TVs (✔ p. 25), with analog and digital signals converging to offer TV with Internet access and electronic mail.

For instance, over the next few years, Tele-Communications Inc. and other big cable-TV operators plan to put in place millions of set-top boxes that will zap all kinds of digital fare to consumers. This would include additional digital TV channels, high-resolution movies, home banking services, interactive TV, e-mail, and high-speed Internet access.[6–8]

5.3 Pointing Devices

KEY QUESTION

How do the different types of pointing devices work?

Preview & Review: Pointing devices include mice, trackballs, pointing sticks, and touchpads; light pens; digitizing tablets; and pen computers.

One of the most natural of all human gestures, the act of pointing is incorporated in several kinds of input devices. The most prominent ones are the following: *mice, trackballs, pointing sticks,* and *touchpads; light pens; digitizing tablets;* and *pen-based systems.*

Mice, Trackballs, Pointing Sticks, & Touchpads

The principal pointing tools used with microcomputers are the mouse or its variants—the trackball, the pointing stick, and the touchpad.

Mouse

- Mouse: You are probably already familiar with the mouse. **A *mouse* is a device that is rolled about on a desktop and directs a pointer on the computer's display screen. The *mouse pointer* is the symbol that indicates the position of the mouse on the display screen.** It may be an arrow, a rectangle, or even a representation of a person's pointing finger. The pointer may change to the shape of an I-beam to indicate that it is a cursor and shows the place where text may be entered.

  On the bottom side of the mouse is a ball that translates the mouse movement into digital signals. On the top side are one to four buttons. The first button is used for common functions, such as clicking and dragging. The functions of the second, third, and fourth buttons are determined by whatever software you're using.

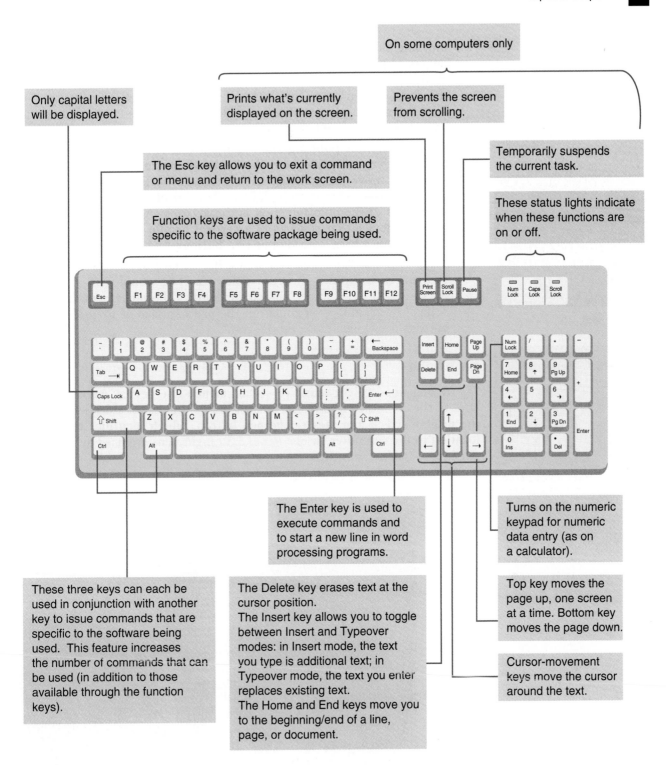

On some computers only

Only capital letters will be displayed.

Prints what's currently displayed on the screen.

Prevents the screen from scrolling.

The Esc key allows you to exit a command or menu and return to the work screen.

Temporarily suspends the current task.

These status lights indicate when these functions are on or off.

Function keys are used to issue commands specific to the software package being used.

The Enter key is used to execute commands and to start a new line in word processing programs.

Turns on the numeric keypad for numeric data entry (as on a calculator).

These three keys can each be used in conjunction with another key to issue commands that are specific to the software being used. This feature increases the number of commands that can be used (in addition to those available through the function keys).

The Delete key erases text at the cursor position.
The Insert key allows you to toggle between Insert and Typeover modes: in Insert mode, the text you type is additional text; in Typeover mode, the text you enter replaces existing text.
The Home and End keys move you to the beginning/end of a line, page, or document.

Top key moves the page up, one screen at a time. Bottom key moves the page down.

Cursor-movement keys move the cursor around the text.

■ **PANEL 5.2**

Common keyboard layout

Trackball

Pointing stick

Touchpad

- Trackball: Another form of pointing device, **the *trackball* is a movable ball, on top of a stationary device, that is rotated with fingers or palm of the hand.** In fact, the trackball looks like the mouse turned upside down. Instead of moving the mouse around on the desktop, you move the trackball with the tips of your fingers. Like the mouse, the trackball has additional buttons whose functions vary depending on the software.

- Pointing stick: **A *pointing stick* is a pointing device that looks like a pencil eraser protruding from the keyboard between the G, H, and B keys.** You move the pointing stick with your forefinger while using your thumb to press buttons located in front of the space bar. A forerunner of the pointing stick is the joystick. **A *joystick* is a pointing device that consists of a vertical handle like a gearshift lever mounted on a base with one or two buttons.**

- Touchpad: **The *touchpad* is a small, flat surface over which you slide your finger, using the same movements as you would with a mouse.** As you move your finger, the cursor follows the movement. You "click" by tapping your finger on the pad's surface or by pressing buttons positioned close by the pad.

Light Pen

The *light pen* **is a light-sensitive stylus, or pen-like device, connected by a wire to the computer terminal. The user brings the pen to a desired point on the display screen and presses the pen button, which identifies that screen location to the computer.** (■ *See Panel 5.3.*) Light pens are used by engineers, graphic designers, and illustrators.

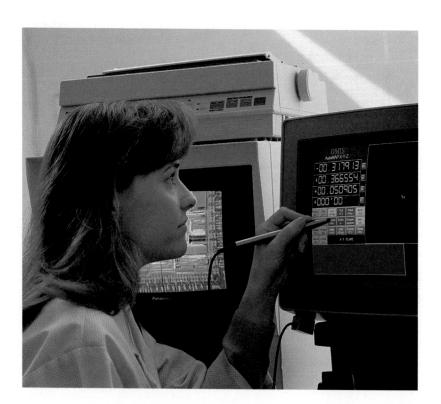

■ PANEL 5.3

Light pen

This person is using a light pen to input instructions to the computer.

■ PANEL 5.4
Digitizing tablet

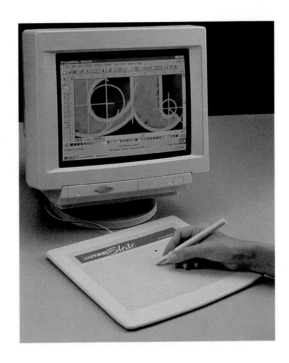

Digitizing Tablet

A *digitizing tablet* **consists of a tablet connected by a wire to a stylus or puck. A** *stylus* **is a pen-like device with which the user "sketches" an image. A** *puck* **is a copying device with which the user copies an image,** such as an architectural drawing or a civil engineering map. (■ *See Panel 5.4.)*

Digitizing tablets are used primarily in design and engineering. When used with drawing and painting software, a digitizing tablet and stylus allow you to do shading and many other effects similar to those artists achieve with pencil, pen, or charcoal. Alternatively, when you use a puck, you can trace a drawing laid on the tablet, and a digitized copy is stored in the computer.

■ PANEL 5.5

Pen-based systems
(Left) Pen-based computer with stylus and color screen. *(Right)* In some hospitals, pen-based computers are used to enter comments to patients' records.

Pen-Based Systems

In the next few years, students will be able to take notes in class without ink and paper, if pen-based computer systems evolve as Depauw University computer science professor David Berque hopes they will. ***Pen-based computer systems*** **use a pen-like stylus to allow people to enter handwriting and marks onto a computer screen rather than typing on a keyboard.** (■ *See Panel 5.5.)* Berque has developed a prototype for a system that would connect an

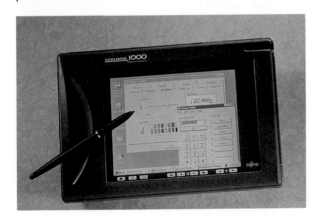

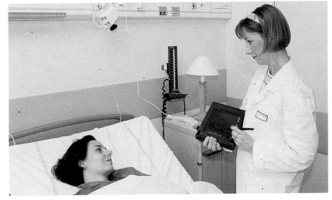

instructor's electronic "whiteboard" on the classroom wall with students' pen computers, so that students could receive notes directly, without having to copy information word for word. "The idea is that this might free the students up to allow them to think about what's going on," Berque says. "They wouldn't have to blindly copy things that maybe would distract them from what's going on."[9]

5.4 Common Hardware for Source Data-Entry: Scanner, Audio, Video, & Photographic Input

KEY QUESTIONS

What are the devices commonly used for source data-entry, and how do they work?

Preview & Review: Scanning devices include four types: bar-code readers, mark- and character-recognition devices, fax machines, and imaging systems. Mark-recognition and character-recognition devices include magnetic-ink character recognition (MICR), optical mark recognition (OMR), and optical character recognition (OCR). Fax machines may be dedicated machines or fax modems. Imaging systems convert text and images to digital form.

Audio-input devices may digitize audio sound by means of an audio board or a MIDI board.

Video-input devices may use frame-grabber or full-motion video cards.

Digital cameras use light-sensitive silicon chips to capture photographic images.

Source data-input devices do not require keystrokes in order to input data to the computer. Rather data is entered directly from the *source;* people do not need to act as typing intermediaries. In this section, we discuss common source data-entry devices. First, we cover *scanning devices—bar-code readers, mark- and character-recognition devices, fax machines,* and *imaging systems.* We then describe *audio-input devices.* Finally, we discuss *video* and *photographic input.*

Scanning Devices: Bar-Code Readers

Scanners use laser beams and reflected light to translate images of text, drawings, photos, and the like into digital form. The images can then be processed by a computer, displayed on a monitor, stored on a storage device, or communicated to another computer. Scanning devices include readers for **bar codes, the vertical zebra-striped marks you see on most manufactured retail products**—everything from candy to cosmetics to comic books. (■ *See Panel 5.6.*) In North America, supermarkets, food manufacturers, and others have agreed to use a bar-code system called the *Universal Product Code.* Other kinds of bar-code systems are used on everything from FedEx packages, to railroad cars, to the jerseys of long-distance relay runners.

Bar codes are read by **bar-code readers, photoelectric scanners that translate the bar-code symbols into digital code.** The price of a particular item is set within the store's computer and appears on the salesclerk's point-of-sale terminal and on your receipt. Records of sales are input to the store's computer and used for accounting, restocking store inventory, and weeding out products that don't sell well.

Universal Product Code bar code

Scanning Devices: Mark-Recognition & Character-Recognition Devices

There are three types of scanning devices that sense marks or characters. They are usually referred to by their abbreviations *MICR, OMR,* and *OCR.*

■ PANEL 5.6

Bar-code readers
(Left) This NCR scanner is popular with specialty and general merchandise store retailers. *(Right)* This self-checkout system includes an ATM and an NCR scanner scale. Shoppers can scan, bag, and pay for purchases without cashier assistance.

- **Magnetic-ink character recognition:** *Magnetic-ink character recognition (MICR)* **reads the strange-looking numbers printed at the bottom of checks.** MICR characters, which are printed with magnetized ink, are read by MICR equipment, producing a digitized signal. This signal is used by a bank's reader/sorter machine to sort checks.

- **Optical mark recognition:** *Optical mark recognition (OMR)* **uses a device that reads pencil marks and converts them into computer-usable form.** The most well-known example is the OMR technology used to read the College Board Scholastic Aptitude Test (SAT) and the Graduate Record Examination (GRE).

- **Optical character recognition:** *Optical character recognition (OCR)* **uses a device that reads preprinted characters in a particular font (typeface design) and converts them to digital code.** Examples of the use of OCR characters are utility bills and price tags on department-store merchandise. The wand reader is a common OCR scanning device. (■ *See Panel 5.7.*)

■ PANEL 5.7

Optical character recognition
Special typefaces can be read by a scanning device called a *wand reader*.

OCR-A	
NUMERIC	0123456789
ALPHA	ABCDEFGHIJKLMNOPQRSTUVWXYZ
SYMBOLS	>$/-+-#"

OCR-B	
NUMERIC	00123456789
ALPHA	ACENPSTVX
SYMBOLS	<+>-¥

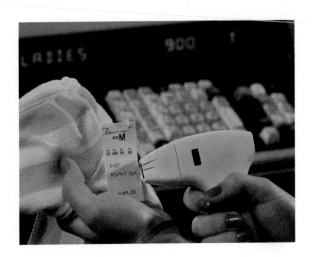

Scanning Devices: Fax Machines

A *fax machine*—or *facsimile transmission machine*—scans an image and sends it as electronic signals over telephone lines to a receiving fax machine, which re-creates the image on paper (✔ p. 22). There are two types of fax machines—*dedicated fax machines* and *fax modems.*

- Dedicated fax machines: **Dedicated fax machines** are specialized devices that do nothing except send and receive fax documents. These are what we usually mean when we say "fax machine." They are found not only in offices and homes but also alongside regular phones in public places such as airports.

- Fax modems: **A *fax modem* is installed as a circuit board inside the computer's system cabinet. It is a modem with fax capability that enables you to send signals directly from your computer to someone else's fax machine or computer fax modem.** With this device, you don't have to print out the material from your printer and then turn around and run it through the scanner on a fax machine. The fax modem allows you to send information much more quickly than if you had to feed it page by page into a machine.

  The fax modem is another feature of mobile computing, although it's more powerful as a receiving device. Fax modems are installed inside portable computers, including pocket PCs and PDAs. (■ *See Panel 5.8.*) You can also link up a cellular phone to a fax modem in your portable computer and thereby send and receive wireless fax messages no matter where you are in the world.

  The main disadvantage of a fax modem is that you cannot scan in outside documents. Thus, if you have a photo or a drawing that you want to fax to someone, you need an image scanner, as we describe next.

Scanning Devices: Imaging Systems

Anthony J. Scalise, 80, of Utica, New York, found a 1922 picture of his father and other immigrants from the Italian city of Scandale. "It was wonderful, all those people with walrus mustaches," he said. He immediately had prints made for friends and relatives. This is easy to do with the self-service Kodak imaging systems now found in many photo stores.[10]

An *imaging system*—or *image scanner* or *graphics scanner*—converts text, drawings, and photographs into digital form that can be stored in a com-

■ PANEL 5.8

PDA

This personal digital assistant not only is a notepad and address book but also can send and receive fax messages.

■ PANEL 5.9

Image scanner
Two workers at the U.S. National Research Center for the Identification of Missing Children scanning a missing child's photo into a computer.

puter system and then manipulated, output, or sent via modem to another computer. (■ *See Panel 5.9.*) The system scans each image—color or black and white—with light and breaks the image into light and dark dots or color dots, which are then converted to digital code. An example of an imaging system is the type used in desktop publishing. This device scans in artwork or photos that can then be positioned within a page of text, using desktop publishing software.

Imaging-system technology has led to a whole new art or industry called *electronic imaging*. **Electronic imaging is the software-controlled combining of separate images, using scanners, digital cameras, and advanced graphic computers.** This technology has become an important part of multimedia.

Audio-Input Devices

An *audio-input device* **records analog sound and translates it for digital storage and processing.** An analog sound signal represents a continuously variable wave within a certain frequency range (✔ p. 5). Such continuous fluctuations are usually represented with an analog device such as a cassette player. For the computer to process them, these variable waves must be converted to digital 0s and 1s. The principal use of audio-input devices is to provide digital input for multimedia computers, which incorporate text, graphics, sound, video, and animation in a single digital presentation.

There are two ways by which audio is digitized:

● **Audio board:** Analog sound from, for instance, a cassette player or a microphone goes through a special circuit board called an audio board (or card). An *audio board* is an add-on circuit board in a computer that converts analog sound to digital sound and stores it for further processing and/or plays it back, providing output directly to speakers or an external amplifier.

- **MIDI board:** A *MIDI board*—MIDI, pronounced "middie," stands for *Musical Instrument Digital Interface*—provides a standard for the interchange of musical information between musical instruments, synthesizers, and computers.

Video-Input Cards

As with sound, most film and videotape is in analog form, with the signal a continuously variable wave. To be used by a computer, the signals that come from a VCR or a camcorder must be converted to digital form through a special digitizing card—a *video-capture card*—that is installed in the computer.

Two types of video cards are frame-grabber video and full-motion video:

- **Frame-grabber video card:** Some video cards, called *frame grabbers,* can capture and digitize only a single frame at a time.
- **Full-motion video card:** Other video cards, called *full-motion video cards* or *adapters,* can convert analog to digital signals at the rate of up to 30 frames per second, giving the effect of a continuously flowing motion picture.

Digital camera

Digital Cameras

Digital cameras are particularly interesting because they foreshadow major change for the entire industry of photography. Instead of using traditional (chemical) film, **a *digital camera* uses a light-sensitive processor chip to capture photographic images in digital form on a small diskette inserted in the camera or on flash-memory chips (✔ p. 125).** The bits of digital information can then be copied right into a computer's hard disk for manipulation and printing out.

5.5 More Hardware for Source Data-Entry: Sensor, Radio-Frequency Identification, Voice, & Human-Biology Input Devices

KEY QUESTION

What are some of the more advanced devices for source data-entry?

Preview & Review: Other source data-entry devices are sensors, radio-frequency identification, voice-recognition, and human-biology input devices. Sensors collect specific kinds of data directly from the environment. Radio-frequency identification devices enable tracking. Voice-recognition systems convert human speech into digital code. Human-biology input devices include biometric systems and line-of-sight systems.

There are some even more intriguing source data-entry devices beyond those we have discussed. In this section, we describe *sensors, radio-frequency identification devices, voice-recognition devices,* and *human-biology input devices.*

Sensors

A *sensor* is a type of input device that collects specific kinds of data directly from the environment and transmits it to a computer. Although you are unlikely to see such input devices connected to a PC in an office, they exist all around us, often in nearly invisible form. Sensors can be used for detecting all kinds of things: speed, movement, weight, pressure, temperature, humidity, wind, current, fog, gas, smoke, light, shapes, images, and so on.

Besides being used to detect the speed and volume of traffic and adjust traffic lights, sensors are used on mountain highways in wintertime in the

Sierra Nevada as weather-sensing devices to tell workers when to roll out snowplows.[11] In California, sensors have been planted along major earthquake fault lines in an experiment to see whether scientists can predict major earth movements. (■ *See Panel 5.10.*) In aviation, sensors are used to detect ice buildup on airplane wings or to alert pilots to sudden changes in wind direction.

Radio-Frequency Identification Devices

***Radio-frequency identification technology,* or RF-ID tagging, consists of (1) a "tag" containing a microchip that contains code numbers that (2) can be read by the radio waves of a scanner linked to a database.** Drivers with RF-ID tags can breeze through the tollbooths without having to even roll down their windows, and the toll is charged to their accounts with the toll authority.[12] Radio-readable ID "tags" are also being used by the Postal Service to monitor the flow of mail through its system. They are being used in inventory control and warehousing. They are being used in the railroad industry to keep track of rail cars. They are even being injected into dogs and cats, so that veterinarians with the right scanning equipment can identify them if the pets become separated from their owners.[13]

Voice-Recognition Input

When you speak to a computer, can it tell whether you want it to "recognize speech" or "wreck a nice beach"? Voice-recognition systems, whereby you dictate input via a microphone, have faced considerable hurdles: different voices, pronunciations, and accents. Recently, however, the systems have measurably improved. Current accuracy rates are at about 90–95%.

A ***voice-recognition system,* using a microphone (or a telephone) as an input device, converts a person's speech into digital code by comparing the electrical patterns produced by the speaker's voice with a set of prerecorded patterns stored in the computer.**

Voice-recognition systems are finding many uses. Warehouse workers are able to speed inventory-taking by recording inventory counts verbally. Traders on stock exchanges can communicate their trades by speaking to computers. Radiologists can dictate their interpretations of X-rays directly into transcription machines. Nurses can fill out patient charts by talking to a computer. Speakers of Chinese can speak to machines that will print out Chinese characters. (■ *See Panel 5.11, next page.*) Indeed, for many disabled individuals, a computer isn't so much a luxury or a simple productivity tool as it is a necessity. It provides freedom of expression, independence, and empowerment.

Human-Biology Input Devices

Characteristics and movements of the human body, when interpreted by sensors, optical scanners, voice recognition, and other technologies, can become forms of input. Some examples:

● Biometric systems: **Biometrics is the science of measuring individual body characteristics.** *Biometric security devices* identify a person through a fingerprint, voice intonation, or other biological characteristic. For example, retinal-identification devices use a ray of light to identify the distinctive network of blood vessels at the back of one's eyeball.

■ PANEL 5.10

Earthquake sensor
Sensor instruments of a telemetered weak motion seismic station (earthquake motion detection)

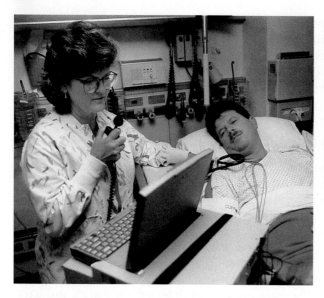

■ PANEL 5.11

Voice-recognition technology

(Left) A registered nurse tests a voice-recognition system designed to help fill out patient charts. *(Right)* Taiwanese scientist Lee Lin-shan displays a computer that can listen to continuous speech in Chinese (Mandarin) and then print out the words at the rate of three characters a second.

- **Line-of-sight systems:** *Line-of-sight systems* enable a person to use his or her eyes to "point" at the screen, a technology that allows some physically disabled users to direct a computer. For example, the Eyegaze System from LC Technologies allows you to operate a computer by focusing on particular areas of a display screen. A camera mounted on the computer analyzes the point of focus of the eye to determine where you are looking. You operate the computer by looking at icons on the screen and "press a key" by looking at one spot for a specified period of time.

5.6 Output Hardware

KEY QUESTION

What is the difference between softcopy and hardcopy output?

Preview & Review: Output devices translate information processed by the computer into a form that humans can understand. The two principal kinds of output are softcopy, such as material shown on a display screen, and hardcopy, which is printed.

Output devices include display screens; printers, plotters, and multifunction devices; devices to output sound, voice, and video; virtual reality; and robots.

The principal kinds of output are *softcopy* and *hardcopy*. (■ *See Panel 5.12.*)

- **Softcopy:** *Softcopy* **refers to data that is shown on a display screen or is in audio or voice form.** This kind of output is not tangible; it cannot be touched.

- **Hardcopy:** *Hardcopy* **refers to printed output.** The principal examples are printouts, whether text or graphics, from printers. Film, including microfilm and microfiche, is also considered hardcopy output.

■ PANEL 5.12
Summary of output devices

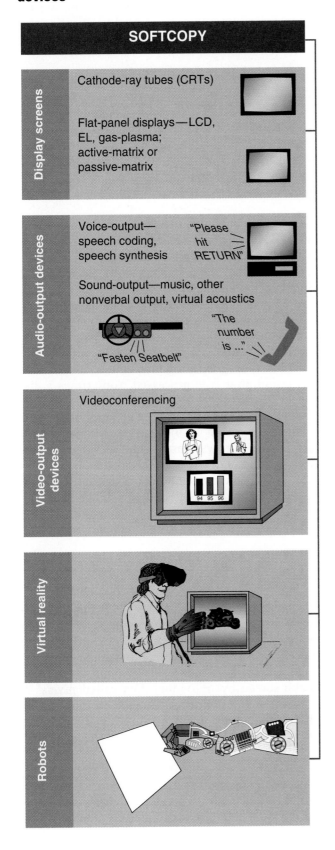

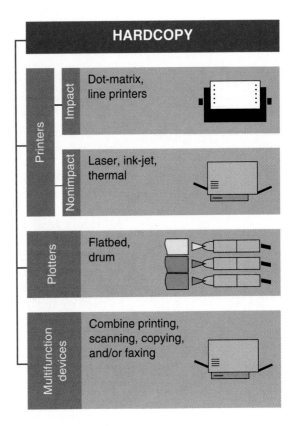

	SOFTCOPY
Display screens	Cathode-ray tubes (CRTs)
	Flat-panel displays—LCD, EL, gas-plasma; active-matrix or passive-matrix
Audio-output devices	Voice-output—speech coding, speech synthesis "Please hit RETURN"
	Sound-output—music, other nonverbal output, virtual acoustics "Fasten Seatbelt" "The number is ..."
Video-output devices	Videoconferencing
Virtual reality	
Robots	

	HARDCOPY	
Printers	**Impact**	Dot-matrix, line printers
	Nonimpact	Laser, ink-jet, thermal
Plotters		Flatbed, drum
Multifunction devices		Combine printing, scanning, copying, and/or faxing

There are several types of output devices. In the following three sections, we discuss, first, *softcopy hardware—display screens*; second, *hardcopy hardware—printers, plotters, multifunction devices*, and *microfilm* and *microfiche devices*; and, third, *other output hardware—sound-output devices, voice-output devices, video-output devices, virtual-reality devices*, and *robots*.

5.7 Softcopy Output: Display Screens

KEY QUESTION

What are the different types of display screens and video display adapters?

Preview & Review: Display screens are either CRT (cathode-ray tube) or flat-panel display. CRTs use a vacuum tube like that in a TV set. Flat-panel displays are thinner, weigh less, and consume less power than CRTs, but only recently have some LCD screens become as clear as CRT screens. The principal flat-panel displays are liquid crystal display (LCD), electroluminescent (EL) display, and gas-plasma display.

Various video display adapters allow various kinds of resolution and colors.

All things great and small—we are now at the point where we can have both in computer displays. Fujitsu has developed a hang-on-the-wall monitor that measures 42 inches corner to corner but is only 4 inches thick.[14] Kopin Corporation is making a screen that is a mere ¼ inch diagonally, so tiny (less than the diameter of a dime) that a lens must be included; the device may be used to display Web pages in cellular phones.[15] Display screens are among the principal windows of information technology. As more and more refinements are made, we can expect to see them adapted to many innovative uses.

Display screens—also variously called *monitors*, *CRTs*, or simply *screens*—are output devices that show programming instructions and data as they are being input and information after it is processed. Sometimes a display screen is also referred to as a *VDT*, for *video display terminal*, although technically a VDT includes both screen and keyboard. The size of a screen is measured diagonally from corner to corner in inches, just like television screens. For terminals on large computer systems and for desktop microcomputers, 14- to 17-inch screens are a standard size, although 19- and 21-inch screens are not uncommon. Notebook and subnotebook computers have screens ranging from 6.1 inches to 14.4 inches, with 11.3 and 12.1 inches the two most popular in-between sizes.

Display screens are of two types: *cathode-ray tubes* and *flat-panel displays*.

Cathode-Ray Tubes (CRTs)

The most common form of display screen is the CRT. **A *CRT*, for *cathode-ray tube*, is a vacuum tube used as a display screen in a computer or video display terminal.** This same kind of technology is found not only in the screens of desktop computers but also in television sets and flight-information monitors in airports.

Images are represented on the screen by individual dots called *pixels*. **A *pixel*, for "picture element," is the smallest unit on the screen that can be turned on and off or made different shades.**

Flat-Panel Displays

If CRTs were the only existing technology for computer screens, we would still be carrying around 25-pound "luggables" instead of lightweight notebooks, subnotebooks, and pocket PCs. CRTs provide bright, clear images, but they add weight and consume space and power.

Compared to CRTs, flat-panel displays are much thinner, weigh less, and consume less power. Thus, they are better for portable computers, although they are becoming available for desktop computers as well. ***Flat-panel displays* are made up of two plates of glass with a substance in between them, which is activated in different ways.**

Flat-panel displays are distinguished in two ways: (1) by the substance between the plates of glass and (2) by the arrangement of the transistors in the screens.

- **Substances between plates—LCD, EL, and gas plasma:** The types of technology used in flat-panel display are *liquid crystal display, electroluminescent display,* and *gas-plasma display.* (■ *See Panel 5.13.)*

    ***Liquid crystal display (LCD)* consists of a substance called *liquid crystal*, the molecules of which line up in a way that alters their optical properties. As a result, light—usually backlighting behind the screen—is blocked or allowed through to create an image.**

    ***Electroluminescent (EL) display* contains a substance that glows when it is charged by an electric current.** A pixel is formed on the screen when current is sent to the intersection of the appropriate row and column. The combined voltages from the row and column cause the screen to glow at that point.

    ***Gas-plasma display* is like a neon bulb, in which the display uses a gas that emits light in the presence of an electric current.** That is, the technology uses predominantly neon gas and electrodes above and below the gas. When electric current passes between the electrodes, the gas glows. Although gas-plasma technology has high resolution, it is expensive. The 42-inch Fujitsu hang-on-the-wall display mentioned above uses gas-plasma display technology.

- **Arrangements of transistors—active-matrix or passive-matrix:** Flat-panel screens are either active-matrix or passive-matrix displays, according to where their transistors are located.

■PANEL 5.13

Flat-panel displays
(Left) Active-matrix LCD, Planar System's CleanScreen compact computer for hospital information systems. *(Top right)* Planar EL screen. *(Bottom right)* Fujitsu 42-inch QFTV gas-plasma display.

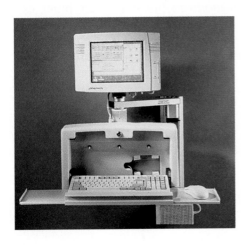

In an *active-matrix display,* **each pixel on the screen is controlled by its own transistor.** Active-matrix screens are much brighter and sharper than passive-matrix screens, but they are more complicated and thus more expensive.

In a *passive-matrix display,* **a transistor controls a whole row or column of pixels.** Passive matrix provides a sharp image for one-color (monochrome) screens but is more subdued for color. The advantage is that passive-matrix displays are less expensive and use less power than active-matrix displays.

Screen Clarity

Whether CRT or flat-panel display, screen clarity depends on three qualities: *resolution, dot pitch,* and *refresh rate.*

- Resolution: **The image sharpness of a display screen is called its *resolution;* the more pixels there are per square inch, the finer the level of detail attained.** Resolution is expressed in terms of the formula *horizontal pixels × vertical pixels.* Each pixel can be assigned a color or a particular shade of gray. Thus, a screen with 640 × 480 pixels multiplied together equals 307,200 pixels. This screen will be less clear and sharp than a screen with 800 × 600 (equals 480,000) or 1024 × 768 (equals 786,432) pixels.

- Dot pitch: **Dot pitch is the amount of space between the centers of adjacent pixels; the closer the dots, the crisper the image.** A .28 dot pitch, for instance, means dots are 28/100ths of a millimeter apart. Generally, a dot pitch of less than .31 will provide clear images. Multimedia and desktop-publishing users typically use .25-millimeter dot-pitch monitors.

- Refresh rate: *Refresh rate* is the number of times per second that the pixels are recharged so that their glow remains bright. Refresh is necessary because the phosphors hold their glow for just a fraction of a second. The higher the refresh rate, the more solid the image looks on the screen—that is, doesn't flicker. In general, displays are refreshed 45–100 times per second.

Monochrome Versus Color Screens

Display screens can be either monochrome or color. *Monochrome display screens* display only one color on a background. Although they are dying out, you may encounter them in text-based mainframe systems.

Color display screens, also called *RGB monitors* (for red, green, blue), can display between 16 colors and 16.7 million colors, depending on the type. Most software today is developed for color, and—except for some pocket PCs—most microcomputers today are sold with color display screens.

Bitmapped Displays: Both Text & Graphics Capability

At one time, computers could display only text. Today's computers can display both text and graphics—that is, not only letters and numbers but also charts, graphs, drawings, and icons. This is because PCs now use bitmapping as a standard.

The computer uses bits (0s and 1s) to describe each pixel's color and position. On monochrome displays, one bit represents one pixel on the screen. On color displays, several bits represent one pixel. ***Bitmapped display* screens**

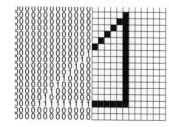

Bitmapping

permit **the computer to manipulate pixels on the screen individually,** enabling software to create a greater variety of images.

Video Display Adapters

To display graphics, a display screen must have a video display adapter. **A *video display adapter,* also called a *video graphics card,* is a circuit board that determines the resolution, number of colors, and speed with which images appear on the display screen.** Video display adapters come with their own memory chips (RAM, or *VRAM,* for *video RAM*), which determine how fast the card processes images, the resolution of the images displayed, and how many colors it can display. At a resolution of 640 × 480, a video display adapter with 256 kilobytes of memory will provide 16 colors; one with 1 megabyte will support 16.7 million colors.

In notebook computers, the video display adapter is built into the motherboard (✔ p. 121); in desktop computers, it is an expansion card that plugs into an expansion slot (✔ p. 127). Video display adapters embody certain standards. Today's microcomputer monitors commonly use VGA and SVGA standards.

- VGA: ***VGA,* for *Video Graphics Array,* will support 16–256 colors, depending on resolution.** At 320 × 200 pixels it will support 256 colors; at the sharper resolution of 640 × 480 pixels it will support 16 colors. VGA is called *4-bit color.*

- SVGA: ***SVGA,* for *Super Video Graphics Array,* will support 256 colors at higher resolution than VGA.** SVGA has two graphics modes: 800 × 600 pixels and 1024 × 768. SVGA is called *8-bit color.*

- XGA: Also referred to as *high-resolution display,* ***XGA,* for *Extended Graphics Array,* supports up to 16.7 million colors at a resolution of 1024 × 768 pixels.** Depending on the video display adapter memory chip, XGA will support 256, 65,536, or 16,777,216 colors. At its highest quality, XGA is called *24-bit color* or *true color.*

For any of these displays to work, video display adapters and monitors must be compatible. Your computer's software and the video display adapter must also be compatible. Thus, if you are changing your monitor or your video display adapter, be sure the new one will still work with the old equipment.

5.8 Hardcopy Output: Printers, Plotters, Multifunction Devices, & Microfilm & Microfiche Devices

KEY QUESTION

What are the different types of hardcopy output devices?

Preview & Review: Printers, plotters, and multifunction devices produce printed text or images on paper.

Printers may be desktop or portable, impact or nonimpact. The most common impact printers are dot-matrix printers. Nonimpact printers include laser, ink-jet, and thermal printers.

Plotters are flatbed or drum.

Multifunction devices combine capabilities such as printing, scanning, copying, and faxing.

Computer output microfilm and microfiche can solve storage problems.

A *printer* is an output device that prints characters, symbols, and perhaps graphics on paper or another hardcopy medium. Printers are categorized according to whether or not the image produced is formed by physical contact of the print mechanism with the paper. *Impact printers* do have contact; *nonimpact printers* do not.

Impact Printers

An *impact printer* **forms characters or images by striking a mechanism such as a print hammer or wheel against an inked ribbon, leaving an image on paper.** You may come in contact with one of the many dot-matrix impact printers that are still around. **A *dot-matrix printer* contains a print head of small pins, which strike an inked ribbon against paper, forming characters or images.** Print heads are available with 9, 18, or 24 pins, with the 24-pin head offering the best quality. Dot-matrix printers can print *draft quality*, a coarser-looking 72 dots per inch vertically, or *near-letter-quality (NLQ)*, a crisper-looking 144 dots per inch vertically. The machines print between 40 and 300 characters per second and print graphics as well as text. However, they are noisy.

Nonimpact Printers

Nonimpact printers are faster and quieter than impact printers because they have fewer moving parts. **Nonimpact printers form characters and images without making direct physical contact between printing mechanism and paper.** Two types of nonimpact printers often used with microcomputers are *laser printers* and *ink-jet printers*. A third kind, the *thermal printer*, is seen less frequently, except with ultraportable printers.

- Laser printer: Similar to a photocopying machine, **a *laser printer* uses the principle of dot-matrix printers of creating images with dots. These images are created on a drum, treated with a magnetically charged ink-like toner (powder), and then transferred from drum to paper.** (■ *See Panel 5.14.*)

    There are good reasons that laser printers are one of the most common types of nonimpact printer. They produce sharp, crisp images of both text and graphics. They are quiet and fast, able to

■ PANEL 5.14

Laser printer
A small laser beam is bounced off a mirror millions of times per second onto a positively charged drum. The spots where the laser beam hits become neutralized, enabling a special toner (powder) to stick to them and then print out on paper. The drum is then recharged for the next cycle.

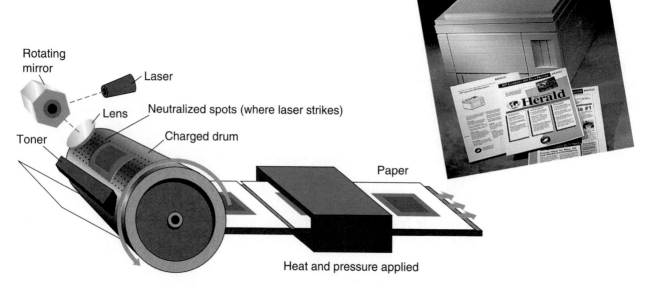

Rotating mirror
Laser
Lens
Neutralized spots (where laser strikes)
Toner
Charged drum
Paper
Heat and pressure applied

print 4–32 text-only pages per minute for individual microcomputers and up to 200 pages per minute for mainframes. They can print in different *fonts*—that is, type styles and sizes. The more expensive models can print in different colors.

To be able to manage graphics and complex page design, a laser printer works with a page description language. **A *page description language* is software that describes the shape and position of characters and graphics to the printer.** PostScript (from Adobe Systems) is one common type of page description language; Hewlett-Packard Graphic Language (HPGL) is another.

- **Ink-jet printer:** Like laser and dot-matrix printers, ink-jet printers also form images with little dots. ***Ink-jet printers* spray small, electrically charged droplets of ink from four nozzles through holes in a matrix at high speed onto paper.** (■ *See Panel 5.15.*)

  The advantages of ink-jet printers are that they can print in color, are quieter, and are much less expensive than color laser printers. The disadvantages are that they print in a somewhat lower resolution than laser printers and they are slower. Printing a document with high-resolution color graphics can take as long as 10 minutes or more for a single page.

- **Thermal printer:** For people who want the highest-quality color printing available with a desktop printer, thermal printers are the answer. ***Thermal printers* use colored waxes and heat to produce images by burning dots onto special paper.** The colored wax sheets

■ PANEL 5.15

Ink-jet printer operations

❶ Four removable ink cartridges are attached to print heads with 64 firing chambers and nozzles apiece.

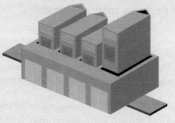

❷ As the print heads move back and forth across the page, software instructs them where to apply dots of ink, what colors to use, and in what quantity.

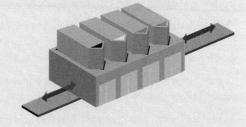

❸ To follow those instructions, the printer sends electrical pulses to thin resistors at the base of the firing chambers behind each nozzle.

Resistor
Vapor bubble
Ink

❹ The resistor heats a thin layer of ink, which in turn forms a vapor bubble. That expansion forces ink through the nozzle and onto the paper at a rate of about 6,000 dots per second.

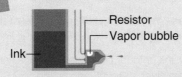

❺ A matrix of dots forms characters and pictures. Colors are created by layering multiple color dots in varying densities.

are not required for black-and-white output. However, thermal printers are expensive, and they require expensive paper.

Black & White Versus Color Printers

Today prices have plummeted for laser and ink-jet printers, so that the cheap but noisy dot-matrix printer may well be going the way of the black-and-white TV set. Your choice in printers may come down to how much you print and whether you need color.

Lasers, which print a page at a time, can handle thousands of black-and-white pages a month. Moreover, compared to ink-jets, laser printers are faster and crisper (though not by much) at printing black-and-white copies and a cent or two cheaper per page. Finally, a freshly printed page from a laser won't smear, as one from an ink-jet might.

Ink-jets, which spray ink onto the page a line at a time, can give you both high-quality black-and-white text and high-quality color graphics. The rock-bottom price for ink-jets is only about $150, although if you print a lot of color, you'll find color ink-jets much slower and more expensive to operate than color laser printers. Still, the initial cost of a color ink-jet printer is considerably less than a color laser printer.

Some questions to consider when choosing a printer for a microcomputer are given in the box below. (■ *See Panel 5.16.*)

Plotters

A *plotter* is a specialized output device designed to produce high-quality graphics in a variety of colors. Plotters are especially useful for creating maps

■ PANEL 5.16

Questions to consider when choosing a printer for a microcomputer

Do I need color, or will black-only do? Are you mainly printing text or will you need to produce color charts and illustrations (and, if so, how often)? If you print lots of black text, consider getting a laser printer. If you might occasionally print color, get an ink-jet that will accept cartridges for both black and color.

Do I have other special output requirements? Do you need to print envelopes or labels? special fonts (type styles)? multiple copies? transparencies or on heavy stock? Find out if the printer comes with envelope feeders, sheet feeders holding at least 100 sheets, or whatever will meet your requirements.

Is the printer easy to set up? Can you easily put the unit together, plug in the hardware, and adjust the software (the "driver" programs) to make the printer work with your computer?

Is the printer easy to operate? Can you add paper, replace ink/toner cartridges or ribbons, and otherwise operate the printer without much difficulty?

Does the printer provide the speed and quality I want? Will the machine print at least three pages a minute of black text and two pages a minute of color? Are the blacks dark enough and the colors vivid enough?

Will I get a reasonable cost per page? Special paper, ink or toner cartridges (especially color), and ribbons are all ongoing costs. Ink-jet color cartridges, for example, may last 100–500 pages and cost $25–$30 new. Laser toner cartridges are cheaper. Ribbons for dot-matrix printers are cheaper still. Ask the seller what the cost per page works out to.

Does the manufacturer offer a good warranty and good telephone technical support? Find out if the warranty lasts at least 2 years. See if the printer's manufacturer offers telephone support in case you have technical problems. The best support systems offer toll-free numbers and operate evenings and weekends as well as weekdays.

Plotter

and architectural drawings, although they may also produce less complicated charts and graphs.

The two principal kinds of plotters are *flatbed* and *drum.*

- Flatbed plotter: **A *flatbed plotter* is designed so that paper lies flat on a table-like surface.** The size of the bed determines the maximum size of the sheet of paper. Under computer control, between one and four color pens move across the paper, and the paper moves beneath the pens.

- Drum plotter: **A *drum plotter* works like a flatbed plotter except that the paper is output over a drum,** enabling continuous output that is useful, for example, to track earthquake activity.

Multifunction Printer Technology: Printers That Do More Than Print

Multifunction devices **combine several capabilities, such as printing, scanning, copying, and faxing, all in one device.** (■ *See Panel 5.17.*) Both Xerox and Hewlett-Packard make machines that combine four pieces of office equipment in one—photocopier, fax machine, scanner, and laser printer. By doing the work of four separate office machines at a price below the combined cost of buying these devices separately, the multifunction machine offers budgetary and space advantages.

Computer Output Microfilm & Microfiche

If you take your time getting rid of old newspapers, you know it doesn't take long for them to pile up—and to take up space. No wonder, then, that libraries try to put newspaper back issues on microfilm or microfiche. One ounce of microfilm can store the equivalent of 10 pounds of paper.

Computer output microfilm **is computer output produced as tiny images on rolls of microfilm; microfiche uses sheets instead of rolls.** The images are up to 48 times smaller than those produced on a printer. The principal disadvantage, however, is that a microfilm or microfiche reader is needed to read this type of output.

■ **PANEL 5.17**

The multifunction device
This machine combines four functions in one—printer, copier, fax machine, and scanner.

The Paper Glut: Whither the "Paperless Office"?

Supposedly, computers were going to make the use of paper obsolete, providing us with "the paperless office." Has this happened? Not exactly. In 1996, the average American used 213 pounds of paper—double the amount in 1966. Says *Newsweek* economics writer Robert J. Samuelson, "the more high-tech we become, the more low-tech paper we use."[16]

Why don't we simply leave information in electronic form, as on a 3½-inch diskette, holding the equivalent of 240 sheets of paper? "People like to hold paper; they like printouts," says Stanford University professor Clifford Nass, who studies social patterns and technology. "If the information exists only in the computer, where is it? You can't tell people it's being stored as a bunch of ones and zeros. They want to touch it."[17]

We make printouts because we are afraid "anything can happen to a computer." Moreover, we get physical comfort from handling paper, from marking it up with colored pens, and from filing it away. As a result, however, there has been a paper explosion such as the world has never seen.

5.9 More Output Devices: Audio, Video, Virtual Reality, & Robots

KEY QUESTION

How do audio, video, virtual reality, and robots operate?

Preview & Review: Other output hardware includes devices for sound output, voice output, and video output; virtual-reality and simulation devices; and robots.

Sound output includes music and other nonverbal sounds. Voice-output technology uses speech-synthesis devices that convert digital data into speech-like sounds.

Video output includes videoconferencing.

Virtual reality is a kind of computer-generated artificial reality.

Robots perform functions ordinarily ascribed to human beings.

How long until speech robots call you during the dinner hour and use charming voices to get you to part with a charitable donation through your credit card? Perhaps sooner than you think. Already University of Iowa scientists have created a computer program and audio output that simulates 90% of the acoustic properties made by one man's voice. "What we have now are extremely human-like speech sounds," says Brad H. Story, the lead researcher and also the volunteer whose vocal tract was analyzed and simulated. "We can produce vowels and consonants in isolation." A harder task, still to be accomplished, is to recreate the transitions between key linguistic sounds—what researchers call "running speech."[18]

Voice output is only one of the many other forms of output technology that remain to be discussed. In this section, we describe *sound-output devices, voice-output devices, video-output devices, virtual-reality devices,* and *robots.*

Sound-Output Devices

***Sound-output devices* produce digitized sounds, ranging from beeps and chirps to music.** All these sounds are nonverbal. PC owners can customize their machines to greet each new program with the sound of breaking glass or to moo like a cow every hour. Or they can make their computers issue the distinctive sounds available (from the book-disk combination *Cool Mac Sounds*) under the titles "Arrgh!!!" or "B-Movie Scream." To exercise these possibilities, you need both the necessary software and sound card, or digital audio circuit board (such as Sound Blaster). The sound card plugs into an expansion slot in your computer; on newer computers, it is integrated with the motherboard. A sound card is also required in making computerized music.

Voice-Output Devices

***Voice-output,* or *speech-synthesis,* devices convert digital data into speech-like sounds.** You hear such forms of voice output on telephones ("Please hang up and dial your call again"), in soft-drink machines, in cars, in toys and games, and recently in mapping software for vehicle-navigation devices.

Some uses of speech output are simply frivolous or amusing. You can replace your computer start-up beep with the sound of James Brown screaming "I feel gooooooood!" But some uses are quite serious. For people with physical disabilities, computers help to level the playing field.

Video-Output Devices

Want to have a meeting with someone across the country and go over some documents—without having to go there? ***Videoconferencing* is a method whereby people in different geographical locations can have a meeting—and see and hear one another—using computers and communications.**

Videoconferencing systems range from small videophones to group conference rooms with cameras and multimedia equipment.[19] You can also do it yourself using a desktop PC system. Say you're on the West Coast and want to go over a draft of a client proposal with your boss on the East Coast. The first thing you need for such a meeting is a high-capacity telephone line or a high-quality Internet connection. To this you link your PC to which you have added a small video camera that sits atop your display monitor, a circuit board, and software that turns your microcomputer into a personal conferencing system.

Your boss's image appears in one window on your computer's display screen, and the document you're working on together is in another window. Although the display screen images are choppier than those on a standard TV set, they're clear enough to enable both of you to observe facial expressions and most body language. The software includes drawing tools and text tools for adding comments. Thus, you can go through and edit paragraphs and draw crude sketches on the proposal draft.

Virtual-Reality & Simulation Devices

***Virtual reality (VR)* is a kind of computer-generated artificial reality that projects a person into a sensation of three-dimensional space.** (■ *See Panel 5.18, next page.*) To put yourself into virtual reality, you need special headgear, gloves, and software. The headgear—which is called *head-mounted display*—has two small video display screens, one for each eye, that create the sense of three-dimensionality. Headphones pipe in stereophonic sound or even "3-D" sound. Three-dimensional sound makes you think you are hearing sounds not only near each ear but also in various places all around you. The glove has sensors that collect data about your hand movements. Software gives the wearer of this special headgear and glove the interactive sensory experience that feels like an alternative to real-world experiences.

You may have seen virtual reality used in arcade-type games, such as Atlantis, a computer simulation of The Lost Continent. However, there are far more important uses, one of them being in simulators for training.

Simulators are devices that represent the behavior of physical or abstract systems. Virtual-reality simulation technologies are applied a great deal in training. For instance, they have been used to create lifelike bus control panels and various scenarios such as icy road conditions to train bus drivers. They are used to train pilots on various aircraft and to prepare air-traffic controllers for equipment failures. Surgeons-in-training can rehearse their craft

■ PANEL 5.18

Virtual reality

(Top left) Man wearing interactive sensory headset and glove. When the man moves his head, the 3-D stereoscopic views change. *(Top right)* When the man moves his glove, sensors collect data about his hand movements. The view then changes so that the man feels he is "moving" over to the bookshelf and "grasping" a book. *(Middle right)* What the man is looking at—a simulation of an office. *(Bottom left)* During a virtual reality experiment in Chapel Hill, North Carolina, a man uses a treadmill to walk through a virtual reality environment. *(Bottom right)* Two medical students study the leg bones of a virtual cadaver.

through simulation on "digital patients." Virtual-reality therapy has been used for autistic children and in the treatment of phobias, such as extreme fear of public speaking or of being in public places or high places.

Robots

More than 40 years ago, in *Forbidden Planet*, Robby the Robot could sew, distill bourbon, and speak 187 languages. We haven't caught up with science-fiction movies, but maybe we'll get there yet.

Basically, **a *robot* is an automatic device that performs functions ordinarily ascribed to human beings or that operates with what appears to be almost human intelligence.** ScrubMate—a robot equipped with computerized controls, ultrasonic "eyes," sensors, batteries, three different cleaning and scrubbing tools, and a self-squeezing mop—can clean bathrooms. Rosie the Help-Mate delivers special-order meals from the kitchen to nursing stations in hospitals. Robodoc is used in surgery to bore the thighbone so that a hip implant can be attached. A driverless harvester, guided by satellite signals and artificial vision system, is used to harvest alfalfa and other crops.

Robots are also used for more exotic purposes such as fighting oil-well fires, doing nuclear inspections and cleanups, and checking for mines and booby traps. An eight-legged, satellite-linked robot called Dante II was used to explore the inside of Mount Spurr, an active Alaskan volcano, sometimes without human guidance. A six-wheeled robot vehicle named Sojourner was used in NASA's 1997 Pathfinder exploration of Mars to sample the planet's atmosphere and soil and to radio data and photos to Earth.

5.10 In & Out: Devices That Do Both

KEY QUESTION

What three devices are both input and output hardware?

Preview & Review: Some hardware devices perform both input and output. Three common ones are terminals, smart cards and optical cards, and touch screens.

Terminals

People working on large computer systems are usually connected to the main, or host, computer via terminals. **A *terminal* is an input/output device that uses a keyboard for input and a monitor for output.** They come in two varieties: dumb or intelligent.

Dumb terminals used by airline clerks

- **Dumb:** The most common type of terminal is dumb. A *dumb terminal* can be used only to input data to and receive information from a computer system. That is, it cannot do any processing on its own. An example of a dumb terminal is the type used by airline clerks at airport ticket and check-in counters.

- **Intelligent:** An *intelligent terminal* has built-in processing capability and RAM but does not have its own storage capacity. Intelligent terminals are not as powerful as microcomputers and are not designed to operate as stand-alone machines. Intelligent terminals are often found in local area networks in offices. Users share applications software and data stored on a server.

One example of an intelligent terminal is the *automated teller machine (ATM)*, which is used to retrieve information on bank balances, make deposits, transfer sums between accounts, and withdraw cash. Usually the cash is disbursed in $20 bills. Some Nevada gambling casinos have machines that dispense only $100 bills. In airports, variations on ATMs called *electronic ticketing machines (ETMs)* help travelers buy their own tickets, helping them avoid lines. Some teller machines, called *electronic kiosks*, act like vending machines, selling theater tickets, traveler's checks, stamps, phone cards, and other documents.

Another example of an intelligent terminal is a **_point-of-sale (POS)_ terminal, which is used much like a cash register. It records customer transactions at the point of sale but also stores data for billing and inventory purposes.** POS terminals are found in most department stores.

POS terminal

Smart Cards & Optical Cards

Today in the United States most ATM cards and credit cards are the old-fashioned magnetic-stripe cards. A magnetic-stripe card has a stripe of magnetically encoded data on its back. The encoded data might include your name, account number, and PIN (personal identification number). Two other kinds of cards, *smart cards* and *optical cards*, hold by far more information.

- Smart cards: **A *smart card* looks like a credit card but contains a microprocessor and memory chip.** When inserted into a reader, it transfers data to and from a central computer, and it can store some basic financial records. Smart cards can be used as telephone debit cards. You insert the card into a slot in the phone, wait for a tone, and dial the number. The time of your call is automatically calculated on the chip inside the card and deducted from the balance. Recently, various credit-card companies and banks have begun to promote smart cards, combining ATM, credit, and debit cards in one instrument.

- Optical cards: The conventional magnetic-stripe credit card holds the equivalent of a half page of data. The smart card with a microprocessor and memory chip holds the equivalent of 250 pages. The optical card presently holds about 2000 pages of data. Optical cards use the same type of technology as music compact disks but look like silvery credit cards. **Optical cards are plastic, laser-recordable, wallet-type cards used with an optical-card reader.** Because they can cram so much data (6.6 megabytes) into so little space, they may become popular in the future. With an optical card, for instance, there's enough room for a person's health card to hold not only his or her medical history and health-insurance information but also digital images, such as electrocardiograms.

Touch Screens

A *touch screen* is a video display screen that has been sensitized to receive input from the touch of a finger. (■ *See Panel 5.19.*) The screen is covered with a plastic layer, behind which are invisible beams of infrared light. You can input requests for information by pressing on buttons or menus displayed. The answers to your requests are displayed as output in words or pictures on the screen. (There may also be sound.)

Because touch screens are easy to use, they can convey information quickly. You find touch screens in kiosks, ATMs, airport tourist directories, hotel TV screens (for guest checkout), and campus information kiosks making available everything from lists of coming events to (with proper ID and personal code) student financial-aid records and grades.

5.11 Input & Output Technology & Quality of Life: Health & Ergonomics

KEY QUESTION

What are the principal health and ergonomics issues related to using computers?

Preview & Review: The use of computers and communications technology can have important effects on our health. Some of these are repetitive strain injuries such as carpal tunnel syndrome, eyestrain and headaches, and backstrain.

Negative health effects have increased interest in the field of ergonomics, the study of the relationship of people to a work environment.

Susan Harrigan, a financial reporter for *Newsday*, a daily newspaper based on New York's Long Island, had to learn to write her stories using a voice-acti-

☑ **PANEL 5.19**

Touch screen
The staff in many restaurants and bars use touch screens for placing orders.

vated computer. She did not do so by choice, nor was she as efficient as she used to be. She did it because she was too disabled to type at all. After 20 years of writing articles with deadline-driven fingers at the keyboard, she had developed a crippling hand disorder. At first the pain was so severe she couldn't even hold a subway token. "Also, I couldn't open doors," she said, "so I'd have to stand in front of doors and ask someone to open them for me."[20]

Health Matters

Harrigan suffers from one of the computer-induced disorders classified as repetitive stress injuries (RSIs). The computer is supposed to make us efficient. Unfortunately, it has made some users—journalists, postal workers, data-entry clerks—anything but. The reasons are repetitive strain injuries, eyestrain and headache, and back and neck pains. In this section we consider these health matters, along with the effects of electromagnetic fields and noise.

- Repetitive stress injuries: ***Repetitive stress (or strain) injuries (RSIs)*** **are several wrist, hand, arm, and neck injuries resulting when muscle groups are forced through fast, repetitive motions,** such as when typing on a computer, playing certain musical instruments, or moving grocery items over a scanner during checkout. The Bureau of Labor Statistics says 25% of all injuries that result in lost work time are due to RSI problems.[21] People who use computer keyboards—some of whom make as many as 21,600 keystrokes *an hour*—account for about 12% of RSI cases that result in lost work time.[22]

  RSIs cover a number of disorders. Some, such as muscle strain and tendinitis, are painful but usually not crippling. These injuries, often caused by hitting the keys too hard, may be cured by rest, anti-inflammatory medication, and change in typing technique. However, carpal tunnel syndrome is disabling and often requires surgery. *Carpal tunnel syndrome (CTS)* consists of a debilitating condition caused by pressure on the median nerve in the wrist, producing damage and pain to nerves and tendons in the hands.

It's important to point out, however, that scientists still don't know what causes RSIs. They don't know why some people operating keyboards develop upper body and wrist pains and others don't. The working list of possible explanations for RSI includes "wrist size, stress level, relationship with supervisors, job pace, posture, length of workday, exercise routine, workplace furniture, [and] job security."[23]

- **Eyestrain and headaches:** Vision problems are actually more common than RSI problems among computer users.[24,25] Computers compel people to use their eyes at close range for a long time. However, our eyes were made to see most efficiently at a distance. It's not surprising, then, that people develop *computer vision syndrome (CVS)*, which consists of eyestrain, headaches, double vision, and other problems caused by improper use of computer display screens. By "improper use," we mean not only staring at the screen for too long but also failing to employ the technology as it should be employed. This includes allowing faulty lighting and screen glare, and using screens with poor resolution.

- **Back and neck pains:** Many people use improper chairs or position keyboards and display screens in improper ways, leading to back and neck pains. All kinds of adjustable, special-purpose furniture and equipment is available to avoid or diminish such maladies.

- **Electromagnetic fields:** Like kitchen appliances, hairdryers, and television sets, many devices related to computers and communications generate low-level electromagnetic field emissions. *Electromagnetic fields (EMFs)* are waves of electrical energy and magnetic energy.

  In recent years, stories have appeared in the mass media reflecting concerns that high-voltage power lines, cellular phones, and CRT-type computer monitors might be harmful. There have been worries that monitors might be linked to miscarriages and birth defects, and that cellular phones and power lines might lead to some types of cancers. Is there anything to this? The answer is: so far no one is sure, although investigation is continuing.

  As for CRT monitors, those made since the early 1980s produce very low emissions. Even so, users are advised to not work closer than arm's length to a CRT monitor. The strongest fields are emitted from the sides and backs of terminals. Alternatively, you can use laptop computers, because their liquid crystal display (LCD) screens emit negligible radiation.

- **Noise:** The chatter of impact printers or hum of fans in computer power units can be stressful to many people. Sound-muffling covers are available for impact printers. Some system units may be placed on the floor under the desk to minimize noise from fans.

Ergonomics: Design with People in Mind

Previously workers had to fit themselves to the job environment. However, health and productivity issues have spurred the development of a relatively new field, called *ergonomics*, that is concerned with fitting the job environment to the worker.

Ergonomic keyboard

***Ergonomics* is the study of the physical relationships between people and their work environment.** It is concerned with designing hardware and software, as well as office furniture, that is less stressful and more comfortable to use, that blends more smoothly with a person's body or actions. Examples of ergonomic hardware are tilting display screens, detachable keyboards, and keyboards hinged in the middle so that the user's wrists are presumably in a more natural position.

We address some further ergonomic issues in the Experience Box at the end of Chapter 6.

Summary

What It Is/What It Does	Why It's Important
active-matrix display (p. 156, KQ 5.7) Type of flat-panel display in which each pixel on the screen is controlled by its own transistor.	Active-matrix screens are much brighter and sharper than passive-matrix screens, but they are more complicated and thus more expensive.
audio-input device (p. 149, KQ 5.4) Device that records or plays analog sound and translates it for digital storage and processing.	Audio-input devices, such as audio boards and MIDI boards, are important for multimedia computing.
bar code (p. 146, KQ 5.4) Vertical striped marks of varying widths that are imprinted on retail products and other items; when scanned by a bar-code reader, the code is converted into computer-acceptable digital input.	Bar codes may be used to input data from many items, from food products to overnight packages to railroad cars, for tracking and data manipulation.
bar-code reader (p. 146, KQ 5.4) Photoelectric scanner, found in many supermarkets, that translates bar code symbols on products into digital code.	With bar-code readers and the appropriate computer system, retail clerks can total purchases and produce invoices with increased speed and accuracy; and stores can monitor inventory with greater efficiency.
biometrics (p. 151, KQ 5.5) Science of measuring individual body characteristics.	Biometric systems are used in lieu of typed passwords to identify people authorized to use a computer system.
bitmapped display (p. 156, KQ 5.7) Display screen that permits the computer to manipulate pixels on the screen individually, enabling software to create a greater variety of images.	Bitmapped display screens allow the software to show text and graphics built pixel by pixel rather than in character blocks, so that a greater variety of images is possible. The more bits represented by a pixel, the higher the resolution.
cathode-ray tube (CRT) (p. 154, KQ 5.7) Vacuum tube used as a display screen in a computer or video display terminal. Images are represented on the screen by individual dots or "picture elements" called *pixels*.	This technology is found not only in the screens of desktop computers but also in television sets and flight-information monitors in airports.
computer output microfilm/microfiche (p. 161, KQ 5.8) Computer output produced as tiny images on rolls or sheets of microfilm.	This fast and inexpensive process can store a lot of data in a small amount of space.
dedicated fax machine (p. 148, KQ 5.4) Specialized machine for scanning images on paper documents and sending them as electronic signals over telephone lines to receiving fax machines or fax-equipped computers; a dedicated fax machine will also received faxed documents.	Unlike fax modems installed inside computers, dedicated fax machines can scan paper documents.

What It Is/What It Does	**Why It's Important**

digital camera (p. 150, KQ 5.4) Type of electronic camera that uses a light-sensitive silicon chip to capture photographic images in digital form on a small diskette or flash-memory chip.

Digital cameras can produce images in digital form that can be transmitted directly to a computer's hard disk for manipulation, storage, and printing out.

digitizing tablet (p. 145, KQ 5.3) Tablet connected by a wire to a pen-like stylus with which the user sketches an image, or to a puck with which the user copies an image.

A digitizing tablet can be used to achieve shading and other artistic effects or to "trace" a drawing, which can be stored in digitized form.

display screen (p. 154, KQ 5.7) Also variously called *monitor, CRT,* or simply *screen;* softcopy output device that shows programming instructions and data as they are being input and information after it is processed. Sometimes a display screen is also referred to as a VDT, for video display terminal, although technically a VDT includes both screen and keyboard. The size of a screen is measured diagonally from corner to corner in inches, just like television screens.

Display screens enable users to immediately view the results of input and processing.

dot-matrix printer (p. 158, KQ 5.8) Printer that contains a print head of small pins that strike an inked ribbon, forming characters or images. Print heads are available with 9, 18, or 24 pins, with the 24-pin head offering the best quality.

Dot-matrix printers can print draft quality, a coarser-looking 72 dots per inch vertically, or near-letter-quality (NLQ), a crisper-looking 144 dots per inch vertically. They can also print graphics.

dot pitch (p. 156, KQ 5.7) Amount of space between pixels (dots); the closer the dots, the crisper the image.

Dot pitch is one of the measures of display screen clarity.

drum plotter (p. 161, KQ 5.8) Output device that places paper on a moving drum below one to four color pens that move across the paper

Drum plotters allow continuous recording, useful for recording data like earthquake activity.

electroluminescent (EL) display (p. 155, KQ 5.7) Flat-panel display that contains a substance that glows when it is charged by an electric current. A pixel is formed on the screen when current is sent to the intersection of the appropriate row and column.

Flat-panel display technologies including EL provide thinner, lighter display screens that use less power than CRTs, so they are well suited to portable computers.

electronic imaging (p. 149, KQ 5.4) The combining of separate images, using scanners, digital cameras, and advanced graphic computers; software controls the process.

Electronic imaging has become an important part of multimedia.

ergonomics (p. 169, KQ 5.11) Study of the physical and psychological relationships between people and their work environment.

Ergonomic principles are used in designing computers, software, and office furniture to further productivity while avoiding stress, illness, and injuries.

What It Is/What It Does	**Why It's Important**

Extended Graphics Array (XGA) (p. 157, KQ 5.7) Graphics board display standard, also referred to as *high resolution, 24-bit color,* or *true color;* supports up to 16.7 million colors at a resolution of 1024 × 768 pixels. Depending on the video display adapter memory chip, XGA will support 256, 65,536, or 16,777,216 colors.

Extended Graphics Array offers the most sophisticated standard for color and resolution.

fax machine (p. 148, KQ 5.4) Short for *facsimile transmission machine;* input device for scanning an image and sending it as electronic signals over telephone lines to a receiving fax machine, which re-creates the image on paper. Fax machines may be dedicated fax machines or fax modems.

Fax machines enable the transmission of text and graphic data over telephone lines quickly and inexpensively.

fax modem (p. 148, KQ 5.4) Modem with fax capability installed as a circuit board inside a computer; it can send and receive electronic signals via telephone lines directly to/from a computer similarly equipped or to/from a dedicated fax machine.

With a fax modem, users can send information much more quickly than they would if they had to feed it page by page through a dedicated fax machine. However, fax modems cannot scan paper documents for faxing.

flatbed plotter (p.161, KQ 5.8) An output device designed so that paper lies flat on a table-like surface while one to four color pens move across the paper, and the paper moves beneath the pens.

Flatbed plotters can produce high-quality graphics such as maps and architectural drawings.

flat-panel display (p. 155, KQ 5.7) Refers to display screens that are much thinner, weigh less, and consume less power than CRTs. Flat-panel displays are made up of two plates of glass with a substance between them that is activated in different ways. Three types of substance used are liquid crystal, electroluminescent, and gas plasma. Flat-panel screens are either active-matrix or passive-matrix displays. Images are represented on the screen by individual dots, or picture elements called *pixels.*

Flat-panel displays are used in portable computers and recently became available for desktop PCs.

gas-plasma display (p. 155, KQ 5.7) Type of flat-panel display in which the display uses a gas that emits light in the presence of an electric current, like a neon bulb. The technology uses predominantly neon gas and electrodes above and below the gas. When electric current passes between the electrodes, the gas glows.

Gas-plasma displays offer better resolution than LCD displays, but they are more expensive.

hardcopy (p. 152, KQ 5.6) Refers to printed output (as opposed to softcopy). The principal examples are printouts, whether text or graphics, from printers. Film, including microfilm and microfiche, is also considered hardcopy output.

Hardcopy is convenient for people to use and distribute; it can be easily handled or stored.

What It Is/What It Does

imaging system (p. 148, KQ 5.4) Also known as *image scanner,* or *graphics scanner;* input device that converts text, drawings, and photographs into digital form that can be stored in a computer system.

impact printer (p. 158, KQ 5.8) Type of printer that forms characters or images by striking a mechanism such as a print hammer or wheel against an inked ribbon, leaving an image on paper.

ink-jet printer (p. 159, KQ 5.8) Nonimpact printer that forms images with little dots. Ink-jet printers spray small, electrically charged droplets of ink from four nozzles through holes in a matrix at high speed onto paper.

input hardware (p. 140, KQ 5.1) Devices that take data and programs that people can read or comprehend and convert them to a form the computer can process. Devices are of three types: keyboards, pointing devices, and source data-entry devices.

joystick (p. 144, KQ 5.3) Pointing device that consists of a vertical handle like a gearshift lever mounted on a base with one or two buttons; it directs a cursor or pointer on the display screen.

keyboard (p. 140, KQ 5.1, 5.2) Input device that converts letters, numbers, and other characters into electrical signals that the computer's processor can "read."

laser printer (p. 158, KQ 5.8) Nonimpact printer similar to a photocopying machine; images are created as dots on a drum, treated with a magnetically charged ink-like toner (powder), and then transferred from drum to paper.

light pen (p. 144, KQ 5.3) Light-sensitive pen-like device connected by a wire to a computer terminal; the user brings the pen to a desired point on the display screen and presses the pen button, which identifies that screen location to the computer.

liquid crystal display (LCD) (p. 155, KQ 5.7) Flat-panel display that consists of a substance called *liquid crystal,* the molecules of which line up in a way that alters their optical properties. As a result, light—usually backlighting behind the screen—is blocked or allowed through to create an image.

Why It's Important

Image scanners have enabled users with desktop-publishing software to readily input images into computer systems for manipulation, storage, and output.

Dot-matrix printers are the most common impact printers for microcomputer users. For large computers, line printers provide high-speed output.

Ink-jet printers can print in color and cost much less than color laser printers and are quieter. However, they are slower than laser printers and may have lower resolution (300–720 dots per inch compared to 300–1200 for laser).

Input hardware enables data to be put into computer-processable form.

Joysticks are used principally in video games and in some computer-aided design systems.

Keyboards are the most popular kind of input device.

Laser printers produce much better image quality than dot-matrix printers do and can print in many more colors; they are also quieter. Laser printers, along with page description languages, enabled the development of desktop publishing.

Light pens are used by engineers, graphic designers, and illustrators for making drawings.

LCD is useful not only for portable computers and new flat-panel display screens for desktop PCs but also as a display for various electronic devices, such as watches and radios.

What It Is/What It Does	Why It's Important

magnetic-ink character recognition (MICR) (p. 147, KQ 5.4) Type of scanning technology that reads magnetized-ink characters printed at the bottom of checks and converts them to computer-acceptable digital form.

MICR technology is used by banks to sort checks.

mouse (p. 142, KQ 5.3) Input device that is rolled about on a desktop to position a cursor or pointer on the computer's display screen, which indicates the area where data may be entered or a command executed.

For many purposes, a mouse is easier to use than a keyboard for communicating commands to a computer. With microcomputers, a mouse is needed to use most graphical user interface programs and to draw illustrations.

mouse pointer (p. 142, KQ 5.3) Symbol on the display screen whose movement is directed by moving a mouse on a flat surface, such as a table top.

The position of the mouse pointer indicates where information may be entered or a command (such as clicking, dragging, or dropping) may be executed. Also, the shape of the pointer may change, indicating a particular function that may be performed at that point.

multifunction device (p. 161, KQ 5.8) Single hardware device that combines several capabilities, such as printing, scanning, copying, and faxing.

A multifunction machine can do the work of several separate office machines at a price below the combined cost of buying these devices separately.

nonimpact printer (p. 158, KQ 5.8) Printer that forms characters and images without making direct physical contact between printing mechanism and paper. Two types of nonimpact printers often used with microcomputers are laser printers and ink-jet printers. A third kind, the thermal printer, is seen less frequently.

Nonimpact printers are faster and quieter than impact printers because they have fewer moving parts. They can print text, graphics, and color, but they cannot be used to print on multipage forms.

optical card (p. 166, KQ 5.10) Plastic, wallet-type card using laser technology like music compact disks, which can be used to store data.

Because they hold so much data, optical cards have considerable uses, as for a health card holding a person's medical history, including digital images such as X-rays.

optical character recognition (OCR) (p. 147, KQ 5.4) Type of scanning technology that reads preprinted characters in a particular font and converts them to computer-usable form. A common OCR scanning device is the wand reader.

OCR technology is frequently used with utility bills and price tags on department-store merchandise.

optical mark recognition (OMR) (p. 147, KQ 5.4) Type of scanning technology that reads pencil marks and converts them into computer-usable form.

OMR technology is frequently used for grading multiple-choice and true/false tests, such as parts of the College Board Scholastic Aptitude Test.

page description language (p. 159, KQ 5.8) Software used in desktop publishing that describes the shape and position of characters and graphics to the printer.

Page description languages, used along with laser printers, gave birth to desktop publishing. They allow users to combine different types of graphics with text in different fonts, all on the same page.

What It Is/What It Does	Why It's Important

passive-matrix display (p. 156, KQ 5.7) Type of flat-panel display in which each transistor controls a whole row or column of pixels.

Although passive-matrix displays are less bright and less sharp than active-matrix displays, they are less expensive and use less power.

pen-based computer system (p. 145, KQ 5.3) Input system that uses a pen-like stylus to enter handwriting and marks onto a computer screen.

Pen-based computer systems benefit people who don't know how to or who don't want to type or need to make routinized kinds of inputs such as checkmarks.

pixel (p. 154, KQ 5.7) Short for *picture element;* smallest unit on the screen that can be turned on and off or made different shades. A stream of bits defining the image is sent from the computer (from the CPU) to the CRT's electron gun, where the bits are converted to electrons.

Pixels are the building blocks that allow graphical images to be presented on a display screen.

plotter (p. 160, KQ 5.8) Specialized hardcopy output device designed to produce high-quality graphics in a variety of colors. The two principal kinds of plotters are flatbed and drum.

Plotters are especially useful for creating maps and architectural drawings, although they may also produce less complicated charts and graphs.

pointing device (p. 140, KQ 5.1, 5.3) Input device that controls the position of the cursor or pointer on the screen. Includes mice, trackballs, pointing sticks, touchpads, light pens, digitizing tablets, and pen-based systems.

Pointing devices allow the user to quickly choose from selections rather than having to remember commands, and some pointers allow the user to input drawing or handwriting to the computer.

pointing stick (p. 144, KQ 5.3) Input device used instead of a mouse; looks like a pencil eraser protruding from the keyboard between the G, H, and B keys. The user moves the stick with a forefinger while using the thumb to press buttons located in front of the space bar.

A pointing stick and the related buttons work like a mouse and don't require desktop space to move around, so they are well suited for laptop computers.

point-of-sale (POS) terminal (p. 165, KQ 5.10) Smart terminal used much like a cash register.

POS terminals record customer transactions at the point of sale but also store data for billing and inventory purposes.

printer (p. 157, KQ 5.8) Output device that prints characters, symbols, and perhaps graphics on paper or another medium. Printers are categorized according to whether the image produced is formed by physical contact of the print mechanism with the paper. Impact printers have contact; nonimpact printers do not.

Printers provide one of the principal forms of computer output.

puck (p. 145, KQ 5.3) Copying device with which the user of a digitizing table may copy an image.

With a puck, users may "trace" (copy) a drawing and store it in digitized form.

radio-frequency identification technology (p. 151, KQ 5.5) Also called *RF-ID tagging;* a source data-entry technology that uses a tag containing a microchip with code numbers that can be read by the radio waves of a scanner linked to a database.

The radio waves that read RF-ID tags don't need line-of-sight contact with the tag. Thus the tags are being used, for example, as tollbooth passes that can be read without stopping traffic.

What It Is/What It Does	Why It's Important

repetitive stress (strain) injuries (RSI) (p. 167, KQ 5.11) Several kinds of wrist, hand, arm, and neck injuries that can result when muscle groups are forced through fast, repetitive motions.

Computer users may suffer RSIs such as muscle strain and tendinitis, which are not disabling, or carpal tunnel syndrome, which is.

resolution (p. 156, KQ 5.7) Clarity or sharpness of a display screen; the more pixels there are per square inch, the finer the level of detail. Resolution is expressed in terms of the formula *horizontal pixels × vertical pixels*. A screen with 640 × 480 pixels multiplied together equals 307,200 pixels. This screen will be less clear and sharp than a screen with 800 × 600 (equals 480,000) or 1024 × 768 (equals 786,432) pixels.

Users need to know what screen resolution is appropriate for their purposes.

robot (p. 164, KQ 5.9) Automatic device that performs functions ordinarily ascribed to human beings or that operate with what appears to be almost human intelligence.

Robots are of several kinds—industrial robots, perception systems, and mobile robots. They are performing more and more functions in business and the professions.

scanners (p. 146, KQ 5.4) Input devices that use laser beams and reflected light to translate images such as optical marks, text, drawings, and photos into digital form.

Scanning devices—bar-code readers, mark- and character-recognition devices, fax machines, imaging systems—simplify the input of complex data.

sensor (p. 150, KQ 5.5) Type of input device that collects specific kinds of data directly from the environment and transmits it to a computer.

Sensors can be used for detecting speed, movement, weight, pressure, temperature, humidity, wind, current, fog, gas, smoke, light, shapes, images, and so on.

smart card (p. 166, KQ 5.10) Wallet-type card containing a microprocessor and memory chip that can be used to store data and transfer data to and from a computer.

In many countries, telephone users may buy a smart card that lets them make telephone calls until the total cost limit programmed into the card has been reached.

softcopy (p. 152, KQ 5.6) Refers to data that is shown on a display screen or is in audio or voice form. This kind of output is not tangible; it cannot be touched. Virtual reality and robots might also be considered softcopy devices.

This term is used to distinguish nonprinted output from printed output.

sound-output device (p. 162, KQ 5.9) Output device that produces digitized, nonverbal sounds, ranging from beeps and chirps to music. It includes software and a sound card or digital audio circuit board.

PC owners can customize their machines to greet each new program with particular sounds. Sound output is also used in multimedia presentations.

What It Is/What It Does	**Why It's Important**

source data-entry device (p. 141, KQ 5.1, 5.4, 5.5) Also called *source-data automation;* device other than keyboard or pointer that creates machine-readable data on magnetic media or paper or feeds it directly into the computer's processor. The category includes scanning devices; sensors; voice-recognition devices; audio-input devices; video-input devices; electronic cameras; and human-biology input devices.

Source data-entry devices lessen reliance on keyboards for data entry and can make data entry more accurate. Some also enable users to draw graphics on screen and create other effects not possible with a keyboard.

stylus (p. 145, KQ 5.3) Pen-like device with which the user of a digitizing tablet "sketches" an image.

With a stylus, users can achieve artistic effects similar to those achieved with pen or pencil.

Super Video Graphics Array (SVGA) (p. 157, KQ 5.7) Graphics board display standard that supports 256 colors at higher resolution than VGA. SVGA has two graphics modes: 800×600 pixels and 1024×768. Also called *8-bit color.*

Super VGA is a higher-resolution version of Video Graphics Array (VGA), introduced in 1987.

terminal (p. 165, KQ 5.10) Input and output device that uses a keyboard for input, a monitor for output, and a communications line to a main computer system.

A terminal is generally used to input data to, and receive visual data from, a mainframe computer system. An intelligent terminal also has processing capability and RAM.

thermal printer (p. 159, KQ 5.8) Nonimpact printer that uses colored waxes and heat to produce images by burning dots onto special paper.

The colored wax sheets are not required for black-and-white output because the thermal print head will register the dots on the paper.

touchpad (p. 144, KQ 5.3) Input device used instead of a mouse; the user slides a finger over the small, flat surface to move the cursor on the display screen, and taps a finger on the pad's surface or presses buttons positioned nearby to perform the same tasks done with the mouse buttons.

Touchpads fit readily on a laptop computer and give the user a pointing device that is convenient to use in a confined space, although they can be more difficult to control than a mouse.

touch screen (p. 166, KQ 5.10) Video display screen that has been sensitized to receive input from the touch of a finger. It is often used in automated teller machines and in directories conveying tourist information.

Because touch screens are easy to use, they can convey information quickly and can be used by people with no computer training; however, the amount of information offered is usually limited.

trackball (p. 144, KQ 5.3) Input device used instead of a mouse; a movable ball on top of a stationary device is rotated with the fingers or palm of the hand to move the cursor or pointer on the display screen, and buttons are positioned nearby.

Unlike a mouse, a trackball is especially suited to portable computers, which are often used in confined places.

videoconferencing (p. 163, KQ 5.9) A method of communicating whereby people in different geographical locations can have a meeting—and see and hear one another—using computers and communications technologies.

Videoconferencing technology enables people to conduct business meetings without having to travel.

What It Is/What It Does	**Why It's Important**

video display adapter (p. 157, KQ 5.7) Also called a *video graphics card;* circuit board that contains its own video RAM and determines the resolution, number of colors, and how fast images appear on the display screen.

Video display adapters determine how fast the card processes images and how many colors it can display.

Video Graphics Array (VGA) (p. 157, KQ 5.7) Graphics board display standard that supports 16 to 256 colors, depending on resolution. At 320 × 200 pixels it will support 256 colors; at the sharper resolution of 640 × 480 pixels it will support 16 colors. Also called *16-bit color.*

VGA and SVGA are the most common video standards used today.

virtual reality (p. 163, KQ 5.9) Computer-generated artificial reality that projects user into sensation of three-dimensional space. Interactive sensory equipment consists of headgear, glove, and software. The headgear has small video display screens, one for each eye, to create a three-dimensional sense, and headphones to pipe in stereo or 3-D sound. The glove has sensors that collect data about hand movements. The software gives the wearer the interactive sensory experience.

Virtual reality is used most in entertainment, as in arcade-type games, but has applications in architectural design and training simulators.

voice-output device (p. 163, KQ 5.9) Output device that converts digital data into speech-like sounds.

Voice-output devices are a common technology, found in telephone systems, soft-drink machines, and toys and games.

voice-recognition system (p. 151, KQ 5.5) Input system that converts a person's speech into digital code; the system compares the electrical patterns produced by the speaker's voice with a set of prerecorded patterns stored in the computer.

Voice-recognition technology is useful for inputting data in situations in which people are unable to use their hands or need their hands free for other purposes.

Exercises

Self-Test

1. A(n) _____ terminal is entirely dependent for all of its processing activities on the computer system to which it is hooked up.
2. _____ is the study of the physical relationships between people and their work environment.
3. A(n) _____ is an input device that is rolled about on a desktop and directs a pointer on the computer's display screen.
4. A device that translates images of text, drawings, photos, and the like into digital form is called a(n) _____.
5. The smallest unit on the screen that can be turned on and off is called a(n) _____.

Short-Answer Questions

1. What does a voice-recognition system do?
2. What three characteristics determine the clarity of a computer screen?
3. What is the main difference between a dedicated fax machine and a fax modem?
4. What is an imaging system?
5. What is a terminal?

Multiple-Choice Questions

1. Which of the following characteristics affect how bright images appear on a computer screen?
   a. resolution
   b. dot pitch
   c. refresh rate
   d. screen size
   e. All of the above

2. Which of the following should you consider using if you have to work in a confined space?
   a. mouse
   b. digitizing tablet
   c. trackball
   d. keyboard
   e. None of the above

3. Which of the following should you purchase if you have a limited amount of space in your office but need to be able to print, make photocopies, scan images, and fax documents?
   a. printer
   b. fax machine
   c. scanner
   d. multifunction device
   e. All of the above

4. A _____ looks like a credit card but contains a microprocessor and memory chip.
   a. sound card
   b. smart card
   c. touch card
   d. point-of-sale card
   e. None of the above

5. Which of the following gathers information from the environment and then transmits it to a computer?
   a. human-biology input device
   b. digital camera
   c. display screen
   d. sensor
   e. None of the above

True/False Questions

T F   1. Photos taken with a digital camera can be downloaded to a computer's hard drive.

T F   2. On a computer screen, the more pixels that appear per square inch, the higher the resolution.

T F   3. In your future, you will likely see better and cheaper display screens.

T F   4.   A Touch-Tone telephone can be used like a dumb terminal to send data to a computer.

T F   5.   Terminals are either dumb or intelligent.

Knowledge in Action

1. If you could buy any printer you want, what type (make, model, etc.) would you choose? Does the printer need to fit into a small space? Does it need to print across the width of wide paper (11 × 14 inches)? In color? On multicarbon forms? How much printer RAM would you need? Review some of the current computer publications for articles or advertisements relating to printers. How much does the printer cost? Your needs should be able to justify the cost of the printer (if necessary, make up what your needs might be).

2. What uses can you imagine for voice output and/or sound output in your planned job or profession?

3. *Paperless office* is a term that has been appearing in computer-related journals and books for over 5 years. However, the paperless office has not yet been achieved. Do you think the paperless office is a good idea? Do you think it's possible? Why do you think it has not yet been achieved?

4. Research the current uses of smart card technology and how companies hope to implement smart card technology in the future. Will smart cards have an effect on shopping over the Internet? The transportation industry? What other industries might be affected? Conduct your research using current periodicals and/or the Internet.

Storage & Databases

Foundations for Interactivity, Multimedia, & Knowledge

Chapter 6

key questions

You should be able to answer the following questions:

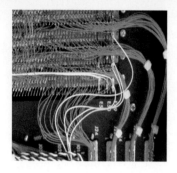

W

hat is now the driving force behind most innovations in personal computers?

Entertainment, suggests Keith McCurdy, the director for North America of the video game company Electronic Arts.[1] Once it was word processing and spreadsheets that were the "killer apps"—the application programs that helped fuel the personal computer market's growth and technological advancement. Now it is advancements in video games—better performance, creativity, and animated realism—that are spinning off business applications, such as animated graphics and other multimedia for corporate presentations.

"The CD-ROM market was first embraced and, as a result, ushered in by video game software," says McCurdy. "While business applications normally [had] little need to store software on a huge 650-megabyte CD-ROM, it is just such a CD-ROM that is essential for video games and their vast array of full-screen animation, live-video footage, digital music, and multiple levels of game play."

The engine of entertainment has made "interactivity" and "multimedia" among the most overused marketing words of recent times. *Interactivity* refers to the user's back-and-forth interaction with a computer program. In other words, the user's actions and choices affect what the software does. *Multimedia* refers to the use of a variety of media—text, sound, video—to deliver information, whether on a computer disk or via the anticipated union of computers, telecommunications, and broadcasting technologies.

Interactive programs and multimedia programs require machines that can handle and store enormous amounts of data. For this reason, the capacities of storage hardware, called *secondary storage* or just *storage*, seem to be increasing almost daily. This chapter covers the most common types of secondary storage, as well as their uses. First, however, we need to go over the fundamentals that relate to the whole topic of secondary storage.

6.1 Storage Fundamentals

KEY QUESTIONS

What are the units of storage measurement, data access methods, and criteria for distinguishing storage devices?

Preview & Review: Storage capacity is measured in multiples of bytes. In addition, there are two main types of data access. Storage capacity, access speed, transfer rate, size, removability, and cost are all factors in rating secondary-storage devices.

As discussed previously (✔ p. 116), when you are, for example, working on a word processing document, the data you are working on is stored in RAM (primary storage) during processing. Because that data in RAM is an electrical state, when you turn off the power to your computer, the data there disappears. Therefore, before you turn your computer off, you must save your work onto a storage device that stores data permanently (until it is changed or erased), such as a diskette or a hard disk.

In addition to data, computer software programs must be stored in a computer-usable form. A copy of software instructions must be retrieved from a secondary-storage device and placed into RAM before processing can begin. The computer's operating system determines where and how programs are stored on the secondary-storage devices.

Units of Measurement for Storage

Nearly every recent development in special effects in movie making—from the stampeding dinosaurs of *Jurassic Park* to the digital water of *Titanic* and *Deep Impact* to the 20-story high reptile in *Godzilla*—has been made possible because of great leaps in secondary-storage technology. *Jurassic Park*, for example, contains about 100 billion bytes, or 100 gigabytes. To get a sense of how big a gigabyte is, suppose that, starting at age 10, you rigorously kept a journal consisting of two double-spaced typewritten pages a day. By the time you were close to 96 years old, you would have a gigabyte's worth of data—a manuscript of 62,500 pages, which would be 21 feet tall if stacked.[2]

We explained the meaning of gigabytes and other measurements in the discussion of processing hardware (✔ p. 119). The same terms are also used to measure the data capacity of storage devices. To repeat:

- **Kilobyte:** A *kilobyte* (abbreviated K or KB) is equivalent to 1024 bytes.
- **Megabyte:** A *megabyte* (abbreviated M or MB) is about 1 million bytes.
- **Gigabyte:** A *gigabyte* (G or GB) is about 1 billion bytes.
- **Terabyte:** A *terabyte* (T or TB) is about 1 trillion bytes.

The amount of data being held in a file in your personal computer might be expressed in kilobytes or megabytes. The amount of data being stored in a remote database accessible to you over a communications line might be expressed in gigabytes or terabytes.

Data Access Methods

Before we move on to discuss individual secondary-storage devices, we need to mention one more aspect of storage fundamentals—data access storage methods. The way that a secondary-storage device allows access to the data stored on it affects its speed and its usefulness for certain applications. The two main types of data access are sequential and direct.

- **Sequential storage:** *Sequential storage* **means that data is stored in sequence,** such as alphabetically. Tape storage falls in the category of sequential storage. Thus, you would have to search a tape past all the information from A to J, for example, before you got to K. Or, if you are looking for employee number 8888, the computer will have to start with 0001, then go past 0002, 0003, and so on, until it finally comes to 8888. This data access method is less expensive than other methods because it uses magnetic tape, which is cheaper than disks. The disadvantage of sequential file organization is that searching for data is slow.
- **Direct access storage:** *Direct access storage* **means that the computer can go directly to the information you want.** The data is retrieved (accessed) according to a unique data identifier called a *key field*, as we will discuss. This method of file organization is used with hard disks and other types of disks. It is ideal for applications such as airline reservation systems or computer-based directory-assistance operations. In these cases, there is no fixed pattern to the requests for data.

  Direct file access is much faster than sequential access for finding specific data. However, because the method requires hard disk or other type of disk storage, it is more expensive to use than sequential access (magnetic tape).

Criteria for Rating Secondary-Storage Devices

To evaluate the various devices, ranging from disk to flash-memory cards to tape to online storage, it's helpful to have the following information:

- **Storage capacity:** As we mentioned earlier, high-capacity storage devices are desirable or required for many sophisticated programs and large databases. However, as capacity increases, so does price. Some users find compression software to be an economical solution to storage-capacity problems. Hard disks can store more data than diskettes, and optical disks can store more than hard disks.

- **Access speed:** *Access speed* refers to the average time needed to locate data on a secondary-storage device. Access speed is measured in milliseconds (thousandths of a second). Hard disks are faster than optical disks, which are faster than diskettes. Disks are faster than magnetic tape. However, the slower media are more economical.

- **Transfer rate:** *Transfer rate* refers to the speed at which data is transferred from secondary storage to main memory (primary storage). It is measured in megabytes per second.

- **Size:** Some situations require compact storage devices (for portability); others don't. Users need to know what their options are.

- **Removability:** Storage devices that are sealed within the computer may suffice for some users; other users may also need removable storage media.

- **Cost:** As we have indicated, the cost of a storage device is directly related to the previous five factors.

Now let's take an in-depth look at the following types of secondary-storage devices: *diskettes, hard disks, optical disks, flash-memory cards, magnetic tape,* and *online storage.*

6.2 Diskettes

KEY QUESTION

What are diskettes, their principal features, and rules for taking care of them?

Preview & Review: Diskettes are round pieces of flat plastic that store data and programs as magnetized spots. A disk drive copies, or reads, data from the disk and writes, or records, data to the disk.

Components of a diskette include tracks and sectors; diskettes come in various densities. All have write-protect features.

Care must be taken to avoid destroying data on disks, and users are advised to back up, or duplicate, the data on their disks.

A *diskette,* or *floppy disk,* **is a removable round, flat piece of mylar plastic 3½ inches across that stores data and programs as magnetized spots.** More specifically, data is stored as electromagnetic charges on a metal oxide film that coats the mylar plastic. Data is represented by the presence or absence of these electromagnetic charges, following standard patterns of data representation (such as ASCII, ✔ p. 120). The disk is contained in a plastic case to protect it from being touched by human hands. It is called "floppy" because the disk within the case is flexible, not rigid.

The Disk Drive

To use a diskette, you need a disk drive. **A *disk drive* is a device that holds, spins, and reads data from and writes data to a diskette.**

The words *read* and *write* (✔ p. 14) have exact meanings:

- Read: *Read* means that the data represented on the secondary-storage medium is converted to electronic signals and transmitted to primary storage (RAM). That is, *read* means that data is *copied from* the diskette, disk, or other type of storage.
- Write: *Write* means that the electronic information processed by the computer is transferred to a secondary-storage medium.

Disk drive

How a Disk Drive Works

A diskette is inserted into a slot, called the *drive gate* or *drive door*, in the front of the disk drive. This clamps the diskette in place over the spindle of the drive mechanism so the drive can operate. An access light goes on when the disk is in use. After using the disk, you can retrieve it by pressing an eject button beside the drive. (Note: *Do not remove the disk when the access light is on.*)

The device by which the data on a disk is transferred to the computer, and from the computer to the disk, is the disk drive's *read/write head.* The diskette spins inside its case, and the read/write head moves back and forth over the *data access area,* which is under the diskette's metal protective plate. Disk drive operations are illustrated below. (■ *See Panel 6.1.*)

How it works:

1. When a diskette is inserted into the drive, it presses against a system of levers. One lever opens the metal plate, or shutter, to expose the data access area.

2. Other levers and gears move two read/write heads until they almost touch the diskette on both sides.

3. The drive's circuit board receives signals, including data and instructions for reading/writing that data from/to disk, from the drive's controller board. The circuit board translates the instructions into signals that control the movement of the disk and the read/write heads.

4. A motor located beneath the disk spins a shaft that engages a notch on the hub of the disk, causing the disk to spin.

5. When the heads are in the correct position, electrical impulses create a magnetic field in one of the heads to write data to either the top or bottom surface of the disk. When the heads are reading data, they react to magnetic fields generated by the metallic particles on the disk.

■ PANEL 6.1

Cutaway view of a disk drive

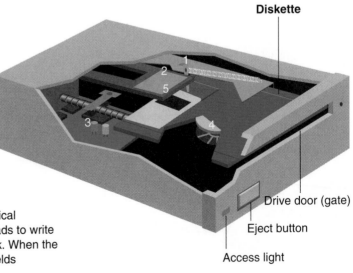

Diskette

Drive door (gate)

Eject button

Access light

Characteristics of Diskettes

Diskettes have the following characteristics:

- **Tracks and sectors:** On a diskette, **data is recorded in rings called *tracks.*** Unlike on a phonograph record, these tracks are neither visible grooves nor a single spiral. Rather, they are closed concentric rings. (■ *See Panel 6.2.*)

  Each track is divided into sectors. ***Sectors* are invisible wedge-shaped sections used for storage reference purposes.** When you save data from your computer to a diskette, the data is distributed by tracks and sectors on the disk. That is, the system software uses the point at which a sector intersects a track to reference the data location in order to spin the disk and position the read/write head.

- **Unformatted versus formatted disks:** When you buy a new box of diskettes to use for storing data, the box may state that it is "unformatted" (or say nothing at all). This means you have a task to perform before you can use the disks with your computer and disk drive. *Unformatted* disks are manufactured without tracks and sectors in place. *Formatting*—or *initializing,* as it is called on the Macintosh —means that you must prepare the disk for use so that the operating

■ PANEL 6.2

Anatomy of a 3½-inch diskette

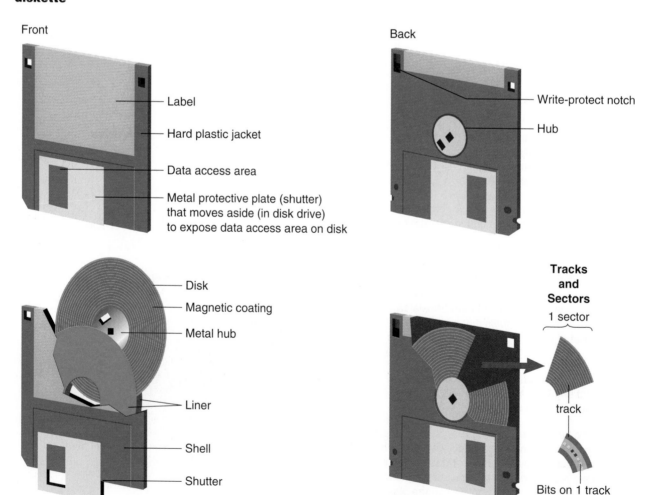

Front

- Label
- Hard plastic jacket
- Data access area
- Metal protective plate (shutter) that moves aside (in disk drive) to expose data access area on disk

Back

- Write-protect notch
- Hub

- Disk
- Magnetic coating
- Metal hub
- Liner
- Shell
- Shutter

Tracks and Sectors

1 sector

track

Bits on 1 track

system can write information on it. Formatting is done quickly by using a few simple software commands (described in the user manual that comes with your computer).

Alternatively, when you buy a new box of diskettes, the box may state that they are "formatted IBM" or "formatted Macintosh." This means that you can simply insert a disk into the drive gate of your PC or Macintosh and use it immediately.

- **Data capacity—sides and densities:** Not all disks hold the same amount of data. Diskettes are *double-sided*, called "DS" or "2," capable of storing data on both sides. However, a disk's capacity depends on its recording density. *Recording density* refers to the number of bits per inch that can be written onto the surface of the disk. Thus, diskettes are either *high-density (HD)* or *extended density (ED)*. A high-density 3½-inch diskette can store 1.44 megabytes. An extended density diskette can store 2.8 megabytes. (Note: You need an ED drive to use ED diskettes; an ED drive will also accept HD disks.)

- **Write-protect features:** The *write-protect feature* allows you to **protect a diskette from being written to,** which would replace data on the disk. To write-protect a 3½-inch diskette, you press a slide lever toward the edge of the disk, uncovering a hole (which appears on the lower right side, viewed from the back). (■ *See Panel 6.3.)*

Taking Care of Diskettes

Diskettes need at least the same amount of care that you would give to an audiotape or music CD. In fact, they need more care than that if you are dealing with difficult-to-replace data or programs.

There are a number of rules for taking care of diskettes:

- **Don't touch disk surfaces:** Don't touch anything visible through the protective case, such as the data access area. Don't manipulate the metal shutter.

- **Handle disks gently:** Don't try to bend diskettes or put heavy weights on them.

- **Avoid risky physical environments:** Disks don't do well in sun or heat (such as in glove compartments or on top of steam radiators). They should not be placed near magnetic fields (including those created by

■ PANEL 6.3

Write-protect features for 3½-inch diskette

For data to be written to this diskette, a small piece of plastic must be closed over the tiny window on one side of the disk. To protect the disk from being written to, you must open the window. (Using the tip of a pen helps.)

Writable

Write-protect window closed

Write-protected

Write-protect window open

nearby telephones or electric motors). They also should not be exposed to chemicals (such as cleaning solvents) or spilled beverages.

- **Don't leave the diskette in the drive:** Take the diskette out of the drive when you're done. If you leave the diskette in the drive, the read/write head remains resting on the diskette surface.

Other suggestions for care of diskettes are given at the end of this chapter in the Experience Box.

6.3   Hard Disks

KEY QUESTION

What are hard disks and their various features and options?

Preview & Review: Hard disks are rigid metal platters that hold data as magnetized spots.

Usually a microcomputer hard-disk drive is located inside the system unit, but external hard-disk drives are available, as are removable hard-disk cartridges.

Large computers use removable-pack hard disk systems, fixed-disk drives, or RAID storage systems.

***Hard disks* are thin but rigid metal platters covered with a substance that allows data to be held in the form of magnetized spots.** Hard disks are tightly sealed within an enclosed hard-disk-drive unit to prevent any foreign matter from getting inside. Data may be recorded on both sides of the disk platters.

When users with the early microcomputers that had only diskette drives switched to machines with hard disks, they found the difference was like moving a household all at once with an enormous moving van instead of doing it in several trips in a small sportscar. Whereas a high-density 3½-inch diskette holds 1.44 megabytes, for a few hundred dollars you can get a hard-disk drive that holds as much as 16 gigabytes.

We'll now describe the following aspects of hard-disk technology:

- Microcomputer hard-disk drives
- Hard-disk connections—SCSI and EIDE
- Defragmentation to speed up hard disks
- Virtual memory
- Microcomputer hard-disk variations
- Hard-disk technology for large computer systems

Microcomputer Hard-Disk Drives

In microcomputers, *hard disks* are one or more platters sealed inside a hard-disk drive that is located inside the system unit and cannot be removed. The drive is installed in a drive bay, a shelf or opening in the computer cabinet. The disks may be 5¼ inches in diameter, although today they are more often 3½ inches, some even smaller. From the outside of a microcomputer, a hard-disk drive is not visible; it is hidden behind a front panel on the system cabinet. Inside, however, is a disk mechanism the size of a small sandwich containing disk platters on a drive spindle, read/write heads mounted on an actuator (access) arm that moves back and forth, and power connections and circuitry. (■ *See Panel 6.4.*) The operation is much the same as for a diskette drive, with the read/write heads locating specific pieces of data according to track and sector.

Hard disks have a couple of real advantages over diskettes—and at least one significant disadvantage.

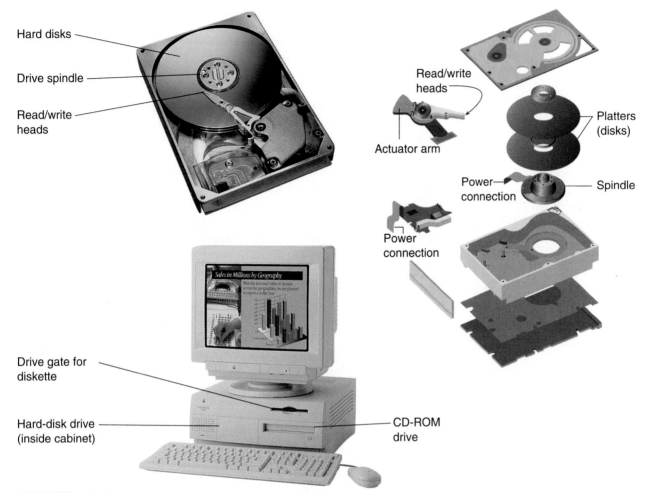

Hard disks

Drive spindle

Read/write heads

Read/write heads

Actuator arm

Platters (disks)

Power connection

Spindle

Power connection

Sales in Millions by Geography

Drive gate for diskette

Hard-disk drive (inside cabinet)

CD-ROM drive

■ PANEL 6.4

Microcomputer internal hard-disk drive

(Top left) A hard-disk drive that has been removed from the system cabinet. *(Right)* Anatomy of a hard-disk drive. *(Bottom left)* The hard-disk drive is sealed inside the system cabinet and is not accessible. The drive gate is for inserting a diskette.

- **Advantages—capacity and speed:** We mentioned that hard disks have a data storage capacity that is significantly greater than that of diskettes. Newer microcomputer hard-disk drives now typically hold 6–9 gigabytes. As for speed, hard disks allow faster access to data than do diskettes because a hard disk spins several times faster than a diskette. A 2.1-gigabyte hard disk will spin at 5600–7800 revolutions per minute, a diskette drive at only 360 rpm.

- **Disadvantage—possible "head crash":** In principle a hard disk is quite a sensitive device. The read/write head does not actually touch the disk but rather rides on a cushion of air about 0.000001 inch thick. The disk is sealed from impurities within a container, and the whole apparatus is manufactured under sterile conditions. Otherwise, all it would take is a smoke particle, a human hair, or a fingerprint to cause what is called a *head crash*. **A *head crash* happens when the surface of the read/write head or particles on its surface come into contact with the disk surface, causing the loss of some or all of the data on the disk.** This can also happen when you bump a computer too hard or drop something heavy on the system cabinet. An incident of this sort could, of course, be a disaster if the data has not been backed up. There are firms that specialize in trying to retrieve (for a hefty price) data from crashed hard disks, though this cannot always be done.

Hard-Disk Connections: SCSI & EIDE

SCSI and EIDE are simply terms that describe two kinds of technological connections by which a hard disk is attached to a microcomputer.

- SCSI: **SCSI (for *small computer system interface*), pronounced "scuzzy," allows you to plug a number of peripheral devices into a single expansion board in your computer by linking these devices end to end in a sort of daisy chain.** Thus, you could link up to 15 peripheral devices, such as a hard disk plus a tape drive plus a scanner. SCSI is the drive-interface connection used on the Macintosh computer and higher-end PCs.

- EIDE: **EIDE (for *enhanced integrated drive electronics*) connects hard drives to a microcomputer by using a flat ribbon cable attached to an expansion board—called a host adapter—that plugs into an expansion slot on the motherboard.** EIDE is popular because of its low cost, and it is increasingly being used to connect CD-ROM drives and tape drives. An inexpensive EIDE host adapter can control two to four hard drives (one of which may be a CD-ROM or optical disk drive), two diskette drives, two serial ports, a parallel port, and a game port.

Fragmentation & Defragmentation: Speeding Up Slow-Running Hard Disks

Like diskettes, for addressing purposes hard disks are divided into a number of tracks and typically nine invisible pie-shaped sectors. Data is stored within the tracks and sectors in groups of clusters. A *cluster* is the smallest storage unit the computer can access, and it always refers to a number of sectors, usually two to eight. (Among other things, cluster size depends on the operating system.)

With a brand-new hard disk, the computer will try to place the data in clusters that are contiguous—that is, that are adjacent (next to one another). Thus, data would be stored on track 1 in sectors 1, 2, 3, 4, and so on. However, as data files are updated and the disk fills up, the operating system stores data in whatever free space is available. Thus, files become fragmented. *Fragmentation* means that a data file becomes spread out across the hard disk in many noncontiguous clusters.

Fragmented files cause the read/write head to go through extra movements to find data, thus slowing access to the data. This means that the computer runs more slowly than it would if all the data elements in each file were stored in contiguous locations. To speed up the disk access, you must defragment the disk. *Defragmentation* means that data on the hard disk is reorganized so that data in each file is stored in contiguous clusters. Programs for defragmenting are available on some operating systems or as separate (external) software utilities (✔ p. 96).

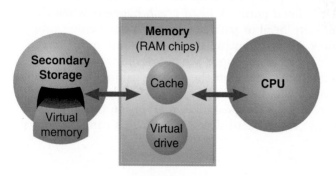

Virtual Memory

Sometimes the computer uses hard-disk space called *virtual memory* to expand RAM. When RAM space is limited, the use of virtual memory can let users run more software at once, if the computer's CPU and operating system are equipped to use it. The system does this by using some free hard-disk space as an extension of

RAM—that is, the computer *swaps* parts of the program and/or data between the hard disk and RAM as needed.

Microcomputer Hard-Disk Variations: Power & Portability

If you have an older microcomputer or one with limited hard-disk capacity, some variations are available that can provide additional power or portability:

- **Miniaturization:** Newer hard-disk drives are less than half the height of older drives ($1\frac{1}{2}$ inches versus $3\frac{1}{2}$ inches high) and so are called *half-height drives.* Thus, you could fit two disk drives into the bay in the system cabinet formerly occupied by one. In addition, the diameter of the disks has been getting smaller. Instead of $3\frac{1}{2}$ inches, some platters are as small as 1 inch in diameter.

- **External hard-disk drives:** If you don't have room in the system unit for another internal hard disk but need additional storage, consider adding an external hard-disk drive. Some detached external hard-disk drives, which have their own power supply and are not built into the system cabinet, can store gigabytes of data.

- **Removable hard disks or cartridge systems:** **Hard-disk cartridges, or removable hard disks, consist of one or two platters enclosed along with read/write heads in a hard plastic case. The case is inserted into an internal or detached external cartridge drive connected to a microcomputer.** (■ *See Panel 6.5.*) One of these is Iomega's Zip drive, whose cartridges each store 100 megabytes. Other popular hard-disk cartridge systems are the Avatar Shark drive (250-megabyte cartridges), the SyQuest SyJet drive (1-gigabyte cartridges), and the Iomega Jaz drive (2-gigabyte cartridges).

  The drives are available in several configurations: EIDE, SCSI, or for parallel ports. A cartridge, which is removable and easily transported in a briefcase, may hold as much as 2 gigabytes of data. These cartridges are often used to transport huge files, such as desktop-publishing files with color and graphics and large spreadsheets. They are also frequently used for backing up data.

■ PANEL 6.5

Removable hard-disk cartridges and drives
Each cartridge has self-contained disks and read/write heads. The entire cartridge, which may store from 100 megabytes to 2 gigabytes of data, may be removed for transporting or may be replaced by another cartridge. *(Left)* Iomega Jaz cartridges and drive, and Zip cartridges and drive. *(Right)* SyQuest drive and cartridge.

Hard-Disk Technology for Large Computer Systems

As a microcomputer user, you may regard secondary-storage technology for large computer systems as being of only casual interest. However, this technology forms the backbone of the revolution in making information available to you over communications lines. The large databases offered by such organizations as America Online and through the Internet and World Wide Web depend to a great degree on secondary-storage technology.

Secondary-storage devices for large computers consist of the following:

- **Removable packs:** A *removable-pack hard disk system* **contains 6–20 hard disks, of 10½- or 14-inch diameter, aligned one above the other in a sealed unit.** Capacity varies, with some packs ranging into the terabytes. These removable hard-disk packs resemble a stack of phonograph records, except that there is space between disks to allow access arms to move in and out. Each access arm has two read/write heads—one reading the disk surface below, the other the disk surface above. However, only *one* of the read/write heads is activated at any given moment.

- **Fixed-disk drives:** *Fixed-disk drives* **are high-speed, high-capacity disk drives that are housed (sealed) in their own cabinets.** Although not removable or portable, they generally have greater storage capacity and are more reliable than removable packs, and so they are used more often. A single mainframe computer might have 20–100 such fixed-disk drives attached to it.

- **RAID storage system:** A fixed-disk drive sends data to the computer along a single path. A *RAID storage system*, which consists of anywhere from 2 to 100 disk drives within a single cabinet, sends data to the computer along several parallel paths simultaneously. Response time is thereby significantly improved. RAID stands for redundant array of independent disks.

   The advantage of a RAID system is that it not only holds more data than a fixed-disk drive within the same amount of space, but it also is more reliable because if one drive fails, others can take over.

RAID unit

6.4 Optical Disks

KEY QUESTION

What are the differences among the four principal types of optical disks?

Preview & Review: Optical disks are removable disks on which data is written and read using laser technology. Four types of optical disks are CD-ROM, CD-R, erasable, and DVD.

By now optical-disk technology is well known to most people. **An *optical disk* is a removable disk on which data is written and read through the use of laser beams.** There is no mechanical arm, as with diskettes and hard disks. The most familiar type of optical disk is the one used in the music industry. An audio CD uses digital code and looks like a miniature phonograph record. Such a CD holds up to 74 minutes (2 billion bits' worth) of high-fidelity stereo sound.

A single optical disk of the type used on computers, called CD-ROM, can hold up to about 700 megabytes of data. This works out to about 269,000 pages of text, or more than 7500 photos or graphics, or 20 hours of speech, or 77 minutes of video. Although some disks are used strictly for digital data storage, many are used to distribute multimedia programs that combine text, visuals, and sound.

In the principal types of optical-disk technology, a high-power laser beam is used to represent data by burning tiny pits into the surface of a hard plas-

■ PANEL 6.6

Optical disks

(Top) Recording (Writing) data—a high-powered laser beam records data by burning tiny pits in an encoded pattern onto the surface of a disk. *(Bottom)* Reading data—a low-powered laser beam is used to read data because it reflects off smooth areas, which are interpreted as 1 bits, but does not reflect off pitted areas, which are interpreted as 0 bits.

Recording data

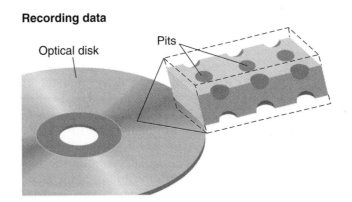

Optical disk   Pits

Reading data

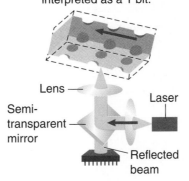

Reading "1":
The laser beam reflects off the smooth surface, which is interpreted as a 1 bit.

Lens
Semi-transparent mirror
Laser
Reflected beam

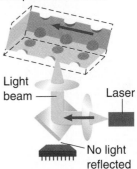

Reading "0":
The laser beam enters a pit and is not reflected, which is interpreted as a 0 bit.

Light beam
Laser
No light reflected

tic disk. To read the data, a low-power laser light scans the disk surface: Pitted areas are not reflected and are interpreted as 0 bits; smooth areas are reflected and are interpreted as 1 bits. (■ *See Panel 6.6.*) Because the pits are so tiny, a great deal more data can be represented than is possible in the same amount of space on a diskette and many hard disks.

The optical-disk technology used with computers consists of four types:

● CD-ROM disks
● CD-R disks
● Erasable disks (CD-E)
● DVD disks

CD-ROM Disks

For microcomputer users, the best-known type of optical disk is the CD-ROM. **CD-ROM, which stands for *compact disk–read-only memory,* is an optical-disk format that is used to hold prerecorded text, graphics, and sound.** Like music CDs, a CD-ROM is a read-only disk. *Read-only* means the disk's content is recorded at the time of manufacture and cannot be written on or erased by the user. You as the user have access only to the data imprinted by the disk's manufacturer. Current microcomputers are being sold with built-in CD-ROM drives, either in a SCSI or an EIDE configuration.

Laptop with CD-ROM drive

At one time a CD-ROM drive was only a single-speed drive. Now there are four-, eight-, ten-, twelve-, sixteen-, twenty-four-, and thirty-two-speed drives (known as 4x, 8x, 10x, 12x, 16x, 24x, and 32x, respectively). A single-speed drive will access data at 150 kilobytes per second, a 16x drive at 2400 kbps, and a 32x drive at 4800 kbps. The faster the drive spins, the more quickly it can deliver data to the processor. There are also multidisk drives that can handle up to 100 disks (*jukeboxes*, or *CD changers*).

There are many uses for CD-ROMs, including the following:

- **Data storage:** Among the top-selling titles are road maps, typeface and illustration libraries for graphics professionals, and video and audio clips. Publishers are also mailing CD-ROMs on such subjects as medical literature, patents, and law.

  Want to have access to every issue in the first 108 years of *National Geographic* magazine? They're now available on 30 CD-ROMs "that include every article, photograph, and even advertisement that has appeared in the magazine during its ... history," according to one report.[3]

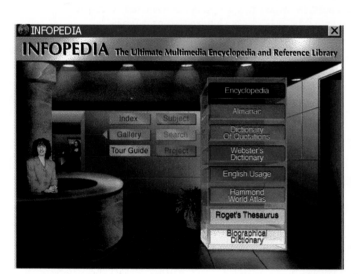

- **Encyclopedias and atlases:** The principal CD-ROM encyclopedias are *Britannica CD*, *Collier's Encyclopedia*, *Compton's Interactive Encyclopedia*, *Encarta Encyclopedia* from Microsoft, *Grolier Multimedia Encyclopedia*, *Infopedia*, and *World Book Multimedia Encyclopedia.* Each packs the entire text of a traditional multivolume encyclopedia onto a single disk, accompanied by pictures, maps, animation, and snippets of audio and video. All have pull-down menus and buttons to trigger search functions.

  CD-ROMs are also turning atlases into multimedia extravaganzas. Mindscape's *World Atlas & Almanac*, for instance, combines the maps, color photos, geographical information, and demographic statistics of a traditional book-style atlas with video, sounds, and the ability to immediately find what you want.

- **Catalogs:** Publishers have also discovered that CD-ROMs can be used as electronic catalogs, or even "megalogs." One, for instance, offers a multimedia catalog of movies available on videotape.

- **Entertainment and games:** As you might expect, CD-ROM has been a hugely successful medium for entertainment and games. Examples are 25 years of Garry Trudeau's comic strip, *Doonesbury* (on one disk), as well as games such as *Myst*, *Doom II*, *Dark Forces*, and *Sherlock Holmes, Consulting Detective.*

- **Music, culture, and films:** In *Xplora 1: Peter Gabriel's Secret World*, you can not only hear rock star Gabriel play his songs but also create "jam sessions" in which you can match up musicians from around the world and hear the result. Other examples of such CD-ROMs are *Bob Dylan: Highway 61 Interactive; Multimedia Beethoven;* and *A Passion for Art.* Several films are on CD-ROM, such as the 1964 Beatles movie *A Hard Day's Night, This Is Spinal Tap,* and *The Day After Trinity.*

- **Education and training:** Want to learn photography? You could buy a pair of CD-ROMs by Bryan Peterson called *Learning to See Creatively* (about composition) and *Understanding Exposure* (discussing the science of exposure). With these disks in your computer, you can practice on-screen with lenses, camera settings, and film speeds.

  You may also explore the inner workings of the human body in *Body Voyage*, a 15-gigabyte CD-ROM package based on Joseph Paul Jernigan, a condemned prisoner executed in 1993. Jernigan gave scientists permission to freeze his body and then cut it into 1878 slices, 1 millimeter each, which were then photographed and scanned into a computer.

- **Edutainment:** *Edutainment software* consists of programs that look like games but actually teach, in a way that feels like fun. An example for children ages 3–6 is *Yearn 2 Learn Peanuts,* which teaches math, geography, and reading.

- **Books:** Book publishers have hundreds of CD-ROM titles, ranging from *Discovering Shakespeare* and *The Official Super Bowl Commemorative Edition* to business directories such as *ProPhone Select* and *11 Million Businesses Phone Book.*

- **Applications and systems software:** Finally, we need to mention that today a great deal of software, such as Windows 98 and Office 97, comes on CD-ROMs rather than diskettes.

Clearly CD-ROMs are not just a mildly interesting technological improvement. They have evolved into a full-fledged mass medium of their own, on the way to becoming as important as books or films.

CD-ROMs & Multimedia

CD-ROMs have enabled the development of the multimedia business. However, as the use of CD-ROMs has burgeoned, so has the vocabulary, creating difficulty for consumers. Much of this confusion arises in conjunction with the words *interactive* and *multimedia.*

As we mentioned earlier, **interactive means that the user controls the direction of a program or presentation on the storage medium.** That is, there is back-and-forth interaction, as between a player and a video game. You could create an interactive production of your own on a diskette. However, because of its limited capacity, you would not be able to present full-motion video and high-quality audio. The best interactive storage media are those with high capacity, such as CD-ROMs and DVD-ROMs.

Multimedia refers to technology that presents information in more than one medium, including text, graphics, animation, video, sound, and voice. As used by telephone, cable, broadcasting, and entertainment companies, *multimedia* also refers to the so-called Information Superhighway. On this avenue various kinds of information and entertainment will presumably be delivered to your home through wired and wireless communication lines.

There are many different CD-ROM formats, some of which work on computers and some of which work only on TVs or special monitors. The majority of nongame CD-ROM disks are available for Macintosh or for Windows-based microcomputers.

CD-R Disks: Recording Your Own CDs

CD-R, which stands for *compact disk—recordable,* is a CD format that allows users to use a peripheral CD recorder to write data (only once) onto

Photo CD

a specially manufactured disk that can then be read by any compatible CD-ROM drive.

CD-R is often used by companies for archiving. However, one of the most interesting examples of CD-R technology is the Photo CD system. Developed by Eastman Kodak, *Photo CD* is a technology that allows photographs taken with an ordinary 35-millimeter camera to be stored digitally on an optical disk. You can shoot up to 100 color photographs and take them to a local photo shop for processing. Then, an hour or so later, your photos will be available online for you to download, or, a bit later than that, you can pick up a CD-ROM with your images. You can then view the disk using any compatible CD-ROM drive—PC, Macintosh, or one of Kodak's own Photo CD players, which attaches directly to a television set.

Erasable Optical Disks

An *erasable optical disk (CDE),* or *rewritable optical disk (CD-RW),* **allows users to record and erase data so that the disk can be used over and over again.** The most common type of erasable or rewritable optical disk is probably the *magneto-optical (MO) disk,* which uses aspects of both magnetic-disk and optical-disk technologies. Such disks are useful to people who need to save successive versions of large documents, handle databases, back up large amounts of data and information, or work in multimedia production or desktop publishing.

DVD: The "Digital Convergence" Disk

A DVD is a silvery, 5-inch optically readable digital disk that looks like an audio compact disk. But, as one writer points out, "DVDs encompass much

DVD disk and drive

more: multiple dialogue tracks and screen formats, and best of all, smashing sound and video."[4] **The *DVD* represents a new generation of high-density CD-ROM disks, which are read by laser and which have both write-once and rewritable capabilities.** According to the various industries sponsoring it, DVD stands for either "digital video disk" or "digital versatile disk."

DVDs can store much more data than standard CDs. The single-sided, single-layer DVD has a capacity of 4.7 gigabytes per side. Single-sided dual-layer DVDs hold 8.5 gigabytes per side. Double-sided DVDs hold 9.4 gigabytes if they are single-layer, and 17 gigabytes if they are dual-layer.

How does a DVD work? Like a CD or CD-ROM, the surface of a DVD contains microscopic pits, which represent the 0s and 1s of digital code that can be read by a laser. The pits on the DVD, however, are much smaller and closer together than those on a CD, allowing far more information to be represented there. Also, the technology uses a new generation of lasers that allows a laser beam to focus on pits roughly half the size of those on current audio CDs. Another important development is that the DVD format allows for two layers of data-defining pits, not just one. Finally, engineers have succeeded in squeezing more data into fewer pits, principally through data compression.[5]

DVDs (and their variant, Divxs) have enormous potential to replace CDs for archival storage, mass distribution of software, and entertainment.[6] Indeed, many new computer systems now come with a DVD drive as standard equipment; these drives can also take standard CD-ROM disks.

6.5 Flash-Memory Cards

KEY QUESTION

What is a flash-memory card?

Preview & Review: Flash-memory cards consist of circuitry on PC cards that can be inserted into slots in a microcomputer.

Disk drives, whether for diskettes, hard disks, CD-ROMs, or DVDs, all involve moving parts—and moving parts can break. Flash-memory cards (✔ p. 125), by contrast, are variations on conventional computer-memory chips, which have no moving parts. **Flash-memory cards consist of circuitry on PC cards that can be inserted into slots connecting to the motherboard.** Flash RAM is one of the options available with PC (PCMCIA) cards. Used as a supplement to or replacement for a hard disk in a portable computer, each flash memory card can hold up to 100 megabytes of data.

6.6 Magnetic Tape

KEY QUESTION

What are the main uses of magnetic tape?

Preview & Review: Magnetic tape is thin plastic tape on which data can be represented with magnetized spots. Tape is used mainly for archiving and backup.

Magnetic tape is thin plastic tape that has been coated with a substance that can be magnetized. Data is represented by magnetized spots (representing 1s) or nonmagnetized spots (representing 0s). On large computers, tapes are used on magnetic-tape units or reels, and in cartridges. On microcomputers, tapes are used only in cartridges.

Today, "mag tape" is used mainly for backup and archiving—that is, for maintaining historical records—where there is no need for quick access.

Cartridge tape units, also called *tape streamers,* are one method used to back up data from a microcomputer hard disk onto a tape cartridge. A cartridge tape unit using ¼-inch cassettes *(QIC, or quarter-inch cassettes)* fits into a standard slot in the microcomputer system cabinet and uses minicartridges that can store up to 17 gigabytes of data on a single tape. A more advanced form of cassette, adapted from technology used in the music industry, is the digital audiotape (DAT), which uses 2- or 3-inch cassettes and stores 2–4 gigabytes. Redesigned DATs called *Traven* technology are expected to hold as much as 8 gigabytes.

6.7 Online Secondary Storage

KEY QUESTIONS

How does online storage work, and what are its advantages?

Preview & Review: Online storage can be used as a secondary-storage method, particularly for stripped-down network computers but also for additional security backup for standard microcomputers. There are advantages and disadvantages to online storage.

Suppose that the network computer actually becomes as popular as its promoters hope it will. This device, you'll recall, consists of a small computer with just a keyboard, display screen, processor, and connecting ports for network or phone cables. The gadget doesn't have any secondary storage. Rather, the Internet itself becomes, in effect, your hard disk.

With or without a network computer, you can use the Internet today as a storage vehicle. This may be particularly useful for backup purposes. Online backup services include Connected Online Backup *(http://www.con-nected.com)*, Network Associates (formerly McAfee) Quick Backup to Personal Vault *(http://www.mcafee.com)* and SafeGuard Interactive *(http://www.sgii.com)*. Monthly prices are generally in the $10–$15 range. When you sign up with the service, you usually download free software from a Web site that lets you upload whatever files you wish to the company's server. For security, you are given a password, and the files are supposedly encrypted to guard against anyone giving them an unwanted look.

From a practical standpoint, online backup should be used only for vital files. Removable hard-disk cartridges are the best medium for backing up entire hard disks, including files and programs.

6.8 Compression & Decompression

KEY QUESTIONS

What is compression, and why is it important?

Preview & Review: Compression is a method of removing redundant elements from a computer file so that it requires less storage space and less time to transmit across the Internet. The two principal compression techniques are "lossless" and "lossy." The principal lossy compression schemes are JPEG for still images and MPEG-1, MPEG-2, and MPEG-4 for moving images.

"Like Gargantua, the computer industry's appetite grows as it feeds," says one writer. "So the smartest software engineers [have been] looking for ways

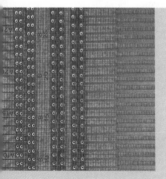

README

Practical Matters: How Long Will Digitized Data Last?

Digital storage has a serious problem: It isn't as long-lived as older forms of data storage. Today's books printed on "permanent" (low-acid, buffered) paper may last up to 500 years. Even books printed on crumbling paper will still be readable. By contrast, data stored on diskettes, magnetic tape, and optical disks is subject to two hazards:[7]

● **Short life span of storage media:** The storage media themselves have a short life expectancy, and often the degradation is not apparent until it's too late. The maximum time seems to be 50 years, the longevity of a high-quality CD-ROM. Some average-quality CD-ROMs won't last 5–10 years, according to tests run at the National Media Laboratory.[8]

The magnetic tapes holding government records, which are stored in the National Archives in Washington, D.C., need to be "refreshed"—copied onto more advanced tapes—every 10 years.

● **Hardware and software obsolescence:** Even when tapes and disks remain intact, the hardware and software needed to read them may no longer be available.

Without the programs and computers used to encode data, digital information may no longer be readable.

"Eight-inch floppy disks and drives, popular as recently as a dozen years ago, are now virtually extinct," says one article, "and their 5¼-inch successors are rapidly disappearing. Optical and magnetic disks recorded under nonstandard storage schemes will be increasingly useless because of the lack of working equipment to read them."[9]

What about the personal records you would store on your own PC, such as financial records, inventories, genealogies, and photographs? *New York Times* technology writer Stephen Manes has a number of suggestions:[10] (1) Choose your storage media carefully. CD-R disks are probably best for archiving—especially if you also keep a paper record. (2) Keep it simple. Store files in a standard format, such as text files and uncompressed bitmapped files. (3) Store data along with the software that created it. (4) Keep two copies, stored in separate places, preferably cool, dry environments. (5) Use high-quality media, not off brands. (6) When you upgrade to a new hardware or software product, have a strategy for transferring the old data.

to shrink the data-meals computers consume, without reducing their nutritional value."[11]

What this writer is referring to is the "digital obesity" brought on by the requirements of the multimedia revolution for putting pictures, sound, and video onto disk or sending them over a communications line. For example, a 2-hour movie contains so much sound and visual information that if stored without modification on a standard CD-ROM, it would require 360 disk changes during a single showing. A broadcast of *Oprah* that presently fits into one conventional, or analog, television channel would require 45 channels if sent in digital language.[12]

The solution for putting more data into less space comes from the mathematical process called compression. **Compression, or *digital-data compression*, is a method of removing redundant (repetitive) elements from a file so that the file requires less storage space and less time to transmit.** After the data is stored or transmitted and is to be used again, it is decompressed. The techniques of compression and decompression are sometimes referred to as *codec* (for *compression/decompression*) techniques.

"Lossless" Versus "Lossy" Compression

There are two principal methods of compressing data—*lossless* and *lossy*. The trade-off between these two techniques is basically data quality versus storage space.

- **"Lossless" techniques:** *Lossless compression* uses mathematical techniques to replace repetitive patterns of bits with a kind of coded summary. During decompression, the "summaries" are replaced with the original patterns of bits. That is, the data that comes out is every bit the same as what went in; it has merely been repackaged for purposes of storage or transmission. Lossless techniques are used for cases in which it's important that *nothing* be lost—as for computer data, database records, spreadsheets, and word processing files.

- **"Lossy" techniques:** *"Lossy" compression techniques* permanently discard some data during compression. Lossy data compression involves a certain loss of accuracy in exchange for a high degree of compression (shrinking material down to as little as 5% of the original file size). This type of compression is often used for graphics files and sound files. Thus, a lossy codec might discard shades of color that a viewer would not notice or soft sounds that are masked by louder ones. In general, most viewers or listeners would not notice the absence of these details.

Compression Standards

Several standards exist for compression, particularly of visual data. If you record and compress in one standard, you cannot play it back in another. The main reason for the lack of agreement is that different industries have different priorities. What will satisfy the users of still photographs, for instance, will not work for the users of movies.

Lossless compression schemes are used for text and numeric data files. Lossy compression schemes are used with graphics and video files. The principal lossy compression schemes are *JPEG* and *MPEG*.

- **Still images—JPEG:** Techniques for storing and transmitting still photographs require that the data remain of high quality. The leading standard for still images is *JPEG* (pronounced "jay-peg"), for the Joint Photographic Experts Group of the International Standards Organization. The JPEG codec looks for a way to squeeze a single image, mainly by eliminating repetitive pixels, or picture-element dots, within the image. Unfortunately, there are more than 30 kinds of JPEG programs. "Unless the decoder in your computer recognizes the version that was used to compress a particular image," noted one reporter, "the result on your computer screen will be multimedia applesauce."[13]

- **Moving images—MPEG:** People who work with videos are less concerned with the niceties of preserving details than are those who deal with still images. They are interested mainly in storing or transmitting an enormous amount of visual information in economical form. A group called *MPEG* ("em-peg"), for Motion Picture Experts Group, was formed to set standards for weeding out redundancies between neighboring images in a stream of video. Three MPEG standards have been developed for compressing visual information—MPEG-1, MPEG-2, and MPEG-4.

The vast streams of bits and bytes of text, audio, and visual information threaten to overwhelm us. Compression/decompression has become a vital technology for rescuing us from the swamp of digital data.

6.9 Organizing Data in Secondary Storage: Databases

KEY QUESTIONS

What is the definition of database, what does a database manager do, and what are the data storage hierarchy and key field?

Preview & Review: A database is an organized collection of integrated files. Examples of databases are personal, public, and private. Databases may also be shared or distributed. Organizations usually appoint a database administrator to manage the database and related activities.

Data in storage is organized as a hierarchy: bits, bytes, fields, records, and files, which are the elements of a database. A key field uniquely identifies each record, making its role in data organization very important.

Many types of files exist. Here we are concerned with *database files,* the type used for keeping records. A *database* is an organized collection of integrated files. This makes them usable in more ways than traditional filing systems (computerized or not), as we shall see.

A database may be small, contained entirely within your own personal computer. Or it may be massive, available online through computer and telephone connections. Such online databases are of special interest to us in this book because they offer us phenomenal resources that until recently were unavailable to most ordinary computer users.

Microcomputer users can set up their own databases using popular database management software. Examples are Paradox, Access, dBASE 5, and Fox-Pro. Such programs are used, for example, by graduate students to conduct research, by salespeople to keep track of clients, by purchasing agents to monitor orders, and by coaches to keep watch on other teams and players.

Some databases are so large that they cannot possibly be stored in a microcomputer. Some of these can be accessed by going online. Such databases, sometimes called *information utilities,* represent enormous compilations of data, any part of which is available, for a fee, to the public.

Examples of well-known information utilities—more commonly known as *online services*—are America Online, CompuServe, and Microsoft Network. As we will describe in Chapter 7, these offer access to news, weather, travel information, home shopping services, reference works, and a great deal more. Some public databases are specialized, such as Lexis, which gives lawyers access to local, state, and federal laws.

Other types of large databases are collections of records shared or distributed throughout a company or other organization. Generally, the records are available only to employees or selected individuals and not to outsiders.

Shared Versus Distributed Databases

A database may be *shared* or *distributed.*

A *shared database* is shared by users in one company or organization in one location. The company owns the database, which is often stored on a minicomputer or mainframe. Users are linked to the database through terminals or microcomputer workstations.

A *distributed database* is one that is stored on different computers in different locations connected by a client/server network (✔ p. 21). For example, sales figures for a chain of discount stores might be located in computers at the various stores, but they would also be available to executives in regional offices or at corporate headquarters. An employee using the database would not know where the data is coming from. However, all employees would still use the same commands to access and use the database.

The Database Administrator

The information in a large database—such as a corporation's patents, formulas, advertising strategies, and sales information—is the organization's lifeblood. Someone needs to manage all activities related to the database. This person is the *database administrator (DBA),* a person who coordinates all related activities and needs for a corporation's database.

The responsibilities include the following:

- **Database design, implementation, and operation:** At the beginning, the DBA helps determine the design of the database. Later he or she determines how space will be used on secondary-storage devices, how files and records may be added and deleted, and how changes are documented.
- **Coordination with users:** The DBA determines user access privileges; sets standards, guidelines, and control procedures; assists in establishing priorities for requests; prioritizes conflicting user needs; and develops user documentation and input procedures.
- **System security:** The DBA sets up and monitors a system for preventing unauthorized access to the database.
- **Backup and recovery:** Because loss of data or a crash in the database could vitally affect the organization, the DBA needs to make sure the system is regularly backed up. He or she also needs to develop plans for recovering data or operations should a failure or disaster occur.
- **Performance monitoring:** The DBA monitors the system to make sure it is serving users appropriately. A standard complaint is that the system is too slow, usually because too many users are trying to access it.

The Data Storage Hierarchy

Data can be grouped into a hierarchy of categories, each increasingly more complex. **The *data storage hierarchy* consists of the levels of data stored in** a computer file: bits, bytes (characters), fields, records, files, and databases. (■ *See Panel 6.7.*)

Computers, we have said, are based on the principle that electricity may be "on" or "off." Thus, individual items of data are represented by the bits 0 for off and 1 for on. Bits and bytes are the building blocks for representing data, whether it is being processed, stored, or telecommunicated. Bits and bytes are what the computer hardware deals with, and you need not be concerned with them. You will, however, be dealing with characters, fields, records, files, and databases.

- Field: **A *field* is a unit of data consisting of one or more characters (bytes).** An example of a field is your name, your address, or your Social Security number.
- Record: **A *record* is a collection of related fields.** An example of a record would be your name *and* address *and* Social Security number.
- File: **A *file* is a collection of related records.** An example of a file is data collected on everyone employed in the same department of a company, including all names, addresses, and Social Security numbers.

■ **PANEL 6.7**

Data storage hierarchy: how data is organized
Bits are organized into bytes, bytes into fields, fields into records, records into files. Related files may be organized into a database.

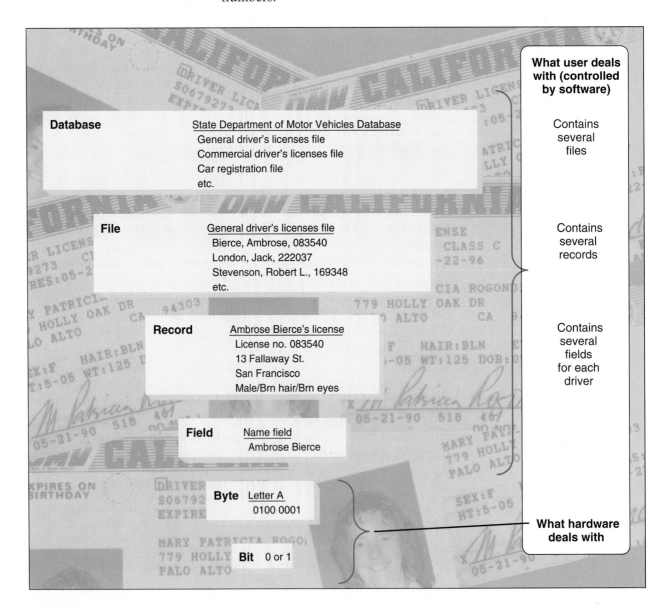

Database   State Department of Motor Vehicles Database
General driver's licenses file
Commercial driver's licenses file
Car registration file
etc.

What user deals with (controlled by software)

Contains several files

File   General driver's licenses file
Bierce, Ambrose, 083540
London, Jack, 222037
Stevenson, Robert L., 169348
etc.

Contains several records

Record   Ambrose Bierce's license
License no. 083540
13 Fallaway St.
San Francisco
Male/Brn hair/Brn eyes

Contains several fields for each driver

Field   Name field
Ambrose Bierce

Byte   Letter A
0100 0001

Bit   0 or 1

What hardware deals with

- Database: **A *database* is an organized collection of integrated files.** A company database might include files on all past and current employees in all departments. There would be various files for each employee: payroll, retirement benefits, sales quotas and achievements (if in sales), and so on.

The Key Field

An important concept in data organization is that of the *key field*. **A *key field* is a field that is chosen to uniquely identify a record so that it can be easily retrieved and processed.** The key field is often an identification number, Social Security number, customer account number, or the like. The primary characteristic of the key field is that it is *unique.* Thus, numbers are clearly preferable to names as key fields because there are many people with common names like James Johnson, Susan Williams, Ann Wong, or Roberto Sanchez, whose records might be confused.

6.10 File Management: Basic Concepts

KEY QUESTIONS

What are the basic types of files, batch and real-time processing, a master file, and a transaction file?

Preview & Review: Common types of files are program, data, ASCII, image, audio, and video files. Transaction files are used to update master files. Files may be processed by batch processing or by real-time processing. Batch processing tends to favor off-line storage. Online, or real-time, processing requires online storage.

How is data stored and accessed? To understand this, first we consider *types of files* and how the computer *keeps track of files.*

Types of Files: Program Files, Data Files, & Others

There are many kinds of files, but perhaps the two principal ones are program files and data files.

- Program files: ***Program files* are files containing software instructions.** Examples are word processing or spreadsheet programs, which are made up of several different program files. The two most important are source program files and executable files. *Source program files* contain high-level computer instructions in the original form written by the programmer.

  For the processor to use source program instructions, they must be translated into machine language (✔ p. 120). The files that contain the machine-language instructions are called *executable files.*

- Data files: ***Data files* are files that contain data**—content such as a report you've created using word processing applications software.

Other common types of files are ASCII files, image files, audio files, and video files; the last three are used in multimedia.

- ASCII files: ASCII (✔ p. 120) is a common binary coding scheme used to represent data in a computer. *ASCII ("as-key") files* are text-only files that contain no graphics and no formatting, such as boldface or italics. This format is used to transfer documents between incompatible computers, such as PC and Macintosh.

- Image files: If ASCII files are for text, *image files* are for digitized graphics, such as art or photographs.

- Audio files: *Audio files* contain digitized sound and are used for conveying sound in CD-ROM multimedia and over the Internet.
- Video files: *Video files* contain digitized video images and are used for such purposes as to convey moving images over the Internet.

Two Types of Data Files: Master File & Transaction File

Among the several types of data files, two are commonly used to update data: a master file and a transaction file.

- Master file: The *master file* is a data file containing relatively permanent records that are generally updated periodically. An example of a master file would be the address-label file for all students currently enrolled at your college.
- Transaction file: The *transaction file* is a temporary holding file that holds all changes to be made to the master file: additions, deletions, revisions. For example, in the case of the address labels for your college, a transaction file would hold new names and addresses to be added (because over time new students enroll) and names and addresses to be deleted (because students leave). It would also hold revised names and addresses (because students change their names or move). Each month or so, the master file would be *updated* with the changes called for in the transaction file.

Batch Versus Online Processing

Updating can be done in two ways: (1) "later," via *batch processing,* or (2) "right now," via *online (real-time) processing.*

- Batch processing: **In *batch processing,* data is collected over several days or weeks and then processed all at one time, as a "batch," against a master file.** Thus, if users need to make some request of the system, they may have to wait until the batch has been processed. Batch processing is less expensive than online processing and is suitable for work in which immediate answers to queries are not needed.
  An example of batch processing is that done by banks for balancing checking accounts. When you deposit a check in the morning, the bank will make a record of it. However, it will not compute your account balance until the end of the day, after all checks have been processed in a batch.
- Online processing: ***Online processing,* also called *real-time processing,* means entering transactions into a computer system as they take place and updating the master files as the transactions occur.** For example, when you use your ATM card to withdraw cash from an automated teller machine, the system automatically computes your account balance then and there. Airline reservation systems also use online processing.

Offline Versus Online Storage

Whether it's on magnetic tape or on some form of disk, data may be stored either offline or online.

- **Offline:** *Offline storage* **means that data is not directly accessible for processing until the tape or disk it's on has been loaded onto an input device.** That is, the storage is not under the direct, immediate control of the central processing unit.

- **Online:** *Online storage* **means that stored data is directly accessible for processing.** That is, storage is under the direct, immediate control of the central processing unit. You need not wait for a tape or disk to be loaded onto an input device.

For processing to be online, the storage must be online and *fast*. This nearly always means storage on disk rather than magnetic tape. With magnetic tape, it is not possible to go directly to the required record; instead, the read/write head has to search through all the records that precede it, which takes time. This is *sequential storage* (✔ p. 183). With disk, however, the system can go directly and quickly to the record—just as a CD player can go directly to a particular spot on a music CD. This is *direct access storage*.

6.11 File Management Systems Versus Database Management Systems

KEY QUESTIONS

What is a database management system, and what are its advantages?

Preview & Review: Files may be retrieved through a file management system, one file at a time. Database management systems are an improvement over file management systems. They use database management system (DBMS) software, which controls the structure of a database and access to the data.

The advantages of databases are reduced data redundancy, improved data integrity, more program independence, increased user productivity, and increased security. However, installing and maintaining a database management system can be expensive.

In the 1950s, when commercial use of computers was just beginning, magnetic tape was the storage medium and records and files were stored sequentially. To work with these files, a user needed a file management system.

A *file management system,* **or** *file manager,* **is software for creating, retrieving, and manipulating files, one file at a time.** Traditionally, a large organization such as a university would have different files for different purposes. For you as a student, for example, there might be one file on you for course grades, another for student records, and a third for tuition billing. Each file would be used independently to produce its own separate reports. If you changed your address, someone had to make the change separately in each file. The arrangement meant more time was required to maintain files. It also prevented a programmer from writing a single program that would access all the data in multiple files.

When magnetic tape began to be replaced by magnetic disk, sequential access storage then began to be replaced by direct access storage. The result was a new technology and new software: the database management system. As mentioned, a *database* is a collection of integrated files, meaning that the file records are logically related, or cross-referenced, to one another. Thus, even though all the pieces of data on a topic are kept in records in different files, they can easily be organized and retrieved with simple requests.

The software for manipulating databases is *database management system (DBMS) software,* **or a** *database manager,* **a program that controls the structure of a database and access to the data.** With a DBMS, then, a large organization such as a university might still have different files for different purposes. As a student, you might have had the same files as you would have had in a file management system (one for course grades, another for student records, and a third for tuition billing). However, in the database management system, data elements are integrated (cross-referenced) and shared among different files. Thus, your address data would need to be in only one file because it can be automatically accessed by the other files.

Advantages of a DBMS

The advantages of databases and DBMS software are as follows:

- **Reduced data redundancy:** *Data redundancy* means that the same data fields appear in many different files and often in different formats. In a file management system, separate files tend to repeat some of the same data over and over. A student's course grades file and tuition billing file would both contain similar data (name, address, telephone number). When data fields are repeated in different files, they waste storage space.

  In a database the information appears just once. The single biggest advantage of a database is that the *same* information is available to *different* users. Moreover, reduced redundancy lowers the expense of storage media and hardware because more data can be stored on the media.

- **Improved data integrity:** *Data integrity* means that data is accurate, consistent, and up to date. However, when the same data fields (a student's address and phone number, for example) must be changed in different files, as in a file management system, some files may be missed or mistakes in some files may go unnoticed. The result is that some reports will be produced with erroneous information.

  In a DBMS, reduced redundancy increases the chances of data integrity—that the data is accurate, consistent, and up to date—because each updating change is made in only one place.

- **More program independence:** With file management systems, different files were often written by different programmers using different file formats. Thus, the files were not *program-independent*. With a database management system, the program and the file formats are the same, so that one programmer or even several programmers can spend less time maintaining files.

- **Increased user productivity:** Database management systems are fairly easy to use, so that users can get their requests for information answered without having to resort to technical manipulations. In addition, users don't have to wait for a computer professional to provide what they need.

- **Increased security:** Although various departments may share data in common, access to specific information can be limited to selected users. Thus, through the use of passwords, a student's financial, medical, and grade information in a university database is made available only to those who have a legitimate need to know.

Disadvantages of a DBMS

Although there are clear advantages to having databases, there are still some disadvantages:

- **Cost issues:** Installing and maintaining a database is expensive, particularly in a large organization. In addition, there are costs associated with training people to use it correctly.

- **Security issues:** Although databases can be structured to restrict access, it's always possible unauthorized users will get past the safeguards. And when they do, they may have access to *all* the files, not just a few. In addition, if a database is destroyed by fire, earthquake, theft, or hardware or software problems, it could be fatal to an organization's business activities—unless steps have been taken to regularly make backup copies of the files and store them elsewhere.

- **Privacy issues:** Databases may hold information they should not and be used for unintended purposes, perhaps intruding on people's privacy. Medical data, for instance, may be used inappropriately in evaluating an employee for a job promotion

6.12 Types of Database Organization

KEY QUESTIONS

What are four types of database organization?

Preview & Review: Types of database organization are hierarchical, network, relational, and object-oriented.

Just as files can be organized in different ways (sequentially or directly, for example), so can databases. The four most common arrangements for database management systems are *hierarchical, network, relational,* and *object-oriented.*

Hierarchical Database

In a *hierarchical database,* fields or records are arranged in related groups resembling a family tree, with lower-level records subordinate to higher-level records. *(■ See Panel 6.8, next page.)* A lower-level record is called a *child,* and a higher-level record is called a *parent.* The parent record at the top of the database is called the *root record.*

Used principally on mainframes, hierarchical DBMSs are the oldest of the four forms of database organization, but they are still used in some types of passenger reservation systems. Also, accessing or updating data is very fast because the relationships have been predefined. However, because the structure must be defined in advance, it is quite rigid. There may be only one parent per child and no relationships among the child records. Moreover, adding new fields to database records requires that the entire database be redefined.

Network Database

A *network database* is similar to a hierarchical DBMS, but each child record can have more than one parent record. *(■ See Panel 6.9, next page.)* Thus, a child record, which in network database terminology is called a *member,* may be reached through more than one parent, which is called an *owner.*

Also used principally with mainframes, the network database is more flexible than the hierarchical one because different relationships may be established between different branches of data. However, it still requires that the structure be defined in advance. Moreover, there are limits to the number of links that can be made among records.

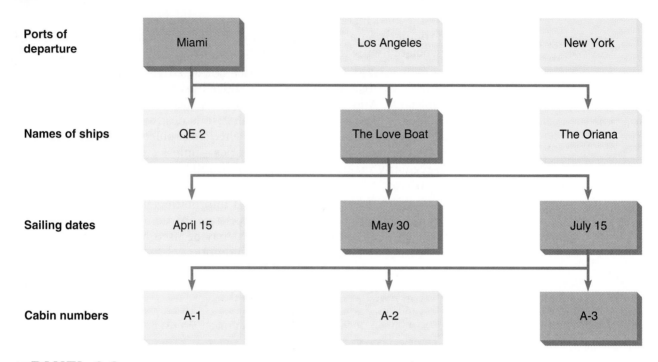

■ PANEL 6.8

Hierarchical database: example of a cruise ship reservation system

Records are arranged in related groups resembling a family tree, with "child" records subordinate to "parent" records. Cabin numbers (A-1, A-2, A-3) are children of the parent July 15. Sailing dates (April 15, May 30, July 15) are children of the parent The Love Boat. The parent at the top, Miami, is called the "root parent."

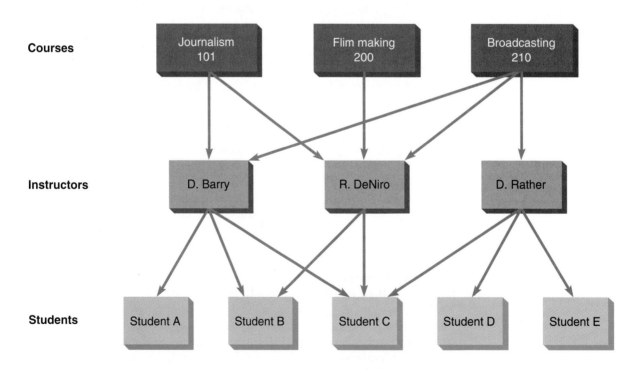

■ PANEL 6.9

Network database: example of a college class scheduling system

This is similar to a hierarchical database, but each child, or "member," record can have more than one parent, or "owner." For example, Student B's owners are instructors D. Barry and R. DeNiro. The owner Broadcasting 210 has three members—D. Barry, R. DeNiro, and D. Rather.

Relational Database

More flexible than hierarchical and network database models, **the *relational database* relates, or connects, data in different files through the use of a key field, or common data element.** (■ *See Panel 6.10.*) In this arrangement there are no access paths down through a hierarchy. Instead, data elements are stored in different tables made up of rows and columns. In database terminology, the tables are called *relations* (files), the rows are called *tuples* (records), and the columns are called *attributes* (fields). All related tables must have a key field that uniquely identifies each row.

The advantage of relational databases is that the user does not have to be aware of any "structure." Thus, they can be used with little training. Moreover, entries can easily be added, deleted, or modified. A disadvantage is that some searches can be time-consuming. Nevertheless, the relational model has become popular for microcomputer DBMSs, such as Paradox and Access.

Object-Oriented Database

The previous three types of databases deal with *structured data*—that is, data that can be neatly classified into fields, rows, and columns. Object-oriented databases can handle new data types, including graphics, audio, and video, which can be combined with text into a multimedia format. Object-oriented databases, then, are important in businesses related to technological convergence and storage of data in multimedia form.

An *object-oriented database system (OODBMS)* uses "objects," software written in small, reusable chunks, as elements within database files. An *object* consists of (1) data in the form of text, sound, video, and pictures and (2) instructions on the action to be taken on the data. A hierarchical or network database would contain only numeric and text data about a student—identification number, name, address, and so on. By contrast, an object-oriented database might also contain the student's photograph, a "sound bite" of his or her voice, and even a short piece of video. Moreover, the object

■ PANEL 6.10

Relational database: example of a state department of motor vehicles database

This kind of database relates, or connects, data in different files through the use of a key field, or common data element. The relational database does not require predefined relationships.

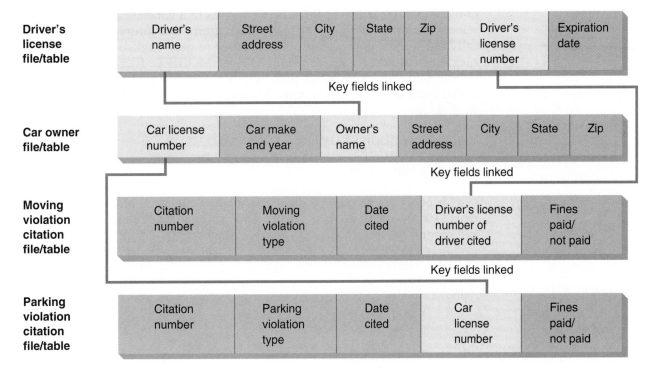

would store operations, called *methods*, programs that objects use to process themselves—for example, how to calculate the student's grade-point average and how to display or print the student's record.

6.13 Features of a DBMS

KEY QUESTION

What are some features of a DBMS?

Preview & Review: Features of a database management system include (1) a data dictionary, (2) utilities, (3) a query language, (4) a report generator, (5) access security, and (6) system recovery.

A database management system may have a number of components, including the following.

Data Dictionary

Some databases have a ***data dictionary*, a procedures document or disk file that stores the data definitions or a description of the structure of data used in the database.** The data dictionary may monitor the data being entered to make sure it conforms to the rules defined during data definition, such as field name, field size, type of data (text, numeric, date, and so on). The data dictionary may also help protect the security of the database by indicating who has the right to gain access to it.

Utilities

The *DBMS utilities* are programs that allow you to maintain the database by creating, editing, and deleting data, records, and files. The utilities allow people to monitor the types of data being input and to adjust display screens for data input, for example.

Query Language

Also known as a *data manipulation language,* **a *query language* is an easy-to-use computer language for making queries to a database and for retrieving selected records,** based on the particular criteria and format indicated. Typically, the query is in the form of a sentence or near-English command, using such basic words as SELECT, DELETE, or MODIFY. There are several different query languages, each with its own vocabulary and procedures. One of the most popular is *Structured Query Language,* or *SQL.* An example of an SQL query is as follows:

SELECT PRODUCT-NUMBER, PRODUCT-NAME
FROM PRODUCT
WHERE PRICE < 100.00

This query selects all records in the product file for products that cost less than $100.00 and displays the selected records according to product number and name—for example:

A-34   Mirror
C-50   Chair
D-168   Table

Report Generator

A *report generator* is a program users may employ to produce an on-screen or printed document from all or part of a database. You can specify the format of the report in advance—row headings, column headings, page headers, and so on. With a report generator, even nonexperts can create attractive, readable reports on short notice.

Access Security

At one point in *Disclosure,* the Michael Douglas/Demi Moore movie, Douglas's character, the beleaguered division head suddenly at odds with his company, types SHOW PRIVILEGES into his desktop computer, which is tied to the corporate network. To his consternation, the system responds by showing him downgraded from PRIOR USER LEVEL: 5 to CURRENT USER LEVEL: 0, shutting him out of files to which he formerly had access.

This is an example of the use of *access security,* a feature allowing database administrators to specify different access privileges for different users of a DBMS. For instance, one kind of user might be allowed only to retrieve (view) data whereas another might have the right to update data and delete records. The purpose of this security feature, of course, is to protect the database from unauthorized access and sabotage.

Physical security is also important, and one of the most effective strategies is to simply *isolate* a database system to protect it from threats. For example, backup copies of databases on removable magnetic disks could be stored in a guarded vault, with authorized employees admitted only by producing a badge with their encoded personal voice prints.

System Recovery

Some advanced database management systems should have *system recovery* features that enable the database administrator to recover contents of the database in the event of a hardware or software failure.

6.14 The Ethics of Using Storage & Databases: Concerns About Accuracy & Privacy

KEY QUESTION

What are some ethical concerns about the uses of databases?

Preview & Review: Users of information technology must weigh the effects of the digital manipulation of sound, photos, and video in art and journalism. Databases may contain inaccuracies or be incomplete. They also may endanger privacy—in the areas of finances, health, employment, and commerce. There may be a danger of certain information becoming monopolized that perhaps should not be.

Ethics

The giant capacities of today's storage devices has given photographers, graphics professionals, and others a new tool—the ability to manipulate images at the level of pixels (✔ p. 156). For example, photographers can easily do *morphing*—transforming one image into another. **In *morphing*, a film or video image is displayed on a computer screen and altered pixel by pixel, or dot by dot. The result is that the image metamorphoses into something else**—a pair of lips into the front of a Toyota, for example.

The ability to manipulate digitized output—images and sounds—has brought a wonderful new tool to art. However, it has created some big new

problems in the area of credibility, especially for journalism. How can we now know that what we're seeing or hearing is the truth? Consider the following.

Manipulation of Sound

Frank Sinatra's 1994 album *Duets* paired him through technological tricks with singers like Barbra Streisand, Liza Minnelli, and Bono of U2. Sinatra recorded solos in a recording studio. His singing partners, while listening to his taped performance on earphones, dubbed in their own voices. This was done not only at different times but often, through distortion-free phone lines, from different places. The illusion in the final recording is that the two singers are standing shoulder to shoulder.

Newspaper columnist William Safire called *Duets* "a series of artistic frauds." Said Safire, "The question raised is this: When a performer's voice and image can not only be edited, echoed, refined, spliced, corrected, and enhanced—but can be transported and combined with others not physically present—what is performance? . . . Enough of additives, plasticity, virtual venality; give me organic entertainment."[14] Some listeners feel that the technology changes the character of a performance for the better. Others, however, think the practice of assembling bits and pieces in a studio drains the music of its essential flow and unity.

Whatever the problems of misrepresentation in art, however, they pale beside those in journalism. Could not a radio station edit a stream of digitized sound to achieve an entirely different effect from what actually happened?

Manipulation of Photos

When O. J. Simpson was arrested in 1994 on suspicion of murder, the two principal American newsmagazines both ran pictures of him on their covers.[15,16] *Newsweek* ran the mug shot unmodified, as taken by the Los Angeles Police Department. *Time,* however, had the shot redone with special effects as a "photo-illustration" by an artist working with a computer. Simpson's image was darkened so that it still looked like a photo but, some critics said, with a more sinister cast to it.

Should a magazine that reports the news be taking such artistic license? Should *National Geographic* in 1982 have photographically moved two Egyptian pyramids closer together so that they would fit on a vertical cover? Was it even right for *TV Guide* in 1989 to run a cover showing Oprah Winfrey's head placed on Ann-Margret's body? In another case, to show what can be done, a photographer digitally manipulated the famous 1945 photo showing the meeting of the leaders of the wartime Allied powers at Yalta. Joining Stalin, Churchill, and Roosevelt are some startling newcomers: Sylvester Stallone and Groucho Marx. The additions are done so seamlessly it is impossible to tell the photo has been altered. (■ *See Panel 6.11.*)

■ PANEL 6.11

Photo manipulation
In this 1945 photo, World War II Allied leaders Joseph Stalin, Winston Churchill, and Franklin D. Roosevelt are shown from left to right. Digital manipulation has added Sylvester Stallone standing behind Roosevelt and Groucho Marx seated at right.

The potential for abuse is clear. "For 150 years, the photographic image has been viewed as more persuasive than written accounts as a form of 'evidence,'" says one writer. "Now this authenticity is breaking down under the assault of technology."[17] Asks a former photo editor of the *New York Times Magazine*, "What would happen if the photograph appeared to be a straightforward recording of physical reality, but could no longer be relied upon to depict actual people and events?"[18]

Many editors try to distinguish between photos used for commercialism (advertising) versus for journalism, or for feature stories versus for news stories. However, this distinction implies that the integrity of photos applies only to some narrow definition of news. In the end, it can be argued, altered photographs pollute the credibility of all of journalism.

Manipulation of Video

The technique of morphing, used in still photos, takes a massive jump when used in movies, videos, and television commercials. Morphing and other techniques of digital image manipulation have had a tremendous impact on filmmaking. Director and digital pioneer Robert Zemeckis *(Death Becomes Her)* compares the new technology to the advent of sound in Hollywood.[19] It can be used to erase jet contrails from the sky in a western and to make digital planes do impossible stunts. It can even be used to add and erase actors. In *Forrest Gump*, many scenes involved old film and TV footage that had been altered so that the Tom Hanks character was interacting with historical figures.

Films and videotapes are widely thought to accurately represent real scenes (as evidenced by the reaction to the amateur videotape of the Rodney King beating by police in Los Angeles). Thus, the possibility of digital alterations raises some real problems. One is the possibility of doctoring videotapes supposed to represent actual events. Another concern is for film archives: Because digital videotapes suffer no loss in resolution when copied, there are no "generations." Thus, it will be impossible for historians and archivists to tell whether the videotape they're viewing is the real thing or not.[20]

Matters of Accuracy & Completeness

Databases—including public databases such as Nexis/Lexis, Dialog, and Dow Jones News/Retrieval—can provide you with *more* facts and *faster* facts but not always *better* facts. Penny Williams, professor of broadcast journalism at Buffalo State College in New York and formerly a television anchor and reporter, suggests there are five limitations to bear in mind when using databases for research:[21]

- **You can't get the whole story:** For some purposes, databases are only a foot in the door. There may be many facts or aspects to the topic you are looking into that are not in a database. Reporters, for instance, find a database is a starting point, but it may take old-fashioned shoe leather to get the rest of the story.

- **It's not the gospel:** Just because you see something on a computer screen doesn't mean it's accurate. Numbers, names, and facts may need to be verified in other ways.

- **Know the boundaries:** One database service doesn't have it all. For example, you can find full text articles from the *New York Times* on Lexis/Nexis, from the *Wall Street Journal* on Dow Jones News/ Retrieval, and from the *San Jose Mercury News* on America Online, but no service carries all three.

- **Find the right words:** You have to know which keywords (search words) to use when searching a database for a topic. As Lynn Davis, a professional researcher with ABC News, points out, in searching for stories on guns, the keyword "can be guns, it can be firearms, it can be handguns, it can be pistols, it can be assault weapons. If you don't cover your bases, you might miss something."[22]

- **History is limited:** Most public databases, Davis says, have information going back to 1980, and a few into the 1970s, but this poses problems if you're trying to research something that happened or was written about earlier.

Matters of Privacy

***Privacy* is the right of people to not reveal information about themselves.** Who you vote for in a voting booth and what you say in a letter sent through the U.S. mail are private matters. However, the ease with which databases and communications lines may pull together and disseminate information has put privacy under extreme pressure.

As you've no doubt discovered, it's no trick at all to get your name on all kinds of mailing lists. Theo Theoklitas, for instance, has received applications for credit cards, invitations to join video clubs, and notification of his finalist status in Ed McMahon's $10 million sweepstakes. Theo is a 6-year-old black cat who's been getting mail ever since his owner sent in an application for a rebate on cat food.[23] A whole industry has grown up of professional information gatherers and sellers, who collect personal data and sell it to fund-raisers, direct marketers, and others.

In the 1970s, the Department of Health, Education, and Welfare developed a set of five Fair Information Practices. These rules have since been adopted by a number of public and private organizations. The practices also led to the enactment of a number of laws to protect individuals from invasion of privacy. (■ *See Panel 6.12.*)

▪ PANEL 6.12

The five Fair Information Practices and important federal privacy laws

The Fair Information Practices were developed by the U.S. Department of Health, Education, and Welfare in the early 1970s. They have been adopted by many public and private organizations since.

Fair Information Practices

1. There must be no personal data record-keeping systems whose existence is a secret from the general public.
2. People have the right to access, inspect, review, and amend data about them that is kept in an information system.
3. There must be no use of personal information for purposes other than those for which it was gathered without prior consent.
4. Managers of systems are responsible and should be held accountable and liable for the reliability and security of the systems under their control, as well as for any damage done by those systems.
5. Governments have the right to intervene in the information relationships among private parties to protect the privacy of individuals.

Important Federal Privacy Laws

Freedom of Information Act (1970): Gives you the right to look at data concerning you that is stored by the federal government. A drawback is that sometimes a lawsuit is necessary to pry it loose.

Fair Credit Reporting Act (1970): Bars credit agencies from sharing credit information with anyone but authorized customers. Gives you the right to review and correct your records and to be notified of credit investigations for insurance or employment. A drawback is that credit agencies may share information with anyone they reasonably believe has a "legitimate business need." Legitimate is not defined.

Privacy Act (1974): Prohibits federal information collected about you for one purpose from being used for a different purpose. Allows you the right to inspect and correct records. A drawback is that exceptions written into the law allow federal agencies to share information anyway.

Family Educational Rights and Privacy Act (1974): Gives students and their parents the right to review, and to challenge and correct, students' school and college records; limits sharing of information in these records.

Right to Financial Privacy Act (1978): Sets strict procedures that federal agencies must follow when seeking to examine customer records in banks; regulates financial industry's use of personal financial records. A drawback is that the law does not cover state and local governments.

Privacy Protection Act (1980): Prohibits agents of federal government from making unannounced searches of press offices if no one there is suspected of a crime.

Cable Communications Policy Act (1984): Restricts cable companies in the collection and sharing of information about their customers.

Computer Fraud and Abuse Act (1986): Allows prosecution for unauthorized access to computers and databases. A drawback is that people with legitimate access can still get into computer systems and create mischief without penalty.

Electronic Communications Privacy Act (1986): Makes eavesdropping on private conversations illegal without a court order.

Computer Security Act (1987): Makes actions that affect the security of computer files and telecommunications illegal.

Computer Matching and Privacy Protection Act (1988): Regulates computer matching of federal data; allows individuals a chance to respond before government takes adverse actions against them. A drawback is that many possible computer matches are not affected, such as those done for law-enforcement or tax reasons.

Video Privacy Protection Act (1988): Prevents retailers from disclosing video-rental records without the customer's consent or a court order.

Privacy concerns don't stop with the use or misuse of information in databases. It also extends to privacy in communications. Although the government is constrained by several laws on acquiring and disseminating information, and listening in on private conversations, privacy advocates still worry. In recent times, the government has tried to impose new technologies that would enable law-enforcement agents to gather a wealth of personal information. Proponents have urged that Americans must be willing to give up some personal privacy in exchange for safety and security. We discuss this matter in Chapter 10.

Monopolizing Information

"We want to capture the entire human experience throughout history," says Corbis Corporation chief executive officer Doug Rowan.[24] Corbis was formed in 1989 by software billionaire Bill Gates to acquire digital rights to fine art and photographic images that can be viewed electronically—in everything from electronic books to computerized wall hangings.[25] In 1995 Corbis acquired the Bettmann Archive of 17 million photographs, for scanning into its digital database.[26] Its founder, Dr. Otto Bettmann, called his famous collection a "visual story of the world," and indeed many of the images are unique. They include tintypes of black Civil War soldiers, the 1937 crash of the *Hindenburg* dirigible, and John F. Kennedy Jr. saluting the casket of his assassinated father.

However, when Rowan says Corbis wants to capture all of human experience, he means not just photos and art works from the likes of the National Gallery in London and the State Hermitage Museum in St. Petersburg, Russia, for which Corbis also owns digital imaging rights. "Film, video, audio," he says. "We are interested in those fields too."

Are there any ethical problems with one company having in its database the exclusive digital rights to our visual and audio history? Like many museums and libraries (such as the Library of Congress), Corbis joins a trend toward democratizing art and scholarship by converting the images and texts of the past into digital form and making them available to people who could never travel to, say, London or St. Petersburg.

However, when Gates acquired the Bettmann images, for example, the move put their future use "into the hands of an aggressive businessman who, unlike Dr. Bettmann, is planning his own publishing ventures," points out one reporter. "While Mr. Gates's initial plans will make Bettmann images more widely accessible, this savvy competitor now ultimately controls who can use them—and who can't."[27]

Good Habits: Protecting Your Computer System, Your Data, & Your Health

Whether you set up a desktop computer and never move it or tote a portable PC from place to place, you need to be concerned about protection. You don't want your computer to get stolen or zapped by a power surge. You don't want to lose your data. And you certainly don't want to lose your health for computer-related reasons. Here are some tips for taking care of these vital areas.

Protecting Your Computer System

Computers are easily stolen, particularly portables. They also don't take kindly to fire, flood, or being dropped. Finally, a power surge through the power line can wreck the insides.

Guarding Against Hardware Theft & Loss Portable computers—laptops, notebooks, and subnotebooks—are easy targets for thieves. Obviously, anything conveniently small enough to be slipped into your briefcase or backpack can be slipped into someone else's. Never leave a portable computer unattended in a public place.

It's also possible to simply lose a portable, as in forgetting it's in the overhead-luggage bin in an airplane. To help in its return, use a wide piece of clear tape to tape a card with your name and address to the outside of the machine. You should tape a similar card to the inside also. In addition, scatter a few such cards in the pockets of the carrying case.

Desktop computers are also easily stolen. However, for under $25, you can buy a cable and lock, like those used for bicycles, that secure the computer, monitor, and printer to a work area. For instance, you can drill a quarter-inch hole in your equipment and desk, then use a product called LEASH-IT (from Z-Lock, Redondo Beach, California) to connect them together. LEASH-IT consists of two tubular locks and a quarter-inch aircraft-grade stainless steel cable.

If your hardware does get stolen, its recovery may be helped if you have inscribed your driver's license number, Social Security number, or home address on each piece. Some campus and city police departments lend inscribing tools for such purposes. (And the tools can be used to mark some of your other possessions.)

Finally, insurance to cover computer theft or damage is surprisingly cheap. Look for advertisements in computer magazines. (If you have standard tenants' or homeowners' insurance, it may not cover your computer. Ask your insurance agent.)

Guarding Against Heat, Cold, Spills, & Drops "We fried them. We froze them. We hurled them. We even tried to drown them," proclaimed *PC Computing,* in a story about its sixth annual "torture test" of notebook computers. "And only about half survived."[28]

The magazine put 16 notebook computers through durability trials. One approximated putting these machines in a car trunk in the desert heat (2 hours at 180 degrees), another with leaving them outdoors in a Chicago winter (2 hours at 0 degrees). A third test simulated sloshing coffee on a keyboard, and a fourth dropped them 29 inches to the floor. All passed the bake and freeze tests. Some keyboards failed the coffee-spill test, although most revived after drying out and/or cleaning. Seven failed one of the two drop tests (flat drop and edge drop). Of the 16, nine ultimately survived (although some required reformatting after the drop tests).

This gives you an idea of how durable computers are. Designed for portability, notebooks may be hardier than desktop machines. Even so, you really don't want to tempt fate by dropping your computer, which could cause your hard-disk drive to fail. And you really shouldn't drink around your notebook. Or, if you do, take your coffee black, since sugar and cream do the most damage.

Guarding Against Power Fluctuations Electricity is supposed to flow to an outlet at a steady voltage level. No doubt, however, you've noticed instances when the lights in your house suddenly brighten or, because a household appliance kicks in, dim momentarily. Such power fluctuations can cause havoc with your computer system, although most computers have some built-in protection. An increase in voltage may be a spike, lasting only a fraction of a second, or a surge, lasting longer. A surge can burn out the power supply circuitry in the system unit. A decrease may be a momentary voltage sag, a longer brownout, or a complete failure or blackout. Sags and brownouts can produce a slowdown of the hard-disk drive or a system shutdown.

Power problems can be handled by plugging your computer, monitor, and other devices into a surge protector or surge suppressor or a UPS. If you're concerned about a lightning storm sending a surge to your system, simply unplug all your hardware until the storm passes.

Guarding Against Damage to Software System software and applications software generally come on CD-ROM disks or flexible diskettes. The unbreakable rule is simply this: Copy the original disk, either onto your hard-disk drive or onto another diskette. Then store the original disk in a safe place. If your computer gets stolen or your software destroyed, you can retrieve the original and make another copy.

Protecting Your Data

Computer hardware and commercial software are nearly always replaceable, although perhaps with some expense and difficulty. Data, however, may be major trouble to replace or even be irreplaceable. (A report of an eyewitness account, say, or a complex spreadsheet project might not come out the same way when you try to reconstruct it.) The following are some precautions to take to protect your data.

Backup Backup Backup Almost every microcomputer user sooner or later has the experience of accidentally wiping out or losing material and having no backup copy. This is what makes people true believers in backing up their data. If you're working on a research paper, for example, it's fairly easy to copy your work onto a diskette at the end of your work session. You can then store that disk in another location. If your computer is destroyed by fire, at least you'll still have the data (unless you stored your disk right next to the computer).

If you do lose data because your disk has been physically damaged, you may still be able to recover it by using special software.

Treating Diskettes with Care Diskettes can be harmed by any number of enemies. These include spills, dirt, heat, moisture, weights, and magnetic fields and magnetized objects. Here are some diskette-maintenance tips:

- Insert the diskette *carefully* into the disk drive.
- Do not manipulate the metal "shutter" on the diskette; it protects the surface of the magnetic material inside.
- Do not place heavy objects on the diskette.
- Do not expose the diskette to excessive heat or light.
- Do not use or place diskettes near a magnetic field, such as a telephone or paper clips stored in magnetic holders. Data can be lost if exposed.
- Do not clean diskettes.
- Instead of leaving disks scattered on your desk, where they can be harmed by dust or beverage spills, it's best to store them in their boxes.
- From time to time it's best to clean the diskette drive, because dirt can get into the drive and cause data loss. You can buy an inexpensive drive-cleaning kit, which includes a disk that looks like a diskette and cleans the drive's read/write heads.

Note: No disk lasts forever. Experts suggest that a diskette that is used properly might last 10 years. However, if you're storing data for the long term, you should copy the data onto new disks every 2 years (or use tape for backup). Note also that over the long run, software compatibility may become an issue if you are trying to use diskettes written in an old program.

Guarding Against Viruses Computer viruses are programs—"deviant" programs—that can cause destruction to computers that contract them. They are spread from computer to computer in two ways: (1) They may be passed by way of an "infected" diskette, such as one a friend gives you containing a copy of a game you want. (2) They may be passed over a network or an online service. They may then attach themselves to software on your hard disk, adding garbage to or erasing your files or wreaking havoc with the system software. They may display messages on your screen (such as "Jason Lives") or they may evade detection and spread their influence elsewhere.

Each day, viruses are getting more sophisticated and harder to detect. The best protection is to install antivirus software. Some programs prevent viruses from infecting your system, others detect the viruses that have slipped through, and still others remove viruses or institute damage control. (Some of the major antivirus programs are Norton AntiVirus, Dr. Solomon's Anti-Virus Toolkit, McAfee Associates' Virus Scan, and Webscan.)

Protecting Your Health

More important than any computer system and (probably) any data is your health. What adverse effects might computers cause? As we discussed earlier in the chapter, the most serious are painful hand and wrist injuries, eyestrain and headache, and back and neck pains. Some experts also worry about the long-range effects of exposure to electromagnetic fields and noise. All these matters can be addressed by *ergonomics,* the study of the physical relationships between people and their work environment. Let's see what you can do to avoid these problems.

Protecting Your Hands & Wrists To avoid difficulties, consider employing the following:

- **Hand exercises:** You should warm up for the keyboard just as athletes warm up before doing a sport in order to prevent injury. There are several types of warm-up exercises. You can gently massage the hands, press the palm down to stretch the underside of the forearms, or press the fist down to stretch the top side of the forearm. Experts advise taking frequent breaks, during which time you should rotate and massage your hands.

- **Work-area setup:** Many people set up their computers in the same way as they would a typewriter. However, the two machines are for various reasons ergonomically different. With a computer, it's important to set up your work area so that you sit with both feet on the floor, thighs at right angles to your body. The chair should be adjustable and support your lower back. Your forearms should be parallel to the floor. You should look down slightly at the screen. (■ *See Panel 6.13.*) This setup is particularly important if you are going to be sitting at a computer for hours.

- **Wrist position:** To avoid wrist and forearm injuries, you should keep your wrists straight and hands relaxed as you type. Instead of putting the keyboard on top of a desk, therefore, you should put it on a low table or in a keyboard drawer under the desk. Otherwise the nerves in your wrists will rub against the sheaths surrounding them, possibly leading to RSI pains. Some experts also suggest using a padded, adjustable wrist rest, which attaches to the keyboard.

Various kinds of ergonomic keyboards are also available, such as those that are hinged in the middle.

Guarding Against Eyestrain, Headaches, & Back & Neck Pains Eyestrain and headaches usually arise because of improper lighting, screen glare, and long shifts staring at the screen. Make sure your windows and lights don't throw a glare on the screen, and that your computer is not framed by an uncovered window. Headaches may also result from too much noise, such as listening for hours to an impact printer printing out.

Back and neck pains occur because furniture is not adjusted correctly or because of heavy computer use. Adjustable furniture and frequent breaks should provide relief here.

Some people worry about emissions of electromagnetic waves and whether they could cause problems in pregnancy or even cause cancer. The best approach is to simply work at an arm's length from computers with CRT-type monitors.

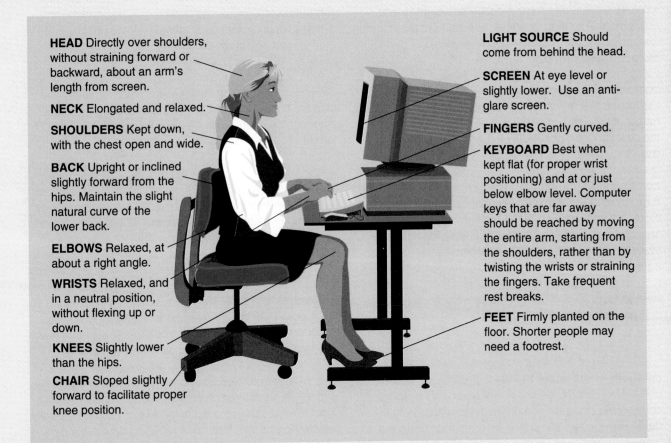

HEAD Directly over shoulders, without straining forward or backward, about an arm's length from screen.

NECK Elongated and relaxed.

SHOULDERS Kept down, with the chest open and wide.

BACK Upright or inclined slightly forward from the hips. Maintain the slight natural curve of the lower back.

ELBOWS Relaxed, at about a right angle.

WRISTS Relaxed, and in a neutral position, without flexing up or down.

KNEES Slightly lower than the hips.

CHAIR Sloped slightly forward to facilitate proper knee position.

LIGHT SOURCE Should come from behind the head.

SCREEN At eye level or slightly lower. Use an anti-glare screen.

FINGERS Gently curved.

KEYBOARD Best when kept flat (for proper wrist positioning) and at or just below elbow level. Computer keys that are far away should be reached by moving the entire arm, starting from the shoulders, rather than by twisting the wrists or straining the fingers. Take frequent rest breaks.

FEET Firmly planted on the floor. Shorter people may need a footrest.

■ **PANEL 6.13**

How to set up your computer work area

Summary

What It Is/What It Does

batch processing (p. 204, KQ 6.10) Method of processing whereby data is collected over several days or weeks and then processed all at one time, as a "batch" used to update the master file.

compact disk–read-only memory (CD-ROM) (p. 193, KQ 6.4) Optical-disk form of secondary storage that holds more data than diskettes; used to hold prerecorded text, graphics, sound, and video. Like music CDs, a CD-ROM is a read-only disk.

compact disk—recordable (CD-R) (p. 195, KQ 6.4) CD format that allows users to write data onto a specially manufactured disk inserted in a peripheral CD recorder; the disk can then be read by a compatible CD-ROM drive.

compression (digital-data compression) (p. 199, KQ 6.8) Process of removing redundant and unnecessary elements from a file so that it requires less storage space or can be easily transmitted. After the data is stored or transmitted it can be decompressed and used again.

database (p. 203, KQ 6.9) Integrated collection of files in a computer system.

database management system (DBMS) (p. 205, KQ 6.11) Also called a *database manager;* software that controls the structure of a database and access to the data; allows users to manipulate more than one file at a time (as opposed to file managers).

Why It's Important

With batch processing, if users need to make a request of the system, they must wait until the batch has been processed. Batch processing is less expensive than online processing and is suitable for work in which immediate answers to queries are not needed.

CD-ROM disks are being used to sell off-the-shelf microcomputer software, books and magazines, and multimedia games, encyclopedias, atlases, movie guides, and training and education programs.

CD-R is often used by business for archiving, but it is also the basis for Kodak's Photo CD technology, and it allows home users to do their own recordings in CD format.

Storage and transmission of digital data—particularly of graphics—requires a huge amount of electronic storage capacity, and transmission is difficult to accomplish over copper wire. Thus compression programs are necessary to reduce the size of these files.

Businesses and organizations build databases to help them keep track of and manage their affairs. In addition, users with online connections to database services have enormous research resources at their disposal.

This software enables: sharing of data (same information is available to different users); economy of files (several departments can use one file instead of each individually maintaining its own files, thus reducing data redundancy, which in turn reduces the expense of storage media and hardware); data integrity (changes made in the files in one department are automatically made in the files in other departments); security (access to specific information can be limited to selected users).

data dictionary (p. 210, KQ 6.13) File that stores data definitions and descriptions of database structure. It may also monitor new entries to the database as well as user access to the database.

The data dictionary monitors the data being entered to make sure it conforms to the rules defined during data definition. The data dictionary may also help protect the security of the database by indicating who has the right to gain access to it.

data files (p. 203, KQ 6.10) Files that contain data, not programs.

Data files contain content that a user has created and stored using applications propgrams. The program may add an extension, such as .DAT.

data storage hierarchy (p. 201, KQ 6.9) The levels of data stored in a computer file: bits, bytes (characters), fields, records, files, and databases.

Bits and bytes are what the computer hardware deals with, so users need not be concerned with them. They will, however, deal with characters, fields, records, files, and databases.

DBMS utilities (p. 210, KQ 6.13) Programs that allow the maintenance of databases by creating, editing, and deleting data, records, and files.

DBMS utilities allow people to establish what is acceptable input data, to monitor the types of data being input, and to adjust display screens for data input.

direct access storage (p. 183, KQ 6.1) Method of storage that allows the computer to go directly to the information sought. Any record can be found quickly by entering its key field, such as a Social Security number, so direct access saves time compared to sequential storage when there is no pattern to searches.

Although the storage media—hard disks and other kinds of disks—is more expensive than tape, the cost is justified by the much quicker random searches.

disk drive (p. 185, KQ 6.2) Computer hardware device that holds, spins, reads from, and writes to magnetic or optical disks.

Users need disk drives in order to use their disks. Disk drives can be internal (built into the computer system cabinet) or external (connected to the computer by a cable).

diskette (p. 184, KQ 6.2) Also called *floppy disk;* secondary-storage medium; removable round, flexible mylar disk that stores data as electromagnetic charges on a metal oxide film that coats the mylar plastic. Data is represented by the presence or absence of these electromagnetic charges, following standard patterns of data representation (such as ASCII). The 3½-inch-wide disk is contained in a square plastic case to protect it from being touched by human hands. It is called "floppy" because the disk within the envelope or case is flexible, not rigid.

Diskettes are used on all microcomputers.

DVD (digital video, or versatile, disk) (p. 196, KQ 6.4) A new generation of high-density compact disk that is read by laser and has both write-once and rewritable capabilities. The five-inch optical disk looks like a regular audio CD, but with dual layers, more tightly spaced pits, and the more precise laser that reads it, a DVD can store up to 17 gigabytes.

DVDs provide great storage capacity, studio-quality images, and theater-like surround sound. However, competing DVD standards and a new challenger, Divx, have so far kept DVDs from taking over the place of CD-ROMs.

What It Is/What It Does	Why It's Important

enhanced integrated drive electronics (EIDE) (p. 190, KQ 6.3) An interface that connects hard drives to a microcomputer by using a flat ribbon cable attached to an expansion board (the host adapter) that plugs into an expansion slot on the motherboard. Also used increasingly to connect CD-ROM and tape drives.

EIDE is popular because of its low cost; one inexpensive host adapter can control two to four hard drives, two diskette drives, two serial ports, a parallel port, and a game port.

erasable optical disk (CDE) (p. 196, KQ 6.4) Also called a *rewritable optical disk (CD-RW);* optical disk that allows users to erase data so that the disk can be used over and over again (as opposed to CD-ROMs, which can be read only).

The most common type of erasable and rewritable optical disk is probably the magneto-optical disk, which uses aspects of both magnetic-disk and optical-disk technologies. Such disks are useful to people who need to save successive versions of large documents, handle enormous databases, or work in multimedia production or desktop publishing.

field (p. 202, KQ 6.9) Unit of data consisting of one or more characters (bytes). An example of a field is your name, your address, *or* your Social Security number.

A collection of fields make up a record. *Also see key field.*

file (p. 202, KQ 6.9) In a database, a collection of related records. An example of a file is collected data on everyone employed in the same department of a company, including all names, addresses, and Social Security numbers.

Integrated files make up a database.

file management system (file manager) (p. 205, KQ 6.11) Software for creating, retrieving, and manipulating files, one file at a time.

In the 1950s, magnetic tape was the storage medium and records and files were stored sequentially. File managers were created to work with these files. Today, however, database managers are more common.

fixed-disk drive (p. 192, KQ 6.3) High-speed, high-capacity disk drive housed in its own cabinet.

Although fixed disks are not removable or portable, these units generally have greater storage capacity and are more reliable than removable disk packs. A single mainframe computer might have 20–100 such fixed disk drives attached to it.

flash-memory card (p. 197, KQ 6.5) Circuitry on credit-card-size cards (PC cards) that can be inserted into slots in the computer that connect to the motherboard.

Flash-memory cards are variations on conventional computer-memory chips; however, unlike standard RAM chips, flash memory is nonvolatile—it retains data even when the power is turned off. Flash memory can be used not only to simulate main memory but also to supplement or replace hard-disk drives for permanent storage.

hard disk (p. 188, KQ 6.3) Secondary-storage medium; thin but rigid metal platter covered with a substance that allows data to be held in the form of magnetized spots. Hard disks are tightly sealed within an enclosed hard-disk-drive unit to prevent any foreign matter from getting inside. Data may be recorded on both sides of the disk platters. In a microcomputer, the drive is inside the system unit and not removable.

Hard disks hold much more data than diskettes do. Nearly all microcomputers now use hard disks as their principal secondary-storage medium.

hard-disk cartridge (p. 191, KQ 6.3) One or two hard-disk platters enclosed along with read/write heads in a hard plastic case. The case is inserted into an external or detached cartridge system connected to a microcomputer.

A hard-disk cartridge, which is removable and easily transported in a briefcase, may hold gigabytes of data. Hard-disk cartridges are often used for transporting large graphics files and for backing up data.

head crash (p. 189, KQ 6.3) Disk disturbance that occurs when the surface of a read/write head or particles on its surface come into contact with the disk surface, causing the loss of some or all of the data on the disk.

Head crashes can spell disaster if the data on the disk has not been backed up.

hierarchical database (p. 207, KQ 6,12) One of the four common arrangements for database management systems; fields or records are arranged in related groups resembling a family tree, with "child" records subordinate to "parent" records. A parent may have more than one child, but a child always has only one parent. To find a particular record, one starts at the top with a parent and traces down the chart to the child.

Hierarchical DBMSs work well when the data elements have an intrinsic one-to-many relationship, as might happen with a reservations system. The difficulty, however, is that the structure must be defined in advance and is quite rigid. There may be only one parent per child and no relationships among the child records.

interactive (p. 195, KQ 6.4) Refers to a situation in which the user controls the direction of a program or presentation on the storage medium; that is, there is back-and-forth interaction between the user and the computer or communications device. The best interactive storage media are those with high capacity, such as CD-ROMs and DVDs.

Interactive devices allow the user to be an active participant in what is going on instead of just reading to it.

key field (p. 203, KQ 6.9) Field that contains unique data used to identify a record so that it can be easily retrieved and processed. The key field is often an identification number, Social Security number, customer account number, or the like. The primary characteristic of the key field is that it is *unique.*

Key fields are needed to identify and retrieve specific records in a database.

magnetic tape (p. 197, KQ 6.6) Thin plastic tape coated with a substance that can be magnetized; data is represented by the magnetized or nonmagnetized spots. Tape can store files only sequentially.

Tapes are used in reels, cartridges, and cassettes. Today "mag tape" is used mainly to provide backup, or duplicate storage.

morphing (p. 211, KQ 6.14) Process in which a film or video image is displayed on a computer screen and altered pixel by pixel (dot by dot) so that it metamorphoses into something else, such as a toddler into a grandfather.

Morphing is frequently used in advertising and helps photo professionals further their range, but it also threatens the credibility of photographs.

multimedia (p. 195, KQ 6.4) Refers to technology that presents information in more than one medium, including text, graphics, animation, video, sound effects, music, and voice.

Use of multimedia is becoming more common in business, the professions, and education as a means of adding depth and variety to presentations, such as those in entertainment and education. *Multimedia* also refers to the so-called Information Superhighway, the delivery of information and entertainment to users' homes through wired and wireless communication lines.

network database (p. 207, KQ 6.12) One of the four common arrangements for database management systems; it is similar to a hierarchical DBMS, but each child record can have more than one parent record. Thus, a child record may be reached through more than one parent.

This arrangement is more flexible than the hierarchical one. However, it still requires that the structure be defined in advance. Moreover, there are limits to the number of links that can be made among records.

object (p. 209, KQ 6.12) Software written in small, reusable chunks and consisting of (1) data in the form of text, sound, video, and pictures and (2) instructions on the action to be taken on the data.

Once written, the software chunk can readily be reused.

object-oriented database system (OODBMS) (p. 209, KQ 6.12) One of the four common database structures; uses objects as elements within database files.

In addition to textual data, an object-oriented database can store, for example, a person's photo, "sound bites" of her voice, and a video clip, as well as methods for processing and outputting the data.

offline storage (p. 205, KQ 6.10) Refers to data that is not directly accessible for processing until a tape or disk has been loaded onto an input device.

The storage medium and data are not under the immediate, direct control of the central processing unit.

online processing (p. 204, KQ 6.10) Also called *real-time processing;* means entering transactions into a computer system as they take place and updating the master files as the transactions occur; requires direct access storage.

The storage medium and data are not under the immediate, direct control of the central processing unit.

online storage (p. 205, KQ 6.10) Refers to stored data that is directly accessible for processing.

Online processing gives users accurate information from an ATM machine or an airline reservations system, for example.

optical disk (p. 192, KQ 6.4) Removable disk on which data is written and read through the use of laser beams. The most familiar form of optical disk is the CD used in the music industry.

Optical disks hold much more data than magnetic disks. Optical disk storage is expected to dramatically affect the storage capacity of microcomputers.

What It Is/What It Does	Why It's Important

privacy (p. 214, KQ 6.14) Right of people to not reveal information about themselves.

The ease with which databases and communications lines may pull together and disseminate information has put privacy under extreme pressure.

program files (p. 203, KQ 6.10) Files containing software instructions.

This term is used to differentiate program files from data files.

query language (p. 210, KQ 6.13) Easy-to-use computer language for making queries to a database and retrieving selected records.

Query languages make it easier for users to deal with databases. To retrieve information from a database, users make queries—that is, they use a query language. These languages have commands such as SELECT, DELETE, and MODIFY.

record (p. 202, KQ 6.9) Collection of related fields. An example of a record would be your name *and* address *and* Social Security number.

Related records make up a file.

relational database (p. 209, KQ 6.12) One of the four common arrangements for database management systems; relates, or connects, data in different files through the use of a key field, or common data element. In this arrangement there are no access paths down through a hierarchy. Instead, data elements are stored in different tables made up of rows and columns. The tables are called *relations*, the rows are called *tuples*, and the columns are called *attributes*. Within a table, a row resembles a record. All related tables must have a key field that uniquely identifies each row.

The relational database is the most flexible arrangement. The advantage of relational databases is that the user does not have to be aware of any "structure." Thus, they can be used with little training. Moreover, entries can easily be added, deleted, or modified. A disadvantage is that some searches can be time consuming. Nevertheless, the relational model has become popular for microcomputer DBMSs.

removable-pack hard disk system (p. 192, KQ 6.3) Secondary storage with 6–20 hard disks, of 10½- or 14-inch diameter, aligned one above the other in a sealed unit. These removable hard-disk packs resemble a stack of phonograph records, except that there is space between disks to allow access arms to move in and out. Each access arm has two read/write heads—one reading the disk surface below, the other the disk surface above. However, only one of the read/write heads is activated at any given moment.

Such secondary storage systems enable a large computer system to store massive amounts of data.

sectors (p. 186, KQ 6.2) On a diskette, invisible wedge-shaped sections used by the computer for storage reference purposes.

When users save data from computer to diskette, it is distributed by tracks and sectors on the disk. That is, the system software uses the point at which a sector intersects a track to reference the data location in order to spin the disk and position the read/write head.

What It Is/What It Does	**Why It's Important**

sequential storage (p. 183, KQ 6.1) Method of data storage by which data is stored in sequence, such as alphabetically.

Sequential storage is the least expensive form of storage because it uses magnetic tape, which is cheaper than disks. But finding data is time-consuming because it requires searching through all records that precede the record sought, such as searching the A through M records to find an N record.

small computer system interface (SCSI) (p. 190, KQ 6.3) An interface that allows the user to plug a number of peripheral devices linked end to end in a daisy chain into a single expansion board in the computer cabinet.

A SCSI interface allows one board to serve a number of peripherals, such as a tape drive, scanner, and external hard disk. It is used on Macintoshes and higher-end PCs.

tracks (p. 186, KQ 6.2) The rings on a diskette along which data is recorded. Unlike on a phonograph record, these tracks are neither visible grooves nor a single spiral. Rather, they are closed concentric rings. Each track is divided into sectors.

See sectors.

write-protect feature (p. 187, KQ 6.2) Feature of diskettes that prevents the disk from being written to, which would replace its data. By pressing a slide lever to uncover a small hole in the lower right corner of the disk, write-protection is activated; closing the slide allows the disk to be written to again.

This feature allows users to protect data on diskettes from accidental change or erasure.

Exercises

Self-Test

1. A(n) _____ is about 1 trillion bytes.

2. _____ is the data access method used by hard disks.

3. _____, a secondary storage device, is most commonly used for backup and archiving information.

4. A removable hard disk is called a _____ _____.

5. A(n) _____ is a removable disk on which data is written and read through the use of laser beams.

6. According to the data storage hierarchy, databases are composed of:
   a. _____
   b. _____
   c. _____

7. An individual piece of data within a record is called a(n) _____.

8. A special file in the DBMS called the _____ _____ maintains descriptions of the structure of data used in the database.

9. _____ is the right of people not to reveal information about themselves.

10. A(n) _____ _____ coordinates all related activities and needs for an organization's database.

Short-Answer Questions

1. What is the significance of the terms *track* and *sector*?

2. What are some of the uses for CD-ROMs?

3. What kinds of secondary-storage devices do large computer systems use?

4. What are the advantages of a hard disk over a diskette?

5. What is the difference between batch and online processing?

6. What are the main disadvantages of traditional file management systems?

7. What is a query language?

8. Which law protects you against government agencies keeping copies of your personnel records?

Multiple-Choice Questions

1. All diskettes must be _____ before they can store data.
   a. named
   b. saved
   c. retrieved
   d. formatted
   e. All of the above

2. Which of the following optical technologies can be used with the full range of electronic, television, and computer hardware?
   a. CD-ROM
   b. CD-R
   c. CDE
   d. DVD
   e. All of the above

3. Which of the following is considered a disadvantage of online storage?
   a. price
   b. safety
   c. portability
   d. slow speed
   e. None of the above

4. Which of the following is a disadvantage of database management systems?
   a. cost issues
   b. data redundancy
   c. lack of program independence
   d. lack of data integrity
   e. All of the above

5. Which of the following database organizations should you choose if you need to store photos?
   a. hierarchy
   b. network
   c. relational
   d. object-oriented
   e. None of the above

6. Which of the following isn't a feature of a DBMS?

   a. data dictionary

   b. utilities

   c. query language

   d. sequential access storage

   e. report generator

7. Which of the following database structures is similar to the hierarchy structure, except that a child record can have more than one parent record?

   a. network

   b. relational

   c. object-oriented

   d. file-management

   e. None of the above

True/False Questions

T F   1. EIDE and SCSI describe two kinds of connections by which a hard disk is attached to a microcomputer.

T F   2. Hard disks may be affected by a head crash when particles on the read/write heads come into contact with the disk's surface.

T F   3. To use a diskette, you usually need a disk drive, but not always.

T F   4. Magnetic tape can handle only sequential data storage and retrieval.

T F   5. One advantage to using diskettes is that they aren't susceptible to extreme temperatures.

T F   6. Ensuring backup and recovery of a database is not one of the functions of a database administrator.

T F   7. Old file-management methods provided the user with an easy way to establish relationships among records in different files.

T F   8. The use of key fields makes it easier to locate a record in a database.

T F   9. A transaction file contains relatively permanent records that are periodically updated.

T F   10. A database is an organized collection of integrated files.

Knowledge in Action

1. You want to purchase a hard disk for use with your microcomputer. Because you don't want to have to upgrade your secondary-storage capacity in the near future, you are going to buy one with the highest storage capacity you can find. Use computer magazines or visit computer stores and find a hard disk you would like to buy. What is its capacity? How much does it cost? Who is the manufacturer? What are the system requirements? Is it an internal or an external drive? Can you install/connect this unit yourself? Why have you chosen this unit and this storage capacity?

2. What types of storage hardware are currently being used in the computer you use at school or at work? What are the storage capacities of these hardware devices? Would you recommend that alternate storage hardware be used? Why or why not?

3. What optical technologies do you think you will use in your planned career or profession? How do you expect to use this technology? Which optical technologies have you already used? For what?

4. Interview someone who works with or manages a database at your school or university. What types of records make up the database, and which departments use it? What types of transactions do these departments enact? Which database structure is used? What are the types and sizes of the storage devices? Was the software custom-written?

5. Describe the characteristics of an object-oriented database that might be useful to a large number of people, including yourself. What type of objects would this database contain? How would this database be used? Who would typically access this database? Does this type of database exist already? Why? Why not?

Tele-communications

The Uses of Online Resources & the Internet

key questions

You should be able to answer the following questions:

The white line dividing computers and telephones, voice and data, is blurring at last."

Why? Because "of a confluence of technology and demand—driven, to a huge degree, by the Internet phenomenon," says this *Business Week* analysis.[1] Companies that in the 1980s spent millions constructing their own private communications systems are now shifting over to the Internet and the graphics-oriented section of it called the World Wide Web. Because of its standard interfaces and low rates, "the Internet has been the great leveler for communications—the way the PC was for computing," says Boston analyst Virginia Brooks.[2]

This chapter describes the Internet, of course, but it is also concerned with the much wider world of communications—the uses of everything from fax machines to extranets. Just as you can learn to operate a car without knowing much about how it works, so you can learn to use telecommunications. And millions of people do. But to stay in the forefront of your career, it's imperative that you *do* know how things work, so that you can understand what's happening with the changes in the field. Accordingly, in this book we first explain *what* you can do with telecommunications; that's covered in this chapter. Then we go behind the scenes and describe *how* it all works; that's covered in the next chapter. (If you wish, the chapters can be read in reverse order.)

7.1 The Practical Uses of Communications & Connectivity

KEY QUESTION

What are communications and connectivity?

Preview & Review: Communications, also called telecommunications, refers to the electronic collection and transfer of information from one location to another. The ability to connect devices by communications lines to other devices and sources of information is known as connectivity. Communications devices and services range from telephone-related services to computer-related communications.

Clearly, communications is extending into every nook and cranny of civilization—the "plumbing of cyberspace," as it has been called. The term *cyberspace* was coined by William Gibson in his novel *Neuromancer*. In that book it refers to a futuristic computer network that people use by plugging their brains into it. Today *cyberspace* encompasses not only the computer online world and the Internet in particular but also the whole wired and wireless world of communications in general.

Communications & Connectivity

Communications, **also called** *telecommunications*, **refers to the electronic collection and transfer of information from one location to another.** The data being communicated may consist of voice, sound, text, video, graphics, or all of these. The electromagnetic instruments sending the data may be telegraph, telephone, cable, microwave, radio, or television. The distance may be as close as the next room or as far away as the outer edge of the solar system. The ability to connect devices by communications lines to other devices and sources of information is known as *connectivity*.

Tools of Communications & Connectivity

What kinds of options do communications and connectivity give you? Let us consider the possibilities. We will take them in order, more or less, from relatively simpler to more complex activities. (■ *See Panel 7.1, next page.*) They include:

- Telephone-related communications services: fax messages and voice mail
- Video/voice communication: videoconferencing and picture phones
- Online information services
- The Internet
- The World Wide Web part of the Internet
- Shared resources: workgroup computing, Electronic Data Interchange (EDI), intranets, and extranets
- New Internet technologies

7.2 Telephone-Related Communications Services

KEY QUESTION

How do fax and voice mail work?

Preview & Review: Telephone-related communications include fax messages, transmitted by dedicated fax machines and fax boards, and voice mail, voice messages stored in digitized form.

Phone systems and computer systems have begun to fuse together. Services available through telephone connections, whether the conventional wired kind or the wireless cellular-phone type, include *fax messages* and *voice mail.*

Fax Messages

Asking "What is your fax number?" is about as common a question in the work world today as asking for someone's telephone number. Indeed, the majority of business cards include both a telephone number and a fax number. *Fax* stands for "facsimile transmission," or reproduction. A fax may be sent by dedicated fax machine or by fax board (✔ p. 148).

- Dedicated fax machines: **Dedicated fax machines are specialized devices that do nothing except send and receive documents over transmission lines to and from other fax machines.** These are the stand-alone machines nowadays found everywhere, from offices to airports to instant-printing shops.
- Fax boards: **A *fax board,* which is installed as a circuit board inside a computer's system cabinet, is a modem with fax capability. It enables you to send signals directly from your computer to someone else's fax machine or fax board.**

Voice Mail

Like a sophisticated telephone answering machine, **voice mail digitizes incoming voice messages and stores them in the recipient's "voice mailbox" in digitized form. It then converts the digitized versions back to voice messages when they are retrieved.** Messages can be copied and forwarded to other people, saved, or erased.

■ PANEL 7.1

The world of connectivity
Wired or wireless communications links offer several options for information and communications.

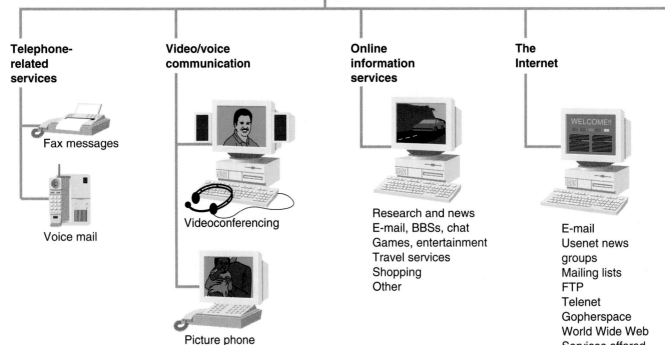

World of Connectivity

Telephone-related services

Fax messages

Voice mail

Video/voice communication

Videoconferencing

Picture phone

Online information services

Research and news
E-mail, BBSs, chat
Games, entertainment
Travel services
Shopping
Other

The Internet

E-mail
Usenet news groups
Mailing lists
FTP
Telenet
Gopherspace
World Wide Web
Services offered by online information service

7.3 Video/Voice Communication: Videoconferencing & Picture Phones

KEY QUESTION

What are the characteristics of videoconferencing and picture phones?

Preview & Review: Videoconferencing is the use of television, sound, and computer technology to enable people in different locations to see, hear, and talk with one another.

Want to have a meeting with people on the other side of the country or the world but don't want the hassle of travel? You may have heard of or participated in a *conference call,* also known as *audio teleconferencing,* a meeting in which people in different geographical locations talk on the telephone. Now we have video plus voice communication, specifically *videoconferencing* and *picture phones.*

"I was a little nervous about going in front of the camera," says Mark Dillard, "but I calmed down pretty quickly after we got going, and it went well."[3] Interviewing for a job can be an uncomfortable event for a lot of people. However, Dillard had just undergone the high-tech version of it: sitting

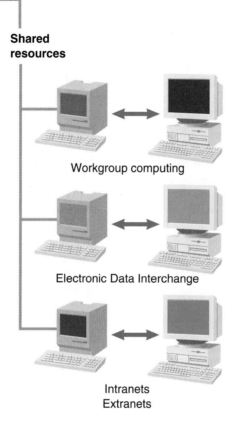

**Shared
resources**

Workgroup computing

Electronic Data Interchange

Intranets
Extranets

Videoconferencing

in front of a video camera in a booth at a local Kinko's store in Atlanta and talking to a job recruiter in New York.

Videoconferencing, **also called** *teleconferencing*, **is the use of television video and sound technology as well as computers to enable people in different locations to see, hear, and talk with one another.** Videoconferencing can consist of people meeting in separate conference rooms or booths with specially equipped television cameras. However, videoconferencing equipment can also be set up on people's desks, with a camera and microphone to capture the person speaking and a monitor and speakers for the person being spoken to. The *picture phone* is a telephone with a TV-like screen and a built-in camera that allows you to see the person you're calling, and vice versa.

The main difficulty with videoconferencing and picture phones is that the standard copper wire in what the telecommunications industry calls POTS—for "plain old telephone service"—has been unable to communicate images very rapidly. Thus, unless you are with an organization that can afford expensive high-speed communications lines, present-day screens will convey a series of jerky, freeze-frame or stop-action still images of the faces of the communicating parties.

7.4 Online Information Services

KEY QUESTIONS

What are online services, and what do they offer?

Preview & Review: Commercial companies called online information services provide software that connects users' computers and modems over phone lines with facilities that provide e-mail, research, shopping, financial services, and Internet connections, among a host of other services.

Before the use of the Internet became common and before the World Wide Web was developed, computer users used online information services to access many sources of information and services. *An online information service* **provides access, for a fee, to all kinds of databases and electronic meeting places to subscribers equipped with telephone-linked microcomputers.** There are several online services, but four are considered the most mainstream. They are *America Online (AOL)*, with nearly 10 million subscribers; *CompuServe*, with about 7.5 million; *Microsoft Network (MSN)*, with about 3 million; and *Prodigy*, with about 1 million.[4]

To gain access to online services, you need a computer and printer so you can download (transfer) and print out online materials. You also need a modem. Finally, you need communications software so your computer can communicate via modem and interact with the online service's computers. (We described the fundamentals of going online with an online service in the Experience Box at the end of Chapter 2.) America Online, CompuServe, and other mainstream services provide subscribers with their own software for going online, but you can also buy communications programs separately, such as ProComm Plus.

Opening an account with an online service requires a credit card, and billing policies resemble those used by cable-TV and telephone companies. As with cable TV, you may be charged a fee for basic service, with additional fees for specialized services. In addition, the online service may charge you for the time spent while on the line. Finally, you will also be charged by your telephone company for your time on the line, just as when making a regular phone call. However, most information services offer local access numbers. Thus, unless you live in a rural area, you will not be paying long-distance phone charges.

The Offerings of Online Services

Although the Internet offers the same information as online services, many users still prefer online services because the information is packaged—organized, filtered, and put in user-friendly form. Some of the options:

- **People connections—e-mail, message boards, chat rooms:** Online services can provide a community through which you can connect with people with similar interests (without identifying yourself, if you prefer). The primary means for making people connections are via e-mail, message boards, and "chat rooms."

  E-mail will be discussed in detail shortly. *Message boards* allow you to post and read messages on any of thousands of special topics. *Chat rooms* are discussion areas in which you may join with others in a real-time "conversation," typed in through your keyboard. The topic may be general or specific, and the collective chat-room conversation scrolls on the screen.

- **Research and news:** The only restriction on the amount of research you can do online is the limit on whatever credit card you are charging your time to, if you are not using a free database. Depending on the online service, you can avail yourself of several encyclopedias. Many online services also offer access, for a fee, to databases of unabridged text from newspapers, journals, and magazines. Indeed, the information resources available online are mind-boggling.

- **Games, entertainment, and clubs:** Online computer games are extremely popular. In single-player games, you play against the computer. In multiplayer games, you play against others, whether someone in your household or someone overseas. Other entertainments include cartoons, sound clips, pictures of show-business celebrities, and reviews of movies and CDs. You can also join online clubs with others who share your interests, whether science fiction, popular music, or cooking.

- **Free software:** Many users download freeware, shareware (✔ p. 65), and commercial demonstration programs from online sources. They can also download software updates (called *patches*).

Online restaurant directory

  - **Travel services:** Online services use Eaasy Sabre or Travelshopper, streamlined versions of the reservations systems travel agents use. You can search for flights and book reservations through the computer and have tickets sent to you by Federal Express. You can also review hotel and restaurant guides, such as the Zagat Restaurant Directory.

  - **Shopping:** If you can't stand parking hassles, limited store hours, and checkout lines, online services may provide a shopping alternative. In some cities it's even possible to order groceries through online services. Peapod Inc. is an online grocery service serving 10,000 households in the Chicago and San Francisco areas. Peapod offers more than 18,000 items, from laundry detergent to lettuce. The orders are delivered in temperature-controlled containers.

  - **Financial management:** Online services also offer access to investment brokerages so that you can invest money and keep tabs on your portfolio and on the stock market.

Will Online Services Survive the Internet?

The online services have a lot to offer. One survey two years ago, for instance, found that *half* of the people on the Net got there through commercial services, which suggests they may be among the easiest ways to get to the Web.[5] In addition, the online services package information so that you can more quickly and easily find what you're looking for. It's also easier to conduct a live "chat" session on an online service than it is on the Web, and it is easier for parents to exert control over the kinds of materials their children may view.

However, as the Internet and particularly the World Wide Web have become easier to navigate, online services have begun to lose customers and content providers—even as they have added their own arrangements for accessing the Internet. Indeed, many of the same kinds of things the online services offer are now directly accessible through the Internet.

7.5 The Internet

KEY QUESTION

What are the Internet, its connections, its addresses, and its features?

Preview & Review: The Internet, the world's biggest network, uses a protocol called TCP/IP to allow computers to communicate. Users can connect to the Internet via direct connections, online information services, and Internet service providers. Its features include e-mail, Usenet newsgroups, mailing lists, FTP, Gopherspace, Telnet, and the World Wide Web.

Called "the mother of all networks," the **Internet, or simply "the Net," is an international network connecting approximately 140,000 smaller networks in more than 200 countries.** Try as you may, you cannot imagine how much data is available on the Internet. (■ *See Panel 7.2.*) Besides e-mail, chat rooms, message boards, games, and free software, there are thousands of databases containing information of all sorts. Here is a sampling, a few droplets from what is a Niagara Falls of information:

The Library of Congress card catalog. The daily White House press releases. Weather maps and forecasts. Schedules of professional sports teams. Weekly Nielsen television ratings. Recipe archives. The Central Intelligence Agency world map. A ZIP Code guide. The National Family Database. Project Gutenberg (offering the complete text of many works of literature). The Alcoholism

■ PANEL 7.2

The Internet
What's available through the network of all networks.

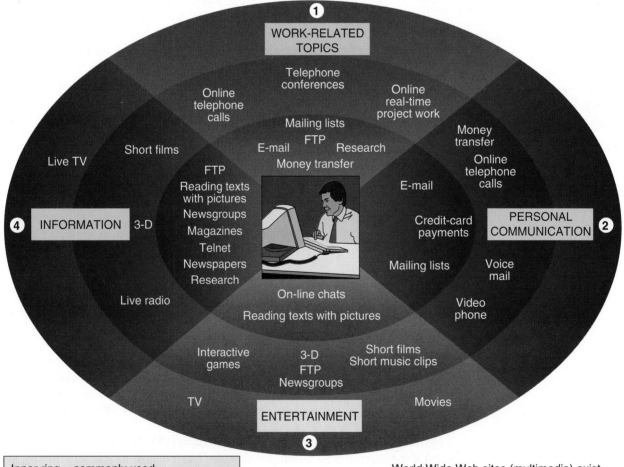

Inner ring = commonly used
Middle ring = less frequently used
Outer ring = technologically not yet in place

World Wide Web sites (multimedia) exist for all areas in the inner two rings.

Research Data Base. Guitar chords. U.S. government addresses and phone (and fax) numbers. *The Simpsons* archive.[6]

To connect with the Internet, you need pretty much the same things you need to connect with online information services: a computer, modem and telephone line (or other network connection), and appropriate communications software.

Created by the U.S. Department of Defense in 1969 (under the name ARPAnet—ARPA was the department's Advanced Research Project Agency), the Internet was built to serve two purposes. The first was to share research among military, industry, and university sources. The second was to provide a diversified system for sustaining communication among military units in the event of nuclear attack. Thus, the system was designed to allow many routes among many computers, so that a message could arrive at its destination by many possible ways, not just a single path. This original network system was largely based on the Unix operating system (✔ p. 93).

With the many different kinds of computers being connected, engineers had to find a way for the computers to speak the same language. The solution developed was *TCP/IP*, the standard since 1983 and the heart of the Internet. *TCP/IP*, for *Transmission Control Protocol/Internet Protocol*, is the standardized set of computer guidelines (protocols) that allow different computers on different networks to communicate with each other efficiently. (We discuss the concept of protocols in Chapter 8.) The effect is to make the Internet appear to the user to operate as a single network.

Connecting to the Internet

There are three ways to connect your microcomputer with the Internet:

- **Through school or work:** Universities, colleges, and most large businesses have high-speed phone lines that provide a direct connection to the Internet. This type of connection is known as dedicated access. *Dedicated access* means a communication line is used that is designed for one purpose. If you're a student, this may be the best deal because the connection is free or low cost. To use a direct connection, your microcomputer must have TCP/IP software and be connected to the local network that has the direct-line connection to the Net.

- **Through online information services:** As mentioned, subscribing to a commercial online information service, which provides you with its own communications software, may not be the cheapest way to connect to the Internet, but in the past, at least, it was one of the easiest. In this case, the online service acts as an electronic "gateway" to the Internet.

- **Through Internet service providers (ISPs): *Internet service providers (ISPs) are local or national companies that will provide public access to the Internet (and World Wide Web) for a flat monthly fee.*** Essentially an ISP is a small network connected to the high-speed communications links that make up the Internet's backbone—the major supercomputer sites and educational and research foundations within the United States and throughout the world.

   Once you have contacted an ISP and paid the required fee, the ISP will provide you with information about phone numbers for a local connection, called a *point of presence (POP)*—a server owned by the

ISP or leased from a common carrier, such as AT&T. The ISP also provides software for setting up your computer and modem to dial into their network of servers, which involves acquiring a user name ("user ID") and a password.

You can ask someone who is already on the Web to access the worldwide list of ISPs at *http://www.thelist.com.* This site presents pricing data and describes the features supported by each ISP.

Internet Addresses

To send and receive e-mail on the Internet and interact with other networks, you need an Internet address. In the *Domain Name System*, the Internet's addressing scheme, an Internet address usually has two sections. (■ *See Panel 7.3.*)

Consider the following address: *president@whitehouse.gov.us*

The first section, the *userID*, tells "who" is at the address—in this case, *president* is the recipient. (Sometimes an underscore, or _, is used between a recipient's first name or initials and last name: bill_clinton, for example.)

The first and second sections are separated by an @ (called "at") symbol.

The second section—in this case, *whitehouse.gov.us*—tells "where" the address is. Components are separated by periods, called "dots." The second section includes the *location* (such as *whitehouse;* the location may have

■ PANEL 7.3

What an Internet address means

How an e-mail message might find its way to a hypothetical address for Albert Einstein in the Physics Department of Princeton University.

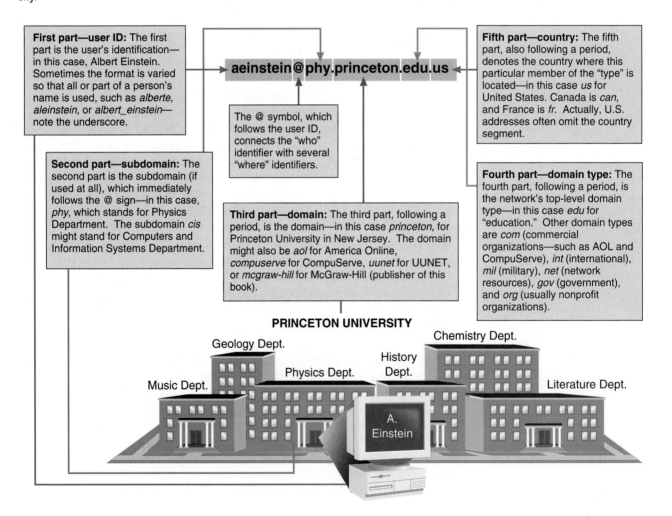

First part—user ID: The first part is the user's identification—in this case, Albert Einstein. Sometimes the format is varied so that all or part of a person's name is used, such as *alberte, aleinstein,* or *albert_einstein*—note the underscore.

Second part—subdomain: The second part is the subdomain (if used at all), which immediately follows the @ sign—in this case, *phy,* which stands for Physics Department. The subdomain *cis* might stand for Computers and Information Systems Department.

aeinstein@phy.princeton.edu.us

The @ symbol, which follows the user ID, connects the "who" identifier with several "where" identifiers.

Third part—domain: The third part, following a period, is the domain—in this case *princeton,* for Princeton University in New Jersey. The domain might also be *aol* for America Online, *compuserve* for CompuServe, *uunet* for UUNET, or *mcgraw-hill* for McGraw-Hill (publisher of this book).

Fifth part—country: The fifth part, also following a period, denotes the country where this particular member of the "type" is located—in this case *us* for United States. Canada is *can,* and France is *fr.* Actually, U.S. addresses often omit the country segment.

Fourth part—domain type: The fourth part, following a period, is the network's top-level domain type—in this case *edu* for "education." Other domain types are *com* (commercial organizations—such as AOL and CompuServe), *int* (international), *mil* (military), *net* (network resources), *gov* (government), and *org* (usually nonprofit organizations).

PRINCETON UNIVERSITY

Geology Dept.   Chemistry Dept.   History Dept.   Physics Dept.   Music Dept.   Literature Dept.

A. Einstein

more than one part), the *top-level domain* (such as *.gov* for government, *.edu* for education, *.com* for commercial, and *.org* for nonprofit organization) and country if required (such as *.us* for United States and *.se* for Sweden).

Features of the Internet

"For many people, the Internet has subsumed the functions of libraries, telephones, televisions, catalogs—even support groups and singles bars," says writer Jared Sandberg. "And that's just a sample of its capabilities."[7] Let us consider the Internet tools at your disposal:

- **E-mail:** "The World Wide Web is getting all the headlines, but for many people the main attraction of the Internet is electronic mail," says technology writer David Einstein.[8] There are millions of users of e-mail in the world, and although half of them are on private corporate networks, a great many of the rest are on the Internet.

  "E-mail is so clearly superior to paper mail for so many purposes," writes *New York Times* computer writer Peter Lewis, "that most people who try it cannot imagine going back to working without it."[9] Says another writer, e-mail "occupies a psychological space all its own: It's almost as immediate as a phone call, but if you need to, you can think about what you're going to say for days and reply when it's convenient."[10]

  E-mail, or *electronic mail*, links computers by wired or wireless connections and allows users, via electronic mailboxes, to send and receive messages. With e-mail, you enter the recipient's e-mail address, type in the subject and the message, then click on the Send icon. The message will be stored in the recipient's mailbox—that is, on a server accessible by the recipient—until it is accessed by that person. To gain access to your mailbox, you connect to your e-mail system and type in your *password*, a secret word or numbers that limit access. You may download (transfer) to your hard disk your mail and read the list of senders. You can discard messages without reading (opening) them, and you can read messages and then discard, save, and/or copy them to other people.

- **Usenet newsgroups—electronic discussion groups:** One of the Internet's most interesting features goes under the name *usenet*, short for "user network," which is essentially a giant, dispersed message board. *Usenet newsgroups* are electronic discussion groups that focus on a specific topic, the equivalent of AOL's or CompuServe's "forums." They are one of the most lively and heavily trafficked areas of the Net. There are more than 15,000 Usenet newsgroup forums and they cover hundreds of topics. Examples are *rec.arts.startrek.info*, *soc.culture.african.american*, and *misc.jobs.offered*.

  Usenet users exchange e-mail and messages ("news"). "Users post questions, answers, general information, and FAQ files on Usenet," says one online specialist. "The flow of messages, or 'articles,' is phenomenal, and you can get easily hooked."[11] Pronounced "fack," a *FAQ*, for *frequently asked questions*, is a file that lays out the basics for a newsgroup's discussion. It's always best to read a newsgroup's FAQ before joining the discussion or posting (asking) questions.

Example of FAQ

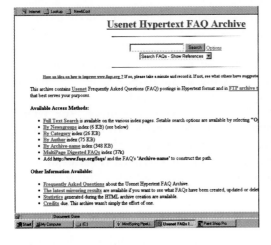

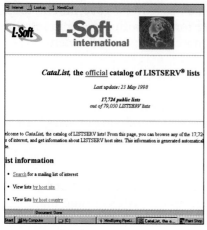

Example of LISTSERV

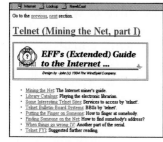

Example of Telnet site

- **Mailing lists—e-mail-based discussion groups:** Combining e-mail and newsgroups, mailing lists—called *listservs*—allow anyone to subscribe (generally free) to an e-mail mailing list on a particular subject or subjects and post messages. The mailing-list sponsor then sends those messages to everyone else on that list. There are more than 3000 electronic mailing-list discussion groups.

- **FTP—for copying all the free files you want:** Many Net users enjoy "FTPing"—cruising the system and checking into some of the tens of thousands of FTP sites, which predate the Web, offering interesting free files to copy (download). *FTP*, for *File Transfer Protocol*, is a method whereby you can connect to a remote computer called an FTP site and transfer publicly available files to your own microcomputer's hard disk. The free files offered cover nearly anything that can be stored on a computer: software, games, photos, maps, art, music, books, statistics.

- **Gopherspace—the hierarchical, text-based menu system:** Several tools exist to help sift through the staggering amount of information on the Internet, but one of the most important has been Gopher, which, like FTP, predates the Web. *Gopher* is a uniform system of menus, or series of lists, that allows users to easily browse and retrieve files stored on different computers by making successive menu selections.

- **Telnet—to connect to remote computers:** *Telnet* is a terminal emulation protocol that allows you to connect (log on) to remote computers. This feature, which allows microcomputers to communicate successfully with mainframes, enables you to tap into Internet computers and access public files as though you were connected directly instead of, for example, through your ISP site. The Telnet feature is especially useful for perusing large databases or library card catalogs. There are perhaps 1000 library catalogs accessible through the Internet.

One last feature of the Internet remains to be discussed—perhaps, for most general users, the most important one: the World Wide Web.

7.6 The World Wide Web

KEY QUESTIONS

What are the attributes of the Web, and how can you find information on it?

Preview & Review: The Web is the graphics-based component of the Internet, which makes it easier to use. Two distinctive features are that it provides information in multimedia form and uses hypertext to link various resources. Information is found using browsers and directories and search engines.

The Web is surely one of the most exciting phenomena of our time. The fastest-growing part of the Internet (growing at perhaps 4% per month in number of users), the World Wide Web is the most graphically inviting and easily navigable section of it. **The *World Wide Web*, or simply "the Web," consists of an interconnected system of sites, or servers, all over the world that can store information in multimedia form—sounds, photos, and video, as well as text. The sites share a form consisting of a hypertext series of links that connect similar words and phrases.**

Note two distinctive features:

1. **Multimedia form:** Whereas Gopher and Telnet deal with text, the Web provides information in *multimedia* form—graphics, video, and audio as well as text.

2. **Use of hypertext:** Whereas Gopher is a menu-based approach to accessing Net resources, the Web uses a hypertext format. *Hypertext* is a system in which documents scattered across many Internet sites are directly linked, so that a word or phrase in one document becomes a connection to a document in a different place.

The Web: A Working Vocabulary

If a Rip Van Winkle fell asleep as recently as 1989 (the year computer scientist Tim Berners-Lee developed the Web software) and awoke today, he would be completely baffled by the new vocabulary that we now encounter on an almost daily basis: *Web site, home page, http://*. Let's see how we would explain to him what these and similar Web terms mean.

- **HTML—instructions for document links:** The format, or language, used on the Web is called hypertext markup language. **Hypertext markup language (HTML) is the set of special instructions, called tags or markups, that are used to specify document structure, formatting, and links to other documents.** Anyone can create HTML documents by using Web-page design software (discussed below).

- **http://—communications standard for the Web:** HTML documents travel back and forth using hypertext transfer protocol. **Hypertext transfer protocol—which is expressed as *http://*—is the communications standard (protocol) used to transfer information on the Web.** This appears as a prefix on Web addresses, such as *http://www.mcgraw_hill.com*. When you use your mouse to point-and-click on a hypertext link—a highlighted word or phrase—it may become a doorway to another place within the same document or to another computer thousands of miles away.

- **Web sites—locations of hyperlinked documents:** The places you visit on the Web are called Web sites, and the estimated number of such sites throughout the world ranges up to 1,250,000. More specifically, a **Web site is the Internet location of a computer or server on which a hyperlinked document is stored.**

  For example, the Parents Place Web site *(http://www.parentsplace. com)* is a resource run by mothers and fathers that includes links to related sites, such as the Computer Museum Guide to the Best Software for Kids and the National Parenting Center.

- **Web pages—hypertext documents:** Information on a Web site is stored on "pages." **A *Web page* is actually a document, consisting of an HTML file. The *home page*, or *welcome page*, is the main page or first screen you see when you access a Web site,** but there are often other pages or screens. "Web site" and "home page" tend to be used interchangeably, although a site may have many pages.

- **Web browsers:** To access a Web site, you use Web browser software (✔ p. 53) and the site's address, called a URL. **A *Web browser*, or simply *browser*, is graphical user interface software that translates HTML documents and allows you to view Web pages on your computer screen.** The main Web browsers are Netscape Navigator and Microsoft Internet Explorer. With a browser, you can surf, browse, or search through the Web. When you connect with a particular Web site, the screen full of information (the home page) is sent to you. You can easily do *Web surfing*—move from one page to another—by using your mouse to click on the hypertext/hypermedia links.

- **URL—the address:** To locate a particular Web site, you type in its address, or *URL.* **The *URL,* for *Uniform Resource Locator,* is an address that points to a specific resource on the Web.** All Web page URLs begin with *http://.* Often a URL looks something like this: *http://www.blah.com/blah.html.* (Here *http* stands for "hypertext transfer protocol"; *www* stands for "World Wide Web"; *html* stands for "hypertext markup language.") The browsers Internet Explorer and Netscape Navigator automatically put the *http://* before any address beginning with *www.* The meaning of the parts of a URL address are explained in the box below. (■ *See Panel 7.4.*)

  A URL, we need to point out, is *not* the same thing as an e-mail address. Some people might type in *president@whitehouse.gov.us* and expect to get a Web site, but it won't happen. The Web site for the White House (which includes presidential information, history, a tour, and guide to federal services) is *http://www.whitehouse.gov*

  Note that URLs, as well as domain-type Internet addresses, are case-sensitive—that is, lowercase and capital letters should be typed as such. This requirement relates to the underlying Unix structure of the Internet.

- **Hyperlinks, history lists, and bookmarks:** Whatever page you are currently viewing will show the hyperlinks to other pages by displaying them in color or with an underline. When you move your mouse pointer over a hyperlink, the pointer will change to a hand. You can then move to that link by clicking on the hyperlink.

  Suppose you want to go back to some Web pages you have viewed. You can use either a history list or a bookmark. With a *history list,*

■ PANEL 7.4

Meaning of a URL address

An example of a URL is that for "Deb&Jen's Land O' Useless Facts," which consists of bizarre trivia submitted by readers.

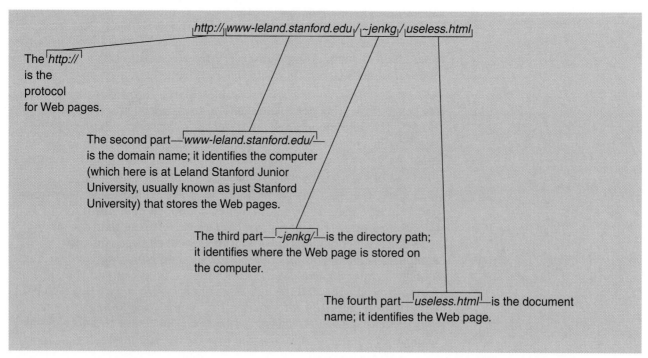

The *http://* is the protocol for Web pages.

The second part—*www-leland.stanford.edu/*—is the domain name; it identifies the computer (which here is at Leland Stanford Junior University, usually known as just Stanford University) that stores the Web pages.

The third part—*~jenkg/*—is the directory path; it identifies where the Web page is stored on the computer.

The fourth part—*useless.html*—is the document name; it identifies the Web page.

the browser records the Web pages you have viewed during a particular connection session. During that session, if you want to return to a site you visited earlier, you can click on that item in the history list. *Bookmarks* consist of titles and URLs of Web pages that you choose to add to your bookmark list because you think you will visit them frequently in the future. With these bookmarks stored in your browser, you can easily return to those pages in a future session by clicking on the listings.

Some common examples of Web page components are shown in the figure below. (■ *See Panel 7.5.*)

What Can You Find on the Web, & How Can You Find It?

There's a Web site for every interest: America's Job Bank, CIA World Factbook, Four11 (phone numbers), Internet Movie Database, Library of Congress, NASA Spacelink, New York Times, Recipe Archives, Rock and Roll Hall of Fame, TV Guide Online, U.S. Census Information, Woody Allen Quotes, and on and on.

Unfortunately, there's no central registry of cyberspace keeping track of the comings and goings and categories of Web sites. However, there are two ways to find information. First, you can buy books (such as *1001 Really Cool Web Sites*), updated every year, that catalog hundreds of popular Web sites. Second, you can use *search tools—directories and search engines—to locate the URLs of sites on topics that interest you* (✔ p. 54):

- Directories: *Directories* are lists of Web sites classified by topic. Directories are created by people submitting Web pages to a group of other people who classify and index them. Yahoo! is an example of a directory.

■ PANEL 7.5

Common examples of Web page components

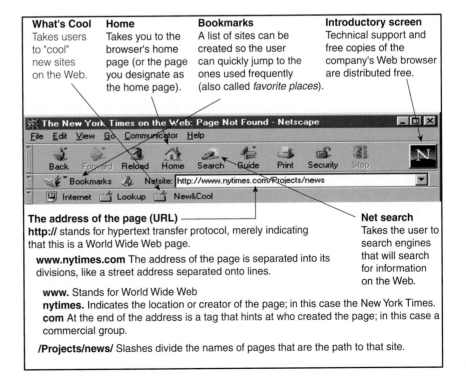

What's Cool
Takes users to "cool" new sites on the Web.

Home
Takes you to the browser's home page (or the page you designate as the home page).

Bookmarks
A list of sites can be created so the user can quickly jump to the ones used frequently (also called *favorite places*).

Introductory screen
Technical support and free copies of the company's Web browser are distributed free.

The address of the page (URL)
http:// stands for hypertext transfer protocol, merely indicating that this is a World Wide Web page.

    www.nytimes.com The address of the page is separated into its divisions, like a street address separated onto lines.

      www. Stands for World Wide Web
      nytimes. Indicates the location or creator of the page; in this case the New York Times.
      com At the end of the address is a tag that hints at who created the page; in this case a commercial group.

    /Projects/news/ Slashes divide the names of pages that are the path to that site.

Net search
Takes the user to search engines that will search for information on the Web.

Search tool	URL address
Yahoo!	www.yahoo.com
Infoseek	www.infoseek.com
AltaVista	www.altavista.com
Lycos	www.lycos.com
Excite	www.excite.com
WebCrawler	www.webcrawler.com
HotBot	www.hotbot.com
Magellan	www.mckinley.com
Galaxy	galaxy.tradewave.com

● Search engines: **Search engines allow you to find specific documents through keyword searches or menu choices.** Search engines find Web pages on their own. Search engines use software indexers (called *spiders*) to "crawl" around the Web and build indexes based on what they find. AltaVista, Excite, HotBot, Infoseek, and Lycos are examples of search engines.

We discussed searching tools and tips for searching in the Experience Box at the end of Chapter 3.

Browser Add-Ons for Multimedia: Plug-Ins

As we've said, what really distinguishes the World Wide Web from the rest of the Internet—and what accounts for a great part of its popularity—is the fact that it provides information in *multimedia* form—graphics, animation, video, and audio as well as text. At the moment, the technology is in a stage of evolution that requires some users to do some extra work in order to activate Web multimedia on their own computers. Thus, you may have to use so-called plug-in programs to run certain multimedia components of a Web page within the browser window. *Plug-ins* are programs that can be attached to your Web browser, giving it additional capabilities. Many plug-ins, which are downloaded from a vendor's Web and enhance your browser, are free, or at least free for a trial period. Often plug-ins are used to improve animation, video, and audio.

Designing Web Pages

To put a business online, you need to design a Web page and perhaps online order forms, determine any hyperlinks, and hire 24-hour-a-day space on a Web server or buy one of your own. Professional Web page designers can produce a page for you, or you can do it yourself using a menu-driven program included with your Web browser or a Web-page design software package such as Microsoft FrontPage or Adobe PageMill. After you have designed your Web page, you can rent space for it on your ISP's server.

Push Technology: Web Sites Come Looking for You

Whereas it used to be that people went out searching the World Wide Web, now the Web is looking for us. The driving force behind this is *push technology,* or "webcasting," defined as software that enables information to find consumers rather than consumers having to retrieve it from the Web using browser programs.[12] "Pull" is basic surfing: You go to a Web site and pull down the information to your desktop. "Push," however, consists of using special software to deliver information from various sites to your PC. Several services offer personalized news and information, based on a profile that you define when you register with them and download their software. You select the categories, or channels, of interest: sports news from the *Miami Herald,* stock updates on Eli Lily, weather reports from Iceland—and the provider sends what you want as soon as it happens or at times scheduled by you.

Portal Sites: The Fight to Be Your Gateway

A recent development has been the attempt by some high-traffic Internet connections and Web sites to redefine themselves as "portals." Representing the first view that a user sees upon directly dialing an Internet service or the first destination once connected, a *portal* is an Internet gateway that offers search tools plus free features such as e-mail, customized news, and chat rooms; revenue comes from online advertising. The movement toward portals attempts to lure more customers—and therefore advertisers—by consolidating content in one location.

7.7 Shared Resources: Workgroup Computing, EDI, & Intranets & Extranets

KEY QUESTION

What are the features of workgroup computing, EDI, intranets and firewalls, and extranets?

Preview & Review: Workgroup computing enables teams of co-workers to use networked microcomputers to share information and cooperate on projects. Electronic data interchange (EDI) is the direct electronic exchange of standard business documents between organizations' computer systems. Intranets and extranets are special-purpose spin-offs of Internet and Web technologies.

When they were first brought into the workplace, microcomputers were used simply as another personal-productivity tool, like typewriters or calculators. Gradually, however, companies began to link a handful of microcomputers together on a network, usually to share an expensive piece of hardware, such as a laser printer. Then employees found that networks allowed them to share files and databases as well. Networking using common software also allowed users to buy equipment from different manufacturers—a mix of workstations from both Sun Microsystems and Hewlett-Packard, for example. Sharing resources has led to workgroup computing.

Workgroup Computing & Groupware

Workgroup computing, also called *collaborative computing,* **enables teams of co-workers to use networks of microcomputers to share information and to cooperate on projects.** Workgroup computing is made possible not only by networks and microcomputers but also by *groupware* (✔ p. 61). Groupware is software that allows two or more people on a network to work on the same information at the same time.

In general, groupware, such as Lotus Notes, permits office workers to collaborate with colleagues and to tap into company information through computer networks. It also enables them to link up with crucial contacts outside their organization.

Electronic Data Interchange

Electronic data interchange (EDI) **is the direct electronic exchange between organizations' computer systems of standard business documents,** such as purchase orders, invoices, and shipping documents. For example, Wal-Mart has electronic ties to major suppliers like Procter & Gamble, allowing both companies to track the progress of an order or other document.

To use EDI, organizations wishing to exchange transaction documents must have compatible computer systems, or else go through an intermediary. For example, many colleges now use EDI to send transcripts and other educational records to do away with standard paper handling.

Intranets & Firewalls

It had to happen: First, businesses found that they could use the World Wide Web to get information to customers, suppliers, or investors. Federal Express, for example, saved millions by putting up a server in 1994 that enabled customers to click through Web pages to trace their parcels, instead of having FedEx customer-service agents do it. It was a short step from that to companies starting to use the same technology inside—in internal Internet networks called *intranets*. **Intranets are internal corporate networks that use the infrastructure and standards of the Internet and the World Wide Web.**

One of the greatest considerations of an intranet is security—making sure that sensitive company data accessible on intranets is protected from the outside world. The means for doing this is a security system called a *firewall*. **A *firewall* is a system of hardware and software that connects the intranet to external networks, such as the Internet. It blocks unauthorized traffic from entering the intranet and can also prevent unauthorized employees from accessing the intranet.**

Extranets

Taking intranet technology a few steps further, extranets offer security and controlled access. However, intranets are internal systems, designed to connect the members of a specific group or a single company. By contrast, **extranets are extended intranets connecting not only internal personnel but also selected customers, suppliers, and other strategic offices.** Ford Motor Company has an extranet that connects more than 15,000 Ford dealers worldwide. Called FocalPt, the extranet supports sales and servicing of cars, with the aim of providing support to Ford customers.

7.8 More Internet Technologies: Phone, Radio, & TV

KEY QUESTION

What are the characteristics of telephone, radio, and TV Internet technologies?

Preview & Review: The Internet has resulted in technologies that combine PC capabilities with telephone, radio, and television.

Where are we headed with the seemingly all-purpose Internet? We describe the Internet and the Web used as phone line, radio network, and television network.

Telephony

With Internet *telephony—using the Net to make phone calls, either one-to-one or for audioconferencing*—it's possible to make long-distance phone calls that are surprisingly inexpensive. Telephony can be performed using a PC with a sound card and a microphone, a modem linked to a standard Internet service provider, and the right software: Netscape Conference (part of Netscape Communicator) or Microsoft NetMeeting (part of Microsoft Internet Explorer).

Radio on the Net

Desktop radio broadcasting is here—both music and spoken programming—and has been since the 1995 unveiling of RealAudio software, which can compress sound so it can be played in real time, even though sent over telephone lines. You can, for instance, listen to 24-hour-a-day net.radio, which features "vintage rock," or English-language services of 19 shortwave outlets from World Radio Network in London.

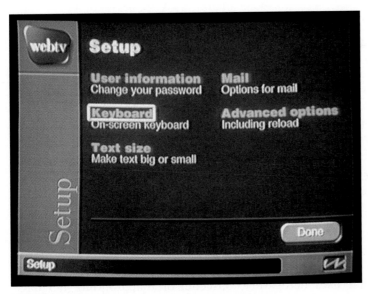

Web TV screen

Television on the Net

You can already visit the Web on television, as with WebTV. But can you get television programs over the Internet? RealPlayer offers live, television-style broadcasts over the Internet for viewing on your PC screen. You download RealPlayer, install it, then point your browser to a site featuring RealVideo. That will produce a streaming-video television image in a window a few inches wide.

READ ME

Practical Matters: Managing Your E-Mail

1. Don't use your electronic mailbox as a things-to-do list. Instead, create a second mailbox or folder for e-mail messages that still need to be answered or acted on. This will prevent important new messages from getting lost.

2. Read all of your e-mail as soon as it arrives and file it away immediately.

3. Don't create too many folders—otherwise, you'll lose messages that you file. Instead, adopt a simple message filing system and stick to it.

4. Don't save long messages with the thought that you will get around to them later. By the time later arrives, you'll have received even more e-mail.

5. Create a new set of folders every year; copy the previous year's correspondence onto a floppy disk. That way, if you change mail providers (or jobs), you won't lose all of your personal letters.

6. You don't have to reply to every e-mail message that you get. If you do, and your correspondents do as well, then the number of messages you get every day will increase geometrically.

7. Do not send chain-letters. If you get a chain-letter, just delete it. They may seem funny, but they clog mail systems and have shut down networks.

8. If somebody sends a request for help to a mailing list that you are on, send your response directly to that person, rather than to the entire list.

9. If you are on a mailing list that has too much traffic for you, don't make things worse by sending mail to the list asking people to send less mail to the list. Just have yourself taken off.

10. If somebody sends you a flame [an insulting message], don't make things worse by broadening the scope of the disaster. If you feel compelled to send mail back to the flamer, send it just to him or her.

—Simson L. Garfinkel, "Managing Your Mail," *San Jose Mercury News*

7.9 Cyberethics: Netiquette, Controversial Material & Censorship, & Privacy Issues

Ethics

Preview & Review: Users of communications technology must weigh standards of behavior and conduct in three areas: netiquette, controversial material and censorship, and privacy.

Communications technology gives us more choices of nearly every sort. Not only does it provide us with different ways of working, thinking, and playing; it also presents us with some different moral choices—determining right actions in the digital and online universe. Here let us consider three important aspects of "cyberethics"—netiquette, controversial material and censorship, and matters of privacy.

Netiquette

A form of speech unique to online communication, *flaming* is writing an online message that uses derogatory, obscene, or inappropriate language. Most flaming happens when someone violates online manners or "netiquette." Many online forums have a set of "FAQs"—frequently asked questions—that newcomers, or "newbies," are expected to become familiar with before joining in any chat forums. Most FAQs offer *netiquette*, or "net etiquette," guides to appropriate behavior while online. Examples of netiquette blunders are typing with the CAPS LOCK key on—the Net equivalent of yelling—discussing subjects not appropriate to the forum, repetition of points made earlier, and improper use of the software. *Spamming*, or sending unsolicited mail, is especially irksome; a spam includes chain letters, advertising, or similar junk mail.

Controversial Material & Censorship

Since computers are simply another way of communicating, there should be no surprise that a lot of people use them to communicate about sex. Yahoo!, the Internet directory company, says that the word "sex" is the most popular search word on the Net.[13] All kinds of online X-rated message boards, chat rooms, and Usenet newsgroups exist. A special problem is with children having access to sexual conversations, downloading hard-core pictures, or encountering criminals tempting them into meeting them. "Parents should never use [a computer] as an electronic baby sitter," says computer columnist Lawrence Magid. People online are not always what they seem to be, he points out, and a message seemingly from a 12-year-old girl could really be from a 30-year-old man. "Children should be warned never to give out personal information," says Magid, "and to tell their parents if they encounter mail or messages that make them uncomfortable."[14]

What can be done about X-rated materials? Some possibilities:

- **Blocking software:** Some software developers have discovered a golden opportunity in making programs like SurfWatch, Net Nanny, and CYBERsitter. These "blocking" programs screen out objectionable matter typically by identifying certain unapproved keywords in a user's request or comparing the user's request for information against a list of prohibited sites.

- **Browsers with ratings:** Another proposal in the works is browser software that contains built-in ratings for Internet, Usenet, and World Wide Web files. Parents could, for example, choose a browser that has been endorsed by the local school board or the online service provider.
- **The V-chip:** The 1996 Telecommunications Law officially launched the era of the V-chip, a device that will be required equipment in most new television sets. The *V-chip* allows parents to automatically block out programs that have been labeled as high in violence, sex, or other objectionable material.

The difficulty with any attempts at restricting the flow of information, perhaps, is the basic Cold War design of the Internet itself, with its strategy of offering different roads to the same place. "If access to information on a computer is blocked by one route," writes the *New York Times*'s Peter Lewis, "a moderately skilled computer user can simply tap into another computer by an alternative route." Lewis points out an Internet axiom attributed to an engineer named John Gilmore: "The Internet interprets censorship as damage and routes around it."[15]

Privacy

Privacy is the right of people not to reveal information about themselves. Technology, however, puts constant pressure on this right.

Consider Web cookies, little pieces of data left in your computer by some sites you visit.[16-18] A *cookie* is a file that a Web server stores on a user's hard-disk drive when the user visits a Web site. Thus, unknown to you, a Web site operator or companies advertising on the site can log your movements within a site. These records provide information that marketers can use to target customers for their products. In addition, however, other Web sites can get access to the cookies and acquire information about you.

There are also other intrusions on your privacy. Think your medical records are inviolable? Actually, private medical information is bought and sold freely by various companies since there is no federal law prohibiting it. (And they simply ignore the patchwork of varying state laws.)

Think the boss can't snoop on your e-mail at work? The law allows employers to "intercept" employee communications if one of the parties involved agrees to the "interception." The party "involved" is the employer. Indeed, employer snooping seems to be widespread.

A great many people are concerned about the loss of their right to privacy. Indeed, one survey found that 80% of the people contacted worried that they had lost "all control" of the personal information being collected and tracked by computers.[19] Although the government is constrained by several laws on acquiring and disseminating information and listening in on private conversations, there are reasons to be alarmed.

Summary

What It Is/What It Does

communications (p. 230, KQ 7.1) Also called *telecommunications;* the electronic transfer of information from one location to another. Also refers to electromagnetic devices and systems for communicating data.

dedicated fax machine (p. 231, KQ 7.2) Specialized device that does nothing except scan in, send, and receive documents over telephone lines to and from other fax machines.

directory (p. 243, KQ 7.6) On the Web, a directory is a list of Web pages classified by topic; it is created by a group that indexes Web pages that people submit.

electronic data interchange (EDI) (p. 245, KQ 7.7) System of direct electronic exchange between organizations' computer systems of standard business documents, such as purchase orders, invoices, and shipping documents.

electronic mail (e-mail) (p. 239, KQ 7.5) System in which computer users, linked by wired or wireless communications lines, may use their keyboards to post messages and their display screens to read responses.

extranet (p. 246, KQ 7.7) An extension of an internal network (intranet) to connect not only internal personnel but also selected customers, suppliers, and other strategic offices.

fax board (p. 231, KQ 7.2) Type of modem installed as a circuit board inside a computer; it exchanges fax messages with another fax machine or fax board.

firewall (p. 246, KQ 7.7) System of hardware and software used to connect internal networks (intranets) to external networks, such as the Internet. It prevents unauthorized people, whether outside or inside the company, from accessing the network.

Why It's Important

Communications systems have helped to expand human communication beyond face-to-face meetings to electronic connections called the *global village.*

Fax machines have enabled people to instantly transmit graphics and documents for the price of a phone call.

Directories are useful for browsing—looking at Web pages in a general category and finding items of interest. *Search engines* may be more useful for hunting specific information.

EDI allows the companies involved to do away with standard paper handling and its costs.

E-mail allows users to send messages to a single recipient's "mailbox"—a file stored on the computer system—or to multiple users. It is a much faster way of transmitting written messages than traditional mail services.

Extranets provide a direct line of communication that makes it easier, for example, to access databases and to send faxes without incurring long-distance phone charges.

The benefit of fax boards is that messages can be transmitted directly from a microcomputer; no paper or scanner is required.

Firewalls are necessary to protect an organization's internal network against theft and corruption.

What It Is/What It Does	**Why It's Important**

home page (p. 241, KQ 7.6) The first page (main page)—that is, the first screen—seen upon accessing a Web site.

The home page provides a menu or explanation of the topics available on that Web site.

hypertext markup language (HTML) (p. 241, KQ 7.6) Set of instructions, called tags or markups, that are used for documents on the Web to specify document structure, formatting, and links to other documents.

HTML makes it relatively simple for computer users to create Web pages and link them to other sites.

hypertext transfer protocol (p. 241, KQ 7.6) Expressed as *http://*; the communications standard used to transfer information on the Web. The abbreviation appears as a prefix on Web addresses.

Hypertext transfer protocol provides a standard for the transfer of multimedia files with hypertext links.

Internet (p. 236, KQ 7.5) Also called "the Net"; international network composed of approximately 140,000 smaller networks in more than 200 countries. Created as ARPAnet in 1969 by the U.S. Department of Defense, the Internet was designed to share research among military, industry, and university sources and to sustain communication in the event of nuclear attack.

Today the Internet is essentially a self-governing and noncommercial community offering both scholars and the public such features as information gathering, electronic mail, and discussion and newsgroups.

Internet service provider (ISP) (p. 237, KQ 7.5) Local or national company that provides unlimited public access to the Internet and the Web for a flat fee.

Unless they are connected to the Internet through an online information service or a direct network connection, microcomputer users need an ISP to connect to the Internet.

intranet (p. 246, KQ 7.7) Internal corporate network that uses the infrastructure and standards of the Internet and the World Wide Web.

Intranets can connect all types of computers.

online information service (p. 234, KQ 7.4) Company that provides access to databases and electronic meeting places to subscribers equipped with telephone-linked microcomputers—for example Prodigy, America Online, and Microsoft Network.

Online information services offer a wealth of services, from electronic mail to home shopping to video games to enormous research facilities to discussion groups.

search engine (p. 244, KQ 7.6) Type of search tool that allows the user to find specific documents through keyword searches or menu choices. It uses software indexers ("spiders") to "crawl" around the Web and build indexes based on what they find in available Web pages.

Search engines allow the user to build an index of Web pages that mention any given topic, so they may be more useful for hunting specific information, whereas a *directory* can provide an index of Web pages on a general area of interest for browsing.

search tool (p. 243, KQ 7.6) Refers to either a *directory* or *search engine* that can locate the URLs (addresses) of sites on topics of interest to the user.

Search tools are an online way of finding Web pages of interest; catalogs and recommendations from other people are another way.

What It Is/What It Does	**Why It's Important**

telephony (p. 246, KQ 7.8) On the Internet, making phone calls to one or more other users; all callers need the same telephonic software, a microcomputer with a microphone, sound card, modem, and a link to an Internet service provider.

ITelephony on the Internet is less expensive than standard phone calls, especially for international calls. It can also support audioconferences in which participants can view and work on documents together.

Uniform Resource Locator (URL) (p. 242, KQ 7.6) Address that points to a specific resource on the Web.

Addresses are necessary to distinguish among Web sites.

videoconferencing (p. 233, KQ 7.3) Also called *teleconferencing;* form of conferencing using television video cameras, monitors, microphones, and speakers as well as computers to allow people at different locations to see, hear, and talk with one another.

Videoconferencing may be done from a special videoconference room or handled with equipment set up on a desk.

voice mail (p. 231, KQ 7.2) System in which incoming voice messages are stored in a recipient's "voice mailbox" in digitized form. The system converts the digitized versions back to voice messages when they are retrieved. With voice mail, callers can direct calls within an office using buttons on their Touch-Tone phone.

Voice mail enables callers to deliver the same message to many people, to forward calls, to save or erase messages, and to dictate replies. The main benefit is that voice mail helps eliminate "telephone tag."

Web browser (p. 241, KQ 7.6) Software that translates HTML documents and allows a user to view a remote Web page; has a graphical user interface.

Browser software lets a user view Web documents and do *Web surfing.*

Web page (p. 241, KQ 7.6) Document in hypertext markup language (HTML) that is on a computer connected to the Internet. The first screen of a Web page is the home page.

Each Web page focuses on a particular topic. The information on a site is stored on "pages." The starting page is called the *home page.*

Web site (p. 241, KQ 7.6) Internet location of a computer or server on which a hyperlinked document (Web page) is stored; also used to refer to the document.

A Web site needs to use a computer that remains turned on, and it's best to have the site on a server with multiple connections so that more than one user at a time can visit.

workgroup computing (p. 245, KQ 7.7) Also called *collaborative computing;* technology that enables teams of co-workers to use networks of microcomputers to share information and cooperate on projects. Workgroup computing is made possible not only by networks and microcomputers but also by groupware.

Workgroup computing permits office workers to collaborate with colleagues, suppliers, and customers and to tap into company information through computer networks.

World Wide Web (p. 240, KQ 7.6) Interconnected system of sites, or servers, of the Internet that store information in multimedia form and share a hypertext form that links similar words or phrases between sites.

Web software allows users to view information that includes not just text but graphics, animation, video, and sound, and to move between related sites via hypertext links.

Exercises

Self-Test

1. The _____ is the most extensive network in the world.

2. _____ is an Internet feature that lets you connect to a remote computer and download files to your computer's hard disk.

3. _____ _____ enables teams of coworkers to collaborate on projects via a network of microcomputers. The software component is referred to as *groupware.*

4. _____ is writing an online message that uses derogatory, obscene, or inappropriate language.

5. Corporate networks that use the infrastructure and standards of the Internet and the World Wide Web are called _____.

Short-Answer Questions

1. List three ways you can connect your microcomputer to the Internet.
2. What is an Internet service provider?
3. What are the principal features of the Internet?
4. What is a firewall?
5. What is meant by the term *connectivity*?

Multiple-Choice Questions

1. Which of the following enables different computers on different networks to communicate with each other?
   a. modems
   b. Internet service provider
   c. TCP/IP software
   d. FTP
   e. All of the above

2. Which of the following would you use to search for and retrieve files stored on different computers?
   a. FTP
   b. Gopher
   c. HTTP
   d. HTML
   e. All of the above

3. Which of the following would you use to write files for the Web?
   a. FTP
   b. Gopher
   c. HTTP
   d. HTML
   e. All of the above

4. Which of the following has the most potential to reduce paper handling?
   a. EDI
   b. Intranets
   c. HTML
   d. All of the above

5. Which of the following addresses might you use to connect to a nonprofit organization?
   a. *clifford@mindspring.com*
   b. *71222.1111@compuserve.com*
   c. *susanh@universe.org*
   d. *help@volunteer.mil*
   e. All of the above

True/False Questions

T F   1. The term *cyberspace* refers to the World Wide Web, but not to most of the other features of the Internet.

T F   2. A picture phone has already been developed by AT&T.

T F   3. With a direct connection to the Internet, you don't need to use a modem.

T F   4. For a fee, you can use an online information service to send e-mail, access databases, and download shareware.

Knowledge in Action

1. You need to purchase a computer to use at home to perform business-related (school-related) tasks. You want to be able to communicate with the network at work (school) and the Internet. Include the following in a report:

   - Description of the hardware and software used at work (school).
   - Description of the types of tasks you will want to perform at home.
   - Name of the computer system you would buy. (Include a detailed description of the computer system, such as the RAM capacity, secondary storage capacity, and modem speed.)
   - The communications software you would need to purchase or obtain.
   - The cost estimate for the system and for the on-line and telephone charges

2. In an effort to reduce new construction costs, some rapidly expanding companies are allowing more and more employees to telecommute several days a week. Offices are shared by several telecommuting employees. One employee will use the office two or three days a week, and another employee will use the same office other days of the week. What advantages does the company gain from this type of arrangement? What advantages do these employees have over the traditional work environment? What are some of the disadvantages to both the company and the employees? Do you think employees' productivity will decline from telecommuting and/or sharing office space with other telecommuting employees? If so, why?

3. What do you think the future holds for online information services? Research your response using current magazines and periodicals and/or on the Internet.

4. "Distance learning," or "distance education," uses electronic links to extend college campuses to people who otherwise would not be able to take college courses. Is your school or someone you know involved in distance learning? If so, research the system's components and uses. What hardware and software do students need in order to communicate with the instructor and classmates?

Communications Technology
Hardware, Channels, & Networks

key questions

You should be able to answer the following questions:

On average, one new telephone area code is added in the United States EVERY MONTH.[1] No wonder the explosive growth in area codes has been called "the trauma of the '90s."[2]

Between 1995 and 1997, 62 new geographic area codes were introduced around the country. Over the next decade, 120 new codes will be implemented.[3] No doubt you already suspect the reasons for the spectacular growth in area codes. Explains economics editor Jonathan Marshall:

> Every time you add an extra phone line for a fax machine, Internet connection, home office, or talkative teenager, you need another number.
>
> Every time you add a pager or a cellular phone to your stockpile of equipment, you add more numbers.
>
> And every time you swipe your credit card through a supermarket or department store register, or put your ATM card into a cash machine, you are making use of a separate "point of sale" phone line and number.
>
> Across the nation, a new customer signs up for cellular phone service every 2.8 seconds. Each one needs a new number.[4]

What is the effect of all these numbers and area codes? Let us take a look at one aspect: some new ways in which work is distributed.

8.1 Portable Work: Telecommuting & Virtual Offices

KEY QUESTION

What are telecommuting and virtual offices?

Preview & Review: Working at home with computer and communications connections between office and home is called telecommuting. The virtual office is a nonpermanent and mobile office run with computer and communications technology.

"In a country that has been moaning about low productivity and searching for new ways to increase it," observed futurist Alvin Toffler, "the single most anti-productive thing we do is ship millions of workers back and forth across the landscape every morning and evening."[5]

Toffler was referring, of course, to the great American phenomenon of physically commuting to and from work. About 96 million Americans commute to work by car, 39 million not to a city's downtown but rather to jobs scattered about in the suburbs.[6] Information technology has responded to the cry of "Move the work instead of the workers!" Computers and communications tools have led to telecommuting and telework centers, the virtual office and "hoteling," and the mobile workplace.

Telecommuting & Telework Centers

Working at home with telecommunications between office and home is called *telecommuting*. The number of telecommuters—those who work at home at least one day a week—has nearly tripled to 11 million in the United States from 4 million in 1990, according to a survey by a market research firm.[7]

Telecommuting has a lot of benefits.[8] The advantages to society are reduced traffic congestion, energy consumption, and air pollution. The advantages to employers include increased productivity because telecommuters experience less distraction at home and can work flexible hours. There are further advantages of improved teamwork and an expanded labor pool because hard-to-get employees don't have to uproot themselves from where they want to live.

Another term for telecommuting, *telework* includes not only those who work at least part time from home but also those who work at remote or satellite offices, removed from organizations' main offices. Such satellite offices are sometimes called *telework centers*. An example is the Riverside Telecommuting Center, in Riverside, California, which provides office space that helps employees avoid lengthy commutes to downtown Los Angeles.

The Virtual Office

The *virtual office* **is an often nonpermanent and mobile office run with computer and communications technology.** Employees work not in a central office but from their homes, cars, and other new work sites. They use pocket pagers, portable computers, fax machines, and various phone and network services to conduct business.

Could you stand not having a permanent office at all? Here's how one variant, called *"hoteling"* or *"alternative officing,"* works. You call ahead to book a room, and speak to the concierge. However, your "hotel" isn't a Hilton, and the "concierge" isn't a hotel employee who handles reservations, luggage, and local tours. Rather, the organization is accounting and management consulting firm Ernst & Young, advertising agency Chiat/Day, or computer maker Tandem Computers, to name three examples. And the concierge is an administrator who handles scheduling of available office cubicles, of which there is perhaps only one for every three workers.[9-11]

Hoteling works for Ernst & Young, for example, because its auditors and management consultants spend 50% to 90% of their time in the field, in the offices of clients. When they need to return to their local E&Y office, they call a few hours in advance. The concierge consults a computerized scheduling program and determines which cubicle is available on the days requested. The concierge then punches a few codes into the phone to program its number and voice mail. When employees come in, they pick up personal effects and files from lockers. They then take them to the cubicles they will use for a few days or weeks.

What makes hoteling possible, of course, is computer and communications technology. Computers handle the cubicle scheduling and reprogramming of phones. They also allow employees to carry their work around with them stored on the hard drives of their laptops. Cellular phones, fax machines, and e-mail permit employees to stay in touch with supervisors and co-workers.

Let us now take a look at the technology that has brought us to this point.

8.2 Using Computers to Communicate: Analog & Digital Signals, Modems, & Other Technological Basics

KEY QUESTIONS

How do analog and digital signals and modems work, and what are alternatives to modems?

Preview & Review: To communicate online through a microcomputer, users need a modem to send and receive computer-generated messages over telephone lines. The modem translates the computer's digital signal of discrete bursts into an analog signal of continuous waves, and vice versa. A modem may have various transmission speeds. Communications software is also required. ISDN lines, DSL lines, T1 lines, and cable modems are faster than conventional PC modems.

Communications, or *telecommunications,* refers to the transfer of data from a transmitter (sender or source) to a receiver across a distance. The data

■ PANEL 8.1

Analog and digital signals

An analog signal represents a continuous electrical signal in the form of a wave. A digital signal is discontinuous, expressed as discrete bursts in on/off electrical pulses.

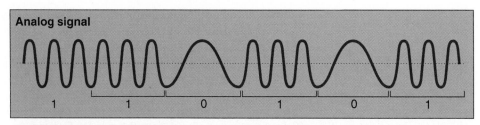

Analog signal

1　　　1　　　0　　　1　　　0　　　1

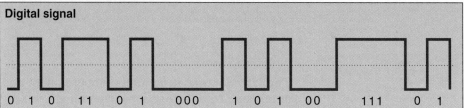

Digital signal

0 1 0　11　0 1　000　1 0 1　00　111　0 1

transferred can be voice, sound, images, video, text, or a combination thereof (multimedia). Some form of electromagnetic energy—electricity, radio waves, or light—is used to represent the data, which is transmitted through a wire, the air, or other physical medium. To set up a path for the data transfer, intermediate devices are put in place, such as microwave towers.

Data is transmitted by two types of signals, each requiring different kinds of communications technology. The two types of signals are *analog* and *digital*. (■ *See Panel 8.1.*)

Analog Signals: Continuous Waves

Telephones, radios, and televisions—the older forms of communications technology—were designed to work with an analog signal (✔ p. 5). **An *analog signal* is a continuous electrical signal in the form of a wave.** The wave is called a *carrier wave.* Two characteristics of analog carrier waves that can be altered are frequency and amplitude.

- Frequency: *Frequency* is the number of times a wave repeats during a specific time interval—that is, how many times it completes a *cycle* in a second.
- Amplitude: *Amplitude* is the height of a wave within a given period of time. Amplitude is actually the strength or volume—the loudness—of a signal.

Both frequency and amplitude can be modified by making adjustments to the wave. Indeed, it is by such adjustments that an analog signal can be made to express a digital signal, as we shall explain.

Digital Signals: Discrete Bursts

A *digital signal* uses on/off or present/absent electrical pulses in discontinuous, or discrete, bursts, rather than a continuous wave. This two-state kind of signal works perfectly in representing the two-state binary language of 0s and 1s that computers use. That is, the presence of an electrical pulse can represent a 1 bit, its absence a 0 bit.

■ PANEL 8.2

How modems work
A sending modem translates digital signals into analog waves for transmission over phone lines. A receiving modem translates the analog signals back into digital signals.

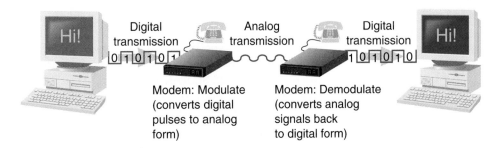

Digital transmission — Modem: Modulate (converts digital pulses to analog form)

Analog transmission — Modem: Demodulate (converts analog signals back to digital form)

Digital transmission

Modems

Digital signals are better—that is, faster and more accurate—at transmitting computer data. However, many of our present communications lines, such as telephone and microwave, are still analog. To get around this problem, we need a *modem*. **A *modem*—short for *modulate/demodulate*—converts digital signals into analog form (a process known as *modulation*) to send over phone lines. A receiving modem at the other end of the phone line then converts the analog signal back to a digital signal (a process known as *demodulation*).** (■ *See Panel 8.2.*)

Two criteria for choosing a modem are whether you want an internal or external one, and what transmission speed you wish:

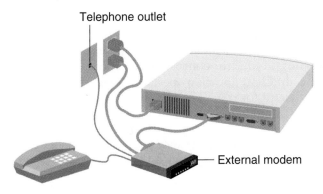

Telephone outlet

External modem

● **External versus internal:** Most modems these days are internal, but some are external.

An *external modem* is a box that is separate from the computer. The box may be large or it may be portable, pocket size. A cable connects the modem to a port in the back of the computer. A second line connects the modem to a standard telephone jack. There is also a power cord that plugs into a standard AC wall socket. The advantage of the external modem is that it can be used with different computers. Thus, if you buy a new microcomputer, you will probably be able to use your old external modem.

An *internal modem* is a circuit board that plugs into a slot inside the system cabinet. Currently most new microcomputers come with an internal modem already installed (some are built right into the motherboard). Advantages of the internal modem are that it doesn't take up extra space on your desk, it is less expensive than an external modem, and it doesn't have a separate power cord.

For laptop computers, there are also easily removable internal modems. That is, modems are available as PC cards (✔ p. 129), which can be slipped in and out of a PCMCIA slot.

● **Transmission speed:** Because most modems use standard telephone lines, users are charged the usual rates by phone companies, whether local or long-distance. Users are also often charged by online services for time spent online. Accordingly, *transmission speed*—the speed at which modems transmit data—becomes an important consideration. The faster the modem, the less time you need to spend on the telephone line.

Today users refer to **bits per second (bps) or, more likely, *kilobits per second (kbps)* to express data transmission speeds.** A 28,800-bps modem, for example, is a 28.8-kbps modem. Today's modems transmit at 1200, 2400, and 4800 (considered slow and not worth using anymore); 9600 and 14,400 bps (moderately fast); and 28,000, 33,600, and 56,000 bps (high speed). A 10-page single-spaced letter can be transmitted by a 2400-bps modem in 2½ minutes, by a 9600-bps modem in 38 seconds, and by a 28,800-bps modem in about 10 seconds. The fastest modem, the 56,000-bps or "56K" modem, doesn't usually operate at 56 kbps. One writer reports that in 60 log-ons, the average was 42.6 kbps.[12]

Communications Software

To communicate via a modem, your microcomputer requires communications software. *Communications software*, or "datacomm software," manages the transmission of data between computers, as we mentioned in Chapter 2 (✔ p. 52). Macintosh users have Smartcom. Windows users have Smartcom, Crosstalk, CommWorks, Crosstalk, ProComm Plus, and Hyper-Terminal. OS/2 Warp users have HyperAccess. Often the software comes on diskettes bundled with (sold along with) the modem. Also, communications software now often comes as part of the system software.

One of the principal uses to which you will put communications software is to download and upload files. *Download* means that you retrieve files from another computer and transfer them to the main memory (RAM) on the hard disk in your computer. *Upload* means that you send files from your computer to another computer.

Besides establishing connections between computers, communications software may perform other functions. One of these is *data compression* (✔ p. 97), which reduces the volume of data in a message, thereby reducing the amount of time required to send data from one modem to another. *Remote-control software* allows you to control a microcomputer from another microcomputer in a different location, perhaps even thousands of miles away. Such software is useful for travelers who want to use their home machines from a distance. *Terminal emulation software* allows you to use your microcomputer to simulate a mainframe's terminal. That is, the software "tricks" the large computer into acting as if it is communicating with a terminal. Your PC needs terminal emulation capability to access computers holding databases of research materials.

ISDN Lines, DSL Lines, T1 Lines, & Cable Modems

Users who have found themselves banging the table in frustration as their 28.8 modem takes 25 minutes to transmit a 1-minute low-quality video from a Web site are getting some relief. Probably the principal contenders to standard phone modems are *ISDN lines, DSL (ADSL), T1 lines, cable modems,* and *satellite dishes.* (■ *See Panel 8.3.*)

- ISDN lines: **ISDN stands for *Integrated Services Digital Network.* It consists of hardware and software that allow voice, video, and data to be communicated as digital signals over traditional copper-wire telephone lines.** Capable of transmitting up to 128 kbps, ISDN lines are more than four times faster than conventional 28.8 modems, or more than double the speed of 56K modems.

    ISDN is not cheap, costing perhaps two or three times as much per month as regular phone service. Nevertheless, with the number of people now working at home and/or surfing the Internet, demand has pushed ISDN orders off the charts. Even so, ISDN's time may have come and gone. The reason: DSL, cable modem, and other technologies threaten to render it obsolete.

■ PANEL 8.3

Connection competitors

Approximate time to transfer a 40-megabyte file.

Technology	Speed	Time
Telephone modem	33.6 kbps	2 hours, 38 minutes
ISDN phone line	128 kbps	41 minutes, 40 seconds
DSL phone line	1.088 Mbps upload 8.192 Mbps download	4 minutes, 54 seconds 39 seconds
T1 phone line	1.544 Mbps	3 minutes, 27 seconds
Cable modem	500 kbps upload 10 Mbps download	10 minutes, 40 seconds 32 seconds
Satellite system	33.6 kbps upload 400 kbps download	2 hours, 38 minutes 13 minutes, 20 seconds

kbps = kilobytes per second; Mbps = megabits per second (a megabit is 1,000,000 kilobytes).

- **DSL (ADSL):** If you were trying to download an approximately 6-minute-long music video from the World Wide Web, it would take you about 4 hours and 45 minutes using a 28.8 modem. An ISDN connection would reduce this to an hour. With DSL (ADSL), however, you would really notice the difference—11 minutes.[13]

  Most modems transmit data in kilobits per second (kbps). **Short for *Digital Subscriber Line, DSL* uses regular phone lines to transmit data in megabits per second (Mbps)—specifically 1.5–8 Mbps.** (ADSL stands for Asymmetric Digital Subscriber Line.) DSL downloads data faster than it uploads data (a 40-megabyte file takes 39 seconds to download but almost 5 minutes to upload). Thus, at present it is not suited to videoconferencing, where conversations need to take place in real time. It is, however, well suited to Web browsing, where the amount of information coming down to your browser is much greater than the amounts you send up, such as e-mail.[14,15]

- **T1 lines:** **A *T1 line* is essentially a traditional trunk line that carries 24 normal telephone circuits and has a speed of 1500 kbps.** Generally, T1 lines are high-capacity communications links found at corporate, government, or academic sites. To get similar speeds, consumers usually use DSL lines.

  Another high-speed digital line is the T3 line, which may cost as much as $40,000 a month and requires a huge investment in equipment. **A *T3 line* transmits at a speed of 4500 kbps.**

- **Cable modems:** If DSL's 11 minutes to move a nearly 6-minute video sounds good, 2 minutes sounds even better. That's the rate of transmission for cable modems. **A *cable modem* connects a personal computer to a cable-TV system that offers online services.**

  The gadgets are still not in common use, and it will probably be a while before internationally standardized cable modems go on sale. The reason: So far probably 90% of U.S. cable subscribers are served by networks that don't permit much in the way of two-way data communications. "The vast majority of today's . . . cable systems can deliver a river of data downstream," says one writer, "but only a cocktail straw's worth back the other way."[16] Nevertheless, Forrester Research Inc. predicts about 6.8 million American homes will have cable modems by 2000.[17]

8.3 Communications Channels: The Conduits of Communications

KEY QUESTION

What are types of wired and wireless channels and some types of wireless communications?

Preview & Review: A channel is the path, either wired or wireless, over which information travels. Various channels occupy various radio-wave bands on the electromagnetic spectrum. Types of wired channels include twisted-pair wire, coaxial cable, and fiber-optic cable. Two principal types of wireless channels are microwave and satellite systems.

Today there are many kinds of communications channels, although they are still wired or wireless. **A *communications channel* is the path—the physical medium—over which information travels in a telecommunications system from its source to its destination.** (Channels are also called *links, lines,* or *media.*) The basis for all telecommunications channels, both wired and wireless, is the electromagnetic spectrum.

The Electromagnetic Spectrum

Telephone signals, radar waves, and the invisible commands from a garage-door opener all represent different waves on what is called the electromagnetic spectrum. **The *electromagnetic spectrum* consists of fields of electrical energy and magnetic energy, which travel in waves.** (■ *See Panel 8.4.*)

All radio signals, light rays, X-rays, and radioactivity radiate an energy that behaves like rippling waves. The waves vary according to two characteristics, frequency and wavelength:

- **Frequency:** As we've seen, *frequency* is the number of times a wave repeats (makes a cycle) in a second. Frequency is measured in hertz (Hz), with 1 Hz equal to 1 cycle per second. One thousand hertz is called a *kilohertz (KHz)*, 1 million hertz is called a *megahertz (MHz)*, and 1 billion hertz is called a *gigahertz (GHz)*.

  Ranges of frequencies are called *bands* or *bandwidths*. The bandwidth is the difference between the lowest and highest frequencies transmitted. Thus, for example, cellular phones are on the 800–900 megahertz bandwidth—that is, their bandwidth is 100 megahertz. The wider the bandwidth, the faster data can be transmitted.

  Why is it important to know this? "Low-frequency waves can travel far and curve with the Earth but can't carry much information," points out technology writer Kevin Maney. "High-frequency waves can travel only a short distance before breaking up and won't curve over the horizon, but they can carry much more information."[18] Thus, different technologies (cell phones versus PCS phones, for instance) are best suited to different purposes, depending on the frequency range—bandwidth—they are in.

- **Wavelength:** Waves also vary according to their length—their *wavelength.* At the low end of the spectrum, the waves are of low frequency and of long wavelength (such as domestic electricity). At the high end, the waves are of high frequency and short wavelength (such as cosmic rays).

The part of the electromagnetic spectrum of principal concern to us is that area in the middle—between 3 million and 300 billion hertz (3 megahertz to 300 gigahertz). This is the portion that is regulated by the government for communications purposes. In the United States, certain bands are assigned by the Federal Communications Commission (FCC) for certain purposes—that is, to be controlled by different types of media equipment or types of users.

■ PANEL 8.4

The electromagnetic spectrum

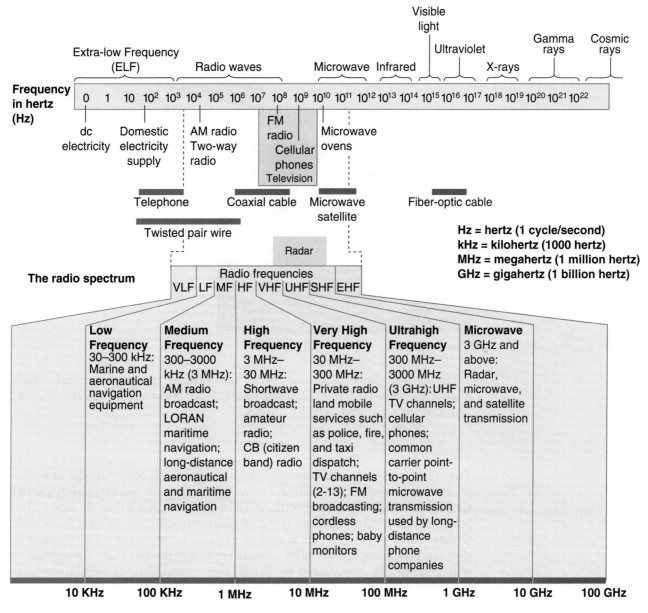

Hz = hertz (1 cycle/second)
kHz = kilohertz (1000 hertz)
MHz = megahertz (1 million hertz)
GHz = gigahertz (1 billion hertz)

Frequencies for wireless data communications

Cellular	Private land mobile	Narrowband PCS	Industrial	Common carrier paging	Point-to-multipoint Point-to-point	PCS	Industrial
824–849 MHz 869–894 MHz	896–901 MHz 930–931 MHz Includes RF packet radio services	901–902 MHz 930–931 MHz	902–928 MHz Unlicensed commercial use such as cordless phones and LANs	931–932 MHz Includes national paging services	932–935 MHz 941–944 MHz	1850–1970 MHz 2130–2150 MHz 2180–2200 MHz	2400–2483.5 MHz Unlicensed commercial use such as LANs

Twisted-pair wire

Coaxial cable

■ PANEL 8.5

Three types of wired communications channels

(Top) Twisted-pair wire. This type does not protect well against electrical interference. *(Middle)* Coaxial cable. This type is shielded against electrical interference. It also can carry more data than most kinds of twisted-pair wire. *(Bottom)* Fiber-optic cable. Thin glass strands transmit pulsating light instead of electricity. These strands can carry computer and voice data over long distances.

Fiber-optic cable

Let us now look more closely at the various types of channels. They include *twisted-pair wire, coaxial cable, fiber-optic cable, microwave and satellite systems,* and *cellular phones.*

Twisted-Pair Wire

The telephone line that runs from your house to the pole outside, or underground, is probably twisted-pair wire. **Twisted-pair wire consists of two strands of insulated copper wire, twisted around each other in pairs.** They are then covered in another layer of plastic insulation. (■ *See Panel 8.5.)* Compared to other forms of wiring or cabling, twisted-pair wire is relatively slow and does not protect well against electrical interference. As a result, it will certainly be superseded by better communications channels, wired or wireless.

Coaxial Cable

Coaxial cable, **commonly called "co-ax," consists of insulated copper wire wrapped in a solid or braided metal shield, then in an external cover.** Co-ax is widely used for cable television. The extra insulation makes coaxial cable much better at resisting noise (static) than twisted-pair wiring. Moreover, it can carry voice and data at a faster rate (up to 200 megabits per second, compared to only 16–100 megabits per second for twisted-pair wire).

Fiber-Optic Cable

A *fiber-optic cable* **consists of hundreds or thousands of thin strands of glass that transmit not electricity but rather pulsating beams of light.** These strands, each as thin as a human hair, can transmit billions of pulses per second, each "on" pulse representing one bit. When bundled together, fiber-optic strands in a cable 0.12 inch thick can support a quarter- to a half-million voice conversations at the same time. Moreover, unlike electrical signals, light pulses are not affected by random electromagnetic interference in the environment. Thus, they have much lower error rates than normal telephone wire and cable. In addition, fiber-optic cable is lighter and more durable than twisted-pair and coaxial cable. A final advantage is that it cannot be easily wiretapped or listened into, so transmissions are more secure.

Microwave & Satellite Systems

Wired forms of communications, which require physical connection between sender and receiver, will not disappear any time soon, if ever. For one thing, fiber-optic cables can transmit data communications 10,000 times faster than microwave and satellite systems can. Moreover, they are resistant to data theft. Still, some of the most exciting developments are in wireless communications. After all, there are many situations in which it is difficult to run physical wires. Here let us consider microwave and satellite systems.

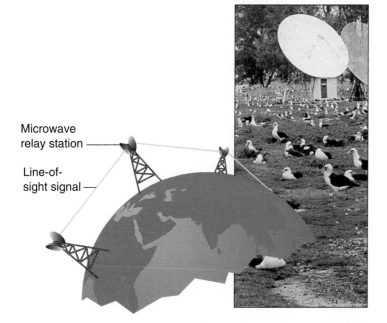

Microwave relay station

Line-of-sight signal

- **Microwave systems:** *Microwave systems transmit voice and data through the atmosphere as super-high-frequency radio waves.* Microwave systems transmit microwaves, of course. *Microwaves* are the electromagnetic waves that vibrate at 1 gigahertz (1 billion hertz) per second or higher. These frequencies are used not only to operate microwave ovens but also to transmit messages between ground-based earth stations and satellite communications systems.

  Today you see dish- or horn-shaped microwave antennas nearly everywhere—on towers, buildings, and hilltops. Why, you might wonder, do people have to intrude on nature by putting a microwave dish on top of a mountain? The reason: microwaves cannot bend around corners or around the earth's curvature; they are "line-of-sight." *Line-of-sight* means there must be an unobstructed view between transmitter and receiver. Thus, microwave stations need to be placed within 25–30 miles of each other, with no obstructions in between. The size of the dish varies with the distance (perhaps 2–4 feet in diameter for short distances, 10 feet or more for long distances). A string of microwave relay stations will each receive incoming messages, boost the signal strength, and relay the signal to the next station.

  More than half of today's telephone system uses dish microwave transmission. However, the airwaves are becoming so saturated with microwave signals that future needs will have to be satisfied by other channels, such as satellite systems.

- **Satellite systems:** To avoid some of the limitations of microwave earth stations, communications companies have added microwave "sky stations"—communications satellites. ***Communications*** *satellites* **are microwave relay stations in orbit around the earth.** Satellite systems may occupy one of three zones in space: *GEO, MEO,* and *LEO.*

The highest level, 22,300 miles up and directly above the equator, is known as *geostationary earth orbit (GEO).* Because they travel at the same speed as the earth, these satellites appear to an observer on the ground to be stationary in space—that is, they are *geostationary.* Consequently, microwave earth stations are always able to beam signals to a fixed location above. The orbiting satellite has solar-powered receivers and transmitters (transponders) that receive the signals, amplify them, and retransmit them to another earth station. This high an earth orbit means that fewer satellites are required for global coverage; however, their quarter-second delay makes two-way telephone conversations difficult. The *medium-earth orbit (MEO),* is 5000–10,000 miles up; it requires more satellites for global coverage than GEO. The *low-earth orbit (LEO)* is 400–1000 miles up and has no signal delay. Satellites may be smaller and are cheaper to launch.

One particularly interesting application of satellite technology is the Global Positioning System. A $10 billion infrastructure developed by the military in the mid-1980s, the *Global Positioning System (GPS),* consists of a series of 24 earth-orbiting satellites 10,600 miles above the earth that continuously transmit timed radio signals that can be used to identify earth locations. A GPS receiver—handheld or mounted in a vehicle, plane, or boat—can pick up transmissions from any four satellites, interpret the information from each, and calculate to within a few hundred feet or less the receiver's longitude, latitude, and altitude. Some GPS receivers include map software for finding your way around, as with the Guidestar system available with some rental cars in cities such as Miami, Los Angeles, and New York.

Cellular Phones

Analog cellular phones **are designed primarily for communicating by voice through a system of ground-area cells.** Each cell is hexagonal in shape, usually 8 miles or less in diameter, and is served by a transmitter-receiving tower. Communications are handled in the bandwidth of 824–894 megahertz. Calls are directed between cells by a mobile telephone switching office (MTSO). Movement between cells requires that calls be "handed off" by the MTSO. (■ *See Panel 8.6.)*

Digital cellular phone **networks turn your voice message into digital bits, which are sent through the airwaves, then decoded back into your voice by the cellular handset.** Unlike analog cellular phones, digital phones can handle short e-mail messages, paging, and some headline news items in addition to voice transmission.

8.4 Communications Networks

KEY QUESTION

What are types, features, and advantages of networks?

Preview & Review: Communications channels and hardware may be used in different layouts or networks, varying in size from large to small: wide area networks (WANs), metropolitan area networks (MANs), and local networks. A network requires a network operating system. Features of networks are hosts, nodes, servers, and clients. Networks allow users to share peripheral devices, programs, and data; to have better communications; to have more secure information; and to have access to databases.

Whether wired, wireless, or both, all the channels we've described can be used singly or in mix-and-match fashion to form networks. **A *network,* or *communications network,* is a system of interconnected computers, telephones, or other communications devices that can communicate with one another and share applications and data.** It is the tying together of so many communications devices in so many ways that is changing the world we live in.

Here let us consider the following: *types of networks, network operating systems, some network features,* and *advantages of networks.*

Types of Networks: Wide Area, Metropolitan Area, & Local

Networks are categorized principally in the following three sizes:

- Wide area network: **A *wide area network (WAN)* is a communications network that covers a wide geographical area, such as a state or a country.** Some examples of computer WANs are Tymnet, Telenet, Uninet, and Accunet. The Internet links together hundreds of computer WANs. Of course, most telephone systems—long-distance, regional Bells, and local—are WANs.

- Metropolitan area network: **A *metropolitan area network (MAN)* is a communications network covering a geographic area the size of a city**

1 A call originates from a mobile cellular phone.

2 The call wirelessly finds the nearest cellular tower using its FM tuner to make a connection.

3 The tower sends the signal to a Mobile Telephone Switching Office (MTSO) using traditional telephone network land lines.

4 The MTSO routes the call over the telephone network to a land-based phone or initiates a search for the recipient on the cellular network.

5 The MTSO sends the recipient's phone number to all its towers, which broadcast the number via radio frequency.

6 The recipient's phone "hears" the broadcast and establishes a connection with the nearest tower. A voice line is established via the tower by the MTSO.

■ PANEL 8.6

Cellular connections

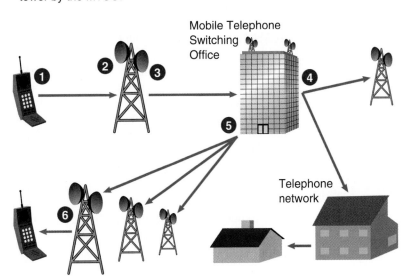

Mobile Telephone Switching Office

Telephone network

or suburb. The purpose of a MAN is often to bypass local telephone companies when accessing long-distance services. Cellular phone systems are often MANs.

● Local network: **A *local network* is a privately owned communications network that serves users within a confined geographical area.** The range is usually within a mile—perhaps one office, one building, or a group of buildings close together, as a college campus. Local networks are of two types: private branch exchanges (PBXs) and local area networks (LANs), as we discuss shortly.

All these networks may consist of various combinations of computers, storage devices, and communications devices.

Network Operating Systems

A network requires a network operating system to support access by multiple users and provide for recognition of users based on passwords and terminal identifications. It may be a completely self-contained operating system, such as NetWare (✔ p. 93). Or it may require an existing operating system in order to function; for example, LAN Manager requires OS/2, and LANtastic requires DOS or Windows.

Some Network Features: Hosts & Nodes, Servers & Clients

Many computer networks, particularly large ones, are served by a host computer. **A *host computer,* or simply a *host,* is the main computer—the central computer that controls the network. A *node* is simply a device that is attached to a network.**

On a local area network, some of the functions of the host may be performed by a server. As discussed in Chapter 1 (✔ p. 21), a *server,* or *network server,* is a central computer that holds databases and programs for many PCs, workstations, or terminals, which are called *clients.* These clients are nodes linked by a wired or wireless network, and the entire network is called a *client/server network.* Applications programs and files on the server are loaded into the main memories of the client machines.

Advantages of Networks

The following advantages are particularly true for LANs, although they apply to MANs and WANs as well.

● Sharing of peripheral devices: Laser printers, disk drives, and scanners are examples of peripheral devices—that is, hardware that is connected to a computer. Any newly introduced piece of hardware is often quite expensive, as was the case with laser or color printers. To justify their purchase, companies want them to be shared by many users. Usually the best way to do this is to connect the peripheral device to a network serving several computer users.

● Sharing of programs and data: In most organizations, people use the same software and need access to the same information. It could be expensive for a company to buy a copy of, say, a word processing program for each employee. Rather, the company will usually buy a network version of that program that will serve many employees.

Organizations also save a great deal of money by letting all employees have access to the same data on a shared storage device. This way the organization avoids such problems as some employees updating customer addresses on their own separate machines while other employees remain ignorant of such changes. It is much easier to update (maintain) software on the server than it is to update it on each user's individual system.

Finally, network-linked employees can more easily work together online on shared projects.

- **Better communications:** One of the greatest features of networks is electronic mail. With e-mail everyone on a network can easily keep others posted about important information.

- **Security of information:** Before networks became commonplace, an individual employee might be the only one with a particular piece of information, stored in his or her desktop computer. If the employee was dismissed—or if a fire or flood demolished the office—no one else in the company might have any knowledge of that information. Today such data would be backed up or duplicated on a networked storage device shared by others.

- **Access to databases:** Networks also enable users to tap into numerous databases, whether the private databases of a company or public databases available online through the Internet.

8.5 Local Networks

KEY QUESTION

What are local networks and the types, components, topologies, and impact of LANs?

Preview & Review: Local networks may be private branch exchanges (PBXs) or local area networks (LANs). LANs may be client/server or peer-to-peer and include components such as network cabling, network interface cards, an operating system, other shared devices, and bridges and gateways. The topology, or shape, of a network may take five forms: star, ring, bus, hybrid, or FDDI.

Although large networks are useful, many organizations need to have a local network—an in-house network—to tie together their own equipment. Here let's consider the following aspects of local networks:

- Types of local networks—PBXs and LANs
- Types of LANs—client/server and peer-to-peer
- Components of a LAN
- Topology of LANs—star, ring, bus, hybrid, and FDDI
- Impact of LANs

Types of Local Networks: PBXs & LANs

The most common types of local networks are PBXs and LANs.

- **Private branch exchange (PBX):** **A *private branch exchange (PBX)* is a private or leased telephone switching system that connects telephone extensions in-house.** It also connects them to the outside phone system.

    A public telephone system consists of "public branch exchanges"—thousands of switching stations that direct calls to different "branches" of the network. A private branch exchange is essentially the old-fashioned company switchboard. You call in from the outside, a switchboard operator says "How may I direct your call?" (or an automated voice gives you options for directing your call), and you are connected to the extension of the person you wish to talk to.

- **Local area network (LAN):** PBXs may share existing phone lines with the telephone system. Local area networks usually require installation of their own communication channels, whether wired or wireless. **Local area networks (LANs) are local networks consisting of a communications link, network operating system, microcomputers or workstations, servers, and other shared hardware.** Such shared hardware might include printers, scanners, and storage devices.

Types of LANs: Client/Server & Peer-to-Peer

Local area networks are of two principal types: client/server and peer-to-peer. (■ *See Panel 8.7.*)

- **Client/server LANs:** **A *client/server LAN* consists of requesting microcomputers, called *clients*, and supplying devices that provide a service, called *servers*.** The server is a computer that manages shared devices, such as laser printers, or shared files. The server microcomputer is usually a powerful one, running on a high-speed chip such as a Pentium II. Client/server networks, such as those run under Novell's NetWare or Windows NT operating systems, are the most common types of LANs. One piece of the network operating system resides in each client machine, and another resides in each server. The operating system allows the remote hard-disk drives on the servers to be accessed as if they were local drives on the client machine.

  Different servers can be used to manage different tasks—files and programs, databases, printers. The one you may hear about most often is the file server. **A *file server* is a computer that stores the programs and data files shared by users on a LAN.** It acts like a disk drive but is in a remote location.

- **Peer-to-peer:** The word *peer* denotes one who is equal in standing with another (as in the phrases "peer pressure" or "jury of one's peers"). **A *peer-to-peer LAN* is one in which all microcomputers on the network communicate directly with one another without relying on a server.** Peer-to-peer networks are less expensive than client/server networks and work effectively for up to 25 computers. Beyond that they slow down under heavy use. They are thus appropriate for networking in small groups.

Many LANs mix elements from both client/server and peer-to-peer models.

Components of a LAN

Local area networks are made up of several standard components.

- **Connection or cabling system:** LANs do not use the telephone network. Instead, they use some other cabling or connection system, either wired or wireless. Wired connections may be twisted-pair wiring, coaxial cable, or fiber-optic cable. Wireless connections may be infrared or radio-wave transmission. Wireless networks are

■ PANEL 8.7

Two types of LANs: client/server and peer-to-peer

(Top) In a client/server LAN, individual microcomputer users, or "clients," share the services of a centralized computer called a "server." In this case, the server is a file server, allowing users to share files of data and some programs. *(Bottom)* In a peer-to-peer LAN, computers share equally with one another without having to rely on a central server.

Client/server LAN

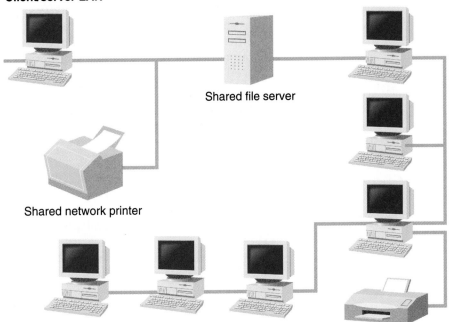

Shared file server

Shared network printer

Local printer

Peer-to-peer LAN

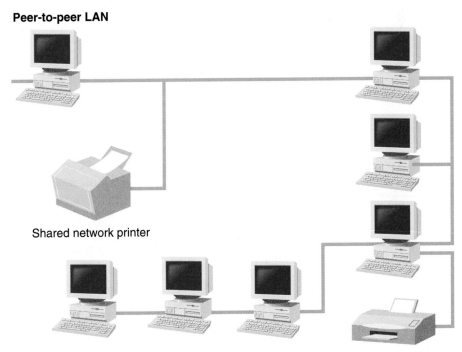

Shared network printer

Local printer

especially useful if computers are portable and are moved often. However, they are subject to interference.

● **Microcomputers with interface cards:** Two or more microcomputers are required, along with network interface cards. A *network interface card,* which is inserted into an expansion slot in a microcomputer, enables the computer to send and receive messages on the LAN. The interface card can also exist in a separate box, which can serve a number of devices.

- Network operating system: As mentioned, the network operating system software manages the activity of the network. Depending on the type of network, the operating system software may be stored on the file server, on each microcomputer on the network, or a combination of both. Examples of network operating systems are Novell's NetWare, Microsoft's Windows NT, and IBM's LAN.

- Other shared devices: Printers, fax machines, scanners, storage devices, and other peripherals may be added to the network as necessary and shared by all users.

- Bridges, routers, and gateways: A LAN may stand alone, but it may also connect to other networks, either similar or different in technology. Network designers determine the types of hardware and software devices necessary—bridges, routers, gateways—to use as interfaces to make these connections.

  A *bridge* is a hardware and software combination used to connect the same types of networks.

  A *router* is a special computer that directs communicating messages when several networks are connected together. High-speed routers can serve as part of the Internet backbone, or transmission path, handling the major data traffic.

  A *gateway* is an interface that enables dissimilar networks to communicate, such as a LAN with a WAN or two LANs based on different topologies or network operating systems.

Topology of LANs

Networks can be laid out in different ways. The logical layout, or shape, of a network is called a *topology*. The five basic topologies are *star, ring, bus, hybrid,* and *FDDI*. (■ *See Panel 8.8.*)

- Star network: **A *star network* is one in which all microcomputers and other communications devices are connected to a central server.** Electronic messages are routed through the central hub to their destinations, so the central hub monitors the flow of traffic. A PBX system is an example of a star network.

- Ring network: **A *ring network* is one in which all microcomputers and other communications devices are connected in a continuous loop.** Electronic messages are passed around the ring until they reach the right destination. There is no central server.

- Bus network: **In a *bus network,* all communications devices are connected to a common channel.** There is no central server. Each communications device transmits electronic messages to other devices. If some of those messages collide, the device waits and tries to retransmit.

- Hybrid network: ***Hybrid networks* are combinations of star, ring, and bus networks.** For example, a small college campus might use a bus network to connect buildings and star and ring networks within certain buildings.

- FDDI network: A newer and higher-speed network is the FDDI, short for Fiber Distributed Data Interface. Capable of transmitting 100–200 megabits per second, **an *FDDI network* uses fiber-optic cable with an adaptation of ring topology using not one but two "token rings."** The FDDI network is being used for such high-tech purposes as electronic imaging, high-resolution graphics, and digital video.

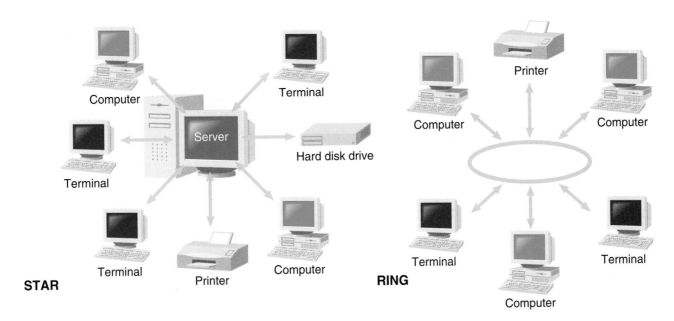

STAR

RING

■ PANEL 8.8

Four LAN topologies

(Top left) In a *star* network, all the network's devices are connected to a central host computer, through which all communications must pass. *(Top right)* In a *ring* network, the network's devices are connected in a closed loop. *(Middle)* In a *bus* network, a single channel connects all communications devices. *(Bottom)* In an *FDDI* network, fiber-optic cable is used in an adaptation of ring topology, using two rings. If one ring fails, the other will keep the network operating.

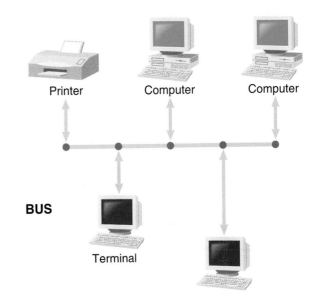

BUS

FDDI

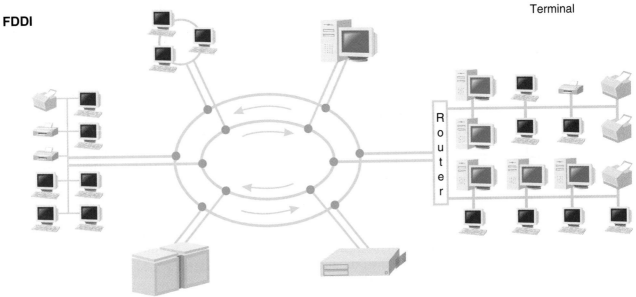

The Impact of LANs

Sales of mainframes and minicomputers have been falling for some time. This is largely because companies have discovered that LANs can take their place for many (though certainly not all) functions, and at considerably less expense. This situation reflects a trend known as *downsizing*. Still, a LAN, like a mainframe, requires a skilled support staff. Moreover, LANs have neither the great storage capacity nor the security that mainframes have, which makes them not useful for some applications.

8.6 Factors Affecting Communications Among Devices

KEY QUESTION

What are the factors affecting data transmission?

Preview & Review: Factors affecting how data is transmitted include the transmission rate (frequency and bandwidth), the line configuration (point-to-point or multipoint), serial versus parallel transmission, the direction of transmission flow (simplex, half-duplex, or full-duplex), transmission mode (asynchronous or synchronous), packet switching, multiplexing, and protocols.

Things are changing, and changing fast. It's not enough to know about the types of communications channels and network configurations available. As the technology moves forward, you'll also want to know what's happening behind the scenes. Several factors affect how data is transmitted, including *transmission rate; line configurations; serial versus parallel transmission; direction of transmission; transmission mode; circuit switching, packet switching,* and *asynchonous transfer mode;* and *protocols.*

Transmission Rate: Higher Frequency, Wider Bandwidth, More Data

Transmission rate is a function of two variables: frequency and bandwidth.

The amount of data that can be transmitted on a channel depends on the wave *frequency*—the cycles of waves per second (expressed in hertz). The more cycles per second, the more data that can be sent through that channel.

The greater a channel's *bandwidth*—the difference (range) between the highest and lowest frequencies—the more frequencies it has available and hence the more data that can be sent through that channel (expressed in bits per second, or bps).

A twisted-pair telephone wire of 4000 hertz might send only 1 kilobyte per second of data. A coaxial cable of 100 megahertz might send 10 megabytes per second. And a fiber-optic cable of 200 trillion hertz might send 1 gigabyte per second.

Line Configurations: Point-to-Point & Multipoint

There are two principal line configurations, or ways of connecting communications lines: point-to-point and multipoint.

- **Point-to-point:** A *point-to-point line* directly connects the sending and receiving devices, such as a terminal with a central computer. This arrangement is appropriate for a private line whose sole purpose is to keep data secure by transmitting it from one device to another.

- **Multipoint:** A *multipoint line* is a single line that interconnects several communications devices to one computer. Often on a multipoint line only one communications device, such as a terminal, can transmit at any given time.

Serial & Parallel Transmission

Data is transmitted in two ways: serially and in parallel.

- **Serial data transmission:** **In *serial data transmission*, bits are transmitted sequentially, one after the other.** This arrangement resembles cars proceeding down a one-lane road. Serial transmission is the way most data flows over a twisted-pair telephone line. Serial transmission is found in communications lines and modems.

- **Parallel data transmission:** **In *parallel data transmission*, bits are transmitted through separate lines simultaneously.** The arrangement resembles cars moving in separate lanes at the same speed on a multilane freeway. Parallel lines move information faster than serial lines do, but they are efficient for up to only 15 feet. Thus, parallel lines are used, for example, to transmit data from a computer's CPU to a printer.

Direction of Transmission Flow: Simplex, Half-Duplex, & Full-Duplex

When two computers are in communication, data can flow in three ways: simplex, half-duplex, or full-duplex. These are fancy terms for easily understood processes.

- **Simplex transmission:** **In *simplex transmission*, data can travel in only one direction.** An example is a traditional television broadcast, in which the signal is sent from the transmitter to your TV antenna. There is no return signal. Some computerized data collection devices also work this way, such as seismograph sensors that measure earthquakes.

- **Half-duplex transmission:** **In *half-duplex transmission*, data travels in both directions but only in one direction at a time.** This arrangement resembles traffic on a one-lane bridge; the separate streams of cars heading in both directions must take turns. Half-duplex transmission is seen with CB or marine radios, in which both parties must take turns talking. This is the most common mode of data transmission used today.

- **Full-duplex transmission:** **In *full-duplex transmission*, data is transmitted back and forth at the same time.** This arrangement resembles automobile traffic on a two-way street. An example is two people on the telephone talking and listening simultaneously. Full-duplex is sometimes used in large computer systems.

Transmission Mode: Asynchronous Versus Synchronous

Suppose your computer sends the word CONGRATULATIONS! to someone as bits and bytes over a communications line. How does the receiving equipment know where one byte (or character) ends and another begins? This matter is resolved through either *asynchronous transmission* or *synchronous transmission*. (■ *See Panel 8.9, next page.*)

ASYNCHRONOUS TRANSMISSION

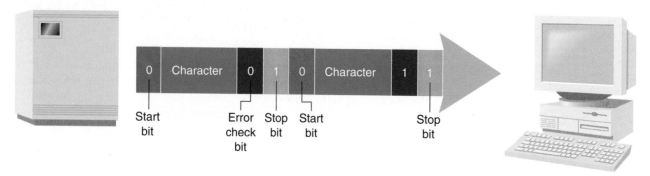

Start bit — Error check bit — Stop bit — Start bit — Stop bit

0 | Character | 0 | 1 | 0 | Character | 1 | 1

SYNCHRONOUS TRANSMISSION

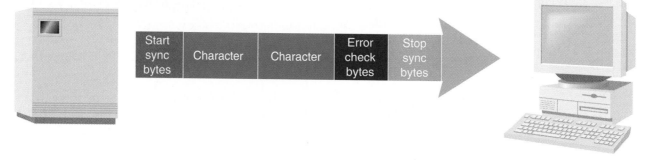

Start sync bytes | Character | Character | Error check bytes | Stop sync bytes

■ PANEL 8.9

Transmission modes
(Top) In asynchronous transmission, each character is preceded by a "start" bit and followed by a "stop" bit.*(Bottom)* In synchronous transmission, messages are sent in blocks with start and stop patterns of bits, called *synch bytes*, before and after the blocks. The synch bytes synchronize the timing of the internal clocks between sending and receiving devices.

- **Asynchronous transmission:** This method, used with most microcomputers, is also called *start-stop transmission.* **In asynchronous transmission, data is sent one byte (or character) at a time. Each string of bits making up the byte is bracketed, or marked off, with special control bits.** That is, a "start" bit represents the beginning of a character, and a "stop" bit represents its end. Transmitting only one byte at a time makes this a relatively slow method. As a result, asynchronous transmission is not used when great amounts of data must be sent rapidly. Its advantage is that the data can be transmitted whenever it is convenient for the sender.

- **Synchronous transmission:** Instead of using start and stop bits, *synchronous transmission* **sends data in blocks. Start and stop bit patterns, called synch bytes, are transmitted at the beginning and end of the blocks.** These start and end bit patterns synchronize internal clocks in the sending and receiving devices so that they are in time with each other. This method is rarely used with microcomputers because it is more complicated and more expensive than asynchronous transmission. It also requires careful timing between sending and receiving equipment. It is appropriate for computer systems that need to transmit great quantities of data quickly.

Circuit Switching, Packet Switching, & Asynchronous Transfer Mode: For Voice, Data, & Both

What is the most efficient way to send messages over a telephone line? That depends on whether the messages are *voice, data,* or *both.*

- **Circuit switching—best for voice:** Circuit switching is used by the telephone company for its voice networks to guarantee steady, consistent service for telephone conversations. **In *circuit switching*, the transmitter has full use of the circuit until all the data has been transmitted and the circuit is terminated.**

● Packet switching—best for data: **A *packet* is a fixed-length block of data for transmission.** The packet also contains instructions about the destination of the packet. ***Packet switching* is a technique for dividing electronic messages into packets for transmission over a wide area network to their destination through the most expedient route.** The benefit of packet switching is that it can handle high-volume traffic in a network. It also allows more users to share a network, thereby offering cost savings. The method is particularly appropriate for sending data long distances, such as across the country.

In packet switching, a sending computer breaks an electronic message apart into packets. The various packets are sent through a communications network—often by different routes, at different speeds, and sandwiched in between packets from other messages. Once the packets arrive at their destination, the receiving computer reassembles them into proper sequence to complete the message.

● Asynchronous transfer mode (ATM)—best for both: **A newer technology, called *asynchronous transfer mode (ATM)*, combines the efficiency of packet switching with some aspects of circuit switching,** thus enabling it to handle both data and real-time voice and video. ATM is designed to run on high-bandwidth fiber-optic cables.

Protocols: The Rules of Data Transmission

Does the foregoing information in this section seem unduly technical for an ordinary computer user? Although you should understand these details, fortunately you won't have to think about them much. Experts will already have taken care of them for you in sets of rules called protocols.

The word *protocol* is used in the military and in diplomacy to express rules of precedence, rank, manners, and other matters of correctness. (An example would be the protocol for who will precede whom into a formal reception.) Here, however, **a *protocol*, or *communications protocol*, is a set of conventions governing the exchange of data between hardware and/or software components in a communications network.**

Protocols are built into the hardware or software you are using. The protocol in your communications software, for example, will specify how receiver devices will acknowledge sending devices, a matter called *handshaking*. Protocols will also specify the type of electrical connections used, the timing of message exchanges, error-detection techniques, and so on.

Summary

What It Is/What It Does

Why It's Important

analog cellular phone (p. 266, KQ 8.3) Mobile telephone designed primarily for communicating by voice through a system of ground-area *cells*. Calls are directed to cells by a mobile telephone switching office (MTSO). Moving between cells requires that calls be "handed off" by the MTSO.

Cellular phone systems allow callers mobility.

analog signal (p. 258, KQ 8.2) Continuous electrical signal in the form of a wave. The wave is called a *carrier wave.* Two characteristics of analog carrier waves that can be altered are frequency and amplitude. Computers cannot process analog signals.

Analog signals are used to convey voices and sounds over wire telephone lines, as well as in radio and TV broadcasting. Computers, however, use digital signals, which must be converted to analog signals in order to be transmitted over telephone wires.

asynchronous transfer mode (ATM) (p. 277, KQ 8.6) Method of communications transmission that combines the efficiency of packet switching with some aspects of circuit switching.

ATM transmission is a recent development using fiber-optic cable to handle both data and real-time voice and video transmissions.

asynchronous transmission (p. 276, KQ 8.6) Also called *start-stop transmission;* data is sent one byte (character) at a time. Each string of bits making up the byte is bracketed with special control bits; a "start" bit represents the beginning of a character, and a "stop" bit represents its end.

This method of communications is used with most microcomputers. Its advantage is that data can be transmitted whenever convenient for the sender. Its drawback is that transmitting only one byte at a time makes it a relatively slow method that cannot be used when great amounts of data must be sent rapidly.

bands (bandwidths) (p. 262, KQ 8.3) Ranges of frequencies. The bandwidth is the difference between the lowest and highest frequencies transmitted.

Different telecommunications systems use different bandwidths for different purposes, whether cellular phones or network television.

bits per second (bps) (p. 259, KQ 8.2) Measurement of data transmission speeds. Modems transmit at 1200, 2400, and 4800 bps (slow), 9600 and 14,400 bps (moderately fast), and 28,800, 33,600, and 56,000 bps (high-speed).

A 10-page single-spaced letter can be transmitted by a 2400-bps modem in 2½ minutes. It can be transmitted by a 9600-bps modem in 38 seconds and by a 56,000-bps modem in about 5 seconds. The faster the modem, the less time online and therefore less expense.

bus network (p. 272, KQ 8.5) Type of network in which all communications devices are connected to a common channel, with no central server. Each communications device transmits electronic messages to other devices. If some of those messages collide, the device waits and tries to retransmit.

The advantage of a bus network is that it may be organized as a client/server or peer-to-peer network. The disadvantage is that extra circuitry and software are needed to avoid collisions between data. Also, if a connection is broken, the entire network may stop working.

What It Is/What It Does

Why It's Important

cable modem (p. 261, KQ 8.2) Modem that connects a PC to a cable-TV system that offers online services as well as TV.

Cable modems transmit data faster than standard modems, but users can't send data nearly as fast as they receive it unless their cable service has upgraded for better two-way communications.

circuit switching (p. 277, KQ 8.6) Method of telephone transmission in which the transmitter has full use of the circuit until all the data has been transmitted and the circuit is terminated.

Used for voice conversations to provide steady service throughout.

client/server LAN (p. 270, KQ 8.5) Type of local area network (LAN); it consists of requesting microcomputers, called *clients,* and supplying devices that provide a service, called *servers.* The server is a computer that manages shared devices, such as laser printers, or shared files.

Client/server networks are the most common type of LAN. Compare with *peer-to-peer LAN.*

coaxial cable (p. 264, KQ 8.3) Type of communications channel; commonly called *co-ax,* it consists of insulated copper wire wrapped in a solid or braided metal shield, then in an external cover.

Coaxial cable is much better at resisting noise than twisted-pair wiring. Moreover, it can carry voice and data at a faster rate.

communications channel (p. 262, KQ 8.3) Also called *links, lines,* or *media;* the physical path over which information travels in a telecommunications system from its source to its destination.

There are many different telecommunications channels, both wired and wireless, some more efficient than others for different purposes.

communications satellites (p. 266, KQ 8.3) Microwave relay stations in orbit above the earth. Microwave earth stations beam signals to the satellite. The satellite has solar-powered receivers and transmitters (transponders) that receive the signals, amplify them, and retransmit them to another earth station.

An orbiting satellite contains many communications channels and receives both analog and digital signals from ground microwave stations.

digital cellular phone (p. 266, KQ 8.3) Mobile phone system that uses cells like an analog cellular phone system but transmits digital signals. Voice messages are decoded by the cellular handset, and short data items can also be transmitted.

Like an analog cellular phone, it offers the user mobility, but digital service also provides lower costs for heavy users, greater privacy, and perhaps clearer sound.

digital signal (p. 258, KQ 8.2) Type of electrical signal that uses on/off or present/absent electrical pulses in discontinuous, or discrete, bursts, rather than a continuous wave.

This two-state kind of signal works perfectly in representing the two-state binary language of 0s and 1s that computers use.

What It Is/What It Does	Why It's Important

Digital Subscriber Line (DSL) (p. 261, KQ 8.2) Data transmission service that uses regular phone lines to transmit data at speeds of 1.5–8 megabits per second (Mbps), and splits the line into three channels for normal voice, outgoing data, and incoming data. Users need a special modem.

DSL service is much faster than ISDN's 128 kbps. Because it's faster for downloading than uploading, it's well suited to receiving Web or other files but not for video-conferencing, where large amounts of data need to travel fast enough to keep up with real time in both directions.

electromagnetic spectrum (p. 262, KQ 8.3) All the fields of electrical energy and magnetic energy, which travel in waves. This includes all radio signals, light rays, X-rays, and radioactivity.

The part of the electromagnetic spectrum of particular interest is the area in the middle, which is used for communications purposes. Various frequencies are assigned by the federal government for different purposes.

FDDI network (p. 272, KQ 8.5) Short for Fiber Distributed Data Interface; a type of local area network that uses fiber-optic cable with an adaptation of ring topology using two "token rings."

The FDDI network is being used for such high-tech purposes as electronic imaging, high-resolution graphics, and digital video.

fiber-optic cable (p. 264, KQ 8.3) Type of communications channel consisting of hundreds or thousands of thin strands of glass that transmit pulsating beams of light. These strands, each as thin as a human hair, can transmit billions of pulses per second, each "on" pulse representing one bit.

When bundled together, fiber-optic strands in a cable 0.12 inch thick can support a quarter- to a half-million simultaneous voice conversations. Moreover, unlike electrical signals, light pulses are not affected by random electromagnetic interference in the environment and thus have much lower error rates than telephone wire and cable.

file server (p. 270, KQ 8.5) Type of computer used on a local area network (LAN) that acts like a disk drive and stores the programs and data files shared by users of the LAN.

A file server enables users of a LAN to all have access to the same programs and data.

full-duplex transmission (p. 275, KQ 8.6) Type of data transmission in which data is transmitted back and forth at the same time, unlike simplex and half-duplex.

Full-duplex is available in some large computer systems and in newer microcomputer modems to support work-group computing.

half-duplex transmission (p. 275, KQ 8.6) Type of data transmission in which data travels in both directions but only in one direction at a time, as with CB or marine radios; the two parties must take turns talking.

Half-duplex is the most common method of data transmission, as when logging onto a bulletin board system.

host computer (p. 268, KQ 8.4) The central computer that controls a network. On a local area network, the host's functions may be performed by a computer called a *server*.

The host is responsible for managing the entire network.

hybrid network (p. 272, KQ 8.5) Type of local area network (LAN) that combines star, ring, and bus networks.

A hybrid network can link different types of LANs. For example, a small college campus might use a bus network to connect buildings and star and ring networks within certain buildings.

What It Is/What It Does

Why It's Important

Integrated Services Digital Network (ISDN) (p. 260, KQ 8.2) Hardware and software that allow voice, video, and data to be communicated as digital signals over traditional copper-wire telephone lines.

The main benefit of ISDN is speed. It allows people to send digital data at 128 kbps, more than double the speed the fastest modems can now deliver on the analog voice network. However, other, faster technologies will probably take over ISDN's role of high-speed data transmission for consumers and small business.

kilobits per second (kbps) (p. 259, KQ 8.2) 1000 bits per second; an expression of data transmission speeds. A 56,000-bps modem is a 56-kbps, or 56K, modem.

See bits per second.

local area network (LAN) (p. 270, KQ 8.5) A network consisting of a communications link, network operating system, microcomputers or workstations, servers, and other shared hardware such as printers or storage devices. LANs are of two principal types: client/server and peer-to-peer.

LANs have replaced mainframes and minicomputers for many functions and are considerably less expensive. However, LANs have neither the great storage capacity nor the security of mainframes.

local network (p. 268, KQ 8.4) Privately owned communications network that serves users within a confined geographical area. The range is usually within a mile.

Local networks are of two types: private branch exchanges (PBXs) and local area networks (LANs).

metropolitan area network (MAN) (p. 267, KQ 8.4) Communications network covering a geographic area the size of a city or suburb. Cellular phone systems are often MANs.

The purpose of a MAN is often to bypass telephone companies when accessing long-distance services.

microwave systems (p. 265, KQ 8.3) Communications systems that transmit voice and data through the atmosphere as super-high-frequency radio waves. Microwaves are the electromagnetic waves that vibrate at 1 billion hertz per second or higher.

Microwave frequencies are used to transmit messages between ground-based earth stations and satellite communications systems. More than half of today's telephone system uses microwave transmission.

modem (p. 259, KQ 8.2) Short for *mo*dulater/*dem*odulater. A device that converts digital signals into a representation of analog form (modulation) to send over phone lines; a receiving modem then converts the analog signal back to a digital signal (demodulation).

A modem enables users to transmit data from one computer to another by using standard telephone lines instead of special communications lines such as fiber optic or cable.

network (communications network) (p. 267, KQ 8.4) System of interconnected computers, telephones, or other communications devices that can communicate with one another.

Networks allow users to share applications and data.

node (p. 268, KQ 8.4) Any device that is attached to a network.

A node may be a microcomputer, terminal, storage device, or some peripheral device, any of which enhance the usefulness of the network.

What It Is/What It Does	Why It's Important

packet (p. 277, KQ 8.6) Fixed-length block of data for transmission. The packet also contains instructions about the destination of the packet.

By creating data in the form of packets, a transmission system can deliver the data more efficiently and economically, as in packet switching.

packet switching (p. 277, KQ 8.6) Technique for dividing electronic messages into packets—fixed-length blocks of data—for transmission over a wide area network to their destination through the most expedient route. A sending computer breaks an electronic message apart into packets, which are sent through a communications network—via different routes and speeds—to a receiving computer, which reassembles them into proper sequence to complete the message.

The benefit of packet switching is that it can handle high-volume traffic in a network. It also allows more users to share a network, thereby offering cost savings.

parallel data transmission (p. 275, KQ 8.6) Method of transmitting data in which bits are sent through separate lines simultaneously.

Unlike serial lines, parallel lines move information fast, but they are efficient for only up to 15 feet. Thus, parallel lines are used, for example, to transmit data from a computer's CPU to a printer.

peer-to-peer LAN (p. 270, KQ 8.5) Type of local area network (LAN); all microcomputers on the network communicate directly with one another without relying on a server.

Peer-to-peer networks are less expensive than client/server networks and work effectively for up to 25 computers. Thus, they are appropriate for networking in small groups.

private branch exchange (PBX) (p. 269, KQ 8.5) Private or leased telephone switching system that connects telephone extensions in-house as well as to the outside telephone system.

Newer PBXs can handle not only analog telephones but also digital equipment, including computers.

protocol (communications protocol) (p. 277, KQ 8.6) Set of conventions governing the exchange of data between hardware and/or software components in a communications network.

Protocols are built into hardware and software to allow different devices to work together, and with OSI standards, protocols have become much more universal.

ring network (p. 272, KQ 8.5) Type of local area network (LAN) in which all communications devices are connected in a continuous loop and messages are passed around the ring until they reach the right destination. There is no central server.

The advantage of a ring network is that messages flow in only one direction and so there is no danger of collisions. The disadvantage is that if a connection is broken, the entire network stops working.

serial data transmission (p. 275, KQ 8.6) Method of data transmission in which bits are sent sequentially, one after the other, through one line.

Serial transmission is found in communications lines, modems, and mice.

simplex transmission (p. 275, KQ 8.6) Type of transmission in which data can travel in only one direction; there is no return signal.

Some computerized data collection devices, such as seismograph sensors that measure earthquakes, use simplex transmission.

What It Is/What It Does	**Why It's Important**

star network (p. 272, KQ 8.5) Type of local area network (LAN) in which all microcomputers and other communications devices are connected to a central hub, such as a file server. Electronic messages are routed through the central hub to their destinations. The central hub monitors the flow of traffic.

The advantage of a star network is that the hub prevents collisions between messages. Moreover, if a connection is broken between any communications device and the hub, the rest of the devices on the network will continue operating.

synchronous transmission (p. 276, KQ 8.6) Type of transmission in which data is sent in blocks. Start and stop bit patterns, called synch bytes, are transmitted at the beginning and end of the blocks. These start and end bit patterns synchronize internal clocks in the sending and receiving devices so that they are in time with each other.

Synchronous transmission is rarely used with microcomputers because it is more complicated and more expensive than asynchronous transmission. It is appropriate for computer systems that need to transmit great quantities of data quickly.

telecommuting (p. 256, KQ 8.1) Way of working at home with telecommunications—phone, fax, and computer—between office and home.

Telecommuting can help ease traffic and the stress of commuting by car, increase productivity and job satisfaction, and let a company hire employees who don't want to move.

twisted-pair wire (p. 264, KQ 8.3) Type of communications channel consisting of two strands of insulated copper wire, twisted around each other in pairs.

Twisted-pair wire has been the most common channel or medium used for telephone systems. It is relatively slow and does not protect well against electrical interference.

T1 line (p. 261, KQ 8.2) A traditional telephone trunk line that carries 24 normal telephone circuits and has a speed of 1500 kbps.

Used as high-capacity communications links at corporate, government, or academic sites.

T3 line (p. 261, KQ 8.2) A digital communications trunk line that transmits at a speed of 4500 kbps.

The digital equivalent of a T1 line, offering three times the speed but at a much higher cost for equipment and service charges.

virtual office (p. 257, KQ 8.1) An often nonpermanent and mobile office run with computer and communications technology.

Employees work not in a central office but from their homes, cars, and customers' offices. They use pocket pagers, portable computers, fax machines, and various phone and network services to conduct business.

wide area network (WAN) (p. 267, KQ 8.4) Type of communications network that covers a wide geographical area, such as a state or a country.

Wide area networks provide worldwide communications systems.

Self-Test Exercises

1. A(n) _____ converts digital signals into analog signals for transmission over phone lines.

2. Before a microcomputer in a LAN can send and receive messages, a(n) _____ _____ must be inserted into an expansion slot in a computer.

3. _____ transmission sends data in both directions simultaneously, similar to two trains passing in opposite directions on side-by-side tracks.

4. A(n) _____ _____ network is a communications network that covers a wide geographical area, such as a state or a country.

5. _____ cable transmits data as pulses of light rather than as electricity.

Short-Answer Questions

1. Why is speed an important consideration when selecting a modem?

2. What is meant by the term *protocol* as it relates to communicating between two computers?

3. What is a hybrid network?

4. When talking about communications, what is the significance of the electromagnetic spectrum?

Multiple-Choice Questions

1. Which of the following functions does communications software perform?
   a. data compression
   b. remote control
   c. terminal emulation
   d. All of the above

2. Which of the following is a standard LAN component?
   a. network operating system
   b. cabling system
   c. network interface cards
   d. shared devices
   e. All of the above

3. Which of the following best describes the telephone line that is used in most homes today?
   a. twisted-pair wire
   b. coaxial cable
   c. fiber-optic cable
   d. modem cable
   e. None of the above

4. Which of the following network configurations always uses a central server?
   a. bus
   b. star
   c. ring
   d. hybrid
   e. All of the above

5. Which of the following do local area networks enable?
   a. sharing of peripheral devices
   b. sharing of programs and data
   c. better communications
   d. access to databases
   e. All of the above

True/False Questions

T F   1. In a LAN, a bridge is used to connect the same types of networks, whereas a gateway is used to enable dissimilar networks to communicate.

T F   2. The current limitation of cable modems is that they don't provide much online interactivity.

T F   3. Transmission rate is a function of two variables: frequency and bandwidth.

T F   4. All communications channels are either wired or wireless.

T F   5. Parallel transmission is faster than serial transmission.

Knowledge in Action

1. Are the computers at your school or work connected to a network? If so, what are the characteristics of the network? What advantages does the network provide in terms of hardware and software support? What types of computers are connected to the network (microcomputers, minicomputers, and/or mainframes)? Specifically, what software/hardware is allowing the network to function?

2. Using current articles, publications, and/or the Web, research the history of cable modems, how they are being used today, and what you think the future holds for them. Do you think you will use a cable modem in the future? Present your findings in a paper or a 15-minute discussion.

3. Describe in more detail the FCC's role in regulating the communications industry. What happens when frequencies are opened up for new communications services? Who gets to use these frequencies?

4. Of the different technologies discussed in this chapter, which do you think will have the biggest impact on you? Why?

Systems

Development, Programming, & Languages

Chapter 9

Organizations can make mistakes, and big organizations can make *really big* mistakes.

California's state Department of Motor Vehicles' databases needed to be modernized, and in 1988 Tandem Computers said they could do it. "The fact that the DMV's database system, designed around an old IBM-based platform, and Tandem's new system were as different as night and day seemed insignificant at the time to the experts involved," said one writer investigating the project later.[1] The massive driver's license database, containing the driving records of more than 30 million people, first had to be "scrubbed" of all information that couldn't be translated into the language used by Tandem computers. One such scrub yielded 600,000 errors. Then the DMV had to translate all its IBM programs into the Tandem language. "Worse, DMV really didn't know how its current IBM applications worked anymore," said the writer, "because they'd been custom-made decades before by long-departed programmers and rewritten many times since." Eventually the project became a staggering $44 million loss to California's taxpayers.

In Denver, airport officials weren't trying to upgrade an old system but to do something completely new. At the heart of the Denver International Airport was supposed to be a high-tech system to whisk baggage between terminals so fast that passengers would practically never have to wait for their luggage. As the system failed test after test, airport officials eventually decided they had to *build a manual baggage system*—at an additional cost of $50 million. Spending the money on old technology, it developed, was cheaper than continuing to spend millions paying interest on construction bonds for a nonoperating airport.[2]

Both these examples show how important planning is, especially when an organization is trying to launch a new kind of system. How do you avoid such mistakes? By employing systems analysis and design.

9.1 Systems Development: The Six Phases of Systems Analysis & Design

KEY QUESTION

What are the six phases of the systems development life cycle?

Preview & Review: Knowledge of systems analysis and design helps you explain your present job, improve personal productivity, and lessen risk of a project's failure. The initiative for suggesting a need to analyze and possibly change an information system may come from users, managers, or technical staff.

The six phases of systems design and analysis are known as the systems development life cycle (SDLC). The six phases are (1) preliminary investigation, (2) systems analysis, (3) systems design, (4) systems development, (5) systems implementation, and (6) systems maintenance.

You may not have to wrestle with problems on the scale of motor-vehicle departments and airports. That's a job for computer professionals. You're mainly interested in using computers and communications to increase your own productivity. Why, then, do you need to know anything about systems analysis and design?

In many types of jobs, you may find your department or your job the focus of a study by a systems analyst. Knowing how systems analysis and design works will help you better explain how your job works or what goals your department is supposed to achieve. In progressive companies, management is always interested in suggestions for improving productivity. This is the method for expressing your ideas.

The Purpose of a System

A *system* is defined as a collection of related components that interact to perform a task in order to accomplish a goal. A system may not work very well, but it is nevertheless a system. The point of systems analysis and design is to ascertain how a system works and then take steps to make it better.

An organization's computer-based information system consists of hardware, software, people, procedures, and data, as well as communications setups. These work together to provide people with information for running the organization.

Getting the Project Going: How It Starts, Who's Involved

All it takes is a single individual who believes that something badly needs changing to get a systems development project rolling. An employee may influence a supervisor. A customer or supplier may get the attention of someone in higher management. Top management on its own may decide to take a look at a system that looks inefficient. A steering committee may be formed to decide which of many possible projects should be worked on.

Participants in the project are of three types:

- Users: The system under discussion should *always* be developed in consultation with users, whether floor sweepers, research scientists, or customers. Indeed, inadequate user involvement in analysis and design can be a major cause of a system's failure.
- Management: Managers within the organization should also be consulted about the system.
- Technical staff: Members of the company's information systems (IS) department, consisting of systems analysts and programmers, need to be involved. For one thing, they may well have to carry out and execute the project. Even if they don't, they may have to work with outside IS people contracted to do the job.

Complex projects will require one or several systems analysts. **A *systems analyst* is an information specialist who performs systems analysis, design, and implementation.** His or her job is to study the information and communications needs of an organization and determine what changes are required to deliver better information to people who need it. "Better" information means information that can be summarized in the acronym "CART"—complete, accurate, relevant, and timely. The systems analyst achieves this goal through the problem-solving method of systems analysis and design.

The Six Phases of Systems Analysis & Design

***Systems analysis and design* is a six-phase problem-solving procedure for examining an information system and improving it.** The six phases make up what is called the systems development life cycle. **The *systems development life cycle (SDLC)* is defined as the step-by-step process that many organizations follow during systems analysis and design.**

Whether applied to a Fortune 500 company or a three-person engineering business, the six phases in systems analysis and design may be said to be as follows. (■ *See Panel 9.1.*)

1. **Preliminary investigation:** Conduct preliminary analysis, propose alternative solutions, and describe the costs and benefits of each solution. Submit a preliminary plan with recommendations.
2. **Systems analysis:** Gather data, analyze the data, and make a written report.
3. **Systems design:** Make a preliminary design and then a detailed design, and write a report.
4. **Systems development:** Acquire the hardware and software and test the system.
5. **Systems implementation:** Convert the hardware, software, and files to the new system and train the users.
6. **Systems maintenance:** Audit the system, request feedback from its users, and evaluate it periodically.

Phases often overlap, and a new one may start before the old one is finished. After the first four phases, management must decide whether to proceed to the next phase. *User input and review is a critical part of each phase.*

■ PANEL 9.1

The systems development life cycle

An SDLC typically includes six phases.

1. *Preliminary investigation:* Conduct preliminary analysis, propose alternative solutions, describe costs and benefits of each solution, and submit a preliminary plan with recommendations.
2. *Systems analysis:* Gather data, analyze the data, and make a written report.
3. *Systems design:* Make a preliminary design and then a detailed design, and write a report.
4. *Systems development:* Acquire the hardware and software and test the system.
5. *Systems implementation:* Convert the hardware, software, and files to the new system and train the users.
6. *Systems maintenance:* Audit the system, and evaluate it periodically.

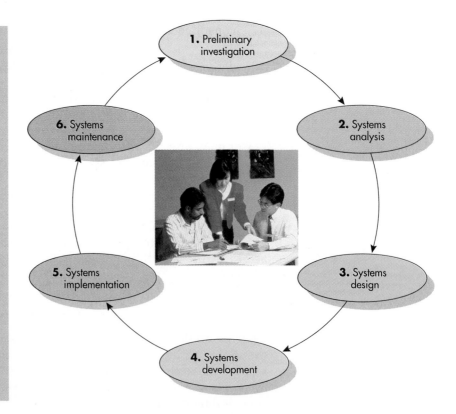

1. Preliminary investigation

2. Systems analysis

3. Systems design

4. Systems development

5. Systems implementation

6. Systems maintenance

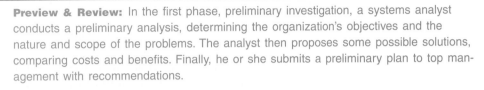

9.2 The First Phase: Conduct a Preliminary Investigation

KEY QUESTION

What does a preliminary investigation involve?

Preview & Review: In the first phase, preliminary investigation, a systems analyst conducts a preliminary analysis, determining the organization's objectives and the nature and scope of the problems. The analyst then proposes some possible solutions, comparing costs and benefits. Finally, he or she submits a preliminary plan to top management with recommendations.

The objective of Phase 1, *preliminary investigation*, is to conduct a preliminary analysis, propose alternative solutions, describe costs and benefits, and submit a preliminary plan with recommendations.

During preliminary investigation, you need to find out what the organization's objectives are and the nature and scope of the problem under study. Even if a problem pertains only to a small segment of the organization, you cannot study it in isolation. You need to find out what the objectives of the organization itself are. Then you need to see how the problem being studied fits in with them.

In delving into the organization's objectives and the specific problem, you may have already discovered some solutions. Other possible solutions can come from interviewing people inside the organization, clients or customers affected by it, suppliers, and consultants. You can also study what competitors are doing. With this data, you then have three choices. You can leave the system as is, improve it, or develop a new system.

Whichever of the three alternatives is chosen, it will have costs and benefits, and you need to indicate what these are. Costs may depend on benefits, which may offer savings. There are all kinds of benefits that may be derived. A process will be speeded up, streamlined through elimination of unnecessary steps, or combined with other processes. Input errors or redundant output may be reduced. Systems and subsystems may be better integrated. Users may be happier with the system. Customers or suppliers may interact better with the system. Security may be improved. Costs may be cut.

Now you need to wrap up all your findings in a written report. The readers of this report will be the executives (probably top managers) who are in a position to decide in which direction to proceed—make no changes, change a little, or change a lot. You should describe the potential solutions, costs, and benefits and indicate your recommendations.

9.3 The Second Phase: Do an Analysis of the System

KEY QUESTION

How is systems analysis carried out?

Preview & Review: In the second phase, systems analysis, a systems analyst gathers data, using the tools of written documents, interviews, questionnaires, and observation. Next he or she analyzes the data, using modeling tools. Finally, the analyst writes a report.

The objective of Phase 2, *systems analysis*, is to gather data, analyze the data, and write a report. In this second phase of the SDLC, you will follow the course that management has indicated after having read your Phase 1 feasibility report. We are assuming that they have ordered you to perform Phase 2—to do a careful analysis or study of the existing system in order to understand how the new system you proposed would differ. This analysis will also consider how people's positions and tasks will have to change if the new system is put into effect. During this phase you will gather data by reviewing written documents, interviewing employees and managers, developing questionnaires, and observing people and processes at work.

Once the data is gathered, you need to come to grips with it and analyze it. Many analytical tools, or modeling tools, are available. *Modeling tools* enable a systems analyst to present graphic, or pictorial, representations of a system. Some of these tools involve creating flowcharts and diagrams on paper.

Once you have completed the analysis, you need to document this phase. This report to management should have three parts. First, it should explain how the existing system works. Second, it should explain the problems with the existing system. Finally, it should describe the requirements for the new system and make recommendations on what to do next.

At this point, not a lot of money will have been spent on the systems analysis and design project. If the costs of going forward seem to be prohibitive, this is a good time for the managers reading the report to call a halt. Otherwise, you will be called upon to move to Phase 3.

9.4 The Third Phase: Design the System

KEY QUESTION

How does systems design proceed?

Preview & Review: In the third phase, systems design, the analyst does a preliminary design, next a detail design, and then writes a report. The preliminary design may be done using CASE tools and project management software. The detail design defines requirements for output, input, storage, and processing, as well as system controls and backup.

The objective of Phase 3, *systems design*, is to do a preliminary design and then a detail design, and write a report. In this third phase of the SDLC, you will essentially create a "rough draft" and then a "detail draft" of the proposed information system.

A *preliminary design*, often called a *logical design*, describes the general functional capabilities of a proposed information system. It reviews the system requirements and then considers major components of the system. Usually several alternative systems (called *candidates*) are considered, and the costs and the benefits of each are evaluated.

Some tools that may be used in the design are *CASE tools* and *project management software.*

- **CASE tools: *CASE* (for *computer-aided software engineering*) tools are programs that automate various activities of the SDLC in several phases.** This technology is intended to speed up the process of developing systems and to improve the quality of the resulting systems. Examples of such programs are Excelerator, Iconix, System Architect, and Powerbuilder. CASE tools may be used at almost any stage of the systems development life cycle, not just design.

  CASE tools may also be used to do prototyping. *Prototyping* refers to using workstations, CASE tools, and other software applications to build working models of system components so that they can be quickly tested and evaluated. Thus, a *prototype* is a limited working system developed to test out design concepts. A prototype, which may be constructed in just a few days, allows users to find out immediately how a change in the system might benefit them.

- **Project management software:** *Project management software* consists of programs used to plan, schedule, and control the people, costs, and resources required to complete a project on time.

A *detail design*, also called a *physical design*, describes how a proposed information system will deliver the general capabilities described in the preliminary design. The detail design usually considers the following parts of the system in this order:

- **Output requirements:** What do you want the system to produce? That is the first requirement to determine. In this first step, the systems analyst determines what media the output will be—whether hardcopy and/or softcopy. He or she will also design the appearance or format of the output, such as headings, columns, menu, and the like.

- **Input requirements:** Once you know the output, you can determine the inputs. Here, too, you must define the type of input, such as keyboard or source data-entry (✔ p. 141). You must determine in what form data will be input and how it will be checked for accuracy. You also need to figure what volume of data the system can be allowed to take in.

- **Storage requirements:** Using the data dictionary (✔ p. 210) as a guide, you need to define the files and databases in the information system. How will the files be organized? What kind of storage devices will be used? How will they interface with other storage devices inside and outside of the organization? What will be the volume of database activity?

- **Processing requirements:** What kind of computer or computers will be used to handle the processing? What kind of operating system will be used? Will the computer or computers be tied to others in a network? Exactly what operations will be performed on the input data to achieve the desired output information?

- **System controls and backup:** Finally, you need to think about matters of security, privacy, and data accuracy. You need to prevent unauthorized users from breaking into the system, for example, and snooping in people's private files. You need to have auditing procedures and set up specifications for testing the new system (Phase 4). You need to institute automatic ways of backing up information and storing it elsewhere in case the system fails or is destroyed.

All the work of the preliminary and detail designs will end up in a large, detailed report. When you hand over this report to senior management, you will probably also make some sort of presentation or speech.

9.5 The Fourth Phase: Develop the System

KEY QUESTION

What is done during systems development?

Preview & Review: The fourth phase, systems development, consists of acquiring the hardware and software and then testing the system.

In Phase 4, *systems development*, **the systems analyst or others in the organization acquire the software, acquire the hardware, and then test the system.** During the design stage, the systems analyst may have had to address what is called the "make-or-buy" decision, but that decision certainly cannot be avoided now. In the *make-or-buy decision*, you decide whether you have to create a program—have it custom-written—or buy it, meaning simply purchase an existing software package. Sometimes programmers decide they can buy an existing program and modify it rather than write it from scratch.

If you decide to create a new program, then the question is whether to use the organization's own staff programmers or hire outside contract programmers. Whichever way you go, the task could take many months.

Once the software has been chosen, the hardware to run it must be acquired or upgraded. It's possible your new system will not require obtaining any new hardware. It's also possible that the new hardware will cost millions of dollars and involve many items: microcomputers, mainframes, monitors, modems, and many other devices. The organization may find it's better to lease rather than to buy some equipment, especially since chip capability has traditionally doubled every 18 months.

With the software and hardware acquired, you can now start testing the system. Testing is usually done in two stages: *unit testing,* then *system testing.*

- **Unit testing:** In *unit testing,* also called *modular testing,* individual parts of the program are tested, using test (made-up, or sample) data. If the program is written as a collaborative effort by multiple programmers, each part of the program is tested separately.

- **System testing:** In *system testing,* the parts are linked together, and test data is used to see if the parts work together. At this point, actual organization data may be used to test the system. The system is also tested with erroneous and massive amounts of data to see if the system can be made to fail ("crash").

At the end of this long process, the organization will have a workable information system, one ready for the implementation phase.

9.6 The Fifth Phase: Implement the System

KEY QUESTIONS

How is the system implemented, and what are the four options?

Preview & Review: The fifth phase, systems implementation, consists of converting the hardware, software, and files to the new system and of training the users. Conversion may proceed in four ways: direct, parallel, phased, or pilot.

Whether the new information system involves a few handheld computers, an elaborate telecommunications network, or expensive mainframes, the fifth phase will involve some close coordination in order to make the system not just workable but successful. **Phase 5, *systems implementation,* consists of converting the hardware, software, and files to the new system and training the users.**

Conversion, the process of converting from an old information system to a new one, involves converting hardware, software, and files.

Hardware conversion may be as simple as taking away an old PC and plunking a new one down in its place. Or it may involve acquiring new buildings and putting in elaborate wiring, climate-control, and security systems.

Software conversion means making sure the applications that worked on the old equipment can be made to work on the new.

File conversion, or *data conversion,* means converting the old files to new ones without loss of accuracy. For example, can the paper contents from the manila folders in the personnel department be input to the system with a scanner? Or do they have to be keyed in manually, with the consequent risk of errors being introduced?

There are four strategies for handling conversion: *direct, parallel, phased,* and *pilot.*

- **Direct approach:** *Direct implementation* means the user simply stops using the old system and starts using the new one. The risk of this method is evident: What if the new system doesn't work? If the old system has been discontinued, there is nothing to fall back on.

- **Parallel approach:** *Parallel implementation* means that the old and new systems are operated side by side until the new system has shown it is reliable, at which time the old system is discontinued. Obviously there are benefits in taking this cautious approach. If the new system fails, the organization can switch back to the old one. The difficulty with this method is the expense of paying for the equipment and people to keep two systems going at the same time.

- **Phased approach:** *Phased implementation* means that parts of the new system are phased in separately—either at different times (parallel) or all at once in groups (direct).

- **Pilot approach:** *Pilot implementation* means that the entire system is tried out but only by some users. Once the reliability has been proved, the system is implemented with the rest of the intended users. The pilot approach still has its risks, since *all* the users of a particular group are taken off the old system. However, the risks are confined to only a small part of the organization.

In general, the phased and pilot approaches are the most favored methods. Phased is best for large organizations in which people are performing different jobs. Pilot is best for organizations in which all people are performing the same task (such as order takers at a direct-mail house).

Training users in the use of a new system is done with a variety of tools. They run from documentation (instruction manuals) to videotapes to live classes to one-on-one, side-by-side teacher-student training. Sometimes training is done by the organization's own staffers; at other times it is contracted out.

9.7 The Sixth Phase: Maintain the System

KEY QUESTION

How is system maintenance accomplished?

Preview & Review: The last phase, systems maintenance, adjusts and improves the system through system audits, user feedback, and periodic evaluations.

Phase 6, *systems maintenance,* adjusts and improves the system by having system audits, user feedback, and periodic evaluations and by making changes based on new conditions. Even with the conversion accomplished and the users trained, the system won't just run itself. There is a sixth—and never-ending—phase in which the information system must be monitored to ensure that it is successful. Maintenance includes not only keeping the machinery running but also updating and upgrading the system to keep pace with new products, services, customers, government regulations, and other requirements.

9.8 Programming: A Five-Step Procedure

KEY QUESTIONS

What is programming, and what are the five steps in accomplishing it?

Preview & Review: Programming is a five-step procedure for producing a program—a list of instructions—for the computer. Coding the program is actually writing the program, choosing the appropriate programming language and following its rules, or syntax.

To see how programming works, consider what a program is. **A *program* is a list of instructions that the computer must follow in order to process data into information.** The instructions consist of *statements* used in a programming language, such as BASIC. Examples are programs that do word processing, desktop publishing, or payroll processing.

The decision whether to buy or create a program is *one* of the phases—Phase 4—in the systems development life cycle. (■ *See Panel 9.2.*) If the decision is made to develop a new system, this requires taking some further steps.

A program, we said, is a list of instructions that the computer must follow in order to process data into information. ***Programming, also called software engineering, is a multistep process for creating that list of instructions.*** Only one of those steps (the step called *coding*) consists of sitting at the keyboard typing words into a computer.

The five steps are as follows.

1. Clarify the problem—include needed output, input, processing requirements.

■ PANEL 9.2

Where programming fits in the systems development life cycle
The fourth phase of the six-phase systems development life cycle has a five-step procedure of its own. These five steps are the problem-solving process called *programming*.

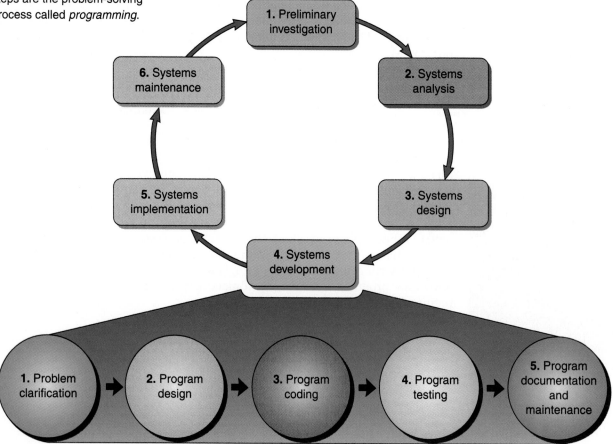

2. Design a solution—use modeling tools to chart the program.

3. Code the program—use a programming language's syntax, or rules, to write the program.

4. Test the program—get rid of any logic errors, or "bugs," in the program ("debug" it).

5. Document and maintain the program—include written instructions for users, explanation of the program, and operating instructions.

Coding is what many people think of when they think of programming, although it is only one of the five steps. Coding consists of translating the logic requirements from pseudocode or flowcharts into a programming language—the letters, numbers, and symbols that make up the program.

A *programming language* is a set of rules that tells the computer what operations to do. Examples of well-known programming languages are BASIC, COBOL, Pascal, FORTRAN, and C. (■ *See Panel 9.3.*) Not all languages are appropriate for all uses. Thus, the language needs to be chosen based on such considerations as what purpose the program is designed to serve and what languages are already being used in the organization or field you are in.

In order for a program to work, you have to follow the *syntax*, the rules of a programming language. Programming languages have their own grammar just as human languages do. But computers are probably a lot less forgiving if you use these rules incorrectly. Even a typographical error can constitute faulty syntax.

Programming languages are also called *high-level languages.* For the computer to be able to "understand" them, they must be translated into the low-level language called machine language. **Machine language is the basic language of the computer, representing data as 1s and 0s.** (■ *See Panel 9.4, opposite page.*) Machine-language programs vary from computer to computer; that is, they are *machine dependent.*

A high-level language allows users to write in a familiar notation, rather than numbers or abbreviations. Most high-level languages are not machine dependent—they can be used on more than one kind of computer. The translator for high-level languages is, depending on the language, either a *compiler* or an *interpreter.*

■ **PANEL 9.3**

Some common programming languages*

Language Name	Sample Code Fragment	Use
FORTRAN (FORmula TRANslator)	IF (XINVO.GT.500.00) THEN	Widely used for mathematical, scientific, and engineering programs.
COBOL (COmmon Business Oriented Language)	IF INVOICE=AMT>500	Most frequently used for business applications.
BASIC (Beginner's All-purpose Symbolic Instruction Code)	IF INV.AMT A>500	Used by nonprofessional and beginning programmers.
Pascal (named after Blaise Pascal)	if INVOICEAMOUNT>500.00 then	Used for teaching purposes at schools.
C	if (invoice_amount>500.00)	Used by many professional programmers.

*These are but a few of *many* languages.

■ PANEL 9.4

Low-level and high-level languages

(Top) Machine language is all binary 0s and 1s—difficult for people to work with. *(Bottom)* COBOL, a high-level language, uses English words that can be understood by people.

Machine language

```
11110010 01110011 1101 001000010000 0111 00000101011
11110010 01110011 1101 001000011000 0111 00000101111
11111100 01010010 1101 001000010010 1101 001000011101
11110000 01000101 1101 001000010011 0000 00000111110
11110011 01000011 0111 000001010000 1101 001000010100
10010110 11110000 0111 000001010100
```

COBOL

```
MULTIPLY HOURS-WORKED BY PAY-RATE GIVING GROSS-PAY ROUNDED
```

- **Compiler—execute later:** A *compiler* is a language translator that converts the entire program of a high-level language into machine language BEFORE the computer executes the program. The programming instructions of a high-level language are called the *source code.* The compiler translates it into machine language, which in this case is called the *object code.* The significance of this is that the object code *can be saved.* Thus, it can be executed later (as many times as desired) rather than run right away. (■ *See Panel 9.5.*)

  Examples of high-level languages using compilers are COBOL, FORTRAN, Pascal, and C.

■ PANEL 9.5

Compiler

This language translator converts the high-level language (source code) into machine language (object code) before the computer can execute the program.

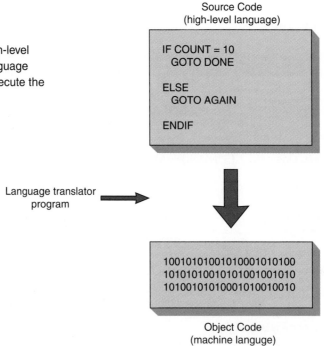

Source Code
(high-level language)

```
IF COUNT = 10
    GOTO DONE

ELSE
    GOTO AGAIN

ENDIF
```

Language translator program

```
10010101001010001010100
10101010010101001001010
10100101010001010010010
```

Object Code
(machine langue)

- Interpreter—execute immediately: **An *interpreter* is a language translator that converts each high-level language statement into machine language and executes it IMMEDIATELY, statement by statement.** No object code is saved, as with the compiler. However, with an interpreter, processing seems to take less time.

An example of a high-level language using an interpreter is BASIC.

9.9 Object-Oriented & Visual Programming

KEY QUESTIONS

How does OOP work?

Preview & Review: Object-oriented programming (OOP) is a programming method that combines data with instructions for processing that data to create a self-sufficient "object," or block of preassembled programming code, that can be used in other programs.

Visual programming is a method of creating programs in which the programmer makes connections between objects by drawing, pointing, and clicking on diagrams and icons.

Two new developments have made things somewhat easier—*object-oriented programming* and *visual programming.*

Object-oriented programming (OOP, pronounced "oop") is a programming method that combines data with the instructions for processing that data, resulting in a self-sufficient "object" that can be used in other programs. The important thing here is the object. An *object* is a block of preassembled programming code that is a self-contained module. The module contains, or encapsulates, both (1) a chunk of data and (2) the processing instructions that may be called on to be performed on that data.

Once you've written a block of program code (that computes overtime pay, for example), it can be reused in any number of programs. Thus, unlike traditional programming, with OOP you don't have to start from scratch—that is, reinvent the wheel—each time. Some examples of OOP programming languages are Smalltalk, C++, and Hypertalk.

***Visual programming* is a method of creating programs in which the programmer makes connections between objects by drawing, pointing, and clicking on diagrams and icons.** Essentially, visual programming takes OOP to the next level. The goal of visual programming is to make programming easier for programmers and more accessible to nonprogrammers by borrowing the object orientation of OOP languages but exercising it in a graphical or visual way. Visual programming enables users to think more about the problem solving than about handling the programming language.

Visual BASIC is the most popular visual programming language. It offers a visual environment for program construction, allowing users to build various application components using drag-and-drop tools, buttons, scroll bars, and menus.

9.10 Internet Programming: HTML, XML, VRML, Java, & ActiveX

KEY QUESTION

What are the features of HTML, XML, VRML, Java, and ActiveX?

Preview & Review: Programming languages used to build linked multimedia sites on the World Wide Web include HTML, XML, VRML, Java, and the set of controls called ActiveX.

Many of the thousands of Internet data and information sites around the world are text-based only; that is, the user sees no graphics, animation, or video and hears no sound. The World Wide Web, however, permits all of this.

One way to build such multimedia sites on the Web is to use some fairly recently developed programming languages and standards: HTML, XML, VRML, Java, and ActiveX.

- **HTML—for creating 2-D Web documents and links:** *HTML (hypertext markup language,* ✔ p. 241*)* is a markup language that lets people create on-screen documents for the Internet that can easily be linked by words and pictures to other documents. HTML is a type of code that embeds simple codes within standard ASCII (✔ p. 120) text documents to provide an integrated, two-dimensional display of text and graphics. In other words, a document created with any word processor and stored in ASCII format can become a Web page with the addition of a few HTML codes.

  One of the main features of HTML is the ability to insert hypertext links into a document. Hypertext links enable you to display another Web document simply by clicking on a link area—usually underlined or highlighted—on your current screen. One document may contain links to many other related documents. The related documents may be on the same server (✔ p. 21) as the first document, or they may be on a computer halfway around the world. A link may be a word, a group of words, or a picture.

- **XML—for making the Web work better:** Whereas HTML makes it easy for humans to read Web sites, *XML (extensible markup language)* makes it easy for machines to read Web sites by enabling Web developers to add more "tags" to a Web page. At present, when you use your browser to click on a Web site, search engines can turn up too much, so that it's difficult to pinpoint the specific site—such as one with a recipe for a low-calorie chicken dish for 12—for you. Says journalist Michael Krantz, "XML makes Web sites smart enough to tell other machines whether they're looking at a recipe, an airline ticket, or a pair of easy-fit blue jeans with a 34-inch waist."[3] XML lets Web site developers put "tags" on their Web pages that describe information in, for example, a food recipe as "ingredients," "calories," "cooking time," and "number of portions." Thus, your browser no longer has to search the entire Web for a low-calorie poultry recipe for 12.

- **VRML—for creating 3-D Web pages:** VRML rhymes with "thermal." *VRML (virtual reality modeling language)* is a type of programming language used to create three-dimensional Web pages. For example, there are 3-D cities that you can tour online. One firm called BigBook has used VRML to create improved telephone-book Yellow Pages. On screen you seem to fly through a three-dimensional rendering of San Francisco, for example, that has the precision of a two-dimensional street map. When you pass your cursor over a building, its address pops up. When you search for the locations of businesses, the buildings housing those businesses are emphasized.[4]

  VRML is not an extension of HTML, and so HTML Web browsers cannot interpret it. Thus, users need a VRML add-on (plug-in), such as Netscape's Live3D, to receive VRML Web pages. Users who are not on a large computer system also need a high-end microcomputer such as a Power Macintosh or Pentium-based PC. Like HTML, VRML is a document-centered ASCII language. Unlike HTML, it tells the computer how to create 3-D worlds. VRML pages can also be linked to other VRML pages.

- **Java—for creating interactive Web pages:** Available from Sun Microsystems and derived from C++, Java is a major departure from the HTML coding that makes up most Web pages. Sitting atop markup languages such as HTML and XML, *Java* is an object-oriented programming language that allows programmers to build applications that can run on any operating system. With Java, big application programs can be broken into mini-applications, or "applets," that can be downloaded off the Internet and run on any computer. Moreover, Java enables a Web page to deliver, along with visual content, applets that when downloaded can make Web pages interactive.

  If the use of Java becomes widespread, the Web will be transformed from the information-delivering medium it is today into a completely interactive computing environment. You will be able to treat the Web as a giant hard disk loaded with a never-ending supply of software applications.

- **ActiveX—also for creating interactive Web pages:** ActiveX was developed by Microsoft as an alternative to Java for creating interactivity on Web pages. Indeed, Java and ActiveX are the two major contenders in the Web-applet war for transforming the Web into a complete interactive environment.

  ActiveX is a set of controls, or reusable components, that enables programs or content of almost any type to be embedded within a Web page. Whereas Java requires you to download an applet each time you visit a Web site, with ActiveX the component is downloaded only once, then stored on your hard drive for later and repeated use.

  Thus, the chief characteristic of ActiveX is that it features *reusable* components—small modules of software code that perform specific tasks (such as a spelling checker), which may be plugged seamlessly into other applications. With ActiveX you can obtain from your hard disk any file that is suitable for the Web—such as a Java applet, animation, or pop-up menu—and insert it directly into an HTML document.

Summary

Summary

What It Is/What It Does

Why It's Important

compiler (p. 298, KQ 9.8) Language translator that converts the entire program of a high-level language (called source code) into machine language (called object code) for execution later. Examples of compiler languages: COBOL, FORTRAN, Pascal, C.

Unlike other language translators (assemblers and interpreters), with a compiler program the object code can be saved and executed later rather than run right away. The advantage of a compiler is that, once the object code has been obtained, the program executes faster.

computer-aided software engineering (CASE) tools (p. 292, KQ 9.4) Software that provides computer-automated means of designing and changing systems.

CASE tools may be used in almost any phase of the SDLC, not just design. So-called *front-end CASE tools* are used during the first three phases—preliminary analysis, systems analysis, systems design—to help with the early analysis and design. So-called *back-end CASE tools* are used during two later phases—systems development and implementation—to help in coding and testing, for instance.

interpreter (p. 299, KQ 9.8) Language translator that converts each high-level language statement into machine language and executes it immediately, statement by statement. An example of a high-level language using an interpreter is BASIC.

Unlike with the language translator called the compiler, no object code is saved. The advantage of an interpreter is that programs are easier to develop.

machine language (p. 297, KQ 9.8) Lowest level of programming language; the language of the computer, representing data as 1s and 0s. Most machine-language programs vary from computer to computer—they are machine dependent.

Machine language, which corresponds to the on and off electrical states of the computer, is not convenient for people to use. Assembly language and higher-level languages were developed to make programming easier.

object-oriented programming (OOP) (p. 299, KQ 9.9) Programming method in which data and the instructions for processing that data are combined into a self-sufficient object—piece of software—that can be used in other programs. Examples of OOP languages: Smalltalk, C++, Hypertalk.

Objects can be reused and interchanged among programs, producing greater flexibility and efficiency than is possible with traditional programming methods.

preliminary investigation (p. 291, KQ 9.2) Phase 1 of the SDLC; the purpose is to conduct a preliminary analysis (determine the organization's objectives, determine the nature and scope of the problem), propose alternative solutions (leave the system as is, improve the efficiency of the system, or develop a new system), describe costs and benefits, and submit a preliminary plan with recommendations.

The preliminary investigation lays the groundwork for the other phases of the SDLC.

What It Is/What It Does

Why It's Important

program (p. 296, KQ 9.8) List of instructions the computer follows to process data into information. The instructions consist of statements written in a programming language (for example, BASIC).

Without programs, data could not be processed into information by a computer.

programming (p. 296, KQ 9.8) Also called *software engineering;* five-step process for creating software instructions: (1) clarify the problem; (2) design a solution; (3) write (code) the program; (4) test the program; (5) document and maintain the program.

Programming is one step in the systems development life cycle.

programming language (p. 297, KQ 9.8) Set of rules that allow programmers to tell the computer what operations to follow. The five levels (generations) of programming languages are (1) machine language, (2) assembly language, (3) high-level (procedural) languages (FORTRAN, COBOL, BASIC, Pascal, C, RPG, etc.), (4) very high-level (nonprocedural) languages (RPG III, SQL, Intellect, NOMAD, FOCUS, etc.), and (5) natural languages.

Not all programming languages are appropriate for all uses. Thus, a language must be chosen to suit the purpose of the program and to be compatible with other languages being used by users.

system (p. 289, KQ 9.1) Collection of related components that interact to perform a task in order to accomplish a goal.

Understanding a set of activities as a system allows one for look for better ways to reach the goal.

systems analysis (p. 291, KQ 9.3) Phase 2 of the SDLC; the purpose is to gather data (using written documents, interviews, questionnaires, observation, and sampling), analyze the data, and write a report.

The results of systems analysis will determine whether the system should be redesigned.

systems analysis and design (p. 289, KQ 9.1) Problem-solving procedure for examining an information system and improving it; consists of the six-phase *systems development life cycle.*

The point of systems analysis and design is to ascertain how a system works and then take steps to make it better.

systems analyst (p. 289, KQ 9.1) Information specialist who performs systems analysis, design, and implementation.

The systems analyst studies the information and communications needs of an organization to determine how to deliver information that is more accurate, timely, and useful. The systems analyst achieves this goal through the problem-solving method of systems analysis and design.

systems design (p. 292, KQ 9.4) Phase 3 of the SDLC; the purpose is to do a preliminary design and then a detail design, and write a report.

Systems design is one of the most crucial phases of the SDLC; at the end of this stage executives decide whether to commit the time and money to develop a new system.

What It Is/What It Does	Why It's Important

systems development (p. 293, KQ 9.5) Phase 4 of the SDLC; hardware and software for the new system are acquired and tested. The fourth phase begins once management has accepted the report containing the design and has approved the way to development.

This phase may involve the organization in investing substantial time and money.

systems development life cycle (SDLC) (p. 289, KQ 9.1) Six-phase process that many organizations follow during systems analysis and design: (1) *preliminary investigation;* (2) *systems analysis;* (3) *systems design;* (4) *systems development;* (5) *systems implementation;* (6) *systems maintenance.* Phases often overlap, and a new one may start before the old one is finished. After the first four phases, management must decide whether to proceed to the next phase. User input and review is a critical part of each phase.

The SDLC is a comprehensive tool for solving organizational problems, particularly those relating to the flow of computer-based information.

systems implementation (p. 294, KQ 9.6) Phase 5 of the SDLC; consists of converting the hardware, software, and files to the new system and training the use295

This phase is important because it involves putting design ideas into operation.

systems maintenance (p. 295, KQ 9.7) Phase 6 of the SDLC; consists of adjusting and improving the system by having system audits, user feedback, and periodic evaluations and by making changes based on new conditions.

This phase is important for keeping a new system operational and useful.

visual programming (p. 299, KQ 9.9) Method of creating programs; the programmer makes connections between objects by drawing, pointing, and clicking on diagrams and icons. Programming is made easier because the object orientation of object-oriented programming is used in a graphical or visual way.

Visual programming enables users to think more about the problem solving than about handling the programming language.

Exercises

Self-Test

1. A _____ is a collection of related components that interact to perform a task in order to accomplish a goal.

2. _____ _____ is when the old system is halted on a given date and the new system is activated.

3. _____ is used for creating 2-D Web documents and links.

4. _____ is used for creating 3-D Web pages.

Short-Answer Questions

1. List the six phases of the SDLC.
2. What is the purpose of the systems development phase of the SDLC?
3. What is visual programming?

Multiple-Choice Questions

1. Which of the following describes the method of trying out a new system on a few users?
   a. direct approach
   b. parallel approach
   c. phased approach
   d. pilot approach
   e. None of the above

2. Assemblers, compilers, and interpreters are types of _____ _____.
   a. programming languages
   b. language translators
   c. alpha testers
   d. application generators
   e. All of the above

True/False Questions

T F 1. The rules for using a programming language are called *syntax*.

T F 2. Objects found in an object-oriented program can be reused in other programs.

T F 3. It is correct to refer to programming as *software engineering*.

T F 4. A syntax error can be caused by a simple typographical error.

Knowledge in Action

1. Interview a student majoring in computer science who plans to become a systems analyst. Why is this person interested in this field? What does he or she hope to accomplish in it? What courses must be taken to satisfy the requirements for becoming an analyst? What major changes in systems design and analysis does this person forecast for the next five years?

2. Does your university/college have an information systems department that is responsible for developing and supporting all the university information systems? If so, interview a management staff member about the services and functions of the department. Can this person identify the various levels of management within the department? What kinds of user input were requested when the department was being set up? Does it use any sophisticated decision support software? What kinds of services does the department offer to students?

3. Visit the computer laboratory at your school.
   a. Identify which high-level languages are available.
   b. Determine if each language processor identified is a compiler or an interpreter.
   c. Determine if the language processors are available for microcomputers, larger computers, or both.
   d. Identify any microcomputer-based electronic spreadsheet software and database management systems software. Have any applications been created with these tools that are used in the lab or by the lab staff?

4. Interview several students who are majoring in computer science and studying to become programmers. What languages do they plan to master? Why? What kinds of jobs do they expect to get? What kinds of future developments do they anticipate in the field of software programming?

5. Check the yellow pages in your phone book, and contact a company that develops custom-designed software. What languages do they use to write the software? Does this company follow the five stages of software development described in this book, or does it use another set of stages? If another set of software-development stages is used, what are its characteristics?

Answers

Self-Test Questions
1. system   2. direct implementation   3. HTML   4. VRML

Short-Answer Questions
1. (1) preliminary investigation, (2) systems analysis, (3) systems design, (4) systems development, (5) systems implementation, (6) systems maintenance   2. In the systems development phase (phase 4), the systems analyst or others in the organization acquire software and hardware, and then test the system. 3. Visual programming is a method of creating programs by using icons that represent common programming routines.

Multiple-Choice Questions
1. d   2. b

True/False Questions
1. t   2. t   3. t   4. t

Chapter 10

Society & the Digital Age

Challenges & Promises

key questions

You should be able to answer the following questions:

Clearly, information technology is driving the new world of jobs, leisure, and services, and nothing is going to stop it. Indeed, predicts one futurist, by 2010 probably 90% of the workforce will be affected by the four principal information technologies—computer networks, imaging technology, massive data storage, and (as we discuss in this chapter) artificial intelligence.[1]

Where will you be in all this? People pursuing careers find the rules are changing very rapidly. Up-to-date skills are becoming ever more crucial. Job descriptions of all kinds are being redefined. Even familiar jobs are becoming more demanding. Today, experts advise, you need to prepare to continually upgrade your skills, prepare for specialization, and prepare to market yourself.

In this chapter, we consider both the challenges and the promises of computers and communications in relation to society. First let us consider the following *challenges* of the Digital Age:

- The blueprint for the Information Superhighway
- Security issues—accidents, hazards, crime, viruses—and security safeguards
- Quality-of-life issues—environment, mental health, the workplace
- Economic issues—employment and the haves/have-nots

We will then consider the following *promises:*

- The roles of intelligent agents and avatars
- Artificial intelligence
- The promised benefits of the Information Revolution

10.1 The Information Superhighway: Is There a Grand Design?

KEY QUESTION

What are the NII, the new Internet, the Telecommunications Act, and the 1997 White House plan?

Preview & Review: The Information Superhighway envisions using wired and wireless capabilities of telephones and networked computers with cable TV. It may evolve following a model backed by the federal government called the National Information Infrastructure, along with newer versions of the Internet—VBNS, Internet 2, and NGI. Or it may evolve out of competition brought on by the deregulation of long-distance and local-telephone companies, cable companies, and television broadcasters created by the 1996 Telecommunications Act. A 1997 White House plan suggests the government should stay out of Internet commerce.

As we said in Chapter 1, the *Information Superhighway* is a vision or a metaphor. It envisions a fusion of the two-way wired and wireless capabilities of telephones and networked computers with cable and satellite TV's capacity to transmit thousands of programs, generally based on the evolving system of the Internet. When completed, it is hoped that the I-way will give us lightning-fast (high-bandwidth) voice and data exchange, multimedia, interactivity, and nearly universal and low-cost access—and that it will do so reliably and securely. You'll be able to participate in telephony, teleconferencing, telecommuting, teleshopping, telemedicine, tele-education, tele-voting, and even tele-psychotherapy, to name a few possibilities.

What shape will the Information Superhighway take? Some government officials hope it will follow a somewhat orderly model, such as that envisioned in the National Information Infrastructure (of which new versions of the Internet are a part). Others hope it will evolve out of competition intended by the passage of the 1996 Telecommunications Act. Still others hope that a White House document, *A Framework for Global Electronic Commerce*, offers a realistic policy. Let us look at these.

The National Information Infrastructure

As portrayed by U.S. government officials, **the *National Information Infrastructure (NII)* is a kind of grand vision for today's existing networks and technologies as well as technologies yet to be deployed. Services would be delivered by telecommunications companies, cable-television companies, and the Internet.** Applications would be varied—education, health care, information access, electronic commerce, and entertainment.[2]

Who would put the pieces of the NII together? The national policy is to let private industry do it, with the government trying to ensure fair competition among phone and cable companies and compatibility among various technological systems.[3] In addition, NII envisions open access to people of all income levels.

The New Internet: VBNS, Internet 2, & NGI

Lately we have been hearing less about NII and more about new Internet networks: *Internet 2*, the *Next Generation Internet*, and *VBNS*. What are these, and does this mean that *three* new networks will be built? Actually, all three names refer to the same network. This will be a new high-speed Internet that will unclog the clogged electronic highway that the present Net has become. Here's what the three efforts represent:[4–9]

- VBNS: **Linking supercomputers and other banks of computers across the nation, *VBNS* (for *Very-high-speed Backbone Network Service*) is the main government component to upgrade the "backbone," or primary hubs of data transmission.** Speeds would be at 1000 times current Internet speeds.

    Financed by the National Science Foundation and managed by telecommunications giant MCI, VBNS will involve only the top 100 research universities, whereas Internet 2 would eventually touch everyone on the line. VBNS has already been underway since 1996, and most of the present members are also members of Internet 2.

- Internet 2: **Internet 2 is a cooperative university-business program to enable high-end users to quickly and reliably move huge amounts of data, using VBNS as the official backbone.** Whereas VBNS would provide data transfer at 1000 times present speeds, Internet 2 would operate at 100 times current Internet speeds.

    In effect, Internet 2 will add "toll lanes" to the Internet that already exists today to speed things up. The purpose is to advance videoconferencing, research, and academic collaboration—to enable a kind of "virtual university." Presently more than 117 universities and about 25 companies are participants.

- Next Generation Internet: **The *Next Generation Internet (NGI)* is the U.S. government's broad new program to parallel the university-and-business-sponsored effort of Internet 2, and is designed to provide money to six government agencies to be used to help tie the campus high-performance backbones into the broader federal infrastructure.** The technical goals for NGI include connecting at least 100 sites, including universities, federal national laboratories, and other research organizations. Speeds, as mentioned, would be 100 times those of today's Internet, and 10 sites would be connected at speeds that are 1000 times as fast.

The 1996 Telecommunications Act

After years of legislative attempts to overhaul the 1934 Communications Act, President Bill Clinton signed into law the *Telecommunications Act of 1996*, which undoes 60 years of federal and state communications regulations and is designed to let phone, cable, and TV businesses compete and combine more freely. The law is supposed to allow greater competition between local and long-distance telephone companies, as well as between the telephone and cable industries.

Is the law successful? "The only point on which all parties agree," says Laurence Tribe, Harvard professor of constitutional law, "is that the law isn't working as intended, and that American consumers are still waiting for free and healthy competition in communications services."[10]

The 1997 White House Plan for Internet Commerce

In July 1997, the Clinton administration unveiled a document that is significant because it endorses a governmental hands-off approach to the Internet—or, as it more grandly calls it, "the Global Information Infrastructure."[11] Behind the title *A Framework for Global Electronic Commerce*, authored by a White House group, was a plan whose gist is this: Government should stay out of the way of Internet commerce.

"Where government is needed," it states, "its aim should be to support and enforce a predictable, minimalist, consistent, and legal environment for commerce."[12] Otherwise, the plan states that private companies, not government, should take the lead in promoting the Internet as an electronic marketplace, in adopting self-regulation, and in devising ratings systems to help parents guide their children away from objectionable online content.

10.2 Security Issues: Threats to Computers & Communications Systems

KEY QUESTION

What are some characteristics of the six key security issues for information technology?

Preview & Review: Information technology can be disabled by a number of occurrences. It may be harmed by human, procedural, and software errors; by electromechanical problems; and by "dirty data." It may be threatened by natural hazards and by civil strife and terrorism. Criminal acts perpetrated against computers include theft of hardware, software, time and services, and information; and crimes of malice and destruction. Computers may be harmed by viruses. Computers can also be used as instruments of crime. Criminals may be employees, outside users, hackers, crackers, and professional criminals.

Security issues go right to the heart of the workability of computer and communications systems. Here we discuss several threats to both computers and communications systems.

Errors & Accidents

In general, errors and accidents in computer systems may be classified as human errors, procedural errors, software errors, electromechanical problems, and "dirty data" problems.

- **Human errors:** Quite often, when experts speak of the "unintended effects of technology," what they are referring to are the unexpected things people do with it. People can complicate the workings of a system in three ways:[13]

  (1) Humans often are not good at assessing their own information needs. Thus, for example, many users will acquire a computer and communications system that either is not sophisticated enough or is far more complex than they need.

  (2) Human emotions affect performance. For example, one frustrating experience with a computer is enough to make some people abandon the whole system. But throwing your computer out the window, of course, isn't going to get you any closer to learning how to use it better.

  (3) Humans act on their perceptions, which in modern information environments are often too slow to keep up with the equipment. You can be so overwhelmed by information overload, for example, that decision making may be just as faulty as if you had too little information.

- **Procedural errors:** Some spectacular computer failures have occurred because someone didn't follow procedures. Consider the 2½-hour shutdown of Nasdaq, the nation's second largest stock market. Nasdaq is so automated that it likes to call itself "the stock market for the next 100 years." A few years ago, Nasdaq was shut down by an effort, ironically, to make the computer system more user-friendly. Technicians were phasing in new software, adding technical improvements a day at a time. A few days into this process, the technicians tried to add more features to the software, flooding the data-storage capability of the computer system. The result was a delay in opening the stock market that shortened the trading day.[14]

- **Software errors:** We are forever hearing about "software glitches" or "software bugs." Recall that a *software bug* is an error in a program that causes it not to work properly.

  An example of a somewhat small error was when a school employee in Newark, New Jersey, made a mistake in coding the school system's master scheduling program. When 1000 students and 90 teachers showed up for the start of school at Central High School, half the students had incomplete or no schedules for classes. Some classrooms had no teachers while others had four instead of one.[15]

- **Electromechanical problems:** Mechanical systems, such as printers, and electrical systems, such as circuit boards, don't always work. They may be improperly constructed, get dirty or overheated, wear out, or become damaged in some other way. Power failures (brownouts and blackouts) can shut a system down. Power surges can burn out equipment.

- **"Dirty data" problems:** When keyboarding a research paper, you undoubtedly make a few typing errors (which, hopefully, you clean up). So do all the data-entry people around the world who feed a continual stream of raw data into computer systems. A lot of problems are caused by this kind of "dirty data." *Dirty data* is data that is incomplete, outdated, or otherwise inaccurate.

Natural & Other Hazards

Some disasters do not merely lead to temporary system downtime; they can wreck the entire system. Examples are natural hazards, and civil strife and terrorism.

- **Natural hazards:** Whatever is harmful to property (and people) is harmful to computers and communications systems. This certainly includes natural disasters: fires, floods, earthquakes, tornadoes, hurricanes, blizzards, and the like. If they inflict damage over a wide area, as have ice storms in eastern Canada or hurricanes in Florida, natural hazards can disable all the electronic systems we take for granted. Without power and communications connections, automated teller machines, credit-card verifiers, and bank computers are useless.

- **Civil strife and terrorism:** We may take comfort in the fact that wars and insurrections seem to take place in other parts of the world. Yet we are not immune to civil unrest, such as the riots that wracked Los Angeles following the 1992 trial of police officers for the beating of Rodney King. Nor are we immune, apparently, to acts of terrorism, such as the 1993 bombing of New York's World Trade Center. In that case, companies found themselves frantically having to move equipment to new offices and reestablishing their computer networks. The Pentagon itself (which has 650,000 terminals and workstations, 100 WANs, and 10,000 LANs) has been taking steps to reduce its own systems' vulnerability to intruders.[16]

Ethics

Crimes Against Computers & Communications

An *information-technology crime* can be of two types. It can be an illegal act perpetrated *against* computers or telecommunications. Or it can be the *use* of computers or telecommunications to accomplish an illegal act. Here we discuss the first type.

Crimes against information technology include theft—of hardware, of software, of computer time, of cable or telephone services, of information. Other illegal acts are crimes of malice and destruction. Some examples are as follows:

- **Theft of hardware:** Stealing of hardware can range from shoplifting an accessory in a computer store to removing a laptop or cellular phone from someone's car. Professional criminals may steal shipments of microprocessor chips off a loading dock or even pry cash machines out of shopping-center walls.

    Eric Avila, 26, a history student at the University of California at Berkeley, had his doctoral dissertation—involving six years of painstaking research—stored on the hard drive of his Macintosh PowerBook when a thief stole the machine out of his apartment. Although he had copied an earlier version of his dissertation (70 pages entitled "Paradise Lost: Politics and Culture in Post-War Los Angeles") onto a diskette, the thief stole that, too. "I'm devastated," Avila said. "Now it's gone, and there is no way I can recover it other than what I have in my head." To make matters worse, he had no choice but to pay off the $2000 loan for a computer he did not have anymore. The moral, as we've said repeatedly in this book: *Always make backup copies of your important data, and store them in a safe place—away from your computer.*

- **Theft of software:** Stealing software can take the form of physically making off with someone's diskettes, but it is more likely to be the copying of programs. Software makers secretly prowl electronic bulletin boards in search of purloined products, then try to get a court order to shut down the bulletin boards. They also look for companies that "softlift"—buying one copy of a program and making copies for as many computers as they have.

  Many pirates are reported by co-workers or fellow students to the "software police," the Software Publishers Association. The SPA has a toll-free number (800-388-7478) for anyone to report illegal copying and initiate antipiracy actions. In mid-1994, two New England college students were indicted for allegedly using the Internet to encourage the exchange of copyrighted software.[17]

  Another type of software theft is copying or counterfeiting of well-known software programs. These pirates often operate in China, Taiwan, Mexico, Russia, and various parts of Asia and Latin America. In some countries, more than 90% of U.S. microcomputer software in use is thought to be illegally copied.[18]

- **Theft of time and services:** The theft of computer time is more common than you might think. Probably the biggest use of it is people using their employer's computer time to play games. Some people also may run sideline businesses.

  For years "phone phreaks" have bedeviled the telephone companies. They have also found ways to get into company voice-mail systems, then use an extension to make long-distance calls at the company's expense. In addition, they have also found ways to tap into cellular phone networks and dial for free.

- **Theft of information:** "Information thieves" have been caught infiltrating the files of the Social Security Administration, stealing confidential personal records and selling the information. Thieves have also broken into computers of the major credit bureaus and have stolen credit information. They have then used the information to charge purchases or have resold it to other people. On college campuses, thieves have snooped into or stolen private information such as grades.

- **Crimes of malice and destruction:** Sometimes criminals are more interested in abusing or vandalizing computers and telecommunications systems than in profiting from them. For example, a student at a Wisconsin campus deliberately and repeatedly shut down a university computer system, destroying final projects for dozens of students. A judge sentenced him to a year's probation, and he left the campus.[19]

Crimes Using Computers & Communications

Ethics

Just as a car can be used to assist in a crime, so can a computer or communications system. For example, four college students on New York's Long Island who met via the Internet used a specialized computer program to steal credit-card numbers, then, according to police, went on a one-year, $100,000 shopping spree. When arrested, they were charged with grand larceny, forgery, and scheming to defraud.[20]

In addition, investment fraud has come to cyberspace. Many people now use online services to manage their stock portfolios through brokerages hooked into the services. Scam artists have followed, offering nonexistent investment deals and phony solicitations and manipulating stock prices.

Worms & Viruses

Worms and viruses are forms of high-tech maliciousness. A *worm* is a program that copies itself repeatedly into memory or onto a disk drive until no more space is left. An example is the worm program unleashed by a student at Cornell University that traveled through an e-mail network and shut down thousands of computers around the country.

A *virus* is a "deviant" program that attaches itself to computer systems and destroys or corrupts data. (■ *See Panel 10.1.*) Viruses are passed in two ways:

- **By diskette:** The first way is via an infected diskette, such as one you might get from a friend or a repair person. It's also possible to get a virus from a sales demo disk.

■ PANEL 10.1   Types of viruses

- **Boot-sector virus:** The boot sector is that part of the system software containing most of the instructions for booting, or powering up, the system. The boot sector virus replaces these boot instructions with some of its own. Once the system is turned on, the virus is loaded into main memory before the operating system. From there it is in a position to infect other files. Any diskette that is used in the drive of the computer then becomes infected. When that diskette is moved to another computer, the contagion continues. Examples of boot-sector viruses: AntCMOS, AntiEXE, Form.A, NYB (New York Boot), Ripper, Stoned.Empire.Monkey.

- **File virus:** File viruses attach themselves to executable files—those that actually begin a program. (In DOS these files have the extensions .com and .exe.) When the program is run, the virus starts working, trying to get into main memory and infecting other files.

- **Multipartite virus:** A hybrid of the file and boot-sector types, the multipartite virus infects both files and boot sectors, which makes it better at spreading and more difficult to detect. Examples of multipartite viruses are Junkie and Parity Boot.

    A type of multipartite virus is the *polymorphic virus,* which can mutate and change form just as human viruses can. Such viruses are especially troublesome because they can change their profile, making existing antiviral technology ineffective.

A particularly sneaky multipartite virus is the *stealth virus,* which can temporarily remove itself from memory to elude capture. An example of a multipartite, polymorphic stealth virus is One Half.

- **Macro virus:** Macro viruses take advantage of a procedure in which miniature programs, known as macros, are embedded inside common data files, such as those created by e-mail or spreadsheets, which are sent over computer networks. Until recently, such documents have typically been ignored by antivirus software. Examples of macro viruses are Concept, which attaches to Word documents and e-mail attachments, and Laroux, which attaches to Excel spreadsheet files. Fortunately, the latest versions of Word and Excel come with built-in macro virus protection.

- **Logic bomb:** Logic bombs, or simply bombs, differ from other viruses in that they are set to go off at a certain date and time. A disgruntled programmer for a defense contractor created a bomb in a program that was supposed to go off two months after he left. Designed to erase an inventory tracking system, the bomb was discovered only by chance.

- **Trojan horse:** The Trojan horse covertly places illegal, destructive instructions in the middle of a legitimate program, such as a computer game. Once you run the program, the Trojan horse goes to work, doing its damage while you are blissfully unaware. An example of a Trojan horse is FormatC.

- **By network:** The second way is via a network, as from e-mail or an electronic bulletin board. This is why, when you're looking into all the freebie games and other software available online, you should use virus-scanning software to check downloaded files.

The virus usually attaches itself to your hard disk. It might then display annoying messages ("Your PC is stoned—legalize marijuana") or cause Ping-Pong balls to bounce around your screen and knock away text. More seriously, it might add garbage to or erase your files or destroy your system software. It may evade your detection and spread its havoc elsewhere.

A variety of virus-fighting programs are available at stores, although you should be sure to specify the viruses you want to protect against. *Antivirus software* scans a computer's hard disk, floppy disks, and main memory to detect viruses and, sometimes, to destroy them. We described some antivirus programs in Chapter 3.

Ethics

Computer Criminals

What kind of people are perpetrating most of the information-technology crime? Over 80% may be employees; the rest are outside users, hackers and crackers, and professional criminals.

- **Employees:** Says Michigan State University criminal justice professor David Carter, who surveyed companies about computer crime, "Seventy-five to 80% of everything happens from inside."[21] Most common frauds, Carter found, involved credit cards, telecommunications, employees' personal use of computers, unauthorized access to confidential files, and unlawful copying of copyrighted or licensed software.

  Workers may use information technology for personal profit or steal hardware or information to sell. They may also use it to seek revenge for real or imagined wrongs, such as being passed over for promotion. Sometimes they may use the technology simply to demonstrate to themselves that they have power over people.

- **Outside users:** Suppliers and clients may also gain access to a company's information technology and use it to commit crimes. Both suppliers and clients have more access as electronic connections such as electronic data interchange (✔ p. 245) systems become more commonplace.

- **Hackers and crackers:** *Hackers* are people who gain unauthorized access to computer or telecommunications systems for the challenge or even the principle of it. For example, Eric Corley, publisher of a magazine called *2600: The Hackers' Quarterly*, believes that hackers are merely engaging in "healthy exploration." In fact, by breaking into corporate computer systems and revealing their flaws, he says, they are performing a favor and a public service. Such unauthorized entries show the corporations involved the leaks in their security systems.[22]

  Crackers also gain unauthorized access to information technology but do so for malicious purposes. (Some observers think the term *hacker* covers malicious intent, also.) Crackers attempt to break into computers and deliberately obtain information for financial gain, shut down hardware, pirate software, or destroy data.

The tolerance for "benign explorers"—hackers—has waned. Most communications systems administrators view any kind of unauthorized access as a threat, and they pursue the offenders vigorously. Educators try to point out to students that universities can't provide an education for everybody if hacking continues. The most flagrant cases of hacking are met with federal prosecution.

● Professional criminals: Members of organized crime rings don't just steal information technology. They also use it the way that legal businesses do—as a business tool, though for illegal purposes. For instance, databases can be used to keep track of illegal gambling debts and stolen goods. Not surprisingly, the old-fashioned illegal bookmaking operation has gone high-tech, with bookies using computers and fax machines in place of betting slips and paper tally sheets.

As information-technology crime has become more sophisticated, so have the people charged with preventing it and disciplining its outlaws. Campus administrators are no longer being quite as easy on offenders and are turning them over to police. Industry organizations such as the Software Publishers Association are going after software pirates large and small. (Commercial software piracy is now a felony, punishable by up to 5 years in prison and fines of up to $250,000 for anyone convicted of stealing at least 10 copies of a program, or more than $2500 worth of software.) Police departments in cities as far apart as Medford, Massachusetts, and San Jose, California, now have police patrolling a "cyber beat." That is, they cruise online bulletin boards looking for pirated software, stolen trade secrets, child molesters, and child pornography.

In 1988, after the last widespread Internet break-in, the U.S. Defense Department created the Computer Emergency Response Team (CERT). Although it has no power to arrest or prosecute, CERT provides round-the-clock international information and security-related support services to users of the Internet. Whenever it gets a report of an electronic snooper, whether on the Internet or on a corporate e-mail system, CERT stands ready to lend assistance. It counsels the party under attack, helps them thwart the intruder, and evaluates the system afterward to protect against future break-ins.

10.3 Security: Safeguarding Computers & Communications

KEY QUESTION

What are the characteristics of the four components of security?

Preview & Review: Information technology requires vigilance in security. Four areas of concern are identification and access, encryption, protection of software and data, and disaster-recovery planning.

The ongoing dilemma of the Digital Age is balancing convenience against security. *Security* **is a system of safeguards for protecting information technology against disasters, systems failure, and unauthorized access that can result in damage or loss.** We consider four components of security.

Identification & Access

Are you who you say you are? The computer wants to know.

There are three ways a computer system can verify that you have legitimate right of access. Some security systems use a mix of these techniques. The systems try to authenticate your identity by determining (1) what you have, (2) what you know, or (3) who you are.

- **What you have—cards, keys, signatures, badges:** Credit cards, debit cards, and cash-machine cards all have magnetic strips or built-in computer chips that identify you to the machine. Many require you to display your signature, which someone may compare as you write it. Computer rooms are always kept locked, requiring a key. Many people also keep a lock on their personal computers. In addition, a computer room may be guarded by security officers, who may need to see an authorized signature or a badge with your photograph before letting you in.

  Of course, credit cards, keys, and badges can be lost or stolen. Signatures can be forged. Badges can be counterfeited.

- **What you know—PINs, passwords, and digital signatures:** To gain access to your bank account through an automated teller machine (ATM), you key in your PIN. **A *PIN, or personal identification number,* is the security number known only to you that is required to access the system.** Telephone credit cards also use a PIN. If you carry either an ATM or a phone card, *never* carry the PIN written down elsewhere in your wallet (even disguised).

  A *password* is a special word, code, or symbol that is required to access a computer system. Passwords are one of the weakest security links, says AT&T security expert Steven Bellovin. Passwords can be guessed, forgotten, or stolen.[23]

- **Who you are—physical traits:** Some forms of identification can't be easily faked—such as your physical traits. Biometrics tries to use these in security devices. ***Biometrics* is the science of measuring individual body characteristics.**

  For example, before a number of University of Georgia students can use the all-you-can-eat plan at the campus cafeteria, they must have their hands read. As one writer describes the system, "a camera automatically compares the shape of a student's hand with an image of the same hand pulled from the magnetic strip of an ID card. If the patterns match, the cafeteria turnstile automatically clicks open. If not, the would-be moocher eats elsewhere."[24]

  Besides handprints, other biological characteristics read by biometric devices are fingerprints (computerized "finger imaging"), voices, the blood vessels in the back of the eyeball, the lips, and even one's entire face.

Some computer security systems have a "call-back" provision. In a *call-back system,* the user calls the computer system, punches in the password, and hangs up. The computer then calls back a certain preauthorized number. This measure will block anyone who has somehow got hold of a password but is calling from an unauthorized telephone.

Ethics

Encryption

PGP is a computer program written for encrypting computer messages—putting them into secret code. ***Encryption, or enciphering, is the altering of data so that it is not usable unless the changes are undone.*** One encryption program that is called *PGP* (for *Pretty Good Privacy*) is so good that it is practically unbreakable; even government experts haven't been able to crack it.

Encryption is clearly useful for some organizations, especially those concerned with trade secrets, military matters, and other sensitive data. Some maintain that the future of Internet commerce is at stake, because transactions cannot flourish over the Net unless they are secure.[25] However, from the standpoint of our society, encryption is a two-edged sword. For instance, police in Sacramento, California, found that PGP blocked them from reading the computer diary of a convicted child molester and finding links to a suspected child pornography ring. *Should* the government be allowed to read the coded e-mail of its citizens? What about its being blocked from surveillance of overseas terrorists, drug dealers, and other enemies?

Protection of Software & Data

Organizations go to tremendous lengths to protect their programs and data. As might be expected, this includes educating employees about making backup disks, protecting against viruses, and so on. Other security procedures include the following:

- **Control of access:** Access to online files is restricted only to those who have a legitimate right to access—because they need them to do their jobs. Many organizations have a transaction log that notes all accesses or attempted accesses to data.

- **Audit controls:** Many networks have *audit controls* that track which programs and servers were used, which files opened, and so on. This creates an *audit trail*, a record of how a transaction was handled from input through processing and output.

- **People controls:** Because people are the greatest threat to a computer system, security precautions begin with the screening of job applicants. That is, résumés are checked to see if people did what they said they did. Another control is to separate employee functions, so that people are not allowed to wander freely into areas not essential to their jobs. Manual and automated controls—input controls, processing controls, and output controls—are used to check that data is handled accurately and completely during the processing cycle. Printouts, printer ribbons, and other waste that may yield passwords and trade secrets to outsiders are disposed of through shredders or locked trash barrels.

Disaster-Recovery Plans

A *disaster-recovery plan* **is a method of restoring information processing operations that have been halted by destruction or accident.** "Among the countless lessons that computer users have absorbed in the hours, days, and weeks after the [1993 New York City] World Trade Center bombing," wrote one reporter, "the most enduring may be the need to have a disaster-recovery plan. The second most enduring lesson may be this: Even a well-practiced plan will quickly reveal its flaws."[26]

Mainframe computer systems are operated in separate departments by professionals, who tend to have disaster plans. Mainframes are usually backed up. However, many personal computers, and even entire local area networks, are not backed up. The consequences of this lapse can be great. It has been reported that on average, a company loses as much as 3% of its gross sales within 8 days of a sustained computer failure. In addition, the average company struck by a computer failure lasting more than 10 days never fully recovers.[27]

A disaster-recovery plan is more than a big fire drill. It includes a list of all business functions and the hardware, software, data, and people to support those functions, as well as arrangements for alternate locations. The disaster-recovery plan includes ways for backing up and storing programs and data in another location, ways of alerting necessary personnel, and training for those personnel.

10.4 Quality-of-Life Issues: The Environment, Mental Health, & the Workplace

KEY QUESTION

How does information technology create environmental, mental-health, and workplace problems?

Preview & Review: Information technology can create problems for the environment, people's mental health (isolation, gambling, Net addiction, and stress), and the workplace (misuse of technology and information overload).

Earlier in this book, we pointed out the worrisome effects of technology on intellectual property rights and truth in art and journalism, on censorship, on health matters and ergonomics, on environmental matters and on privacy. Here we discuss some other quality-of-life issues related to information technology.

Environmental Problems

"This county will do peachy fine without computers," says Micki Haverland, who has lived in rural Hancock County, Tennessee, for 20 years.[28] Telecommunications could bring jobs to an area that badly needs them, but several people moved there precisely because they like things the way they are—pristine rivers, unspoiled forests, and mountain views.

But it isn't just people in rural areas who are concerned. Suburbanites in Idaho and Utah, for example, worry that lofty metal poles topped by cellular-transmitting equipment will be eyesores that will destroy views and property values.[29] City dwellers everywhere are concerned that the federal government's 1996 decision to deregulate the telecommunications industry will lead to a rat's nest of roof antennas, satellite dishes, and above-ground transmission stations. As a result, telecommunications companies are now experimenting with hiding transmitters in the "foliage" of fake trees made of metal.

Political scientist James Snider, of Northwestern University, points out that the problems of the cities could expand well beyond the cities if telecommuting triggers a massive movement of people to rural areas. "If all Americans succeed in getting their dream homes with several acres of land," he writes, "the forests and open lands across the entire continental United States will be destroyed" as they become carved up with subdivisions and roads.[30]

Mental-Health Problems: Isolation, Gambling, Net-Addiction, Stress

Some of the mental health problems involving people and information technology are the following:

- Isolation: Automation allows us to go days without actually speaking with or touching another person, from buying gas to playing games. Even the friendships we make online in cyberspace, some believe, "are likely to be trivial, short lived, and disposable—junk friends." Says one writer, "We may be overwhelmed by a continuous static of information and casual acquaintance, so that finding true soul mates will be even harder than it is today."[31]

- **Gambling:** Gambling is already widespread in North America, but information technology could make it almost unavoidable. Although gambling by wire is illegal in the U.S., all kinds of moves are afoot to get around it. For example, host computers for Internet casinos and sports books have been established in Caribbean tax havens, and satellites, decoders, and remote-control devices are being used so TV viewers can do racetrack wagering from home.

- **Net addiction:** Don't let this happen to you: "A student e-mails friends, browses the World Wide Web, blows off homework, botches exams, flunks out of school."[32] This is a description of the downward spiral of the "Net addict," often a college student—because schools give students no-cost/low-cost linkage to the Internet—though it can be anyone. Some become addicted (although until recently some professionals felt "addiction" was too strong a word) to chat groups, some to online pornography, some simply to the escape from real life.[33,34] Indeed, sometimes the computer replaces one's spouse or boyfriend/girlfriend in the user's affections. In one instance, a man sued his wife for divorce for having an "online affair" with a partner who called himself The Weasel.[35,36]

- **Stress:** In a 1995 survey of 2802 American PC users, three-quarters of the respondents (ranging in age from children to retirees) said personal computers had increased their job satisfaction and were a key to success and learning. However, many found PCs stressful: 59% admitted getting angry at them within the previous year. And 41% said they thought computers have reduced job opportunities rather than increased them.[37]

ARE YOU AN INTERNET ADDICT?

- Do you stay on line longer than you intended?

- Has tolerance developed so that longer periods of time are needed on line?

- Do you call in sick to work, skip classes, go to bed late or wake up early to use the Internet?

- Do you experience withdrawal symptoms (increased depression, moodiness, or anxiety) when you are off line?

- Have you given up recreational, social, or occupational activities because of the Internet?

- Do you continue to use the Internet despite recurrent problems it creates in your real life (work, school, financial, or family problems)?

- Have you made several unsuccessful attempts to cut down the amount of time you use the Internet?

Ethics

Workplace Problems

First the mainframe computer, then the desktop stand-alone PC, and most recently the networked computer were all brought into the workplace for one reason only: to improve productivity. How is it working out? Let's consider two aspects: the misuse of technology, and information overload.

- **Misuse of technology:** "For all their power," says an economics writer, "computers may be costing U.S. companies tens of billions of dollars a year in downtime, maintenance, and training costs, useless game playing, and information overload."[38]

  Consider games. Employees may look busy, staring into their computer screens with brows crinkled. But it could be they're just hard at work playing Doom or surfing the Net. Workers with Internet access average 10 hours a week online.[39] However, fully 23% of computer game players use their office PCs for their fun, according to one survey.[40] A study of employee online use at one major company concluded that the average worker wastes 1½ hours each day.[41]

Another reason for so much wasted time is all the fussing that employees do with hardware and software. One study estimated that microcomputer users waste 5 billion hours a year waiting for programs to run, checking computer output for accuracy, helping co-workers use their applications, organizing cluttered disk storage, and calling for technical support.[42]

Many companies don't even know what kind of microcomputers they have, who's running them, or where they are. The corporate customer of one computer consultant, for instance, swore it had 700 PCs and 15 users per printer. An audit showed it had 1200 PCs with one printer each.[43]

- Information overload: "My boss basically said, 'Carry this pager seven days a week, 24 hours a day, or find another job,'" says the chief architect for a New Jersey school system. (He complied, but pointedly notes that the pager's "batteries run out all the time.")[44] "It used to be considered a status symbol to carry a laptop computer on a plane," says futurist Paul Saffo. "Now anyone who has one is clearly a working dweeb who can't get the time to relax. Carrying one means you're on someone's electronic leash."[45]

The new technology is definitely a two-edged sword. Cellular phones, pagers, fax machines, and modems may untether employees from the office. But they tend to work longer hours under more severe deadline pressure than do their tethered counterparts who stay at the office, according to one study.[46]

What does being overwhelmed with information do to you, besides inducing stress and burnout? One result is that because we have so many choices to entice and confuse us we may become more reluctant to make decisions. "The volume of information available is so great that I think people generally are suffering from a lack of meaning in their lives," says Neil Postman, chair of the department of culture and communication at New York University. "People are just adrift in the sea of information, and they don't know what the information is about or why they need it."[47]

People and businesses are beginning to realize the importance of coming to grips with these problems. Some companies are employing GameCop, a software program that catches unsuspecting employees playing computer games on company time.[48] Some are installing special software (asset-management programs) that tell them how many PCs are on their networks and what they run. Some are imposing strict hardware and software standards to reduce the number of different products they support.[49] To avoid information overload, some people—those who have a choice—no longer carry cell phones or even look at their e-mail. Others are installing so-called *Bozo filters*, software that screens out trivial e-mail messages and cellular calls and assigns priorities to the remaining files. Still others are beginning to employ programs called *intelligent agents* to help them make decisions.

But the real change may come as people realize that they need not be tied to the technological world in order to be themselves, that solitude is a scarce resource, and that seeking serenity means streamlining the clutter and reaching for simpler things.

10.5 Economic Issues: Employment & the Haves/Have-Nots

Preview & Review: Many people worry that jobs are being reduced by the effects of information technology. They also worry that it is widening the gap between the haves and have-nots.

KEY QUESTION

How may technology affect the unemployment rate and the gap between rich and poor?

Ethics

In recent times a number of critics have appeared who have tried to provide a counterpoint to the hype and overselling of information technology. Some of these strike a sensible balance, but some make the alarming case that technological progress is actually no progress at all—indeed, it is a curse. The two biggest charges (which are related) are, first, that information technology is killing jobs and, second, that it is widening the gap between the rich and the poor.

Technology, the Job Killer?

Certainly ATMs do replace bank tellers, fast-pass electronic systems do replace turnpike-toll takers, and Internet travel agents do lure customers away from small travel agencies. There's no question that technological advances play an ambiguous role in social progress.

But is it true, as technology critic Jeremy Rifkin says, that intelligent machines are replacing humans in countless tasks, "forcing millions of blue-collar and white-collar workers into temporary, contingent, and part-time employment and, worse, unemployment"?[50]

This is too large a question to be fully considered in this book. The economy of North America is undergoing powerful structural changes, brought on not only by the widespread diffusion of technology but also by greater competition, increased global trade, the shift from manufacturing to service employment, the weakening of labor unions, more flexible labor markets, more rapid immigration, partial deregulation, and other factors.[51–53]

A counterargument is that jobs don't disappear, they just change. Or the jobs that do disappear represent drudgery. "If your job has been replaced by a computer," says Stewart Brand, "that may have been a job that was not worthy of a human."[54]

Gap Between Rich & Poor

"In the long run," says MIT economist Paul Krugman, "improvements in technology are good for almost everyone. . . . Unfortunately, what is true in the long run need not be true over shorter periods."[55] We are now, he believes, living through one of those difficult periods in which technology doesn't produce widely shared economic gains but instead widens the gap between those who have the right skills and those who don't.

A U.S. Department of Commerce survey of "information have-nots" reveals that about 20% of the poorest households in the U.S. do not have telephones. Moreover, only a fraction of those poor homes that do have phones will be able to afford the information technology that most economists agree is the key to a comfortable future.[56] The richer the family, the more likely it is to have and use a computer.

Schooling—especially college—makes a great difference. Every year of formal schooling after high school adds 5–15% to annual earnings later in life.[57] Being well educated is only part of it, however; one should also be technologically literate. Employees who are skilled at technology "earn roughly 10–15% higher pay," according to the chief economist for the U.S. Labor Department.[58]

Advocates of information access for all find hope in the promises of NII proponents for "universal service" and the wiring of every school to the Net. But this won't happen automatically. Ultimately we must become concerned with the effects of growing economic disparities on our social and political health.

Now that we've considered the challenges, let us discuss some of the promises of information technology not described so far.

10.6 Artificial Intelligence

KEY QUESTION

What are some characteristics of the key areas of artificial intelligence?

Preview & Review: Artificial intelligence (AI) is a research and applications discipline that includes the areas of robotics, expert systems, and natural-language processing. The Turing test has long been used as a standard to determine whether a computer possesses "intelligence." Behind all aspects of AI are ethical questions.

You're having trouble with your new software program. You call the customer "help desk" at the software maker. Do you get a busy signal or get put on hold to listen to music (or, worse, advertising) for several minutes? Technical support lines are often swamped, and waiting is commonplace. Or, to deal with your software difficulty, do you find yourself dealing with . . . other software?

This event is not unlikely. Programs that can walk you through a problem and help solve it are called *expert systems*. As the name suggests, these are systems that are imbued with knowledge by a human expert. Expert systems are one of the most useful applications of an area known as *artificial intelligence*.

Artificial intelligence (AI) is a group of related technologies that attempt to develop machines to emulate human-like qualities, such as learning, reasoning, communicating, seeing, and hearing. Today the main areas of AI are *robotics*, *expert systems*, and *natural language processing*.

▪ PANEL 10.2

Robotics

(Left) Dante II volcano explorer. *(Right)* NASA's Mars Pathfinder, used to explore part of the surface of Mars in 1997.

Robotics

Robotics is a field that attempts to develop machines that can perform work normally done by people. The machines themselves, of course, are called *robots*. A robot is an automatic device that performs functions ordinarily ascribed to human beings or that operates with what appears to be almost human intelligence. Dante II, for instance, is an eight-legged, 10-foot-high, satellite-linked robot used by scientists to explore the inside of Mount Spurr, an active volcano in Alaska. *(See ▪ Panel 10.2.)* Robots may be controlled from afar, as in an experiment at the University of Southern California in

which Internet users thousands of miles away were invited to manipulate a robotic arm to uncover objects in a sandbox.[59]

Expert Systems

An *expert system* **is an interactive computer program that helps users solve problems that would otherwise require the assistance of a human expert.** Such programs simulate the reasoning process of experts in certain well-defined areas. That is, professionals called knowledge engineers interview the expert or experts and determine the rules and knowledge that must go into the system. Programs incorporate not only the experts' surface knowledge ("textbook knowledge") but also deep knowledge ("tricks of the trade"). Expert systems exist in many areas. For example, MYCIN helps diagnose infectious diseases. PROSPECTOR assesses geological data to locate mineral deposits. DENDRAL identifies chemical compounds. Home-Safe-Home evaluates the residential environment of an elderly person. Business Insight helps businesses find the best strategies for marketing a product. REBES (Residential Burglary Expert System) helps detectives investigate crime scenes.

Natural Language Processing

Natural languages are ordinary human languages, such as English. **Natural-language processing is the study of ways for computers to recognize and understand human language,** whether in spoken or written form.

Think how challenging it is to make a computer translate English into another language. In one instance, the English sentence "The spirit is willing, but the flesh is weak" came out in Russian as "The wine is agreeable, but the meat is spoiled." The problem with human language is that it is often ambiguous and often interpreted differently by different listeners.

Today you can buy a handheld computer that will translate a number of English sentences—principally travelers' phrases ("Please take me to the airport")—into another language. This trick is similar to teaching an English-speaking child to sing "Frère Jacques." More complex is the work being done by AI scientists trying to discover ways to endow the computer with an "understanding" of how human language works. This means working with ideas about the instinctual instructions or genetic code that babies are born with for understanding language.

Still, some natural-language systems are already in use. Intellect is a product that uses a limited English vocabulary to help users orally query databases. LUNAR, developed to help analyze moon rocks, answers questions about geology from an extensive database. Verbex, used by the U.S. Postal Service, lets mail sorters read aloud an incomplete address and replies with the correct zip code.

Ethics

Artificial Life, the Turing Test, & AI Ethics

How can we know when we have reached the point where computers have achieved human intelligence? How will you always know, say, if you're on the phone, whether you're talking to a human being or to a computer? Clearly, with the strides made in the fields of artificial intelligence and artificial life, this question is no longer just academic.

Interestingly, this matter was addressed back in 1950 by Alan Turing, an English mathematician and computer pioneer. Turing predicted that by the end of the century computers would be able to mimic human thinking and converse so naturally that their communications would be indistinguishable from a person's. Out of these observations came the Turing test. The *Turing test* is a test or game for determining whether a computer is considered to possess "intelligence" or "self-awareness."

In the Turing test, a human judge converses by means of a computer terminal with two entities hidden in another location. One entity is a person typing on a keyboard. The other is a software program. As the judge types in and receives messages on the terminal, he or she must decide whether the entity is human. In this test, intelligence, the ability to think, is demonstrated by the computer's success in fooling the judge.

Judith Anne Gunther participated as one of eight judges in the third annual Loebner Prize Competition, which is based on Turing's ideas.[60] (There have been other competitions since.) The "conversations" are restricted to predetermined topics, such as baseball. This is because today's best programs have neither the databases nor the syntactical ability to handle an unlimited number of subjects. Conversations with each entity are limited to 15 minutes. At the end of the contest, the program that fools the judges most is the one that wins.

Gunther found that she wasn't fooled by any of the computer programs. The winning program, for example, relied as much on deflection and wit as it did on responding logically and conversationally. (For example, to a judge trying to discuss a federally funded program, the computer said: "You want logic? I'll give you logic: shut up, shut up, shut up, shut up, shut up, now go away! How's that for logic?") However, Gunther *was* fooled by one of the five humans, a real person discussing abortion. "He was so uncommunicative," wrote Gunther, "that I pegged him for a computer."

Behind everything to do with artificial intelligence and artificial life—just as it underlies everything we do—is the whole matter of *ethics.* In his book *Ethics in Modeling,* William A. Wallace, professor of decision sciences at Rensselaer Polytechnic Institute, points out that many users are not aware that computer software, such as expert systems, is often subtly shaped by the ethical judgments and assumptions of the people who create them.[61] In one instance, he points out, a bank had to modify its loan-evaluation software after it discovered that it tended to reject some applications because it unduly emphasized old age as a negative factor. Another expert system, used by health maintenance organizations (HMOs), instructs doctors on when they should opt for expensive medical procedures, such as magnetic resonance imaging tests. HMOs like expert systems because they help control expenses, but critics are concerned that doctors will have to base decisions not on the best medicine but simply on "satisfactory" medicine combined with cost cutting.[62] Clearly, there is no such thing as completely "value-free" technology. Human beings build it, use it, and have to live with the results.

10.7 The Promised Benefits of the Information Revolution

KEY QUESTION

What are the expected future benefits of the Information Revolution?

Preview & Review: The Information Revolution promises great benefits in the areas of education and information, health, commerce and electronic money, entertainment, and government and electronic democracy

Looking ahead to a moment when you are holding in your hand your "information appliance," the gadget that will help you access anybody and anything anywhere, how might this connection affect your life? Let's look at some areas of promise.

Education & Information

The government is interested in reforming education, and technology can assist that effort. Presently the United States has more computers in its classrooms than other countries, but the machines are older and teachers aren't as computer-literate. A recent study shows that 61.2% of urban schools have phone lines they could use for Internet access, while 42% own modems. The poorer the school district, the less likely it is to have modems.[63]

Computers can be used to create "virtual" classrooms not limited by scheduled class time. Several institutions (Stanford, MIT) have been replacing the lecture hall with forms of learning featuring multimedia programs, workstations, and television courses at remote sites. The Internet could be used to enable students to take video field trips to distant places and to pull information from remote museums and libraries.

Of particular interest is distance learning, or the "virtual university." *Distance learning* is the use of computer and/or video networks to teach courses to students outside the conventional classroom. Until recently, distance learning has been largely outside the mainstream of campus life. That is, it concentrates principally on part-time students, those who cannot easily travel to campus, those interested in noncredit classes, or those seeking special courses in business or engineering. However, part-timers presently make up about 45% of all college enrollments. This, says one writer, is "a group for whom 'anytime, anywhere' education holds special appeal."[64]

Health

The government is calling for an expansion of "telemedicine," the use of telecommunications to link health-care providers and researchers, enabling them to share medical images, patient records, and research. Of particular interest would be the use of networks for "teleradiology" (the exchange of X-rays, CAT scans, and the like), so that specialists could easily confer. Telemedicine would also allow long-distance patient examinations, using video cameras and, perhaps, virtual-reality kinds of gloves that would transmit and receive tactile sensations.

Commerce & Electronic Money

Businesses clearly see the Internet as a way to enhance productivity and competitiveness. However, the changes will probably go well beyond this.

The thrust of the original Industrial Revolution was separation—to break work up into its component parts to permit mass production. The effect of computer networks in the Digital Revolution, however, is unification—to erase boundaries between company departments, suppliers, and customers.[65]

Indeed, the parts of a company can now as easily be global as down the hall from one another. Thus, designs for a new product can be tested and exchanged with factories in remote locations. With information flowing faster, goods can be sent to market faster and inventories kept reduced. Says an officer of the Internet Society, "Increasingly you have people in a wide variety of professions collaborating in diverse ways in other places. The whole notion of 'the organization' becomes a blurry boundary around a set of people and information systems and enterprises."[66]

The electronic mall, in which people make purchases online, is already here. Record companies, for instance, are making sound excerpts and videos of new albums available on Web sites; you can sample the album and then order it sent as a cassette or CD. Banks in cyberspace are allowing customers to adopt avatars or personas of themselves and then meet in three-dimensional virtual space on the World Wide Web where they can query bank tellers and officers and make transactions. Wal-Mart Stores and Microsoft have developed a joint online shopping venture that allows shoppers to browse online and buy merchandise.

Cybercash or E-cash will change the future of money. Whether they take the form of smart cards or of electronic blips online, cybercash will probably begin to displace (though not completely supplant) checks and paper currency. This would change the nature of how money is regulated as well as the way we spend and sell.

Entertainment

Among the future entertainment offerings could be movies on-demand, video games, and gaming ("telegambling"). *Video on-demand* would allow viewers to browse through a menu of hundreds of movies, select one, and start it when they wanted. This definition is for true video on-demand, which is like having a complete video library in your house. (An alternative, simpler form could consist of running the same movie on multiple channels, with staggered starting times.) True video on-demand will require a server, a storage system with the power of a supercomputer that would deliver movies and other data to thousands of customers at once.

Government & Electronic Democracy

Will information technology help the democratic process? There seem to be two parts to this. The first is its use as a campaign tool, which may, in fact, skew the democratic process in some ways. The second is its use in governing and in delivering government services.

Santa Monica, California, established a computer system, called Public Electronic Network (PEN), which residents may hook into free of charge. PEN gives Santa Monica residents access to city council agendas, staff reports, public safety tips, and the public library's online catalog. Citizens may also enter into electronic conferences on topics both political and nonpolitical; this has been by far the most popular attraction.

PEN could be the basis for wider forms of electronic democracy. For example, electronic voting might raise the percentage of people who vote. Interactive local-government meetings could enable constituents and town council members to discuss proposals.

The Internet could also deliver federal services and benefits. A few years ago, the government unveiled a program in which Social Security pensioners and other recipients of federal aid without bank accounts could use a plastic automated-teller-machine card to walk up to any ATM and withdraw the funds due them.

Onward

How do most of us view the way change takes place?

We believe it occurs slowly and predictably, like the process of water boiling, says economics writer Robert Samuelson. That is, the water warms gradually, getting hotter until it boils.

Quite often, however, change occurs suddenly, wrenchingly, dramatically—and is quite different from what came before. "Life and history aren't always water coming slowly to a boil," he says. "Sometimes they're a critical mass triggering radical change."[67]

This is what makes predictions difficult. "Hardly anyone foresaw . . . the explosion of the Internet," Samuelson points out, just as hardly anyone foresaw the collapse of Communism or the advent of AIDS. These were all major, world-shaking events, yet they were not on the radar screens of most futurists and planners.

Thus, if change often occurs in abrupt, surprising fashion, how can we really make predictions about the future?

Still, as we said at the beginning of the chapter, in a world of breakneck change, you can still thrive. The most critical knowledge, however, may turn out to be self-knowledge.

This is not the end. It is the beginning.

Job Searching on the Internet & World Wide Web

"If you haven't done a job search in a while, you will find many changes in a modern-day, high-quality search for a new position," says Mary Anne Buckman, consultant at Career Directions Inc.[68] Indeed, technological change has so affected the whole field of job hunting that futurists refer to it as a *paradigm shift.* This means that the change is of such magnitude that the "prevailing structure is radically, rapidly, and unalterably transformed by new circumstances."[69]

Here let's describe how you can use the Internet and the World Wide Web to help you search for jobs. Online areas of interest for the job seeker include:

- Resources for career advice
- Ways for you to find employers
- Ways for employers to find you

Resources for Career Advice

It's 3 A.M. Still, if you're up at this hour (or indeed at any other time) you can still find job-search advice, tips on interviewing and résumé writing, and postings of employment opportunities around the world. One means for doing so is to use your Web browser to use a directory such as Yahoo! *(http://www.yahoo.com)* to obtain a list of popular Web sites. In the menu, you can click on Business and Economy, then Employment, then Jobs. This will bring up a list of sites that offer career advice, résumé postings, job listings, research about specific companies, and other services. (Caution: As might be expected, there is also a fair amount of junk out there: get-rich-quick offers, résumé-preparation firms, and other attempts to separate you from your money.)

Advice about careers, occupational trends, employment laws, and job hunting is also available through online chat groups and bulletin boards, such as those on the online services—America Online, CompuServe, Microsoft Network, and Prodigy. For instance, CompuServe offers career-specific discussion groups, such as the PR Marketing Forum. Through these groups you can get tips on job searching, interviewing, and salary negotiations. In addition, you might wish to check the U.S. Bureau of Labor Statistics Web site *(http://stats.bls.gov/eophome.htm),* which contains employment projections and a list of fastest-growing occupations; Career Magazine *(http://www.careermag.com);* Job Search Advice for College Grads *(http://www.collegegrad.com);* and JobSmart Salary Survey Links for all fields *(http://www.jobsmart.org/tools/salary/sal-prof.htm).*

Ways for You to Find Employers

As you might expect, companies seeking people with technical backgrounds and technical people seeking employment pioneered the use of cyberspace as a job bazaar. However, as the public's interest in commercial services and the Internet has exploded, the technical orientation of online job exchanges has changed. Now, says one writer, "interspersed among all the ads for programmers on the Internet are openings for English teachers in China, forest rangers in New York, physical therapists in Atlanta, and models in Florida."[70] Most Web sites are free to job seekers, although some may require you to fill out an online registration form.

Some jobs are posted on Usenets by individuals, companies, and universities or colleges, such as computer networking company Cisco Systems of San Jose, California, and the University of Utah in Salt Lake City. Others are posted by professional or other organizations, such as the American Astronomical Society, Jobs Online New Zealand, and Volunteers in Service to America (VISTA). Some of the principal organizations posting job listings are listed in the box on the next page. (■ *See Panel 10.4.)*

The difficulty with searching through these resources is that it can mean wading through thousands of entries in numerous databanks, with many of them not being suitable for or interesting to you. An alternative to trying to find an employer is to have employers find you.

Ways for Employers to Find You

Because of the Internet's low (or zero) cost and wide reach, do you have anything to lose by posting your résumé online for prospective employers to view? Certainly you might if the employer happens to be the one you're already working for. In addition, you have to be aware that you lose control over anything broadcast into cyberspace—you're putting your credentials out there for the whole world to see, and you need to be somewhat concerned about who might gain access to them.

Posting your résumé with an electronic jobs registry is certainly worth doing if you have a technical background, since technology companies in particular find this an efficient way of screening and hiring. However, it may also benefit people with less technical backgrounds. Online recruitment "is popular with companies because it pre-screens applicants for at least basic computer skills," says one writer. "Anyone who can master the Internet is likely to know something about word processing, spreadsheets, or database searches, knowledge required in most good jobs these days."[71]

The latest variant is to produce a résumé with hypertext links and/or clever graphics and multimedia effects, then put it on a Web site to entice employers to chase after you. If you don't know how to do this, there are many companies that—for a fee—can convert your résumé to HTML

(✔ p. 326) and publish it on their own Web sites. Some of these services can't dress it up with fancy graphics or multimedia, but since complex pages take longer for employers to download anyway, the extra pizzazz is probably not worth the effort. In any case, for you the bottom line is how much you're willing to pay for these services. For instance, Résumé Innovations *(http://www.resume-innovations.com)* charges $85 to write a résumé and nothing to post it on a Web site. There are a number of Web sites on which you can post your résumé, sometimes for free.

Companies are also beginning to replace their recruiters' campus visits with online interviewing. For example, the firm VIEWnet of Madison, Wisconsin, offers first-round screenings or interviews for summer internships through its teleconferencing "InterVIEW" technology, which allows video signals to be transmitted (at 17 frames per second) via phone lines.

■ PANEL 10.4   Organizations posting job listings on the Web

- **America's Job Bank:** A joint venture of the New York State Department of Labor and the Federal Employment and Training Administration, America's Job Bank *(http://www.ajb.dni.us/index.html)* advertises more than 100,000 jobs of all types. There are links to each state's employment office. More than a quarter of the jobs posted are sales, service, or clerical. Another quarter are managerial, professional, and technical. Other major types are construction, trucking, and manufacturing.

- **Career Mosaic:** A service run by Bernard Hodes Advertising, Career Mosaic *(http://www. careermosaic.com)* offers links to nearly 200 major corporations, most of them high-technology companies. One section is aimed at college students and offers tips on résumés and networking. A major strength is the JOBS database, which lets you fill out forms to narrow your search, then presents you with a list of jobs meeting your criteria.

- **Career Path:** Career Path *(http://www. careerpath.com/)* is a classified-ad employment listing from numerous American newspapers, which you can search either individually or all at once. Major papers include the *Boston Globe,* the *Chicago Tribune,* the *Los Angeles Times,* the *New York Times,* the *San Jose Mercury News,* and the *Washington Post.*

- **E-Span:** One of the oldest and biggest services, the E-Span Interactive Employment Network *(http://www.espan.com)* features all-paid ads from employers.

- **FedWorld:** This bulletin board *(http://www.fedworld. gov)* offers job postings from the U.S. Goverment.

- **Internet Job Locator:** Combining all major job-search engines on one page, the Internet Job Locator *(http://www.joblocator.com/jobs)* lets you do a search of all of them at once.

- **JobHunt:** Started by Stanford University geologist Dane Spearing, JobHunt *(http://www.job-hunt.org)* contains a list of more than 700 sites related to online recruiting.

- **JobTrak:** The nation's leading online job listing service, JobTrak *(http://www.jobtrak.com)* claims to have 35,000 students and alumni visiting the site each day, with more than 300,000 employers and 750 college career centers posting 3000 new jobs daily.

- **JobWeb:** Operated by the National Association of colleges and Employers, Job Web *(http://www. jobweb.org/)* is a college placement service with 1600 U.S. member universities and colleges and 1400 employer organizations. It claims to have served over 1 million college students and alumni.

- **Monster Board:** Not just for computer techies, the Monster Board *(http://www.monster.com)* offers real jobs for real people, although a lot of the companies listed are in the computer industry.

- **NationJob Network:** Based in Des Moines, Iowa, NationJob Network *(http://www.nationjob.com)* lists job opportunities primarily in the Midwest. A free feature called P.J. Scout sends job seekers news of new jobs.

- **Online Career Center:** Based in Indianapolis, Online Career Center *(http:www.occ.com/occ/)* is a nonprofit national recruiting service listing jobs at more than 3000 companies. About 30% of the jobs are nontechnical, with many in sales and marketing and in health care.

- **Workplace:** An employment resource offering staff and administrative positions in colleges and universities, government, and the arts *(http://galaxy.einet.net.galaxy/Community/Workplace. html).*

Summary

What It Is/What It Does	Why It's Important

artificial intelligence (p. 323, KQ 10.6) Group of related technologies that attempt to develop machines to emulate human-like qualities, such as learning, reasoning, communicating, seeing, and hearing.

AI is important for enabling machines to do things formerly possible only with human effort.

biometrics (p. 317, KQ 10.3) Science of measuring individual body characteristics.

Biometrics is used in some computer security systems—for example, to verify individual's fingerprints before allowing access.

disaster-recovery plan (p. 318, KQ 10.3) Method of restoring information processing operations that have been halted by destruction or accident.

Disaster recovery plans are important for companies desiring to resume computer and business operations in short order.

encryption (p. 317, KQ 10.3) Also called *enciphering;* the altering of data so that it is not usable unless the changes are undone.

Encryption is useful for users transmitting trade or military secrets or other sensitive data.

expert system (p. 324, KQ 10.6) Interactive computer program that helps users solve problems that would otherwise require the assistance of a human expert.

Expert systems allow users to solve problems without assistance of a human expert; they incorporate both surface knowledge ("textbook knowledge") and deep knowledge ("tricks of the trade").

information-technology crime (p. 312, KQ 10.2) Crime of one of two types: an illegal act perpetrated against computers or telecommunications; or the use of computers or telecommunications to accomplish an illegal act.

Information-technology crimes cost billions of dollars every year.

Internet 2 (p. 309, KQ 10.1) Cooperative university-business program to upgrade the Internet, allowing high-end users to quickly and reliably move huge amounts of data using "toll lanes" provided by VBNS, the high-speed data transmission system connecting major research centers.

Internet 2 would provide speeds 100 times that of today's Internet. The improvement could advance videoconferencing, research, and academic collaboration among the members—currently more than 117 universities and about 25 companies.

National Information Infrastructure (NII) (p. 309, KQ 10.1) U.S. government vision for the Information Superhighway; services wil be delivered via the networks and technologies of several information providers—the telecommunications companies, cable-TV companies, and the Internet.

Services could include education, health care, information, commerce, and entertainment.

What It Is/What It Does	Why It's Important

natural language processing (p. 324, KQ 10.6) Study of ways for computers to recognize and understand human language, whether in spoken or written form.

Natural language processing could further reduce the barriers to human/computer communications.

Next Generation Internet (p. 310, KQ 10.1) U.S. government's broad program to parallel the university/business effort of Internet-2, helping to tie that high-performance network into the broader federal infrastructure. NGI funds six government agencies' programs directed at the effort.

Using high-speed fiber-optic circuits and sophisticated software, NGI, Internet 2, and VBNS all aim to improve on the original Internet. NGI and Internet 2 are planned to be available by 2003.

password (p. 317, KQ 10.3) Special word, code, or symbol that is required to access a computer system.

One of the weakest links in computer security, passwords can be guessed, forgotten, or stolen.

personal identification number (PIN) (p. 317, KQ 10.3) Security number known only to an individual user, who cannot access the system without it.

PINs are required to access many computer systems and automated teller machines.

robotics (p. 323, KQ 10.6) Field of artificial intelligence that attempts to develop robots, machines that can perform work normally done by people.

Robots are performing more and more functions in business and the professions.

security (p. 316, KQ 10.3) System of safeguards for protecting information technology against disasters, systems failure, and unauthorized access, all of which can result in damage or loss.

With proper security, organizations and individuals can minimize losses caused to information technology from disasters, systems failures, and unauthorized access.

VBNS (Very-High-Speed Backbone Network Service) (p. 309, KQ 10.1) Part of the effort to upgrade the Internet; VBNS is the U.S. government's project to link supercomputers and other banks of computers across the nation at speeds 1000 times faster than the current Internet. Begun in 1996, VBNS will involve only the top 100 research universities in the United States, but it will also have "toll lanes" for other users.

VBNS is the main U.S. government component to upgrade primary hubs of data transmission (the Internet's "backbone"). Most of the present members of VBNS will also be part of Internet 2.

Exercises

Self-Test

1. The purpose of _____ is to scan a computer's disk devices and memory to detect viruses and, sometimes, to destroy them.
2. Data that is incomplete, outdated, or otherwise inaccurate is referred to as _____ _____.
3. List four areas in which the Information Superhighway promises great benefits.
   a _____
   b. _____
   c. _____
   d. _____
4. So that information processing operations can be restored after destruction or accident, a company should adopt a _____.

Short-Answer Questions

1. What is the significance of the 1996 Telecommunications Act?
2. How would you define *information-technology crime*?
3. What is the difference between a hacker and a cracker?

Multiple-Choice Questions

1. Which of the following is an interactive computer program that helps users solve problems?
   a. robot
   b. expert system
   c. natural language
   d. All of the above

2. Which of the following groups perpetrate over 80% of information technology crime?
   a. hackers
   b. crackers
   c. professional criminals
   d. employees
   e. None of the above

True/False Questions

T F 1. A digital signature looks the same as your signature on a check.

T F 2. Encrypted data isn't directly usable.

T F 3. The 1996 Telecommunications Act permits greater competition between local and long-distance telephone companies.

T F 4. Viruses can be passed to another computer by a diskette or through a network.

Knowledge in Action

1. In addition to *2600: The Hacker's Quarterly*, where do hackers find new information about their field? Are support groups available? In what ways do hackers help companies? Does a hacker underground exist? Research your answers using current computer periodicals and/or the Internet.
2. Assuming you have a microcomputer in your home that includes a modem, what security threats, if any, should you be concerned with? List as many ways as you can think of to ensure that your computer is protected.
3. Explore the National Information Infrastructure (NII) in more detail. Create an executive report describing the objectives for the NII, its guiding principles, and its agenda for action. Does the NII exist today or is it a plan for the future? Or both? Research your answers using current periodicals and/or the Internet.

4. What's your opinion about the issue of free speech on an electronic network? Research some recent legal decisions in various countries, as well as some articles on the topic, and then give a short report about what you think. Should the contents of messages be censored? If so, under what conditions?

5. Artificial intelligence professional societies, such as the American Association for Artificial Intelligence (contact info: 415-328-3123 or *http://www.aaai.org*), provide a variety of published material as well as symposia, workshops, conferences, and related services and activities for those involved in various AI fields. These societies can be easily located by using a Web browser and then searching for the phrase "artificial intelligence." Contact one or more societies and obtain information on activities, services, and fees.

Answers

Self-Test Questions
1. *antivirus software* 2. *dirty data* 3. *education and information, health, commerce and electronic money, entertainment, government and electronic democracy* 4. *disaster-recovery plan*

Short-Answer Questions
1. *...It undoes 60 years of federal and state communications regulations enabling phone, cable, and TV businesses to compete and combine more freely.* 2. *An illegal act perpetrated against computers or telecommunications; an illegal act involving the use of computers or telecommunications.* 3. *A hacker gains unauthorized access to a computer or telecommunications system for the challenge of it, whereas a cracker may do the same for malicious reasons.*

Multiple-Choice Questions
1. *b* 2. *d*

True/False Questions
1. *F* 2. *T* 3. *T* 4. *T*

Notes

Chapter 1

1. Thomas A. Stewart, "The Information Age in Charts," *Fortune*, April 4, 1994, pp. 75–79.
2. Donald Spencer, *Webster's New World Dictionary of Computer Terms*, 4th ed. (New York: Prentice Hall, 1992), p. 206.
3. "What Does 'Digital' Mean in Regard to Electronics?" *Popular Science*, August 1997, pp. 91–94.
4. *Wall Street Journal*, November 16, 1992, p. R18–R19.
5. Barbara Simmons and Gary Chapman, "Information Highway Has Many Potholes," *San Francisco Chronicle*, January 17, 1994, p. B3.
6. Blanton Fortson, in "Talking About Portables," 1992.
7. Link Resources, reported in Ilana DeBare, "Telecommuting Sparks Debate Over Safety," *San Francisco Chronicle*, August 4, 1997, pp. B1, B2.
8. IDC/Link, reported in Susan J. Wells, "For Stay-Home Workers, Speed Bumps on the Telecommute," *New York Times*, August 17, 1997, sec. 3, pp. 1, 14.
9. Michael Capochiano, commenting on 1996 USA Today/IntelliQuest Technology Monitor study, reported in Leslie Miller, "Most Users See Internet as Happy Medium," *USA Today*, June 18, 1996, p. 4E.
10. Mike Snider, "Fewer Homes on Line, Study Shows," *USA Today*, September 3, 1997, p. 1D.
11. Study by Dataquest, reported in Jon Swartz, "A Rush to Plug PCs into the Internet," *San Francisco Chronicle*, August 21, 1997, pp. A1, A15.
12. John D. Dvorak, "Avoiding Information Overload," *PC Magazine*, December 17, 1996, p. 87.
13. Tom Forester and Perry Morrison, *Computer Ethics: Cautionary Tales and Ethical Dilemmas in Computing* (Cambridge, MA: The MIT Press, 1990), pp. 1–2.

Chapter 2

1. John Markoff, "A Free and Simple Computer Link," *New York Times*, December 8, 1993, p. C1.
2. Software Publishers Association, reported in Alan Deutschman, "Mac vs. Windows: Who Cares?" *Fortune*, October 4, 1993, p. 114.
3. Claris survey of small businesses, reported in USA Snapshots, "Small-Business Software," *USA Today*, July 17, 1996, p. 1B.
4. Deutschman, 1993.
5. Joan Indiana Rigdon, "Nintendo Catches Up to Sony in Market for Most-Advanced Video-Game Players," *New York Times*, February 3, 1997, p. B3.
6. Steve G. Steinberg, "Back in Your Court, Software Designers," *Los Angeles Times*, December 7, 1995, pp. D2, D11.
7. Rick Tetzeli, "Videogames: Serious Fun," *Fortune*, December 27, 1993, pp. 110–116.
8. Herb Brody, "Video Games That Teach?" *Technology Review*, November/December 1993, pp. 50–57.
9. Jay Sivin-Kachala, Interactive Educational Systems Design, quoted in Nicole Carroll, "How Computers Can Help Low-Achieving Students," *USA Today*, November 20, 1995, p. 5D.
10. Edward Rothstein, "Between the Dream and the Reality Lies the Shadow. Or Is It the Interface?" *New York Times*, December 11, 1995, p. C3.
11. Randall Stross, "Netscape: Inside the Big Software Giveaway," *Fortune*, March 30, 1998, pp. 150–152.
12. Baruch College–Harris Poll, commissioned by *Business Week*; reported in Amy Cortese, "A Census in Cyberspace," *Business Week*, May 5, 1997, pp. 84–85.
13. Jan Norman, "Office Suite Office," *San Francisco Examiner*, November 17, 1996, pp. B-5, B-7.
14. Margaret Trejo, quoted in Richard Atcheson, "A Woman for *Lear's*," *Lear's*, November 1993, p. 87.
15. Bernie Ward, "Computer Chic," *Sky*, April 1993, pp. 84–90.
16. John Ennis, quoted in Peter Plagens and Ray Sawhill, "Throw Out the Brushes," *Newsweek*, September 1, 1997, pp. 76–77.
17. David Kirkpatrick, "Groupware Goes Boom," *Fortune*, December 27, 1993, p. 100.
18. Associated Press, quoted in Ellen Goodman, "Computercide on My Mind," *San Francisco Chronicle*, July 31, 1997, p. A21; reprinted from Boston Globe.
19. Don Clark and David Bank, "Microsoft May Face a Backlash Against 'Bloatware,'" *Wall Street Journal*, November 18, 1996, pp. B1, B4.
20. Stephen Manes, "The Life of a Computer User: One Frustration After Another," *San Jose Mercury News*, November 24, 1996, p. 5F; reprinted from *New York Times*.
21. Denise K. Magner, "Verdict in a Plagiarism Case," *Chronicle of Higher Education*, January 5, 1994, pp. A17, A20.
22. Andy Ihnatko, "Right-Protected Software," *MacUser*, March 1993, pp. 29–30.

Chapter 3

1. Alan Robbins, "Why There's Egg on Your Interface," *New York Times*, December 1, 1996, sec. 3, p. 12.
2. Stuart Card, quoted in Kevin Maney, "Computer Windows May Be Obsolete," *USA Today*, August 25, 1995, p. 2B.
3. Peter H. Lewis, "Champion of MS-DOS, Admirer of Windows," *New York Times*, April 4, 1993, sec. 3, p. 11.
4. Don Clark, "Microsoft Corp. Delays Release of Windows 95 System Upgrade," *Wall Street Journal*, September 16, 1997, p. B10.
5. International Data Corp., reported in Tom Abate, "Novell's Comeback Chief," *San Francisco Chronicle*, September 12, 1997, pp. B1, B2.
6. Ben Smith, quoted in John Montgomery, "Putting Unix in All the Right Places," *Byte*, January 1998, pp. 96I-96N.
7. David Bank, "Microsoft's Gates Urges Clients Focus on Its Windows NT," *Wall Street Journal*, October 3, 1997, p. B5.
8. Tosca Moon Lee, "Utility Software: Your PC's Life Preserver," *PC Novice*, March 1993, pp. 68–73.
9. "A New Model for Personal Computing," *San Jose Mercury News*, August 13, 1995, p. 27A. 6
10. Lee Gomes, "Hollow Dreams," *San Jose Mercury News*, November 12, 1995, pp. 1D, 3D.
11. Joseph Jennings, "The End of Wintel?" *San Francisco Examiner*, December 17, 1995, pp. B-5, B-7.
12. Mark Fleming [letter] and Mike McGowan [letter], "Present at the Creation of the Net," *Business Week*, December 25, 1995, p. 12.
13. Jim Carlton, "Apple to Roll Out New Operating System Gradually, Scrapping Quick Transition," *Wall Street Journal*, October 3, 1997, p. B5.
14. Michael H. Martin, "Digging Data Out of Cyberspace," *Fortune*, April 1, 1996, p. 147.
15. Richard Scoville, "Find It on the Net," *PC World*, January 1996, pp. 125-130.
16. David Haskin, "Power Search," *Internet World*, December 1997, pp. 78-92.
17. Martin, 1996.
18. Scoville, 1996.

Chapter 4

1. Michael S. Malone, "The Tiniest Transformer," *San Jose Mercury News*, September 10, 1995, pp. 1D–2D; excerpted from *The Microprocessor: A Biography* (New York: Telos/Springer Verlag, 1995).
2. Laurence Hooper, "No Compromises," *Wall Street Journal*, November 16, 1992, p. R8.
3. Kevin Maney, "Moore's Law Still Intact," *USA Today*, September 25, 1997, p. 2B.
4. Dean Takahashi, "Intel's Top Chip Architect to Unveil His Latest Creation," *Wall Street Journal*, October 10, 1997, pp. B1, B9.
5. John Markoff, "Intel Is Gambling with a New and More Powerful Set of Chips," *New York Times*, August 27, 1997, p. C8.
6. Craig Barrett, reported in Bloomberg News, "The Intel View of Future PCs," *New York Times*, April 23, 1997, p. C2.
7. Phillip Robinson, "When the Power Fails," *San Jose Mercury News*, December 17, 1995, pp. 1F, 6F.
8. Robinson, 1995.
9. Harry Somerfield, "Surge Protectors Vital to Shield Electronics," *San Francisco Chronicle*, November 22, 1995, sec. Z-1, p. 7.
10. Suzanne Weixel, *Easy PCs*, 2nd ed. (Indianapolis: Que Corp., 1993).
11. Bruce Haring, "Power Outages Give PC Owners an Unpleasant Jolt," *USA Today*, August 19, 1996, p. 3D.
12. Steve Mann, quoted in Judith Gaines, "MIT Graduate's Clothes Make for a Truly Personal Computer," *San Francisco Chronicle*, October 1, 1997, p. A7; reprinted from Boston Globe.
13. Dan Gillmor, "Old Computer Will Mean a Lot to Those in Need," *San Jose Mercury News*, December 24, 1995, p. 1F.
14. Lawrence J. Magid, "Computer Users Can Do Their Part in Recycling," *San Jose Mercury News*, May 26, 1996, pp. 1F, 2F.

Chapter 5

1. Heather Fisher, quoted in Carol Jouzaitis, "Step Right Up, and Pay Your Taxes and Tickets," *USA Today*, October 2, 1997, p. 4A.
2. Connie Guglielmo, "Here Come the Super-ATMs," *Fortune*, October 14, 1996, pp. 232–34.

3. Betsy Wade, "E-Tickets Begin to Catch On," *New York Times*, August 10, 1997, sec. 4, p. 4.
4. Jouzaitis, 1997.
5. David Gelernter, quoted in Associated Press, "Bombing Victim Says He's Lucky to Be Alive," *San Francisco Chronicle*, January 28, 1994, p. A15.
6. David Lieberman, "Do-it-all Box Could Start a Cable Revolution," *USA Today*, December 16, 1997, p. 6B.
7. David Bank, "TCI Uses Hi-Tech 'Layer Cake' to Ward Off Microsoft," *Wall Street Journal*, December 16, 1997, p. B4.
8. Leslie Cauley, "TCI, Others in Pact with NextLevel to Buy Digital-TV Set-Top Devices," *Wall Street Journal*, December 18, 1997, p. B10.
9. David Berquel, quoted in Mary Geraghty, "Pen-Based Computer Seen as Tool to Ease Burden of Note Taking," *Chronicle of Higher Education*, November 9, 1994, p. A22.
10. Claudia H. Deutsch, "There's Gold in Those Old Photos in the Attic," *New York Times*, June 30, 1997, p. C6.
11. Faith Bremner, "Sensors Make Snowy Roads Safer," *Reno Gazette-Journal*, December 6, 1996, pp. 1A, 10A.
12. Matthew L. Wald, "E-Z Pass to Cross George Washington Monday, Heading to Washington," *New York Times*, July 25, 1997, p. A13.
13. Laurie J. Flynn, "High-Technology Dog Tags for More Than Just Dogs," *New York Times*, August 12, 1996, p. C5.
14. "Flat-Panel TV," *Popular Science*, December 1997, p. 34.
15. Paul M. Eng, "A Cyberscreen So Tiny It Fits on a Dime," *Business Week*, April 21, 1997, p. 126C.
16. Robert J. Samuelson, "The Endless Paper Chase," *Newsweek*, December 1, 1997, p. 53.
17. Clifford Nass, quoted in Liz Spayd, "Taming the Paper Jungle," *San Francisco Chronicle*, Sunday Punch, December 19, 1993, p. 2; reprinted from Washington Post.
18. David L. Wheeler, "Recreating the Human Voice," *Chronicle of Higher Education*, January 19, 1996, pp. A8–A9.
19. Jonathan Marshall, "Videophone Finds Niche," *San Francisco Chronicle*, November 6, 1997, pp. D1, D6.
20. Diana Hembree and Ricardo Sandoval, "The Lady and the Dragon," *Columbia Journalism Review*, August 1991, pp. 44–45.
21. Bureau of Labor Statistics, cited in Ellen Neuborne, "Workers in Pain; Employers Up in Arms," *USA Today*, January 9, 1997, pp. 1B, 2B.
22. Edward Felsenthal, "An Epidemic or a Fad? The Debate Heats Up Over Repetitive Stress," *Wall Street Journal*, July 14, 1994, pp. A1, A4.
23. Felsenthal, 1994.
24. Ilana DeBare, "Eyestrain a Bulging Problem," *San Francisco Chronicle*, July 14, 1997, pp. B1, B2.
25. Jane E. Brody, "Reading a Computer Screen Is Different from Reading a Book, and Has Different Effects on the Eyes," *New York Times*, August 7, 1997, p. B6.

Chapter 6

1. Keith McCurdy, "'Killer Apps' of the '90s," *San Francisco Examiner*, January 19, 1997, pp. D-5, D-6.
2. Lawrence M. Fisher, "IBM Plans to Announce Leap in Disk-Drive Capacity," *New York Times*, December 30, 1997, p. C2.
3. Joel Shurkin, "108 Years in a Box," *San Jose Mercury News*, October 19, 1997, p. 3F; reprinted from Detroit News.
4. Edward Baig, "Be Happy, Film Freaks," *Business Week*, May 26, 1997, pp. 172–73.
5. Dennis Normile, "Get Set for the Super Disc," *Popular Science*, February 1996, pp. 55–58.
6. "DVD Stands for DiVideD," *Byte*, January 1998, p. 77.
7. Laura Tangley, "Whoops, There Goes Another CD-ROM," *U.S. News & World Report*, February 16, 1998, pp. 67–68.
8. Marcia Stepanek, "From Digits to Dust," *Business Week*, April 20, 1998, pp. 128-130.
9. Stephen Manes, "Time and Technology Threaten Digital Archives . . . ," *New York Times*, April 7, 1998, p. B15.
10. Stephen Manes, ". . . But with Luck and Diligence, Treasure-Troves of Data Can Be Preserved," *New York Times*, April 7, 1998, p. B15.
11. "Gargantua's 'Lossless' Compression," *The Australian*, March 22, 1994, p. 32; reprinted from *The Economist*.
12. Peter Coy, "Invasion of the Data Shrinkers," *Business Week*, February 14, 1994, pp. 115–16.
13. Coy, 1994.
14. William Safire, "Art vs. Artifice," *New York Times*, January 3, 1994, p. A11.
15. Cover, *Newsweek*, June 27, 1994.
16. Cover, June 27, 1994.
17. Jonathan Alter, "When Photographs Lie," *Newsweek*, July 30, 1990, pp. 44–45.

18. Fred Ritchin, quoted in Alter, 1990.
19. Robert Zemeckis, cited in Laurence Hooper, "Digital Hollywood: How Computers Are Remaking Movie Making," *Rolling Stone*, August 11, 1994, pp. 55–58, 75.
20. Woody Hochswender, "When Seeing Cannot Be Believing," *New York Times*, June 23, 1992, pp. B1, B3.
21. Penny Williams, "Database Dangers," *Quill*, July/August 1994, pp. 37–38.
22. Lynn Davis, quoted in Williams, 1994.
23. Associated Press, "Many Companies Are Willing to Give a Cat a Little Credit," *San Francisco Chronicle*, January 8, 1994, p. C1.
24. Doug Rowan, quoted in Ronald B. Lieber, "Picture This: Bill Gates Dominating the Wide World of Digital Content," *Fortune*, December 11, 1995, p. 38.
25. Kathy Rebello, "The Ultimate Photo Op?" *Business Week*, October 23, 1995, p. 40.
26. Steve Lohr, "Huge Photo Archive Bought by Software Billionaire Gates," *New York Times*, October 11, 1995, pp. A1, C5.
27. Wendy Bounds, "Bill Gates Owns Otto Bettmann's Lifework," *The Wall Street Journal*, January 17, 1996, pp. B1, B2.
28. Marty Jerome, "Boot Up or Die," *PC Computing*, April 1998, pp. 172-86.

Chapter 7

1. Andy Reinhardt, Peter Elstrom, and Paul Judge, "Zooming Down the I-Way," *Business Week*, April 7, 1997, pp. 76–87.
2. Virginia Brooks, quoted in Reinhardt et al., 1997.
3. Mark Dillard, quoted in Marcia Vickers, "Don't Touch That Dial: Why Should I Hire You?" *New York Times*, April 13, 1997, sec. 3, p. 11.
4. Cowles/Simba, reported in "Online," *Popular Science*, March 1998, p. 29.
5. Jesse Kornbluth, "The Truth About the Web," *San Francisco Chronicle*, January 23, 1996, p. C4.
6. David Landis, "Exploring the Online Universe," *USA Today*, October 7, 1993, p. 4D.
7. Jared Sandberg, "What Do They Do On-line?" *Wall Street Journal*, December 9, 1996, p. R8.
8. David Einstein, "What They Want Is E-mail," *San Francisco Chronicle*, February 20, 1996, pp. B1, B6.
9. Peter H. Lewis, "The Good, the Bad and the Truly Ugly Faces of Electronic Mail," *New York Times*, September 6, 1994, p. B7.
10. Robert Rossney, "E-Mail's Best Asset—Time to Think," *San Francisco Chronicle*, October 5, 1995, p. E7.
11. Elizabeth P. Crowe, "The News on Usenet," *Bay Area Computer Currents*, August 8–21, 1995, pp. 94–95.
12. Walter Mossberg, "'Push' Technology Sometimes Pushes News You Can't Use," *Wall Street Journal*, March 27, 1997, p. B1.
13. Yahoo!, cited in Del Jones, "Cyber-porn Poses Workplace Threat," *USA Today*, November 27, 1995, p. 1B.
14. Lawrence J. Magid, "Be Wary, Stay Safe in the On-line World," *San Jose Mercury News*, May 15, 1994, p. 1F.
15. Peter H. Lewis, "Limiting a Medium without Boundaries," *New York Times*, January 15, 1996, pp. C1, C4.
16. John M. Broder, "Making America Safe for Electronic Commerce," *New York Times*, June 22, 1997, sec. 4, p. 4.
17. Margaret Mannix and Susan Gregory Thomas, "Exposed Online," *U.S. News & World Report*, June 23, 1997, p. 59-61.
18. Noah Matthews, "Shareware," *San Jose Mercury News*, October 12, 1997, p. 4F.
19. Survey by Equifax and Louis Harris & Associates, cited in Bruce Horovitz, "80% Fear Loss of Privacy to Computers," *USA Today*, October 31, 1995, p. 1A.

Chapter 8

1. Anthony Ramirez, "Why Phone Numbers Don't Add Up," *New York Times*, August 10, 1997, sec. 4, p. 4.
2. Patrick J. Lyons, "The Trauma of the 90's: Adding New Area Codes," *New York Times*, March 10, 1997, p. C5.
3. The Wahlstrom Report, Stamford, CN, reported in "More Area Codes Needed," *The Futurist*, September-October 1997, p. 5.
4. Marshall, 1997.
5. Alvin Toffler, quoted in Marianne Roberts, "Computers Replace Commuters," *PC Novice*, September 1992, p. 27.
6. Scott Bowles, "Sharing a Ride a Luxury to Some," *USA Today*, January 29, 1998, pp. 1A, 2A.
7. FIND/SVP survey, reported in Patricia Commins, "Telecommuting Accelerates with Tight Job Market," *San Jose Mercury News*, October 12, 1997, pp. 1PC, 2PC.
8. June Langhoff, "Telecommuting Makes Sense (and Cents)," *San Francisco Examiner*, October 19, 1997, pp. D-5, D-7.
9. Alison L. Sprout, "Moving Into the Virtual Office," *Fortune*, May 2, 1994, p. 103.
10. Leon Jaroff, "Age of the Road Warrior," *Time*, Spring 1995, pp. 38–40.
11. James J. Mitchell, "Office Sharing," *San Jose Mercury News*, April 20, 1997, pp. 1D, 2D.
12. Walter S. Mossberg, "Attempts to Speed Up Modem Connections Are Off to a Slow Start," *Wall Street Journal*, March 13, 1997, p. B1.
13. Kevin Maney, "Moving to Fast Lanes on the Net," *USA Today*, October 31, 1996, p. 1B.
14. Gregg Keizer, "Screaming for Bandwidth," *Computerlife*, January 1997, pp. 58–64.
15. Jonathan Marshall, "Reducing the World Wide Wait," *San Francisco Chronicle*, June 4, 1997, pp. D1, D4.
16. Lucien Rhodes, "The Race for More Bandwidth," *Wired*, January 1996, pp. 140–145.
17. Forrester Research Inc., cited in Peter Coy, "The Big Daddy of Data Haulers?" *Business Week*, January 29, 1996, pp. 74–76.
18. Kevin Maney, "'Megahertz' Remains a Mega-Mystery to Most," *USA Today*, February 13, 1997, p. 4B.

Chapter 9

1. Gary Webb, "Potholes, Not 'Smooth Transition,' Mark Project," *San Jose Mercury News*, July 3, 1994, p. 18A.
2. Dirk Johnson, "Denver May Open Airport in Spite of Glitches," *New York Times*, July 17, 1994, p. A12.
3. Michael Krantz, "Keeping Tabs Online," *Time*, November 10, 1997, pp. 81–82.
4. "Big City, BigBook," Newsweek, August 1996, p. 13.

Chapter 10

1. Andy Hines, "Jobs and Infotech," *The Futurist*, January-February 1994, pp. 9–13.
2. Patricia Schnaidt, "The Electronic Superhighway," *LAN Magazine*, October 1993, pp. 6–8.
3. Al Gore, reported in "Toward a Free Market in Telecommunications," *Wall Street Journal*, April 19, 1994, p. A18.
4. Young, 1997.
5. Robyn Meredith, "Building 'Internet 2,' " *New York Times*, February 2, 1998, p. C3.
6. Jon Swartz, "Need for Speed Spawns 2 Internetlets," *San Francisco Chronicle*, July 28, 1997, pp. A1, A13.
7. Mike Snider, "Envisioning the Internet's Next Step," *USA Today*, May 15, 1997, p. 6D.
8. Jeffrey R. Young, "Searching for 'Killer Applications,'" *Chronicle of Higher Education*, August 8, 1997, pp. A22, A23.
9. Colleen Cordes, "Federal Support for New Version of Internet Hinges on 5 Spending Bills," *Chronicle of Higher Education*, September 5, 1997, p. A38.
10. Laurence H. Tribe, "The FCC vs. the Constitution," *Wall Street Journal*, September 9, 1997, p. A8.
11. John M. Broder, "Let It Be," *New York Times*, June 30, 1997, pp. C1, C9.
12. *A Framework for Global Electronic Commerce*, quoted in Steven Levy, "Bill and Al Get It Right," *Newsweek*, July 7, 1997, p. 80.
13. We are grateful to Prof. John Durham for contributing these ideas.
14. Arthur M. Louis, "Nasdaq's Computer Crashes," *San Francisco Chronicle*, July 16, 1994, pp. D1, D3.
15. Joseph F. Sullivan, "A Computer Glitch Causes Bumpy Start in a Newark School," *New York Times*, September 18, 1991, p. A25.
16. John J. Fialka, "Pentagon Studies Art of 'Information Warfare,' to Reduce Its Systems' Vulnerability to Hackers," *Wall Street Journal*, July 3, 1995, p. A10.
17. Thomas J. DeLoughry, "2 Students Are Arrested for Software Piracy," *The Chronicle of Higher Education*, April 20, 1994, p. A32.
18. Suzanne P. Weisband and Seymour E. Goodman, "Subduing Software Pirates," *Technology Review*, October 1993, pp. 31–33.
19. David L. Wilson, "Gate Crashers," *The Chronicle of Higher Education*, October 20, 1993, pp. A22–A23.
20. John T. McQuiston, "4 College Students Charged with Theft Via Computer," *New York Times*, March 18, 1995, p. 38.
21. David Carter, quoted in Associated Press, "Computer Crime Usually Inside Job," *USA Today*, October 25, 1995, p. 1B.
22. Eric Corley, cited in Kenneth R. Clark, "Hacker Says It's Harmless, Bellcore Calls It Data Rape," *San Francisco Examiner*, September 13, 1992, p. B-9; reprinted from Chicago Tribune.
23. Steven Bellovin, cited in Jane Bird, "More than a Nuisance," *The Times* (London), April 22, 1994, p. 31.
24. Eugene Carlson, "Some Forms of Identification Can't Be Handily Faked," *Wall Street Journal*, September 14, 1993, p. B2.
25. Justin Matlkick, "Security of Online Markets Could Well Be at Stake," *San Francisco Chronicle*, September 16, 1997, A21.
26. John Holusha, "The Painful Lessons of Disruption," *New York Times*, March 17, 1993, pp. C1, C5.
27. The Enterprise Technology Center, cited in "Disaster Avoidance and Recovery Is Growing Business Priority," special advertising supplement in *LAN Magazine*, November 1992, p. SS3.
28. Micki Haverland, quoted in Fred R. Bleakley, "Rural County Balks at Joining Global Village," *Wall Street Journal*, January 4, 1996, pp. B1, B2.
29. David Ensunsa, "Proposed Cell-Phone Pole Faces Challenge," *The Idaho Statesman*, June 23, 1995, p. 4B.
30. James H. Snider, "The Information Superhighway as Environmental Menace," *The Futurist*, March-April 1995, pp. 16–21.
31. Andrew Kupfer, "Alone Together," *Fortune*, March 20, 1995, pp. 94–104.
32. Marco R. della Cava, "Are Heavy Users Hooked or Just Online Fanatics?" *USA Today*, January 16, 1996, pp. 1A, 2A.
33. Kenneth Howe, "Diary of an AOL Addict," *San Francisco Chronicle*, April 5, 1995, pp. D1, D3.
34. Kendall Hamilton and Claudia Kalb, "They Log On, but They Can't Log Off," *Newsweek*, December 18, 1995, pp. 60–61.
35. Associated Press, "Husband Accuses Wife of Having Online Affair," *San Francisco Chronicle*, February 2, 1996, p. A3.
36. Karen S. Peterson and Leslie Miller, "Cyberflings Are Heating Up the Internet," *USA Today*, February 6, 1996, pp. 1D, 2D.
37. Survey by Microsoft Corporation, reported in Don Clark and Kyle Pope, "Poll Finds Americans Like Using PCs but May Find Them to Be Stressful," *Wall Street Journal*, April 10, 1995, p. B3.
38. Jonathan Marshall, "Some Say High-Tech Boom Is Actually a Bust," *San Francisco Chronicle*, July 10, 1995, pp. A1, A4.
39. Yahoo!/Jupiter Communications survey, reported in Del Jones, "On-line Surfing Costs Firms Time and Money," *USA Today*, December 8, 1995, pp. 1A, 2A.
40. Coleman & Associates survey, reported in Julie Tilsner, "Meet the New Office Party Pooper," *Business Week*, January 29, 1996, p. 6.
41. Webster Network Strategies survey, reported in Jones, 1995.
42. STB Accounting Systems 1992 survey, reported in Jones, 1995.
43. Ira Sager and Gary McWilliams, "Do You Know Where Your PCs Are?" *Business Week*, March 6, 1995, pp. 73–74.
44. Alex Markels, "Words of Advice for Vacation-Bound Workers: Get Lost," *Wall Street Journal*, July 3, 1995, pp. B1, B5.
45. Paul Saffo, quoted in Laura Evenson, "Pulling the Plug," *San Francisco Chronicle*, December 18, 1994, "Sunday" section, p. 53.
46. Daniel Yankelovich Group report, cited in Barbara Presley Noble, "Electronic Liberation or Entrapment," *New York Times*, June 15, 1994, p. C4.
47. Neil Postman, quoted in Evenson, 1994.
48. Mike Snider, "Keeping PC Play Out of the Office," *USA Today*, January 26, 1995, p. 3D.
49. Sager & McWilliams, 1995.
50. Jeremy Rifkin, "Technology's Curse: Fewer Jobs, Fewer Buyers," *San Francisco Examiner*, December 3, 1995, p. C-19.
51. Michael J. Mandel, "Economic Anxiety," *Business Week*, March 11, 1996, pp. 50–56.
52. Bob Herbert, "A Job Myth Downsized," *New York Times*, March 8, 1996, p. A19.
53. Robert Kuttner, "The Myth of a Natural Jobless Rate," *Business Week*, October 20, 1997, p. 26.
54. Stewart Brand, in "Boon or Bane for Jobs?" *The Futurist*, January-February 1997, pp. 13–14.
55. Paul Krugman, "Long-Term Riches, Short-Term Pain," *New York Times*, September 25, 1994, sec. 3, p. 9.
56. Department of Commerce survey, cited in "The Information 'Have Nots'" [editorial], *New York Times*, September 5, 1995, p. A12.
57. Beth Belton, "Degree-based Earnings Gap Grows Quickly," *USA Today*, February 16, 1996, p. 1B.
58. Alan Krueger, quoted in LynNell Hancock, Pat Wingert, Patricia King, Debra Rosenberg, and Allison Samuels, "The Haves and the Have-Nots," *Newsweek*, February 27, 1995, pp. 50–52.
59. David L. Wilson, "On-Line Treasure Hunt," *The Chronicle of Higher Education*, March 17, 1995, pp. A19–A20.
60. Judith Anne Gunther, "An Encounter With A.I.," *Popular Science*, June 1994, pp. 90–93.
61. William A. Wallace, *Ethics in Modeling*, (New York: Elsevier Science, 1994).
62. Laura Johannes, "Meet the Doctor: A Computer That Knows a Few Things," *Wall Street Journal*, December 18, 1995, p. B1.
63. Tamara Henry, "Many Schools Can't Access Net Offer," *USA Today*, November 3, 1995, p. 7D.
64. Robert L. Johnson, "Extending the Reach of 'Virtual' Classrooms," *The Chronicle of Higher Education*, July 6, 1994, pp. A19–A23.
65. Myron Magnet, "Who's Winning the Information Revolution," *Fortune*, November 30, 1992, pp. 110–117.
66. Tony Rutkowski, quoted in Schnaidt, 1993.
67. Robert J. Samuelson, "The Way the World Works," *Newsweek*, January 12, 1998, p. 52.
68. Mary Anne Buckman, quoted in Carol Kleiman, "Tailor Your Resume for Inclusion in a Company Database," *San Jose Mercury News*, April 14, 1996, pp. PC1–PC2.
69. David Borchard, "Planning for Career and Life," *The Futurist*, January-February 1995, pp. 8–12.
70. Jonathan Marshall, "Surfing the Internet Can Land You a Job," *San Francisco Chronicle*, July 17, 1995, pp. D1, D3.
71. Marshall, 1995.

Index

Photo & Art Credits

Page 1 © Photo Disc; **12** © PhotoDisc; **13** (top) © Photo Disc, (second from top) Intel, (third from top) Sony, (bottom) Hewlett-Packard; **14** © Photo Disc; **Panel 1.5** (left) NEC, (middle) Seagate, (right) Iomega; **15** © PhotoDisc; **16** (top) Adobe, (bottom) Microsoft; **Panel 1.6** clockwise from top left © Karen Kosmanski / Photo Net / PNI, © Tom Tracy / Photo Network / PNI, IBM, IBM, IBM, Adastra Systems, (middle) Intel; **22** (top) Motorola, (bottom) Sharp Electronics Corp.; **25** (top) "Riven" by Cyan Productions; (bottom) IBM; ; **35** © Luciano Galiardi / The Stock Market; **Panel 2.9** (both) IBM; **79** © PhotoDisc; **111** © PhotoDisc; **Panel 4.1** IBM Archives; **114** © Dan McCoy; **123** Intel; **126** (both) Brian K. Williams; **129** Hewlett-Packard; **130** from Steve Man's Web site; **139** © PhotoDisc; **140** IBM; **142** Mouseman by Logitech; **144** (top) Marble FX by Logitech, (middle) IBM, (bottom) Brian K. Williams; **Panel 5.3** FTG Data Systems; **Panel 5.4** Calcomp Ultraslate; **Panel 5.5** both from Stylistic 1000; **Panel 5.6** both courtesy of NCR; **Panel 5.8** Psion; **Panel 5.9** © Arnold Zann / Black, Star; **150** courtsey of Casio; **Panel 5.10** Tom Burdete, U.S. Geological Service; **Panel 5.11** (left) © Liz Hafalia, *San Francisco Chronicle,*(right) Reuters / Archive Photos; **Panel 5.13** (top right, bottom left) Planar, (bottom right) Fujitsu; **Panel 5.14** Hewlett-Packard; **Panel 5.15** Hewlett-Packard; **161** courtesy of Calcomp; **Panel 5.17** Hewlett-Packard; **Panel 5.18** (top left) Autodesk, (top right) UPL Research, Inc., (middle right) Autodesk, (bottom right) © Peter Menzel; (bottom left) © Charles Gupton; **165** (top and botom) © Wernher Krutein / Photovault; **Panel 5.19** AT&T Global Info / Solution; **169** Kinesis; **181** © PhotoDisc; **184** IBM; **Panel 6.5** (left) Iomega, (right) Syquest; **194** APS; **194** Toshiba; **195** Frank Bevans; **196** (top) Kodak, (bottom) Toshiba/The Benjamin Group; **199** IBM; **Panel 6.11** © Paul Higdon, *New York Times;* **229** © PhotoDisc; **233** Intel; **247** Sony Electronics, Inc.; **255** © PhotoDisc; **Panel 8.5** (top left and top right) AT&T, (bottom left) U.S. Sprint; **265** (photo) Brian K. Williams; **Panel 8.6** (photo) © Peter Townes / Photo Network / PNI; **287** © PhotoDisc; **Panel 9.1** © PhotoDisc; **291** (top and bottom), **292**, **293**, **294**, **295** © PhotoDisc; **307** © PhotoDisc; **320** reprinted with permission of Kimberly S. Young; **Panel 10.2** all photos courtesy of the Robotics Institute, Carnegie Melon; photo decoration for all Readme boxes © PhotoDisc.

DEAD ROMEO

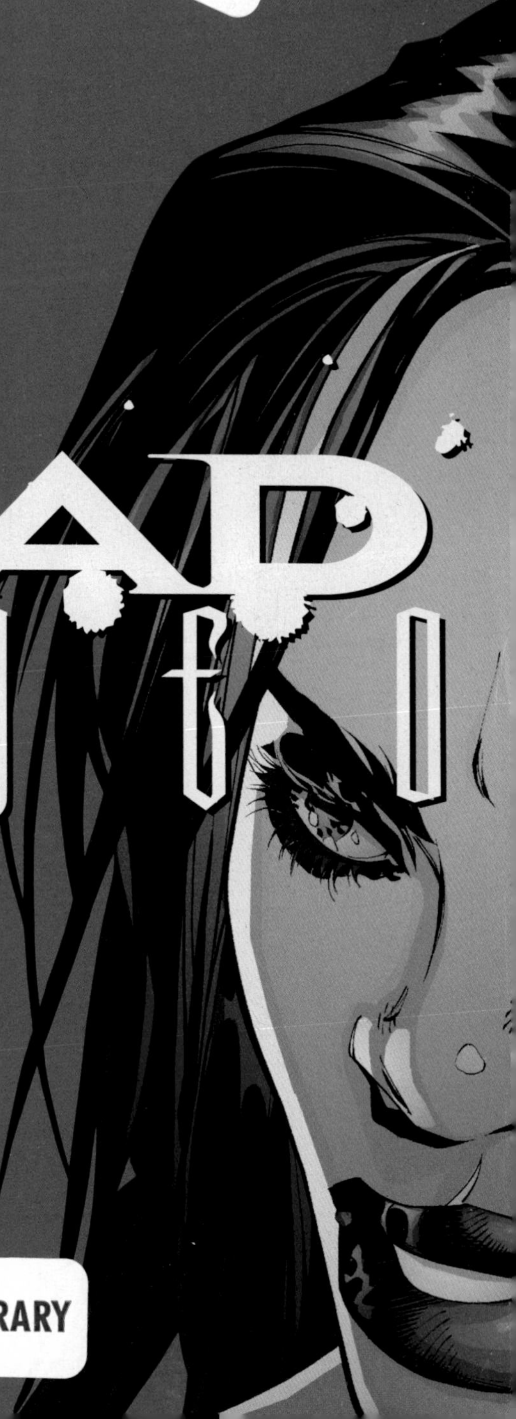

JESSE BLAZE SNIDER WRITER • RYAN BENJAMIN PENCILLER • SALEEM CRAWFORD INKER

ANDRE COELHO ADDITIONAL ART (PAGES 49-54) • RYAN BENJAMIN ADDITIONAL INKS (PAGES 93-114)

JOEL BENJAMIN COLORIST • TRAVIS LANHAM LETTERER • RYAN BENJAMIN ORIGINAL SERIES COVERS

Dan DiDio SVP-Executive Editor **Ian Sattler** Editor-original series **Rachel Gluckstern** Associate Editor-original series
Georg Brewer VP-Design & DC Direct Creative **Bob Harras** Group Editor-Collected Editions **Bob Joy** Editor
Robbin Brosterman Design Director-Books

DC COMICS

Paul Levitz President & Publisher **Richard Bruning** SVP-Creative Director **Patrick Caldon** EVP-Finance & Operations
Amy Genkins SVP-Business & Legal Affairs **Jim Lee** Editorial Director-WildStorm **Gregory Noveck** SVP-Creative Affairs
Steve Rotterdam SVP-Sales & Marketing **Cheryl Rubin** SVP-Brand Management

Cover by **Ryan Benjamin**

DC Comics, 1700 Broadway, New York, NY 10019
A Warner Bros. Entertainment Company
Printed by World Color Press, Inc., St-Romuald, QC, Canada 12/16/09. First Printing.
ISBN: 978-1-4012-2604-6

SUSTAINABLE
FORESTRY
INITIATIVE

Certified Fiber
Sourcing

www.sfiprogram.org

Fiber used in this product line meets the sourcing requirements
of the SFI program. www.sfiprogram.org PWC-SFICOC-260

BUT I'M GETTING AHEAD OF MYSELF.

HOLLYWOOD

CEMETERY

THAT'S *NOT* WHERE THE STORY *BEGINS*.

IT'S NOT EVEN WHERE IT *ENDS*.

OR AS I LIKE TO CALL HIM, *"DEAD ROMEO."*

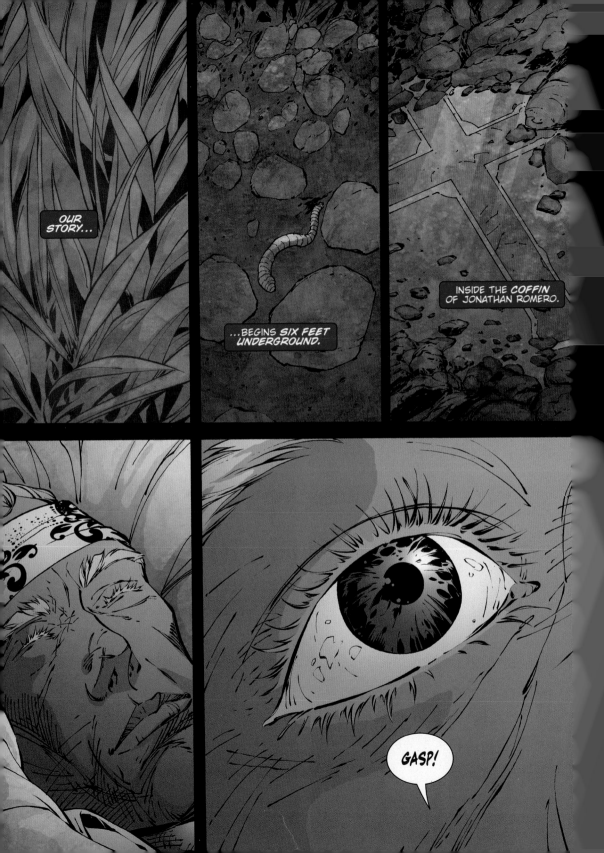

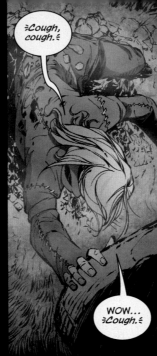

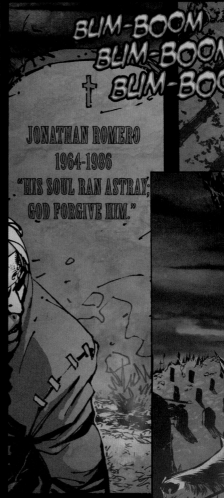

9

DO I LOOK LIKE A DAMSEL IN DISTRESS TO YOU?

NO... YOU LOOK LIKE A GIRL WHO HAS IT *ALL* FIGURED OUT.

GUESS YOU'RE NOT AS *STUPID* AS YOU LOOK IN THOSE *CLOTHES.*

AGAIN WITH THE *CLOTHES,* THAT ALL YOU GOT?

OH, THERE'S PLENTY MORE, BUT I HAVE BETTER THINGS TO DO.

YOU KNOW, I'M STARTING TO THINK YOUR DOG DOESN'T LIKE ME.

HE DOESN'T LIKE *ANYBODY.* AND *NEITHER* DO I.

GRRRRR

BUT YOU *DO* THINK I'M CUTE.

YEAH MAYBE, IF I WAS INTO '80S THROWBACKS, WHICH I'M NOT. *DID* HALLOWEEN COME EARLY THIS YEAR?

OUCH. *THAT* HURT.

WHAT DO YOU WANT?

ME? NOTHING. JUST THOUGHT MAYBE YOU NEEDED SOME HELP, IS ALL.

GRRRRR

LOVE YOU.

TALKING'S OVERRATED, ANYWAY...WE SHOULD MAKE OUT.

OH, GOD...

NOW, ROMEO WAS NOT THE *ONLY* RESURRECTION OF THE NIGHT.

ACROSS TOWN...

BEWARE! HERE LIES DWIGHT PHRY A CRAZY MAN WHO WOULD NOT DIE WAS STABBED WAS SHOT BUT STILL SURVIVED AND SO WE BURIED HIM ALIVE!

...*THREE* MORE *AWAKENINGS* WERE ABOUT TO LEAD TO A *FOURTH*.

HOW'S THAT FOR A CREEPY EPITAPH? HE, HE, HEH.

IT'S GOOD TO BE ALIVE, AIN'T IT, FUZZY?

THIS *SUCKS!*

YEAH, WHO ASKED YA?

HOW COME DWIGHT CAN'T DIG HIMSELF UP LIKE EVERYBODY ELSE? NOBODY DUG *ME* OUT.

OF COURSE NOT, WHO'D WANT TO DIG YOUR UGLY FACE UP?

NOW, SHUT UP AND DIG!

CRACK

YOU MAY BE TOUGHER THAN ME NOW, ERNIE, BUT ONE OF THESE NIGHTS...

...I'M GONNA TEAR YOU IN HALF.

YEAH, YEAH, SO YOU KEEP SAYING.

NOW, DIG!

CRACK

CAN YOU BELIEVE THIS UNGRATEFUL MUTHASUCKER? BACK FROM THE DEAD *TWO HOURS* AND ALREADY COMPLAINING.

ERNIE, WE *DON'T* HAVE *ALL NIGHT.* WE'VE GOT A JOB TO DO AND THE SOONER WE *FINISH IT...* THE SOONER *WE'RE FREE.* SO SHUT YOUR MOUTH AND *HELP...* HIM...*DIG.*

SORRY, BOSS.

AND TO ANSWER *YOUR* QUESTION, *FUZZY...*

...*DWIGHT CAN'T* DIG HIMSELF UP, BECAUSE HE WASN'T BURIED IN A *COFFIN...*

...HE WAS BURIED IN A *PRISON.*

HE LIVED HERE, SIX-FEET-UNDER FOR OVER A *CENTURY.*

THEN HOW'D HE *DIE?*

EVENTUALLY... HE JUST *STARVED TO DEATH?*

JESUS. NO WONDER HE'S SO MESSED UP.

EVINK

WHAT THE HELL?

...BUT BETTER LUCK *NEXT TIME.*

ROMEO SMILES.

BECAUSE HE *KNOWS* THEIR STORY HAS ONLY JUST BEGUN.

AND WITH THAT, ROMEO HEADS TOWARDS HIS FINAL DESTINATION: *THE LAIR, HOME OF THE HOLLYWOOD VAMPIRES!*

AND *THAT...* IS WHERE I COME IN.

ROMEO! WELCOME ACK TO THE LAND OF THE *DYING!* CAN I GET YOU A DRINK?

THAT'S ME BEHIND THE BAR.

DON'T CALL ME "ROMEO." IT'S JOHN, "JOHNNY" IF YOU GOTTA.

FORGIVE ME, BUT CONSIDERING THE CIRCUMSTANCE OF YOUR DEATH, YOUR *NICKNAME* IS *FAR MORE ENTERTAINING* THAN YOUR GIVEN NAME.

BESIDES, YOU KNOW HOW MANY "ROMEOS" I'VE MET IN MY LIFE?

TWO. YOU AND THAT OTHER IDIOT.

SO QUIT YOUR COMPLAINING AND EMBRACE YOUR UNIQUENESS.

SIGN OUTSIDE SAYS "HOME OF THE HOLLYWOOD VAMPIRES" THAT SOME KINDA JOKE?

NAW, JUST A BUNCH OF ROCK STARS WHO USED TO DRINK HERE IN THE '70S, STARTED A CLUB TO SEE WHO WAS THE BIGGEST ALCOHOLIC.

THEY PICK A WINNER?

WELL, HALF OF THEM ARE DEAD NOW, SO I GUESS SO.

DEATH...

...I'M YOUR *LAST* BEST FRIEND.

...YOUR *PATRONS* DON'T CARE A TALKING SKELETON IS SERVING THEIR DRINKS?

NAW, TO THEM I LOOK JUST LIKE YOU...MINUS THE HAIR AND RIDICULOUS OUTFIT.

YEAH...NEVER LET A *ROCK BAND* MAKE YOUR *FUNERAL* ARRANGEMENTS. LESSON LEARNED.

IT'S **GOOD** TO SEE YOU, KID.

GOOD TO SEE YOU TOO.

YOU KNOW, IN MY LINE OF WORK, I GET TO MEET A **LOT** OF PEOPLE.

HELL, I GET TO MEET ALMOST **EVERYONE**... EVENTUALLY.

BUT IT'S **VERY RARE** FOR ME TO **EVER** SEE THOSE PEOPLE A SECOND TIME, AND I ALMOST **NEVER** SEE ONE OF THE **GOOD ONES** AGAIN.

"**GOOD ONES**"?

SOMEONE LIKE YOU, KID. SOMEONE I DIDN'T THINK DESERVED WHAT THEY GOT. SOMEONE WHO I THOUGHT **MAYBE**... SHOULD HAVE GONE THE OTHER WAY.

I DON'T MEET MANY... BUT **YOU** WERE ONE OF THEM.

GUESS I WAS WRONG THOUGH, HUH?

WHY DO YOU **SAY** THAT?

BECAUSE I KNOW ALL THE TERRIBLE THINGS YOU HAD TO DO TO EARN YOUR WAY OUT.

NOTHING I THOUGHT **YOU** WERE CAPABLE OF.

YEAH, WELL I DIDN'T THINK SO EITHER. BUT YOU SPEND ENOUGH TIME IN **THE INFERNO** AND YOU'LL DO ANYTHING TO GET OUT.

ANYTHING.

FAIR ENOUGH, KID. FAIR ENOUGH.

COME ON, THEY'RE WAITING FOR YOU IN THE BACK.

I DIDN'T KNOW WHAT TO SAY TO THE KID.

HIS LIFE WAS **TRAGEDY** ON INFINITE REPEAT...

...AND IT WAS ABOUT TO GET EVEN WORSE.

NOW, IF ROMEO WAS ONE OF THE FEW *"GOOD ONES,"* THEN THESE GUYS WERE SOME OF THE FEW TRULY *"EVIL ONES."*

"THE LAIR" WAS ONCE AGAIN HOME TO "THE HOLLYWOOD *VAMPIRES"* BUT NOW IT WAS QUITE *LITERAL...*

BEFORE HE WAS A VAMPIRE, *"WICKED UNCLE ERNIE"* WAS A PEDOPHILE AND AS YOU CAN SEE...THAT *HASN'T* CHANGED.

...WE *ALMOST* LEFT WITHOUT YOU.

YOU'RE LATE...

HEY ROMEO! WANT SOME GIRL SCOUT *COOKIES?*

OR MAYBE SOME GIRL... *SCOUT!* HE, HE, HE, HE.

"THE END" WAS A STRUGGLING ACTION FILM STAR IN THE 70'S, WHO TURNED TO *VAMPIRISM* FOR AN EDGE. HE WAS QUITE HAPPY WITH THE RESULT, UNTIL HE FOUND OUT THAT VAMPIRES *CAN'T* BE CAUGHT ON *FILM.*

FUZZY WUZZY COULDN'T GET A DATE FOR THE PROM, SO HE BECAME A *RAPIST* AND *"DATED"* WHOEVER HE WANTED, WHENEVER HE WANTED, ON AND ON UNTIL THE DAY HE DIED.

THEN THERE'S *SILVERHAMMER.* WEIGHT LIFTING MADE HIM STRONG, *STEROIDS* MADE HIM STRONGER, BUT *VAMPIRISM* MADE HIM A GOD.

ROMEO IS *NOT* IN HELL ANYMORE.

SOMETHING TO DRINK?

NO, THANKS.

OH, *THAT'S RIGHT.* I *ALMOST* FORGOT.

"ROMEO"... *DOESN'T... DRINK... BLOOD.*

I KNOW...MAYBE WE CAN FIND A *COW* AND YOU CAN SUCK THE MILK STRAIGHT FROM ITS TEAT?

WHERE'S *FEARLESS?*

ON TO THE *NEXT LIFE,* I'M AFRAID.

PROBLEM? 'CAUSE WE DON'T *REALLY* NEED *EIGHT MONSTERS* TO KILL ONE MORTAL... *SEVEN* WOULD DO JUST FINE.

YOU'VE ALREADY MET *DWIGHT PHRY.*

ERNIE... *SHUT UP!*

YOKO IS DWIGHT'S *FAMILIAR,* LIKE A SUCCUBUS OF OLD, SHE CAN MAKE MEN SEE AND DO *WHATEVER* SHE WANTS.

FINALLY, *DESPERADO* WAS THE FASTEST AND MOST ACCURATE GUN IN THE WEST. THEY SAY THAT HE NEVER NEEDED TO SHOOT A MAN MORE THAN *ONCE...*

YOU SEE, HELL IS LIKE PRISON: YOU WANT TO MAKE SURE YOU ALIGN YOURSELF WITH PEOPLE WHO CAN PROTECT YOU.

PROBLEM IS...

NO. NO PROBLEM.

IMMEDIATELY.

...COME ON, BOYS, LET'S GET THIS DONE.

BEFORE YOU GO, *DWIGHT.*

GOOD.

THIS AIN'T GONNA BE LIKE BEFORE THOUGH, NO *WATCHING* FROM AFAR. YOU WANNA RUN WITH US, YOU'RE GONNA HAVE TO START *EARNING* YOUR KEEP.

THE BOYS DOWNSTAIRS WANTED ME TO *STRESS* HOW *IMPORTANT* THE *SUCCESS* OF THIS MISSION IS TO THEM AND *REMIND YOU* THAT YOU HAVE *ONLY TWO DAYS* TO GET THE JOB DONE...

...OR THEY WILL *RADICALLY REVOKE* YOUR *"PAROLE."*

DON'T WORRY, *BOATMAN,* I'VE GOT TWO COINS WITH YOUR NAME ON 'EM...

21

25

YOU'RE **NOT**, I'M FLYING.

OKAY... HOW ARE **YOU** FLYING?

PLEASE JUST **SHUT UP** FOR A SECOND AND LET ME THINK.

LOOK, I DON'T KNOW WHERE **YOU COME FROM**, BUT FOR **ME**... MURDER... FLYING ...AND-AND... PEOPLE WHO-PEOPLE THAT...**PEOPLE EATING OTHER PEOPLE** IS JUST A **BIT** OUT OF THE ORDINARY! SO, I'M **REALLY GONNA NEED**... SOME SORT OF-OF-OF EXPLANATION.

AND YOU'LL **GET IT**...

...BUT IN A FEW SECONDS THOSE **"PEOPLE"** BACK THERE ARE GONNA REALIZE WE **RAN** AND THEY'RE GONNA CHASE US DOWN AND **KILL US!**

SO IF YOU **PLEASE**, ALLOW ME TO SAVE THE "Q & A" PORTION OF OUR SHOW UNTIL **I'VE FOUND** SOMEWHERE FOR US TO HIDE!

QUICK, INSIDE.

CRANK

ROMEO...

...**THANK YOU** FOR HELPING ME.

DON'T THANK ME YE--

CLICK

...GOOSE!!!

SMASH

ARGH!

CRASH

CHOMP

ARRGGHHH!!

SPLTT!!

TASTE LIKE CHICKEN.

DA-ROOL, DA-ROOL!

AARRRGGHHH!!

YOU DON'T MIND IF I HAVE SECONDS... DO YA?

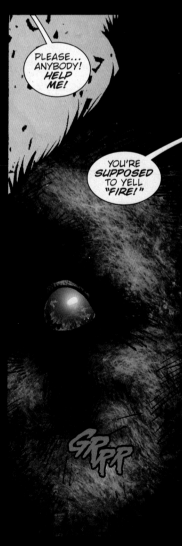

CRASH

BUS STOP

JESUS, ARE YOU OKAY?

I'M FINE... BUT DON'T CALL ME... "JESUS."

THIS IS NO TIME FOR *JOKES!*

YEAH, ≈*Cough*≈ BUT IF I DON'T *LAUGH,* I'M GONNA *CRY.* ≈*Cough*≈

YOU SHOULD *DEFINITELY* ≈*Cough*≈ THINK ABOUT GETTING OUTTA HERE, THOUGH.

I *CAN'T* JUST *LEAVE YOU.*

...YOU DON'T EVEN KNOW ME.

SERIOUSLY...

...*RUN FOR IT.*

I'LL KEEP HIM DISTRACTED.

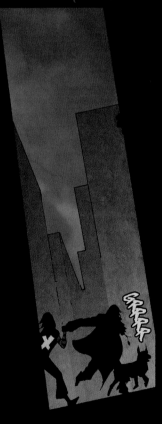

ESPECIALLY, WHEN IT DOESN'T *TAKE* ME ANYWHERE.

HERE WE ARE... *AGAIN.*

DIFFERENT ALLEY...*SAME* QUESTION.

I THINK YOU'RE THE FIRST TO EVER CHOOSE "BE KILLED".

CONGRATS.

GRRRRR

YOU GOT A LOT OF HEART, KID, AND NOW...

...*I'M* GONNA RIP IT OUTTA YOUR CHEST.

LET *SILVERHAMMER* DO 'EM, DWIGHT. SUCKER GOUGED HIS *EYES* OUT!

NO.

NOW IT'S *MY* TURN.

I KNOW THAT THIS IS *HARDLY* A *"FAIR FIGHT,"* BUT A VAMPIRE WHO *DOESN'T FEED* DOESN'T HEAL...AND I CAN *HARDLY* BE HELD RESPONSIBLE FOR YOUR *LACK* OF *LUST.*

BUT YOU KNOW WHAT I *WILL* DO...?

I'LL TUCK ONE ARM BEHIND MY BACK...AND EVEN KEEP ONE EYE *CLOSED.*

NOW...YOU *WATCH*.

LOVE.

ROMEO?

YOU'D BE SURPRISED HOW MUCH TIME CAN LIE IN THAT ONE LITTLE WORD.

LOVE.

"ROMEO" WAS IN "LOVE" AND LOOK WHERE IT GOT HIM.

TAKEN APART PIECE BY PIECE BY THE UNENDING TIDES OF HELL.

IT WAS ENOUGH TO HAVE DIED ONCE.

BUT TO DIE *AGAIN*?

LIKE *THIS*?

SLOWLY.

PAINFULLY.

FOR *LOVE*?

AT THIS POINT, HE'S NOT EVEN SURE HE *LIKES* WHISPER, AND YET HE *KNOWS* HE *LOVES* HER.

NOW HE'S *STUCK*. STUCK BETWEEN *LOVE* AND *GRIEF*.

BECAUSE HE *COULD* SAVE HER. HE COULD SAVE HIMSELF. HE IS A *VAMPIRE* AFTER ALL. HE COULD COME BACK FROM *ALL* OF THIS. ALL HE HAS TO DO...

...IS *FEED*.

BUT HE *CAN'T*.

HE *WON'T*.

NOT AFTER THE *LAST TIME*.

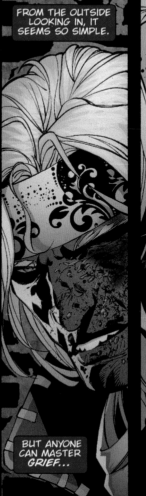

FROM THE OUTSIDE LOOKING IN, IT SEEMS SO SIMPLE.

BUT ANYONE CAN MASTER *GRIEF*...

...SAVE FOR HIM THAT HAS IT.

47

57

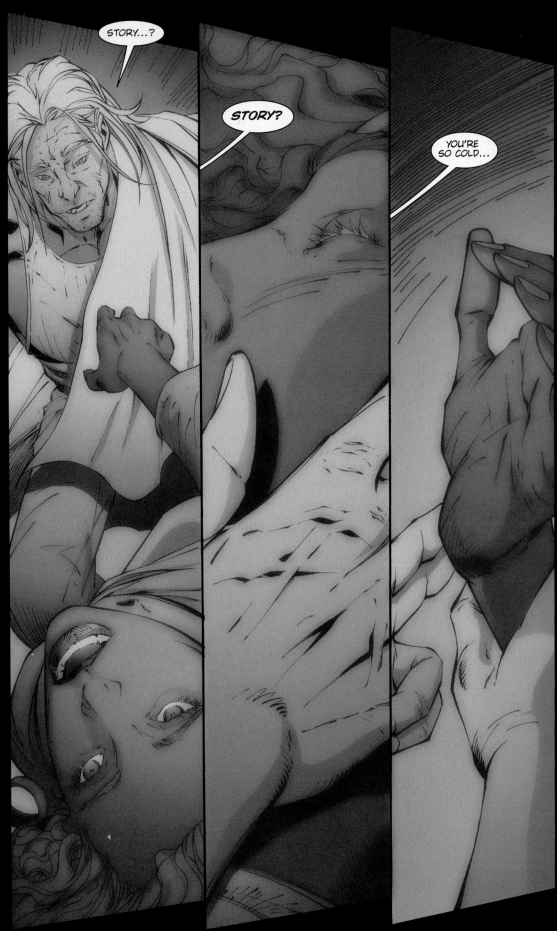

OH, AH... HA, HA, HA, HAH... MEN ARE SO... PREDICTABLE.

"I CONDEMN YOU TO LIVING DEATH," ROMEO...

"TO ETERNAL HUNGER FOR LIVING... BLOOD--"

GGGRRRR

GET OFF ME, GROWLY, SHE'S ONE OF THE BAD GUYS!

CR4CK

SHE'S...

ROMANCE ACT 4: THE DATE

MOST REGRET THEIR PUNISHMENT.

FEW... REGRET THEIR SIN.

GGGRRR

"WISELY AND *SLOW;* THEY STUMBLE THAT RUN FAST."

IT'S JUST ME, BOY.

C'MERE.

TIME TO WAKE UP, ROMEO!

HUH...? WHISPER?!

SHE'S FINE. YOU WERE DREAMING. *TURNING* SOMEONE ISN'T *THAT* SIMPLE.

NO...! MY RING!

LOOKING FOR THIS?

YOU DROPPED IT.

DOUBT YOU CAN REATTACH IT, BUT...*MAYBE* YOU CAN MAKE A *NECKLACE.*

OH, GOD...

WHERE'S WHISPER? IS SHE ALL RIGHT?!

HOW LONG 'TIL *SUNDOWN*?

SHE'S UPSTAIRS, ROOM 550. SHE'S *STABLE*... FOR NOW.

A LITTLE LESS THAN 24 HOURS.

WHAT?! IT'S AFTER DARK?! HOW LONG 'TIL THEY GET HERE?!

THEY'RE HERE ALREADY.

GOD, WHY DIDN'T YOU SAY SOMETHING?!

I JUST DID.

TOOK YOUR SWEET TIME TOO!

IT ADDS TO THE *SUSPENSE.*

"SUSPENSE"?

THIS ISN'T ONE OF YOUR STORIES...

...THIS IS *LIFE!*

MAYBE FOR *YOU.*

WELL, I'M GLAD YOU'RE ENJOYING THE SHOW!!!

I AM.

BUT ONLY 'CAUSE I KNOW IT'LL ALL WORK OUT IN THE END.

HOW DO YOU KNOW THAT?

I JUST HAVE A GOOD FEELING.

OF COURSE, YOU'RE STILL GONNA NEED ALL THE HELP YOU CAN GET.

SHEATH

KEEPING IT FROM BEING KICKED FROM HIS SHOULDERS LIKE A FOOTBALL FELL TO HIM.

THUG

HE WAS MORE WORRIED ABOUT WHAT THE END WOULD DO WHEN HE REALIZED THAT THEY WERE DIRECTLY OUTSIDE OF WHISPER'S HOSPITAL ROOM.

HE COULDN'T POSSIBLY PROTECT HER LIKE THIS; HE NEEDED TO LEAD HIM AWAY FROM WHISPER **AND** IF HE WANTED TO BE OF HELP IN THE FUTURE, HE NEEDED TIME TO HEAL.

QUICKLY, A TWO-PART PLAN WAS CONCEIVED.

PART ONE...

ODDLY ENOUGH, ROMEO WASN'T AS CONCERNED ABOUT THIS AS HE PROBABLY SHOULD HAVE BEEN.

RUN.

PART TWO... *HIDE.*

HEY, A PLAN'S A PLAN, AND THE SIMPLER THE PLAN...

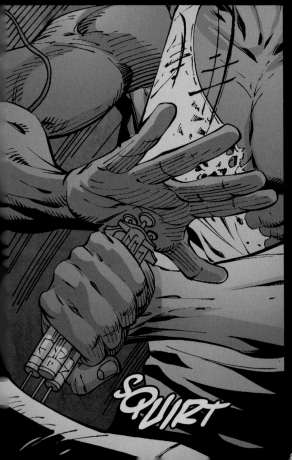

ARE YOU WHISPER...?

NO.

WHAT THE HELL'S WRONG WITH *YOUR* FACE?

ARE YOU WHISPER...?

NO.

WOW... ...WERE YOU *BORN* LIKE THAT?

HEY, ERNIE... ...*I FOUND HER!*

HEY SILVERHAMMER, -:COUGH:- I AIN'T DEAD YE--

WHISPER. NO...

WHAT--?

KA-KLIK

BANG

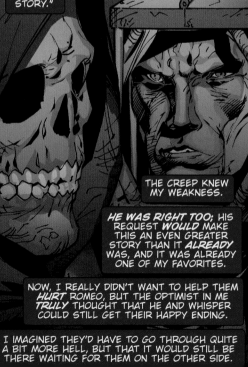

ARGH!

RIIIP

WHAT THE CRAP IS GOING ON?

DEATH...IS WALKING...OVER *YOUR* GRAVE, ERNIE!

WHAT?! I DIDN'T KNOW... I DIDN'T KNOW, MAN.

NO, PLEASE!

ARGGHH!!

THIS ISN'T FAIR, MAN. NOBODY TOLD ME...

NOBODY TOLD ME FUZZY WAS A...

THAT FUZZY WAS A... A...

DID I FORGET TO MENTION...

AAHHH!

THESE ARE WHISPER'S CLOTHES... THINK YOU CAN TRACK HER DOWN BY SCENT?

CRUNCH

...THAT *FUZZY WUZZY*...

...WAS A WERE?
ABSOLUTELY!!!
HOOWWLLL!!
DEAD ROMEO IN
HELTER SKELTER ROMANCE
ACT 5: THEY LOVE
THE END... IS NEAR.

ONCE UPON A TIME...

...THERE WAS A GIRL NAMED **WHISPER**...

...AND A **VAMPIRE** NAMED **ROMEO**...

...WHO BOTH DREAMED OF A "HAPPILY EVER AFTER."

...THE END.

UNFORTUNATELY...

...THERE IS **NO**...

...HAPPILY...

...EVER...

...AFTER.

THERE ARE ONLY **MOMENTS** OF HAPPINESS...

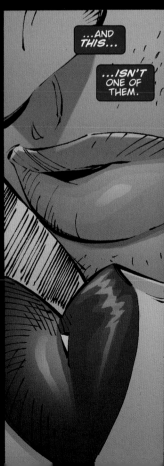

...AND THIS...

...ISN'T ONE OF THEM.

CRASH

WELL, **THAT** WAS CLOSE.

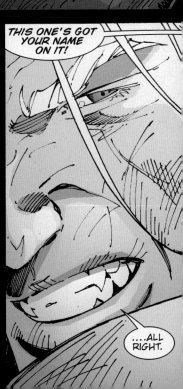

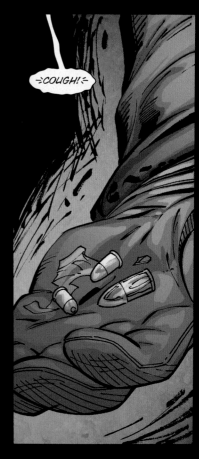

A GLOOMING PEACE THIS MORNING WITH IT BRINGS...

...THE SUN, FOR SORROW, WILL NOT SHOW HIS *HEAD!*

KRAK

GO HENCE, TO HAVE MORE TALK OF THESE SAD THINGS...

...SOME SHALL BE PARDON'D, AND SOME *PUNISHED!*

KRAK

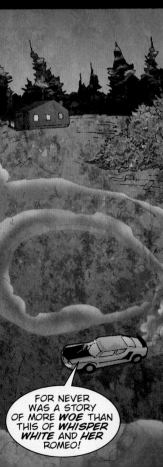

FOR NEVER WAS A STORY OF MORE *WOE* THAN THIS OF *WHISPER WHITE* AND *HER* ROMEO!

TIME TO *LEAVE* THE STAGE... *EXEUNT.*

THE SCENE OF THE CRIME!

I'M SURE THIS BRINGS BACK MEMORIES. I KNOW *I'LL ALWAYS* REMEMBER MY *FIRST KILL.*

ALLOW ME TO HELP *RECREATE* THE MOMENT....

YOU CRY LIKE A LITTLE GIRL...AND I'LL TEAR YOUR *HEART* OUT!

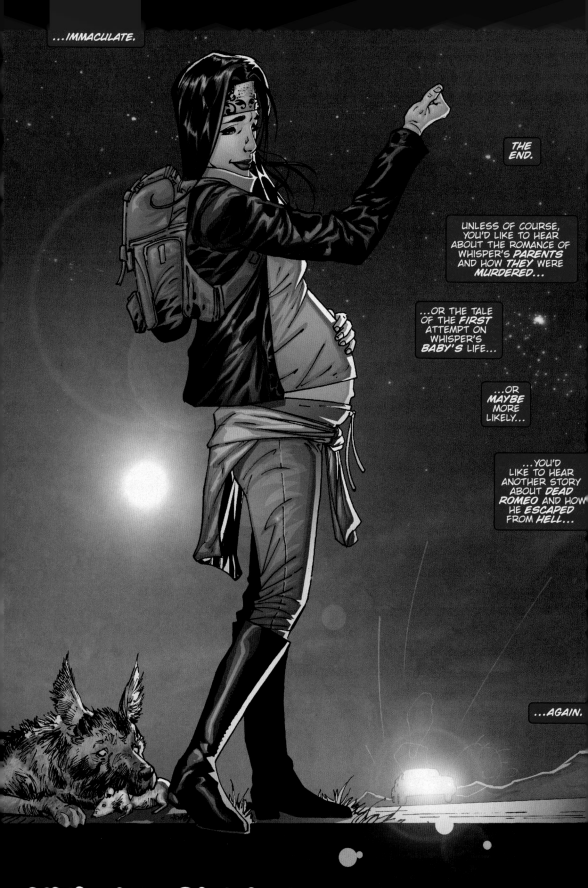

...IMMACULATE.

THE END.

UNLESS OF COURSE, YOU'D LIKE TO HEAR ABOUT THE ROMANCE OF WHISPER'S *PARENTS* AND HOW *THEY* WERE *MURDERED*...

...OR THE TALE OF THE *FIRST* ATTEMPT ON WHISPER'S *BABY'S* LIFE...

...OR *MAYBE MORE LIKELY*...

...YOU'D LIKE TO HEAR ANOTHER STORY ABOUT *DEAD ROMEO* AND HOW HE *ESCAPED* FROM *HELL*...

...AGAIN.

HELTER SKELTER ROMANCE ACT 6
JUNIO